MILLER'S
Collectors
Cars
PRICE GUIDE

⧉BROOKS

WORLD LEADERS

IN THE SALE OF COLLECTORS'

MOTOR CARS AND AUTOMOBILIA

The Brooks team are the world's leading specialists in the sale of collectors' motor cars at auction from Veteran to modern day classics, from the sedate to Formula 1. Brooks' extensive sale calendar for 1997 includes general and specialist sales at famous venues throughout Europe: Goodwood, Beaulieu, The London Motor Show, Monte Carlo, Stuttgart (at the Mercedes-Benz Museum), Geneva and the Nürburgring.

Brooks offers you the services of a formidable but wholly approachable team of enthusiasts whether buying or selling historic collectors' cars, motorcycles or automobilia. We can find or place any important car in the world. We also offer a valuation service for insurance, probate and family division.

To discuss any of Brooks services please call Malcolm Barber, James Knight or Nick Lumby

in London on 0171 228 8000 or Stewart Skilbeck on 01757 638894 (North of England and Scotland)

or Simon Kidston or Anthony Maclean at Brooks Europe in Geneva on +41 (0) 22 300 3160

LONDON 81 Westside, London SW4 9AY Tel: 0171 228 8000 Fax: 0171 585 0830
GENEVA 10 Rue Blavignac, 1227 Carouge-Geneva, Switzerland Tel: +41 (0) 22 300 3160 Fax: +41 (0) 22 300 3035

MILLER'S
Collectors Cars
PRICE GUIDE

1998-99

Volume VII

Consultant: Judith Miller

General Editor: Dave Selby

Foreword by John Surtees

MILLER'S COLLECTORS CARS PRICE GUIDE 1998–99

Created and designed by
Miller's Publications
The Cellars, High Street
Tenterden, Kent TN30 6BN
Telephone: 01580 766411

Consultant: Judith Miller

General Editor: Dave Selby
Editorial and Production Co-ordinator: Sue Boyd
Editorial Assistants: Shirley Reeves, Jo Wood
Design: Kari Reeves, Matthew Leppard
Advertising Executives: Jill Jackson, Melinda Williams
Production Assistants: Gillian Charles, Nancy Charles
Additional Photographers: Ian Booth, Neill Bruce, Jim Bush, Classic & Sportscar,
Simon Clay (National Motor Museum), John Colley, Edward Eves, John Fasal Collection,
Bennett Hall, Jay Hirsch, Bob Masters, Robin Saker, Alan Smith, A. T. Willett,
Tom Wood (National Motor Museum)
Index compiled by: Hilary Bird

First published in 1997
by Miller's
an imprint of Reed Consumer Books Limited
Michelin House, 81 Fulham Road, London SW3 6RB
and Auckland, Melbourne and Singapore

Copyright © 1997 Reed Consumer Books Limited

A CIP catalogue record for this book is
available from the British Library

ISBN 1 84000 008 2

Film output by Perfect Image, Hurst Green, E. Sussex
Illustrations and bromide output by A. S. Group, Ashford, Kent
Colour origination by Scantrans, Singapore
Printed and bound in England by William Clowes Ltd,
Beccles and London

Miller's is a trademark of
Reed Consumer Books Limited

Front cover illustrations:

1931 Ford Model A Cabriolet Model 68-B. **£11,500–12,500** *BKS*
A motor racing poster, by A. Barata, c1955. **£1,000–1,200** *S*
1971 MGB GT. **£3,400–3,800** *H&H*
A racing helmet worn by Ayrton Senna, 1986. **£37,000–40,000** *C*
1952 Jaguar XK120 Roadster. **Est. £35,000–38,000** *S*
A French six-person picnic case, c1920. **£5,500–6,000** *S*
1936 Maserati 6CM. **£162,000–180,000** *COYS*

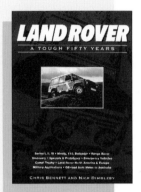

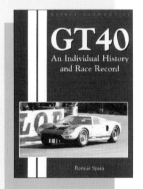

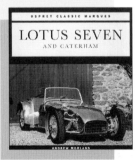
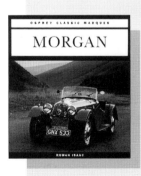

CONTENTS

ACKNOWLEDGEMENTS

The publishers would like to acknowledge the great assistance given by our consultants:

Chris Alford	Newland Cottage, Hassocks, West Sussex BN6 8NU
Darren Banks	Race-Lit, Unit 6, Healey New Mills, Healey Road, Ossett, W. Yorks WF5 8NF
Malcolm Barber	Tel: 0171 228 8000
Stephen Boyd	Scootacar Register, 18 Holman Close, Aylsham, Norfolk NR11 6DD
Paul Foulkes-Halbard	Foulkes-Halbard of Filching, Filching Manor, Jevington Road, Wannock, Polegate, Sussex BN26 5QA
David Hayhoe	Grand Prix Contact Club, 28 Pine Avenue, West Wickham, Kent BR4 OLW
Simon Johnson	Military Vehicle Trust, 7 Carter Fold, Mellor, Lancs BB2 7ER
John Oliver	Jarrots, 62 Albert Road, Ashford, Kent TN24 8NU
Mike Stallwood Tim Fuggle	RR Motor Services Ltd, Bethersden, Ashford, Kent TN26 3DN

We would like to extend our thanks to all auction houses, their press offices, and dealers who have assisted us in the production of this book along with the organisers and press offices of the following events:

Beaulieu September Autojumble & Automart

Louis Vuitton Classic

Goodwood Festival of Speed

RAC British Grand Prix

Coys International Historic Festival

Beltring '97 – The War and Peace Show

KEY TO ILLUSTRATIONS

Each illustration and descriptive caption is accompanied by a letter code. By referring to the following list of Auctioneers (denoted by *), Dealers (•), Clubs and Trusts (§), the source of any item may be immediately determined. Inclusion in this edition no way constitutes or implies a contract or binding offer on the part of any of our contributors to supply or sell the goods illustrated, or similar articles, at the prices stated. Advertisers in this year's directory are denoted by †.

If you require a valuation for an item, it is advisable to check whether the dealer or specialist will carry out this service and if there is a charge. Please mention Miller's when making an enquiry. Having found a specialist who will carry out your valuation it is best to send a photograph and description of the item to the specialist together with a stamped addressed envelope for the reply. A valuation by telephone is not possible. Most dealers are only too happy to help you with your enquiry. However, they are very busy people and consideration of the above points would be welcomed.

ADT/ BRIT *† British Car Auctions Ltd Classic & Historic Automobile Division, Auction Centre, Blackbushe Airport, Blackwater, Camberley, Surrey, GU17 9LG Tel: 01252 878555

AS •† Ashted Service Station of Kenilworth, The Willows Meer End Road, Kenilworth, Warwicks, CV8 1PU Tel: 01676 532289

BBo • Barry Bone, Quoins, Jarvis Lane, Steyning, West Sussex, BN44 3GA Tel: 01903 813355

BC •† Beaulieu Cars Ltd, Beaulieu, Hants, SO42 7YE Tel: 01590 612689

BCA •† Beaulieu Cars Ltd, The Garage, Beaulieu, Hants, SO42 7YE Tel: 01590 612689

BKS *† Brooks, 81 Westside, London, SW4 9AY Tel: 0171 228 8000

BLE •† Ivor Bleaney, PO Box 60, Salisbury, Wiltshire, SP5 2DH Tel: 01794 390895

BLK •† Blackhawk Collection, 3600 Blackhawk Plaza Circle, Danville, California 94506, USA Tel: 510 736 3444

Bon(C)* Bonhams, 65-69 Lots Road, Chelsea, London, SW10 0RN Tel: 0171 393 3900

Bro • John Brown, Between Baldock & Royston, Hertfordshire, SG8 0NL Tel: 01763 852200

C * Christie, Manson & Woods Ltd, 8 King Street, St James's, London, SW1Y 6QT Tel: 0171 839 9060

CARS •† C.A.R.S. (Classic Automobilia & Regalia Specialists), 4-4a Chapel Terrace Mews, Kemp Town, Brighton, Sussex, BN2 1HU Tel: 01273 601960

Car •† Chris Alford Racing and Sportscars, Newland Cottage, Hassocks, Sussex, BN6 8NU Tel: 01273 845966

CC • Collectors Cars, Drakeshill, Birmingham Road, Kenilworth, Warwickshire, CV8 1PT Tel: 01926 857705

CGB • Cars Gone By, Maidstone, Kent Tel: 01622 630220

COB • Cobwebs, 78 Northam Road, Southampton, Hampshire, SO14 0PB Tel: 01703 227458

COR •† Claremont Corvette, Snodland, Kent, ME6 5NA Tel: 01634 244444

COYS* Coys of Kensington, 2/4 Queens Gate Mews, London, SW7 5QJ Tel: 0171 584 7444

CRC § Craven Collection of Classic Motorcycles, Brockfield Villa, Stockton-on-the-Forest, Yorkshire, YO3 9UE Tel: 01904 488461/400493

CRE •† Cresswell Cars, 602 Hagley Road West Quinton, Birmingham, West Midlands, B68 0BS Tel: 0121 421 3494

CSK * Christie's South Kensington Ltd, 85 Old Brompton Road, London, SW7 3LD Tel: 0171 581 7611

CTP •† Classic Trading Post, Longbarn Lewes Road Cross in Hand, Heathfield, East Sussex, TN21 0TP Tel: 01435 863800

DB •† David Baldock, North Road, Goudhurst, Kent, TN17 1AD Tel: 01580 211326

DH • David Howard Cars, Ranvilles Farm, Romsey, Hampshire, SO51 6AA Tel: 01703 814481

DHAM•† Duncan Hamilton & Co Ltd, PO Box 222 Hook, Basingstoke, Hampshire, RG27 9YZ Tel: 01256 765000 Photos © Neill Bruce Tel 01635 278342

DJ * Wealden Auction Galleries, Desmond Judd, 23 Hendly Drive, Cranbrook, Kent, TN17 3DY Tel: 01580 714522

DRC •† D.R.C. (Motors), Herts Tel: 01923 268000

DTR • DTR European Sports Cars, 16F Crown Yard, Crown Road, St Margarets, Twickenham, Middlesex, TW1 3EE Tel: 0181 891 4043

EAE •† Eagle E-Types, Henry Pearman, Brookside Farm Tinkers Lane, Hadlow Down, Sussex Tel: 01825 830966

FHD •† F. H. Douglass, 1a South Ealing Road, Ealing, London, W5 4OT Tel: 0181 567 0570

FHF •† Foulkes-Halbard of Filching, Filching Manor, Filching, Wannock, Polegate, Sussex, BN26 5QA Tel: 01323 487838

FM • Franco Macri, Kent Tel: 01227 700555

FYC § Ford Y&C Model Register, Bob Wilkinson, Castle Farm, Main Street, Pollington, Goole, Humberside, DN14 0DJ Tel: 01405 860836

GAZE* Thomas Wm Gaze & Son, 10 Market Hill, Diss, Norfolk, IP22 3JZ Tel: 01379 651931

GPCC§† Grand Prix Contact Club, David Hayhoe, 28 Pine Avenue, West Wickham, Kent, BR4 0LW Tel: 0181 777 6479

GPT •† Grand Prix Top Gear, The Old Mill, Mill End, Standon, Hertfordshire, SG11 1LR Tel: 01279 843999

GW •† Graham Walker Ltd, Parkgate Road, Mollington, Chester, Cheshire, CH1 6JS Tel: 01244 851144

H&H *† H & H Classic Auctions Ltd, 134 Roseneath Road, Urmston, Manchester, M41 5AZ Tel: 0161 747 0561

Hal * Halls Fine Art Auctions, Welsh Bridge, Shrewsbury, Shropshire, SY3 8LA Tel: 01743 231212

HOLL* Dreweatt Neate Holloways, 49 Parsons Street, Banbury, Oxon, OX16 8PF Tel: 01295 253197

JAR • Jarrotts, Hales Place, Woodchurch Road, High Halden, Kent, TN26 3JQ Tel: 01233 850037

JNic * John Nicholson, The Auction Rooms, Longfield, Midhurst Road, Fernhurst, Surrey, GU27 3HA Tel: 01428 653727

KHP •† Kent High Performance Cars, Unit 1-2 Target Business Centre, Bircholt Road Parkwood Industrial Estate, Maidstone, Kent, ME15 9YY Tel: 01622 663308

KI *† Kruse International, PO Box 190, 5400 County Road 11A, Auburn, Indiana, 46706 USA Tel: 219 925 5600

LE •† Laurence Edscer, The Old House, The Square, Tisbury, Wiltshire, SP3 6JP Tel: 01747 871200

LF * Lambert & Foster, 77 Commercial Road, Paddock Wood, Kent, TN12 6DR Tel: 01892 832325

LHA * Lesley Hindman Auctioneers, 215 West Ohio Street, Chicago, Illinois, 60610 USA Tel: 001 312 670 0010

MAN • Stanley Mann, The Fruit Farm, Common Lane, Radlett, Hertfordshire, WD7 8PW Tel: 01923 852505

MATT• Paul Matty Sports Cars Ltd, 12 Old Birmingham Road, Bromsgrove, Worcs B60 1DE Tel: 01527 835656

MCA * Mervyn Carey, Twysden Cottage, Benenden, Cranbrook, Kent, TN17 4LD Tel: 01580 240283

MEE • Nicholas Mee & Co Ltd, 36-38 Queensgate Place Mews, London, SW7 5BQ Tel: 0171 581 0088

MPG • MotorPost Gallery, 5 Shadwell Park Court, Leeds, Yorkshire, LS17 8TS Tel: 0113 225 3525

MUN •† Munich Legends Ltd, The Ashdown Garage, Chelwood Gate, East Sussex, RH17 7DE Tel: 01825 740456

MVT § Military Vehicle Trust, PO Box 6, Fleet, Hampshire, GU13 9PE

NCC § Naylor Car Club, John W. Taylor (Sec), c/o Naylor Brothers Restoration, Airedale Garage, Hollins Hill, Shipley, Yorkshire, BD17 7QN

P(Sc) * Phillips Scotland, 207 Bath Street, Glasgow G2 4HD Tel: 0141 221 8377

PA *† Parkes Auctions Ltd, 2/4 Station Road, Swavesey, Cambs CB4 5QJ Tel: 01954 232332

PAL •† Palmeira Classic & Sporting Cars, 26/28 St Johns Road, Hove, Sussex, BN3 2FB Tel: 01273 206064

PARA• † Paragon Porsche, Five Ashes, East Sussex, TN20 6HY Tel: 01825 830424

PC Private Collection.

PETT• Dick Pettman, Henley House, Wadhurst Road, Frant, Tunbridge Wells, Kent, TN3 9EJ Tel: 01892 750249

PJF • P. J. Fischer Classic Automobiles, Dyers Lane, Upper Richmond Road, Putney, London, SW15 6JR Tel: 0181 785 6633

RCC •† Real Car Co, Snowdonia Business Park, Coed y Parc, Bethesda, Gwynedd, LL57 4YS Tel: 01248 602649

RRM • RR Motor Services Ltd, Bethersden, Ashford, Kent, TN26 3DN Tel: 01233 820219

RUT •† Melvyn Rutter Ltd, The Morgan Garage, Little Hallingbury, Nr Bishops Stortford, Herts, CM22 7RA Tel: 01279 725725

S * Sotheby's, 34-35 New Bond Street, London, W1A 2AA Tel: 0171 493 8080

S(S) * Sotheby's Sussex, Summers Place, Billingshurst, Sussex, RH14 9AD Tel: 01403 783933

SC •† Sporting Classics, Phil Hacker, The Oast, Shears Farm, North Road, Goudhurst, Kent, TN17 1JR Tel: 01580 211275

ScR § Scootacar Register, Stephen Boyd, Pamanste, 18 Holman Close, Aylsham, Norwich, Norfolk, NR11 6DD Tel: 01263 733861

SJR • Simon J. Robinson (MGA) 1982 Ltd, Ketton Garage, Durham Road, Coatham, Munderville, Darlington, Co. Durham, DL1 3LZ Tel: 01325 311232

SW • Spinning Wheel Garage, Sheffield Road, Sheepbridge, Chesterfield, Derbyshire, S41 9EH Tel: 01246 451772

TALA • Talacrest, 74 Station Road, Egham, Surrey, TW20 9LF Tel: 01784 439797

TVR • David Gerald TVR Sportscars Ltd, Hereford & Worcs Tel: 01386 793237

UMC •† Unicorn Motor Company, Brian R. Chant, M.I.M.I., Station Road, Stalbridge, Dorset, DT10 2RH Tel: 01963 363353

VIC •† Vicarys of Battle Ltd, 32 High St, Battle, Sussex, TN33 0EH Tel: 01424 772425

VIN • Vintage & Sports Car Garage Ltd, 47 West Street, Harrietsham, Kent, ME17 1HX Tel: 01622 859570

WDG * William Doyle Galleries, 175 East 87th Street, New York, NY 10128, USA Tel: 212 427 2730

WYK • Wykenhams, 6 Kendrick Place, Reece Mews, S Kensington, London, SW7 3HF Tel: 0171 589 6894

HOW TO USE THIS BOOK

I t is our aim to make the guide easy to use. Marques are listed alphabetically and then chronologically within each section. Racing Cars, Commercial Vehicles, Military Vehicles, Microcars and Restoration Projects are located after the marques, towards the end of the book. In the Automobilia section objects are grouped alphabetically by type. If you cannot find what you are looking for please consult the index which starts on page 348.

48 AUSTIN-HEALEY

1954 Austin-Healey 100/4, 4 cylinders, 2660cc, thoroughly overhauled, new wiring loom, exterior chrome renovated, new chrome wire wheels, interior, hood and tonneau cover completely re-trimmed.
£15,000–17,000 *COYS*

1959 Austin-Healey Sprite MkI, 4 cylinders, 948cc, extensive restoration, sills replaced, floor-pan overhauled, full respray, chrome replated, steering overhauled, new rear springs, new brake cylinders, shoes and copper pipes, rebuilt radiator and new wiring loom, interior completely re-trimmed, new black fabric hood, perspex sidescreens replaced.
£8,750–9,750 *ADT*

Caption
provides a brief description of the vehicle or item, and could include comments on its history, mileage, any restoration work carried out and current condition.

Miller's Starter Marque

Starter Austin-Healeys: *Austin Healey Sprite MkI 'Frog-eye'; Austin-Healey Sprite MkII–V.*

- Few cars have a cuter face than the cheeky little Austin-Healey Sprite MkI that everyone knows as the 'Frog-eye'. Truth be told, it's not very fast. A contemporary road test in *The Motor* quoted a leisurely 0–60mph time of 20.5 seconds. Acceleration petered out altogether at 84mph. But what it lacked in outright pace it more than made up for with true agility and genuine sporting feel.

- It's a viable restore-while-you-drive car, with basic readily available mechanicals – mostly Austin A35 with a bit of Morris Minor. Many of the same virtues apply to the Sprite MkII–V, which is identical to the MG Midget in all but minor detail. With both makes to choose from the Midget and Sprite MkII–V were made in far larger numbers than the 'Frog-eye' and are that much more affordable and readily available.

Austin Milestones

1866: Herbert Austin born 8 November.
1905: Austin Motor Company founded.
1914: Austin became public company.
1975: British Leyland nationalised.
1980: British Leyland reorganises with Austin-badged cars produced under Austin-Rover Group banner.
1986: 5,000,000th Mini was produced 19 February.
1987: Austin name disappears from remaining models and company name shortened to the Rover Group. The end of Austin.

Source Code
refers to the 'Key to Illustrations' on page 10 which lists the details of where the item was photographed, and whether it is from a dealer or auction house. Advertisers are also indicated on this page.

Miller's Starter Marque
refers to selected marques that offer affordable, reliable and interesting classic motoring.

Information Box
covers relevant information on marques, designers, racing drivers and special events.

1957 Austin-Healey 100/6 BN4, 6 cylinders, 2639cc, 4 speed gearbox with overdrive, bare metal respray, converted to right-hand drive, chrome and wire wheels and interior refurbished.
£12,500–14,000 *H&H*

1963 Austin-Healey 3000 MkIIA, converted to right-hand drive, imported, very good restored condition, including new wheels and tyres, new hood and new tonneau.
£15,000–17,000 *H&H*

AUSTIN HEALEY Model	ENGINE cc/cyl	DATES	CONDITION 1	2	3
100 BN 1/2	2660/4	1953-56	£20,000	£14,000	£8,000
100/6, BN4/BN6	2639/6	1956-59	£18,000	£13,500	£8,000
3000 Mk I	2912/6	1959-61	£20,000	£13,000	£8,500
3000 Mk II	2912/6	1961-64	£22,000	£15,000	£9,000
3000 Mk III	2912/6	1964-68	£24,000	£17,000	£11,000
Sprite Mk I	948/4	1958-61	£5,000	£4,000	£2,000
Sprite Mk II	948/4	1961-64	£3,000	£2,000	£1,000
Sprite Mk IV	1275/4	1966-71	£4,000	£2,000	£1,000

Price Guide
price ranges are worked out by a team of trade and auction house experts, and are based on actual prices realised. Remember that Miller's is a PRICE GUIDE not a PRICE LIST and prices are affected by many variables such as location, condition, desirability and so on. Don't forget that if you are selling it is quite likely you will be offered less than the price range. Price ranges for items sold at auction include the buyer's premium.

Price Boxes
give the value of a particular model, dependent on condition and are compiled by our team of experts, car clubs and private collectors.
Condition 1 refers to a vehicle in top class condition but not *concours d'élégance* standard, either fully restored or in very good original condition.
Condition 2 refers to a good, clean roadworthy vehicle, both mechanically and bodily sound.
Condition 3 refers to a runner, but in need of attention, probably to both bodywork and mechanics. It must have a current MOT.
Restoration projects are vehicles that fail to make the Condition 3 grading.

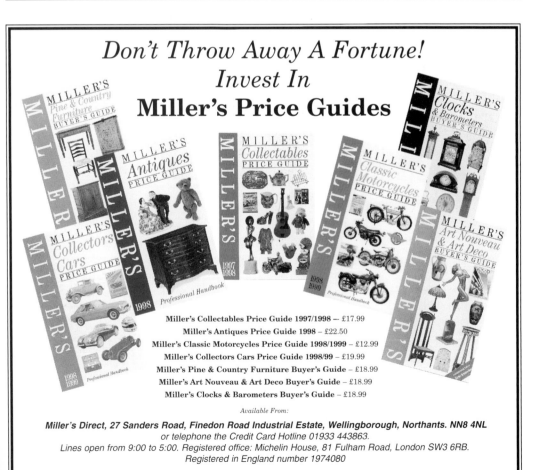

FOREWORD

Miller's Collectors Cars Price Guide is now in its seventh year and I am pleased to once again provide the foreword. There is perhaps no better reflection of the growth of interest in classic and vintage cars than the enthusiastic support worldwide events catering for these machines are attracting. In *Miller's Collectors Cars Price Guide* many wonderful examples of vintage and classic can be seen.

Over the past five years I have seen the attendance figures at the Goodwood Festival of Speed, possibly the best supported and most prestigious event of its kind, grow from five figures to 100,000. Wearing two hats as I do on these occasions, with my career spanning both two and four wheels, it is intriguing and satisfying to see enthusiasts; the young, not so young and many families, gaze in awe over a W125 Mercedes-Benz Grand Prix car of 1937.

In Italy this year I had the pleasure of acquainting myself with the last of the 300SLR Mercedes-Benz sports racing cars that was destined for Juan Manuel Fangio, and it was in his seat that I tackled the Mille Miglia. The event took place on open roads with a lot of police help, and the excitment created by the open exhausts and the silver Mercedes travelling at up to 150mph was enormous. Only in Italy in the midst of Rome could the 50 years of Ferrari have started its celebrations. The masses turned out to support owners and drivers who had brought their pieces of Ferrari history back to Italy for the occasion. Back in the UK where a call to drive the all-conquering Mercedes-Benz W196 from 1954–55 at the British Grand Prix was not to be refused. It is good to see that the multi-million Grand Prix business is taking its history seriously.

Recently, classic cars of 25 years or more were sensibly given exemption from Road Fund Licence, and I would expect to see classic machines of all types play a greater part in leisure activities as the frustrations and burdens associated with everyday motoring increase. The marketplace, however, can be a perilous place and should you make a mistake with a classic or historic vehicle it can be costly to rectify so time spent on research and gaining knowledge pays dividends. *Miller's Collectors Cars Price Guide* is an essential reference book for both enthusiast and professional car owner alike to help with this task. With thousands of illustrations ranging from Abarth to Wolseley you are sure to find what you are looking for.

STATE OF THE MARKET

Up until recently the classic car market in the UK was suffering from a surfeit of cars, many of which were imported from the USA when the dollar was weak in the early 1990s. It seems likely that the large number of sales now being held will finally absorb that surfeit, and the situation may then be reversed. Most leading auction houses have a full calendar of sales. If, however, there should be a shortage of vehicles to meet demand, this will have been exacerbated by recent changes in attitude by HM Customs & Excise towards collectors' cars, which formerly enjoyed a preferential rate of 2½ per cent VAT and nil duty when imported from outside the EU. As a result, imports from the USA, the Antipodes, South Africa and Japan have drastically reduced, and if our EU partners continue buying at the present rate in the UK market then shortages in some sectors appear inevitable. HM Customs are, however, being challenged in a forthcoming tribunal, the outcome of which will be important to both buyers and sellers alike.

Increasing prosperity has been reflected in a buoyant market at all levels in the UK, but particularly in vehicles at the top end of the market. Since the disastrous slump at the beginning of the 1990s, the rate of recovery has been gaining momentum all the time and has recently even shown signs of achieving levels last seen in the closing years of the 1980s.

This is particularly true in the case of Ferraris. The trend was set by Christie's at Pebble Beach when the 1949 Scuderia Ferrari 166MM Barchetta, which won the 1949 Belgian Francorchamps 24-hour Grand Prix, sold for $1,652,500 (£1,032,812), a 1953 Ferrari 212 Inter Coupé sold for $107,000 (£66,875) and a 1959 250GT Spyder made $508,500 (£317,812). It was underlined by Brooks at Geneva in March – £101,054 for a 1965 Ferrari 275GTB Berlinetta, and £92,214 for a 1960 Ferrari 250GT Series II cabriolet. Indeed, top quality sports cars are all doing well. Brooks continued the trend in Monaco when the ex-Wolfgang Siedel 1957 Ferrari 3 litre 250GT Tour de France Berlinetta realised £354,729 and the 1952 Ferrari Tipo 225S Spider by Vignale fetched £302,605. Coys repeated the Ferrari revival, when six cars from this maker sold in their Chiswick sale in May, including another 250GT Series II cabriolet at £83,340.

Somewhat strangely, following the flurry of excitement which greeted the centenary of the British motor industry in 1996, interest in very old vehicles has waned rather, and veteran prices other than for charismatic marques like Mercedes-Benz and Rolls-Royce have remained in the doldrums. Traditional British sports cars are, however, doing well, Coys selling a 1937 Bentley 4¼ litre roadster in Chiswick in May for £101,220, and a 1930 Cricklewood Bentley Speed Six tourer for £348,188.

Single-owner collections continue to attract a premium when they come on the market, and when the 'King Tut's Tomb' syndrome is added for good measure, then success is assured. This was graphically illustrated when Christie's sold a legendary unrestored Stutz collection in the USA, and when Brooks offered the residue of the collection of the late Shah of Iran in Geneva. The Shah's rare 1971 Lamborghini Miura SVJ made £308,578 in Geneva, and in both sales all the single-owner collection cars found new homes.

There has been considerable expansion of British companies in the European auction scene. Both Christie's and Brooks have held sales in Geneva; Brooks has also been to Monaco and Stuttgart and is planning sales in France (a real breakthrough).

Other areas of the market that have witnessed phenomenal growth are Formula 1 memorabilia and microcars. Long considered something of a joke within the classic car world, interest in these peculiar little cars has been steadily increasing in recent years, culminating in the quite sensational prices achieved by Christie's at Nine Elms when the Bruce Weiner Collection was dispersed. It would, however, be premature to read too much into these results: a single-owner collection that included many makes and models never seen before, most of which were restored to a high standard, represented something of a one-off.

Interest, particularly in the classic car era, is healthy at all levels. Although all the major auction houses continue to offer and successfully sell more modestly priced classics as well as supercars, British Car Auctions (formerly ADT) and H&H in Buxton succeeded in finding buyers for most of their more modestly priced collectors cars.

Thematic sales continue to be popular, with Brooks firmly entrenched as an integral part of the hugely successful Goodwood Festival of Speed in June and with the Mercedes-Benz factory in Stuttgart in April, Coys joining forces with Chrysler for the Coys International Historic Festival at Silverstone in July, and Sotheby's continuing their now long-established relationship with the Rolls-Royce Enthusiasts' Club with a sale at the annual concours at Althorp. With Christie's now holding two sales a year in North America, and Brooks holding regular sales as Brooks-Goodman with their associates in Australia and establishing Brooks Europe in Geneva, Stuttgart, Monaco, Nürburgring and Paris, the international nature of the auction world is expanding all the time and the future looks rosy.

Malcolm Barber

A WORLD OF CHOICE

You can, if you insist, try to justify your passion for old cars on grounds of practicality, low insurance premiums, zero road tax for cars over 25 years old, nil depreciation, or even as an investment. But I think that misses the point — that pride of ownership, nostalgic enjoyment, and the investment in pleasure stand up by themselves as justification enough. What's more, as you browse through the pages of this latest addition of *Miller's Collectors Cars Price Guide* you will discover a world of fascinating alternatives to that anonymous modern wipe-clean driving appliance. Below are a few suggestions for fertile hunting grounds for classic car enthusiasts. Classic convertibles are available in a kaleidoscipic range of prices and configurations, left-hand drive sports cars are well worth looking at on grounds of price, widespread availability and re-sale, and if you are after a mainstream classic, auctions are stacked high with many of the most popular models.

Topless Choices

You may think that today's modern convertibles amount to a deluge of dropheads. Truth be told, today's offerings of fresh-air funsters amount to a feeble drip compared with the flood tide that coursed through the classic post-war period from the late 1940s until the drought of the 1970s.

Today, you pay more for less. How times change. In the earliest years of motoring, cars were predominantly open and windscreens and roofs were luxury options. In the inter-war years cars like the MG M-type Midget (and the later T-series Midget) had no direct saloon counterpart. In other cases, like the ubiquitous Austin 7, the open tourers were cheaper than saloons because there was less metal, wood and labour in them. After WWII the trend persisted. Today the sublime XK120 Jaguar roadster is much more highly valued than its fixed-head counterpart. When current though, it was cheaper than the fixed-head coupé.

Another factor was that most cars had separate chassis, so a roof was something you added. However, even into the monocoque era though, cars like the MGB and E-type Jaguar were more expensive new in tin-top form.

Today classic convertibles are uniformly more expensive than fixed heads, the one notable exception being the Mercedes-Benz 300SL 'Gullwing'. That said there's a world of choice to suit all pockets, as you will find when you browse through the following pages.

Left-hand Drives

Not so long ago left-hand drive British classics were looked down upon by most English enthusiasts. In fact your left-hand drive version of the 'proper' right-hand drive car might be worth anything from 10–40 per cent less in the UK. But with growing world interest in old British metal, things are looking up for once-unloved left-hookers. In fact, despite conventional old-car dogma, they even make sense for all sorts of reasons.

They're cheaper to buy in the UK, more prized abroad in left-hand drive form, and there's a huge stock available, in many cases many times larger than right-hand drive offerings.

It all started with the quaint MG TC, that favourite GI jallopy discovered by US servicemen stationed over here in WWII. Of the 10,000 made from 1945 to 1949, two were exported for every one that stayed at home. In 1949 the most feline of all Jaguars, the XK120, blazed an export trail, with 85 per cent of all the 12,000 built until 1954 going abroad. Through the 'export or die' era for British industry the story continued with the Austin-Healeys and TR Triumphs. Three final statistics: of the 387,000 MGB roadsters only 49,000 stayed home; of 101,000 MGAs, 81,000 went to the USA; two thirds of Jaguar E-types went abroad and most of those, of course, to the USA.

In the late 1980s the magnetic pull of the classic car boom brought tons of old left-hand drive metal back to the UK and much of it was converted to right-hand drive. But these days many British enthusiasts are keeping left-hand drive cars intact and original. They are still cheaper to buy in most cases in the UK, although prices are converging. They are convenient for continental touring and when the time comes to sell there's a hungry foreign market for left-hand drive staple British classics.

Popular Auction Choices

With auction activity at an all time high you have every chance of picking up the classic you are after at auction. The most common marque at British classic auctions is Jaguar, very closely followed by MG. However, the most popular single model is the MGB followed by the E-type Jaguar; a testimony to the high survival rate of E-types, their enduring appeal and collectibility, considering more than 500,000 MGBs were made compared to 70,000 E-types.

Triumph is the third most prolific classic marque with the TR models and the Stag which is the most popular Triumph at auction. Just behind Triumph is Mercedes, headed by the SL sports models from the 190SL of the 1950s and early 1960s to the 450SL of the 1970s and 1980s. In at number five is Rolls-Royce, the mainstay models being Silver Clouds and Shadows and their Bentley counterparts. In fact so popular are these models that if you lumped Bentley (seventh in the top 10) and Rolls together they would be the top seller overall. Ford at number six is sandwiched between Rolls and Bentley and the top 10 is completed by Austin, Morris and Ferrari. Considering the miniscule numbers of Ferraris made compared to Austin and Morris this is a strong indication of their enduring appeal.

And with that we wish you happy hunting and enjoyable classic motoring.

Dave Selby

ABARTH

Carlo Abarth initially launched his Turin business as a motor tuning concern in 1950, specialising mostly in the Fiat marque. His first proper car appeared in 1955 and he went on to produce in limited numbers a distinguished series of small-engined sports racers and competition machines. Throughout the 1960s Carlo Abarth squeezed extra performance out of Fiat 500s and 600s. Racing activities propelled the company into liquidation in 1971, when Fiat took over the competition shop and continued to apply the Abarth tag to hot Fiats.

1966 Abarth OT 2000 Coupé, 2 litre, 1946cc, Abarth engine, 215bhp at 7600rpm. **£50,000–55,000** *BKS*

This splendid little Porsche-baiter was intended to be Turin's answer to Stuttgart's Porsche 904 and 906 2 litre GT class endurance championship challengers. Now a very rare example.

Cross Reference
Fiat-Abarth

AC

From its earlier days producing three-wheeled tradesman's vehicles, AC graduated to building four-wheeled cars before WWI and in the 1920s and '30s offered a range of high-quality sporting cars. Immediate post-war products were idiosyncratic, if not inelegant, until the launch of the lovely Ace in 1954. Endowed with a mighty American Ford V8 engine, this dainty sports car was later transformed into the potent and legendary AC Cobra. Cobra mechanics and under-pinnings also spawned the AC 427 and 428,

a luxury GT which this time combined US power and British engineering with an elegant Italian body courtesy of Frua. A mere 80 of these well-bred but macho GTs were built before the fuel crisis of October 1973 dried up demand. In 1979 AC resumed production with the 3 litre, V6, mid-engined 3000ME. It was never beautiful but still looked extremely purposeful although its 120mph top speed did not live up to its aggressive posture. Only 82 were built and they remain an affordable oddball with a certain 'what is it?' appeal.

l. **1924 AC 'SF Edge Special' Sports Two Seater with Dickey,** polished aluminium body, specially-tuned 1991cc, AC 6 with aluminium cylinder head and triple carburettors. **£14,000–18,000** *BKS*

This engine was one of the great perennials of the British motor industry. Designed by engineer John Weller in 1919, it was one of this country's first series-production overhead camshaft engines, and powered successive AC models up to February 1963, when the last Weller 6 was fitted in the final Aceca to leave the factory.

Cross Reference
Restoration Projects

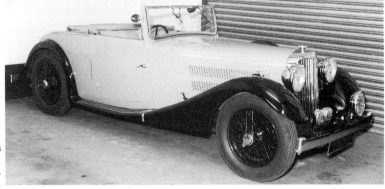

r. **1938 AC 16/60 Tourer,** 2 litre engine, Vanden Plas body, repainted, new hood, excellent original condition. **£18,000–20,000** *SW*

AC Model	ENGINE cc/cyl	DATES	CONDITION		
			1	2	3
Sociable	636/1	1907-12	£10,500	£9,000	£4,500
12/24 (Anzani)	1498/4	1919-27	£14,000	£11,500	£7,500
16/40	1991/6	1920-28	£18,000	£15,000	£11,000
16/60 Drophead/Saloon	1991/6	1937-40	£24,000	£21,000	£15,500
16/70 Sports Tourer	1991/6	1937-40	£35,000	£26,000	£18,000
16/80 Competition 2 Seater	1991/6	1937-40	£55,000	£45,000	£35,000

1939 AC Greyhound 15hp Four Door Saloon, original condition.
£5,000–6,000 *BKS*

Believed to be the 1938 Earls Court Show model, possibly the only one ever built, with less than 90,000 miles documented history. Very good original condition having been stored since the 1960s.

1960 AC Aceca, 2 litre, straight 6 engine, repainted, low mileage.
£28,000–30,000 *C*

One of only a handful of examples to have left the Thames Ditton factory with left-hand drive. Indeed only 55 Aceca's were shipped over to the United States. This is probably one of the most genuine examples in existence.

l. **1963 AC 4.7 Litre V8 Experimental Drophead Coupé,** aluminium coachwork restored to original design, original engine 260cu in replaced with 289cu in unit, Ford GT40 engine, 33,000 miles from new.
£25,000–35,000 *BKS*

The engine is one of a series of 5 Le Mans spec units numbered CP001 to CP005, produced at Cleveland, Ohio. This one is numbered CP003.

1966 AC Cobra 427 Open Sports, 8 cylinders, 6998cc, very good condition, original Goodyear Blue Dot tyres on Halibrand wheels, low mileage.
£120,000–130,000 *COYS*

Over £5,000 has been spent on a comprehensive service.

r. **1988 AC Cobra MkIV Roadster,** 5 litre Ford V8 engine, recorded mileage of under 13,500 miles, as new condition.
£35,000–40,000 *S*

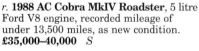

AC Model	ENGINE cc/cyl	DATES	CONDITION 1	2	3
2 litre	1991/6	1947-55	£6,000	£4,000	£1,000
Buckland	1991/6	1949-54	£8,500	£5,500	£2,500
Ace	1991/6	1953-63	£30,000	£25,000	£18,000
Ace Bristol	1971/6	1954-63	£42,000	£30,000	£25,000
Ace 2.6	1553/6	1961-62	£38,000	£32,000	£29,000
Aceca	1991/6	1954-63	£24,000	£17,000	£12,000
Aceca Bristol	1971/6	1956-63	£28,000	£21,000	£16,000
Greyhound Bristol	1971/6	1961-63	£16,000	£13,000	£8,000
Cobra Mk II 289	4735/8	1963-64	£90,000	£80,000	£70,000
Cobra Mk III 427	6998/8	1965-67	£125,000	£100,000	£90,000
Cobra Mk IV	5340/8	1987-	£55,000	£40,000	£32,000
428 Frua	7014/8	1967-73	£19,000	£15,000	£12,000
428 Frua Convertible	7014/8	1967-73	£25,000	£20,000	£16,000
3000 ME	2994/6	1976-84	£15,000	£10,000	£8,000

Racing history for Cobra will put the price to over £100,000–120,000.

ADLER

r. **1937 Adler Rennlimousine
Competition Coupé,** fully restored
to original specification.
£350,000+ *BLK*
*One of 3 competition Adlers built and
this car is the only remaining example.
The front-wheel drive aerodynamic
coupé was the only 1.5 litre Adler to
compete at Le Mans and Spa and these
successes stimulated the creation of
several other streamlined competition
cars. An award winner at the 1996
Pebble Beach Concours d'élégance.*

AEL

1949 AEL St Phall, 4 cylinder, in-line, 1543cc, Citroën traction avant engine, 76bhp at 4900rpm,
1400lbs, maximum speed of approx 112mph.
£1,200–1,500 *C*

*Originally conceived as a light aerodynamic touring car it was well suited to long distance endurance-style
racing. It was designed and built by Dr Andre Le Pelletier, a well-known figure in the pre-war French motor
racing scene. The AEL St Phall was his second post-war car venture and was also destined to be his last.*

ALFA ROMEO

l. **1932 Alfa
Romeo 6C 1750
Gran Sport,**
original Zagato
coachwork,
fully restored.
£225,000+ *BC*

r. **1965 Alfa Romeo 2600 Sprint
Coupé,** 6 cylinder, 2584cc, twin
overhead camshaft engine, 5 speed
all-synchromesh gearbox, 4 seater
Bertone coachwork, all-round disc
brakes, 36,000 recorded miles,
bodywork resprayed.
£4,750–5,500 *BKS*

ALFA ROMEO Model	ENGINE cc/cyl	DATES	CONDITION		
			1	2	3
24HP	4084/4	1910-11	£25,000	£16,000	£12,000
12HP	2413/4	1910-11	£18,000	£11,000	£8,000
40-60	6028/4	1913-15	£32,000	£24,000	£14,000
RL	2916/6	1921-22	£30,000	£24,000	£14,000
RM	1944/4	1924-25	£28,000	£17,000	£13,000
6C 1500	1487/6	1927-28	£50,000*	£20,000	£10,000
6C 1750	1752/6	1923-33	£100,000+	£60,000	-
6C 1900	1917/6	1933	£18,000	£15,000	£12,000
6C 2300	2309/6	1934	£22,000	£18,000	£15,000
6C 2500 SS Cabriolet/Spider	2443/6	1939-45	£100,000	£50,000	£40,000
6C 2500 SS Coupé	2443/6	1939-45	£60,000	£40,000	£30,000
8C 2300 Monza/Short Chassis	2300/8	1931-34	£1,000,000	£400,000	£200,000
8C 2900	2900/8	1935-39	£1,000,000	£500,000	£300,000

Value is very dependent on sporting history, body style and engine type.
*The high price on this model is dependent on whether it is 1500 supercharged/twin overhead cam.

Cross Reference
Restoration Projects

l. **1965 Alfa Romeo Giulia Sprint GT,** 4 cylinders, 1570cc, right-hand drive, excellent overall condition, under 63,000 miles, original toolkit, sales invoice, photographs taken during its respray and large quantity of paperwork.
£5,000–6,000 *ADT*

r. **1967 Alfa Romeo Duetto Spider,** excellent condition.
£10,500–12,000 *FM*

The Alfa Romeo Spider has enjoyed a cult following ever since one was driven by Dustin Hoffman to the strains of Simon and Garfunkel in the film The Graduate. *This particular car was a Concours and Lady's Cup winner.*

1967 Alfa Romeo Duetto Spider, 1750cc, fully restored.
£9,500–10,500 *PC*

Perspex headlamp covers give smoother air-flow and raises top speed a little. However, this type of headlamp was banned in the USA.

l. **1967 Alfa Romeo Duetto Spider,** 1600cc, imported from South Africa, original right-hand drive, resprayed and very good condition.
£8,750–10,000 *H&H*

When the new Spider was first seen at the Geneva Motor Show in 1966, Alfa launched a competition to name the car. After ploughing through 140,000 entries with suggestions like Lollobrigida, Bardot and Nuvolari, they chose Duetto, which neatly summed up the two's-company-three's-a-crowd image.

1968 Alfa Romeo Sprint GT, good condition, well maintained, full history.
£6,500–7,000 *FM*

1970 Alfa Romeo 1300 Junior Zagato.
£8,000–9,000 *FM*

Excellent car on Italian plates.

1972 Alfa Romeo 2000 GTV Bertone, new fuel tank, complete new clutch assembly and silencers fitted.
£2,250–3,000 *PA*

1974 Alfa Romeo Montreal, 2593cc, 200bhp, 4 cam V8, ZF 5 speed gearbox.
£11,500–13,000 *PAL*

First seen in Canada in 1967 – hence the name – the Bertone-styled Montreal offered sparkling performance with a 137mph top speed. Just under 4,000 were produced from 1970–77. A small number of right-hand drive cars, like this example, were produced from 1974.

1975 Alfa Romeo Montreal,
2593cc, V8 twin overhead
camshaft engine, 200bhp and
173lb ft at 6500rpm and
4750rpm respectively,
0–60mph in 7.6 seconds,
maximum speed of 137mph.
£10,500–12,000 *COYS*

*One of approximately 100
right-hand drive cars. Bills
totalling more than £15,000
for restoration work are
supplied and the mileage is
warranted at 57,000.*

r. **1975 Alfa Romeo Montreal,**
2593cc, V8, DOHC, 200bhp,
0-60mph in 7.6 seconds,
maximum speed of 140mph,
reconditioned engine, resprayed,
new clutch and radiator,
black interior, fair condition.
£5,500–6,500 *BRIT*

ALFA ROMEO Model	ENGINE cc/cyl	DATES	CONDITION 1	2	3
2000 Spider	1974/4	1958-61	£15,000	£9,000	£3,000
2600 Sprint	2584/6	1962-66	£11,000	£7,500	£4,000
2600 Spider	2584/6	1962-65	£14,000	£12,000	£5,000
Giulietta Sprint	1290/4	1955-62	£10,000	£7,000	£4,000
Giulietta Spider	1290/4	1956-62	£11,000	£6,000	£4,500
Giulia Saloon	1570/4	1962-72	£5,000	£3,000	£1,500
Giulia Sprint (rhd)	1570/4	1962-68	£10,500	£6,000	£2,000
Giulia Spider (rhd)	1570/4	1962-65	£11,000	£8,000	£5,000
Giulia SS	1570/4	1962-66	£16,000	£13,000	£10,000
GT 1300 Junior	1290/4	1966-77	£7,000	£5,500	£3,000
Giulia Sprint GT (105)	1570/4	1962-68	£7,500	£5,000	£3,000
1600GT Junior	1570/4	1972-75	£7,000	£4,000	£2,000
1750/2000 Berlina	1779/1962/4	1967-77	£4,000	£2,500	£1,500
1750GTV	1779/4	1967-72	£9,000	£7,000	£3,000
2000GTV	1962/4	1971-77	£8,000	£5,500	£3,000
1600/1750 (Duetto)	1570/1779/4	1966-67	£10,000	£7,500	£5,000
1750/2000 Spider (Kamm)	1779/1962/4	1967-78	£9,000	£6,000	£4,000
Montreal	2593/8	1970-77	£10,000	£8,000	£5,000
Junior Zagato 1300	1290/4	1968-74	£10,000	£7,000	£4,000
Junior Zagato 1600	1570/4	1968-74	£11,000	£8,000	£5,000
Alfetta GT/GTV (chrome)	1962/4	1972-86	£4,000	£2,500	£1,000
Alfasud	1186/1490/4	1972-83	£2,000	£1,000	£500
Alfasud ti	1186/1490/4	1974-81	£2,500	£1,200	£900
Alfasud Sprint	1284/1490/4	1976-85	£3,000	£2,000	£1,000
GTV6	2492/6	1981-	£4,000	£2,500	£1,000

1976 Alfa Romeo 1600 GT Junior, 4 cylinders, 1570cc, carefully maintained, 41,000 miles recorded. **£3,750–4,250** *BRIT*

Miller's Starter Marque

Starter Alfa Romeos: *1750 and 2000 GTV; 1300 Junior Spider, 1600 Duetto Spider, 1750 and 2000 Spider Veloce; 1300 and 1600 GT Junior; Alfasud ti and Sprint.*

• Responsive, eager and sweet twin-cam engines, finely balanced chassis, nimble handling and delightful looks are just some of the character traits of classic Alfas from the mid-1960s onwards. They are also eminently affordable. For the kind of money that gets you an MGB or TR Triumph you could be a little more adventurous and acquire an engaging Alfa Romeo sporting saloon or convertible.

1986 Alfa Romeo, 6 cylinder, 2,500cc engine, automatic gearbox, 40,000 miles recorded, air conditioning, power-assisted steering, electric windows, alloy wheels, central locking, engine and gearbox restored, right-hand drive. **£1,700–2,000** *H&H*

l. **c1988 Alfa Romeo Spider Veloce,** 2 litres, European specification. **£7,000–8,000** *CARS*

ALLARD

Sydney Herbert Allard's name has been synonymous with various forms of motor sport since the mid-1930s, when he dominated trials and hillclimbs with his Ford V8 specials. Allard drove his own creation to win the British RAC hillclimb championship in 1949 and the Monte Carlo Rally in 1952. The basis of these specials was to form the new range of Allards that were introduced in 1946 with their box section rigid frame chassis and Ford V8 engines. The export market to America was Allard's future aim, and various tuned V8-engine options were available, ranging from the 3.6 litre Ford or 3.9 Mercury to the fearsome and legendary Cadillac engines. Many cars were exported without engines and transmission, enabling the owners to install their own tuned engines.

1951 Allard P1 Saloon, 3.6 litre, Ford V8 engine, unrestored condition.
£4,500–5,000 *S*

In 1952 Sydney Allard scored an epic victory in the Monte Carle rally in a P1 saloon.

1951 Allard J2 Roadster, 5899cc, specially modified Cadillac V8 engine, 275bhp at 6,300rpm, restored.
£80,000–95,000 *C*

This car is one of the most famous and successful Allards to ever race and was originally sold to Tom Carstens and raced by Bill Pollack.

ALLARD Model	ENGINE cc/cyl	DATES	CONDITION 1	2	3
K/K2/L/M/M2X	3622/8	1947-54	£18,500	£12,000	£8,000
K3	var/8	1953-54	£24,000	£15,000	£11,000
P1	3622/8	1949-52	£19,500	£13,000	£8,000
P2	3622/8	1952-54	£22,000	£18,000	£11,500
J2/J2X	var/8	1950-54	£60,000	£50,000	£35,000
Palm Beach	1508/4, 2262/6	1952-55	£10,000	£7,500	£4,500
Palm Beach II	2252/ 3442/6	1956-60	£22,500	£18,000	£11,000

ALVIS

r. **1929 Alvis Supercharged Two Door Sports Tourer,** front-wheel drive, 4 speed manual gearbox, substantially rebuilt engine, coachwork and interior, fair condition.
£15,500–16,500 *BKS*

Alvis experimented with front-wheel drive from around 1925 onwards, initially with a back-to-front 12/50 engine. In 1928 front-wheel drive cars finished 6th and 9th at Le Mans, in which year limited production commenced.

1937 Alvis 4.3 Litre Sports Tourer, 4387cc, straight 6 cylinder, overhead valve engine, triple SU carburettors rebuilt by specialists, top end of engine rebuilt, including new rings, coachwork by Charlesworth, good condition.
£25,000–30,000 *BKS*

1931 Alvis 12/50 Silver Eagle Four Seater Tourer, coachwork by Cross & Ellis, excellent history.
£22,000–25,000 *UMC*

ALVIS Model	ENGINE cc/cyl	DATES	CONDITION 1	2	3
12/50	1496/4	1923-32	£20,000	£13,000	£7,000
Silver Eagle	2148	1929-37	£14,000	£10,000	£8,000
Silver Eagle DHC	2148	1929-37	£16,000	£11,000	£8,000
12/60	1645/4	1931-32	£15,000	£10,000	£7,000
Speed 20 (tourer)	2511/6	1932-36	£35,000	£28,000	£18,000
Speed 20 (closed)	2511/6	1932-36	£22,000	£15,000	£11,000
Crested Eagle	3571/6	1933-39	£10,000	£7,000	£4,000
Firefly (tourer)	1496/4	1932-34	£12,000	£10,000	£6,000
Firefly (closed)	1496/6	1932-34	£7,000	£5,000	£4,000
Firebird (tourer)	1842/4	1934-39	£13,000	£10,000	£6,000
Firebird (closed)	1842/4	1934-39	£7,000	£5,000	£4,000
Speed 25 (tourer)	3571/6	1936-40	£38,500	£30,000	£20,000
Speed 25 (closed)	3571/6	1936-40	£20,000	£15,000	£12,000
3.5 litre	3571/6	1935-36	£35,000	£25,000	£18,000
4.3 litre	4387/6	1936-40	£44,000	£30,000	£22,000
Silver Crest	2362/6	1936-40	£14,000	£10,000	£7,000
TA	3571/6	1936-39	£18,000	£12,000	£8,000
12/70	1842/4	1937-40	£14,000	£10,000	£7,000

1940 Alvis 12/70 Series II Mulliner Saloon, retrimmed, in need of some restoration.
£4,000–5,000 *UMC*

1950 Alvis TB14 Roadster,
4 cylinders, 1892cc, restored.
£9,500–10,500 *BRIT*

Whilst the styling may have been controversial, the competence of the car was never in doubt and today the model is seen as a period piece and a throw back to the excellent sporting Alvis's of the 1930s. With just 100 produced, this model is rarely seen.

l. **1948 Alvis TA14 Tickford Convertible.**
£9,000–10,000 *AS*

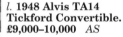

1952 Alvis TA21 Tickford Drophead Convertible, 6 cylinder, 2993cc, overhead valve engine, 4 speed synchromesh gearbox and twin SU carburettors, restored.
£24,500–27,000 *S*
Restored to the highest standards, with receipts totalling £30,000.

l. **1958 Alvis TD21 Two Door Saloon,** coachwork by Park Ward, recently fitted replacement automatic gearbox, original red leather interior, fair condition.
£7,500–8,500 *BKS*

This car would benefit from remedial mechanical and cosmetic work in some areas and an enthusiast's touch.

1961 Alvis TD21 Two Door Saloon, coachwork by Park Ward, original Radiomobile and toolkit, 23,000 miles recorded, resprayed, large collection of documentation.
£7,750–8,750 *HOLL*

1961 Alvis TD21 Series I Saloon, 4 speed manual gearbox, excellent mechanical condition, chassis and body fair, full history.
£5,000–6,000 *UMC*

1961 Alvis TD21 Two Door Saloon, 6 cylinders, 2993cc, overhead valve, automatic gearbox, right-hand drive, 75,580 miles recorded, unused in recent years, requires attention.
£2,000–3,000 *C*

Alvis's last all new model was the 3 litre, launched at the 1950 Geneva Salon which it progressively developed up to the abandonment by the company of private-car production in 1967. For the last 11 years bodies were styled by the Swiss coachbuilder, Graber, with production coachwork entrusted to Park Ward. As perhaps the last of the traditional thoroughbred luxury cars, Alvis T series enjoy a loyal following. Just 1,067 chassis of the TD21 were built between 1959 and 1962.

ALVIS Model	ENGINE cc/cyl	DATES	CONDITION		
			1	2	3
TA14	1892/4	1946-50	£9,500	£8,000	£4,500
TA14 DHC	1892/4	1946-50	£14,000	£12,000	£5,000
TB14 Roadster	1892/4	1949-50	£15,000	£10,000	£8,000
TB21 Roadster	2993/6	1951	£16,000	£10,000	£7,000
TA21/TC21	2993/6	1950-55	£12,000	£9,000	£5,000
TA21/TC21 DHC	2993/6	1950-55	£17,000	£13,000	£10,000
TC21/100 Grey Lady	2993/6	1953-56	£13,000	£11,000	£5,000
TC21/100 DHC	2993/6	1954-56	£19,000	£15,000	£9,000
TD21	2993/6	1956-62	£11,000	£8,000	£6,000
TD21 DHC	2993/6	1956-62	£22,000	£16,000	£10,000
TE21	2993/6	1963-67	£15,000	£10,000	£8,000
TE21 DHC	2993/6	1963-67	£25,000	£16,000	£12,000
TF21	2993/6	1966-67	£16,000	£12,000	£9,500
TF21 DHC	2993/6	1966-67	£28,000	£17,000	£13,000

AMILCAR

The French company's first production model appeared in 1921 and throughout that decade a series of delightful sporting voiturettes and light cars came out of the Paris works. In the 1930s the company changed direction to concentrate on family transport. The company was taken over by Hotchkiss in 1937 before fading away altogether in 1939.

1926 Amilcar-Riley Special, 4 cylinder, 1089cc, twin camshaft Riley 9 engine based on a G type Cabriolet, chassis shortened and fitted with a C6 style body.
£22,000–25,000   *COYS*

This car was discovered in a French farmyard.

1922 Amilcar CC 7.5hp Two Seater Sports,
4 cylinder, 905cc, side valve engine, coachwork by Weymann of Paris, good condition, known history.
£14,000–16,000   *S*

Together with Senechal and Salmson, the Amilcar was the archetypal French small sports car, and dominated the market until the advent of the first MG M-Type Midget at the end of the 1920s. This example is believed to be one of the earliest known survivors of the marque, and the only example with bodywork by Weymann of Paris.

ANGUS-SANDERSON

1921 Angus-Sanderson, 4 cylinders, 2300cc, 14.3hp, chassis-up restoration.
£14,000–15,000   *C*

Only about 2,500 Angus-Sanderson motor cars were made and one of its main strengths was its pretty bodywork. Sales of the 14.3hp continued until 1927, before the company ceased trading.

l. **1921 Angus-Sanderson 14.4hp De Luxe Open Tourer,** 2.3 litre engine, restored to original specification.
£17,000–20,000   *BKS*

The old-established coachbuilding firm of Sir William Angus, Sanderson & Co Ltd commenced motor manufacture in 1918 in Newcastle-upon-Tyne.

ARMSTRONG-SIDDELEY

John Davenport Siddeley was typical of the cycling men whose interest turned to motor cars. The name Siddeley appeared in several motor companies from the Siddeley Autocar Company to Wolseley-Siddeley Cars to the Siddeley-Deasey Motor Car Company Ltd and finally to Armstrong-Siddeley. The Coventry firm emphasised good workmanship and ease of driving, and production on a conservative scale averaged 300 models a year. The last Armstrong-Siddeley was produced in 1959.

1926 Armstrong-Siddeley 18hp Sports Saloon,
short saloon, coachwork by Weymann, good original condition.
£6,000–7,000   *S*

1932 Armstrong-Siddeley, long 15, pre-select gearbox, re-trimmed in blue leather, resprayed, good condition.
£12,000–14,000   *AS*

l. **1936 Armstrong-Siddeley 17hp Four door Tickford Cabriolet,** 6 cylinder overhead valve engine, 2394cc, Wilson pre-selector gearbox, engine recently rebuilt.
£8,500–10,000 *BKS*

This model was available in 3 chassis lengths, and mechanically the cars were conventional for the period, with semi-elliptic springs all-round and mechanical brakes. This particular cabriolet conversion car is believed to be the sole surviving car of this type.

ARMSTRONG-SIDDELEY Model	ENGINE cc/cyl	DATES	CONDITION		
			1	2	3
Hurricane	1991/6	1945-53	£10,000	£7,000	£4,000
Typhoon	1991/6	1946-50	£7,000	£3,000	£2,000
Lancaster/Whitley	1991/ 2306/6	1945-53	£8,500	£6,500	£3,500
Sapphire 234/236	2290/4 2309/6	1955-58	£7,500	£5,000	£3,000
Sapphire 346	3440/6	1953-58	£9,000	£5,000	£3,000
Star Sapphire	3990/6	1958-60	£10,000	£7,000	£4,000

ASA

Autocostruzioni Societa per Azioni of Turin was founded in 1962 by the de Nora family, wealthy industrialists active in the Italian electro-chemical industries. A Bizzarini design based on a proposed 'baby' Ferrari first shown at Turin in 1961, the ASA GT or 'Ferrarina' as it came to be known was powered by a single overhead camshaft 4 cylinder engine of 1032cc, producing 97bhp at 7000rpm. Top speed was in the region of 113mph. The Spider version with Bertone-styled glassfibre bodywork appeared the following year. Unfortunately, ASA ceased production in 1967 after around 80 Coupés and seven Spiders had been built.

1965 ASA 1000 GT Spider, 4 cylinders, 1032cc, producing 97bhp at 7000rpm, Italian racing red, black upholstered interior, good condition, complete with large quantity of original spare parts.
£14,000–16,000 *BKS*

The 14th car to be constructed, this left-hand drive Spider has had only 2 owners.

ASTON MARTIN

Bamford & Martin Ltd was set up in 1913 by engineers Robert Bamford and Lionel Martin from a base in London's South Kensington, initially tuning and developing Singer 10s. In 1919 the first prototype Aston Martins were produced (the name was formed from the Aston Clinton Hillclimb and Lionel Martin's surname), however the cars were not available for sale for another two years or more. Although the company achieved considerable sporting success its financial base was always flimsy, with frequent changes of ownership.

In 1947 the company was taken over by tractor manufacturer David Brown, whose initials gave name to the memorable DB series. With losses of £1 million a year, Brown relinquished ownership and since 1987 Ford has been custodian of one of the most charismatic British sporting marques.

1930 Aston Martin International Four-Seater Short Chassis, 1.5 litre engine, 11.9hp, original Bertelli coachwork, recently recommissioned for the road.
£35,000–40,000 *S*

The famed 1.5 litre Aston Martin International was unveiled in 1928, an 11.9hp sports car with a top speed in excess of 80mph. The International featured dry sump lubrication, Ricardo type combustion chambers and a single overhead camshaft activating inclined overhead valves.

ASTON MARTIN Model	ENGINE cc/cyl	DATES	CONDITION 1	2	3
Lionel Martin Cars	1486/4	1921-25	£26,000	£18,000	£16,000
International	1486/4	1927-32	£30,000	£18,000	£16,000
Le Mans	1486/4	1932-33	£52,000	£38,000	£32,000
Mk II	1486/4	1934-36	£40,000	£30,000	£25,000
Ulster	1486/4	1934-36	£80,000	£50,000	-
2 litre	1950/4	1936-40	£25,000	£18,000	£9,000

Value is dependent upon racing history, originality and completeness.
Add 40% if a competition winner or works team car.

1937 Aston Martin 2 litre Two Door Sports Tourer, 2/4 seater coachwork by Abbott on a 15/98 chassis, subject of considerable work.
£28,500-32,500 *BKS*

The new series of 2 litre Aston Martins made their first appearance at the 1936 Olympia Motor Show. The wet sump engine was described in a contemporary road test as 'softer, quieter and more flexible, whilst acceleration and general suitability for everyday purposes have increased out of all knowledge'.

1950 Aston Martin Prototype DB2 Drophead Coupé, 6 cylinder, 2580cc engine, twin-cams, engine rebuilt in 1983 and in 1989, rewired, chassis, tyres, transmission and gearbox in good condition.
£54,000-59,000 *S*

The acquisition of the company by David Brown in 1947 was followed by the first DB model, DB1, exhibited at Earls Court in 1948. The DB2 version was announced at the New York Show in 1950 and was later available in drophead form. The W.O. Bentley inspired 6 cylinder, 2580cc twin-cam engine was fitted to a space frame of square section tubing, with suspension springs and trailing arms front and rear.

l. **1955 Aston Martin DB2/4 MkI,** 2922cc, 4 speed manual gearbox, alloy sports body, complete restoration.
£24,000-28,000 *H&H*

1953 Aston Martin DB2, meticulously restored, good condition.
£50,000-55,000 *MEE*
This car was originally owned by Lord Brabazon.

1959 Aston Martin DB2/4 MkIII, 6 cylinder, in-line, 2922cc, double overhead camshaft, 162bhp at 5500rpm, 4 speed manual gearbox, trailing link front suspension, live axle with coil springs, radius arms and Panhard rod at rear, disc and drum brakes, left-hand drive, engine rebuilt, stainless steel exhaust system, Swiss-owned from new.
£32,000–35,000 *C*

With its unusual trailing link front suspension and well located live rear axle the DB2/4 Mk III was one of the best handling GT cars of the 1950s. The Autocar December 1957 road test of the Mk III credited the car with a top speed of 120mph with 91mph available in third gear, 0–60mph in 9.3 seconds in second gear at between 16–22mpg.

1960 Aston Martin DB4 Convertible, converted from saloon by Paul Banham, 6 cylinder, 3670cc, 240bhp.
£20,000–23,000 *COYS*

The DB4's performance of 140mph, 0–60mph in around 9 seconds and 0–100mph in 20 seconds ranked it amongst the fastest grand tourers available. Its Connolly leather and Wilton carpeted interior ensured that it was also one of the most luxurious.

1960 Aston Martin DB4 Series IV, special series engine, entensive marque specialist restoration, first class condition.
£47,500–52,500 *MEE*

1960 Aston Martin DB4GT, immaculate condition, complete restoration with marque specialists.
£160,000–170,000 *MEE*

Although the David Brown era is considered by many to be Aston Martin's golden period the company struggled to make a profit on its cars. A friend once asked David Brown if he could buy an Aston Martin at cost price. David Brown replied: 'I would love to sell it to you at cost, but I couldn't possibly charge you that much.'

Aston Martin DB5, 1964–5

Production: 1,058 (898 saloons,
160 convertibles).
1964 price: £4,175. 7s. 1d. (saloon)
Engine: 3995cc, straight 6, with triple SU carbs
(triple Webers on Vantage).
Power output: 282bhp (Vantage: 314bhp).
Transmission: 5 speed ZF gearbox.
Brakes: Girling discs all-round.
0-60mph: 7 seconds. 0–100mph: 15 seconds.
Top speed: 147.6mph (in Vantage tune).

The specs only tell half the story of the classic
series of 6 cylinder DB Astons. The sensational
shape of the DB5 evolved from the DB4 of 1958,
with its sharp new Italian designer suit by
Carrozzeria Touring of Milan. Under the
aluminium body was a platform chassis with
Touring's trademark lightweight steel tube
frame construction known as Superleggera –
super lightweight. The engine evolved from the
Le Mans racing Astons.

In short, the DB4 looked superb and went like
stink. Aston owner, industrialist David Brown –

the DB of the DB Astons – wanted the world to
know it and orchestrated a publicity stunt in
which the DB4 shot to 100mph and rest again
in under 30 seconds. He later trimmed the
time to a remarkable 20 seconds with Girling
disc brakes.

The DB5 was even more powerful, its engine
enlarged from 3.7 to 4 litres and the short
life of the DB5 spanned the glory years for
Aston, or more precisely, the glory year. For the
first and only time in David Brown's ownership
Aston Martin made more than 1,000 cars in
a year. That was in the 1964/5 season and
production in that year virtually matched the
entire production run of 1,110 DB4s produced
from 1958-63. James Bond really did have
that effect.

The DB6 which followed, with its turned-up
rear spoiler, was heavier and yet more powerful.
From 1965–71 only 1,753 were produced and
the arrival of the DBS V8 in 1969 marked the
end of the classic DB series of 6 cylinder Astons.

l. **1961 Aston Martin DB4
Series II,** complete engine rebuild,
excellent condition throughout.
£32,000–35,000 *COYS*

*The DB4 made its debut at the 1958
London Motor Show to great public
acclaim. Successor to the DB MkIII,
it was the first production Aston
Martin to use both Tadek Marek's
new twin overhead camshaft
straight 6 all-alloy engine and an
aluminium body designed by
Touring of Milan using its
Superleggera method of attachment
to a lightweight steel tube frame.*

1962 Aston Martin DB4 Series V Vantage, 6 cylinder, in-line, twin overhead camshaft, 3670cc engine,
266bhp at 5750rpm, 4 speed manual gearbox, 4 wheel disc brakes, all coil spring independent front
suspension, right-hand drive, fully restored.
£38,000–43,000 *C*

*The acquisition of Aston Martin along with Lagonda in the late 1940s by David Brown brought new
security to the 2 companies. It also gave Aston Martin access to W.O. Bentley's splendid twin-cam engine,
a layout favoured on all subsequent 6 cylinder cars. Series V DB4 cars, introduced in September 1962 were
lengthened about 3½in to 15ft, which gave more leg room and luggage space. With a special series (SS) or
Vantage engine using triple SU carburettors and a compression ratio of 9:1 the bhp rose by 16 to 266bhp.*

l. **1964 Aston Martin DB5,**
outstanding original
condition, 51,000 miles
from new.
£55,000–60,000 *MEE*

ASTON MARTIN Model	ENGINE cc/cyl	DATES	CONDITION 1	2	3
DB1	1970/4	1948-50	£30,000	£20,000	£16,000
DB2	2580/6	1950-53	£25,000+	£18,000	£14,000
DB2 Conv	2580/6	1951-53	£35,000	£28,000	£17,000
DB2/4 Mk I/II	2580/ 2922/6	1953-57	£30,000	£18,000	£14,000
DB2/4 Mk II Conv	2580/ 2922/6	1953-57	£35,000	£25,000	£15,000
DB2/4 Mk III	2580/ 2922/6	1957-59	£35,000	£22,000	£15,000
DB2/4 Mk III Conv	2580/ 2922/6	1957-59	£38,000	£26,000	£20,000
DB Mk III Conv	2922/6	1957-59	£46,000	£28,000	£20,000
DB Mk III	2922/6	1957-59	£35,000	£22,000	£18,000
DB4	3670/6	1959-63	£35,000	£22,000	£16,000
DB4 Conv	3670/6	1961-63	£60,000	£35,000	-
DB4 GT	3670/6	1961-63	£100,000+	£80,000	-
DB5	3995/6	1964-65	£35,000	£26,000	£20,000
DB5 Conv	3995/6	1964-65	£48,000+	£38,000	-
DB6	3995/6	1965-69	£30,000	£20,000	£16,000
DB6 Mk I auto	3995/6	1965-69	£28,000	£18,000	£14,000
DB6 Mk I Volante	3995/6	1965-71	£42,000	£32,000	£28,000
DB6 Mk II Volante	3995/6	1969-70	£50,000	£40,000	£30,000
DBS	3995/6	1967-72	£14,000	£12,000	£9,000
AM Vantage	5340/8	1977-78	£16,000	£12,000	£10,000
V8 Vantage Oscar India	5340/8	1978-82	£30,000	£25,000	£20,000
V8 Volante	5340/8	2978-82	£35,000	£30,000	£25,000

1964 Aston Martin DB5 Saloon, re-upholstered in white hide, bare metal respray, new chrome wire wheels, sunroof fitted.
£25,000–28,000 *S*

This model was immortalised by the James Bond film Goldfinger.

1968 Aston Martin DB6 Volante, 6 cylinders, 3995cc, good condition throughout.
£48,000–55,000 *COYS*

The well proven 3995cc engine gave a top speed in excess of 150mph, however, the DB6 was a proper 4 seater as a result of increased length. Other body alterations included a Kamm tail which reduced areodynamic lift. This car is one of only 140 open Volante models.

1964 Aston Martin DB5 Convertible, ex-Sir David Brown, excellent original condition.
£70,000–80,000 *MEE*

1970 Aston Martin DBS, fully restored, many concours wins.
£18,500–22,500 *PA*

1971 Aston Martin DB6 MkII Two Door Saloon, 6 cylinders, 3995cc engine, twin SU carburettors, 282bhp, automatic gearbox, ground-up restoration, Aston Martin Owners Club concours prize winner.
£20,000–25,000 *BKS*

This car was one of the very last DB6s to leave the Newport Pagnell factory.

1980 Aston Martin V8 Vantage Two Door Saloon, 5340cc, double overhead camshaft engine, 5 speed manual gearbox, right-hand drive, considerable work carried out, excellent condition, electrics in working order with the exception of the electric mirror.
£32,000–35,000 *BKS*

Introduced in 1977, by 1986 the V8 Vantage engine was producing 432bhp with 0–60mph in under 6 seconds, and a top speed of 168mph. Some 313 saloons were sold between 1977 and 1989, with the Volante convertible being added in 1986, of which 116 were made.

1979 Aston Martin V8 Volante, 5340cc, 4 Weber carburettors, 300bhp, 3 speed automatic gearbox, upper/lower control arms front suspension, coil springs rear, De Dion axle, trailing arms and coil springs, front and rear disc brakes, left-hand drive, 37,000 miles, full service history.
£30,000–35,000 *C*

In August 1973 the new Aston Martin V8 was unveiled with 4 twin choke 42 DCNF Weber carburettors replacing the previously used Bosch fuel injection. Not only did these Italian carburettors improve the performance with extra torque, but they were good enough to get the car through US emission regulations.

1980 Aston Martin Lagonda Sports Saloon, power steering pump requires attention, requires recommissioning.
£6,000–9,000 *BKS*

Aston Martin, under their new management in 1975, set about producing a new model. First shown at the 1976 British Motor Show the car known as the 'Lagonda' went into production by 1978 featuring the 5.3 litre V8 engine and Chrysler automatic gearbox. Instrumentation was by way of advanced electronic digital displays. These technical advances initially caused some teething problems at the factory and subsequently the first deliveries were delayed, the first car being delivered in April 1978.

l. **1987 Aston Martin V8 Volante,** automatic gearbox, left-hand drive, fully-lined power hood, factory serviced, 13,000km from new.
£45,000–50,000 *BKS*

The Aston Martin V8, which made its debut as the DBS V8 in October 1969, made its last show appearance at the 1988 Geneva Salon. The record-breaking production run saw 2,919 V8s sold to make this the most successful Aston Martin since the company built its first car in 1915.

1988 Aston Martin V8 Volante, 5340cc, low mileage, good condition throughout.
£45,000–50,000 *COYS*

ATALANTA

1939 Atalanta V12 Four Seater Drophead Convertible, 4.2 litre, Lincoln Zephyr V12 engine, fully restored.
£40,000–45,000 *PC*

Atalanta Motors of Staines, Middlesex, produced exciting sports cars between 1937 and 1939. They were technically advanced and, with all-round independent suspension, fine handlers. Only 15 were made and 3 remain in existence.

AUSTIN

From its foundation in 1905 until its demise in 1987 the name of Austin remained a main artery running through the heart of the British motor industry. At various times in its history Austin was the largest British car maker. As for the cars, Austin's greatest legacy must surely be the two modest machines that transformed British motoring: The Austin 7 of 1922 brought motoring en masse to the middle classes, and in 1959 the new Austin Se7en, as it was originally badged, brought motoring to millions in a pocket-sized world-beater better known as the Mini.

1928 Austin 7 Chummy,
good condition.
£4,200–4,900 *CC*

Cross Reference
Commercial Vehicles

1929 Austin Heavy 12/4 Clifton Tourer,
paintwork very good with excellent original leather interior, hood and sidescreens, running order, good original condition.
£11,000–14,000 *DH*

l. **1928 Austin 12/4 Landaulette,**
good condition.
£8,500–10,500 *CC*

Austin Milestones

1866: Herbert Austin born 8 November.
1905: Austin Motor Company founded.
1914: Austin became public company.
1917: Herbert Austin knighted.
1922: Austin 7 launched.
1929: 100,000th Austin 7 built.
1936: Sir Herbert Austin became the first Baron Austin of Longbridge.
1941: Herbert Austin died 23 May.
1946: The millionth Austin built 25 June, an Austin 16.
1952: Austin merged with Morris to form British Motor Corporation (BMC), on 1 April.
1952: A30 Austin's first monocoque car.
1953: 2,000,000th Austin built.
1959: Mini launched on 26 August.
1966: British Motor Corporation becomes British Motor Holdings after merger with Jaguar.
1968: Merger with Leyland results in another name, British Leyland Motor Corporation.
1975: British Leyland nationalised.
1980: British Leyland reorganises with Austin-badged cars produced under Austin-Rover Group banner.
1986: 5,000,000th Mini was produced 19 February.
1987: Austin name disappears from remaining models and company name shortened to the Rover Group. The end of Austin.

1928 Austin 7, Gordon England fabric body, excellent condition.
£5,200–6,200 *CC*

1929 Austin 7, excellent condition.
£3,750–4,450 *CC*

r. **1930 Austin 7 Ulster Replica,** 4 cylinders, 747cc, re-bodied with Ulster-type coachwork in 1976, completely renovated including body-off repaint and replating of brightwork, rewired.
£8,000–9,500 *ADT*

1926 Austin 12/4 Truck.
£8,500–9,500 *FHF*

AUSTIN Model	ENGINE cc/cyl	DATES	CONDITION 1	2	3
25/30	4900/4	1906	£35,000	£25,000	£20,000
20/4	3600/4	1919-29	£20,000	£12,000	£6,000
12	1661/4	1922-26	£8,000	£5,000	£2,000
7/Chummy	747/4	1924-39	£7,000	£4,000	£2,500
7 Coachbuilt/Nippy/Opal etc	747/4	1924-39	£10,000	£9,000	£7,000
12/4	1861/4	1927-35	£5,500	£4,000	£2,000
16	2249/6	1928-36	£9,000	£7,000	£4,000
20/6	3400/6	1928-38	£12,500	£10,000	£8,000
12/6	1496/6	1932-37	£6,000	£4,000	£1,500
12/4	1535/4	1933-39	£5,000	£3,500	£1,500
10 and 10/4	1125/4	1932-47	£4,000	£3,000	£1,000
10 and 10/4 Conv	1125/4	1933-47	£5,000	£3,500	£1,000
18	2510/6	1934-39	£8,000	£5,000	£3,000
14	1711/6	1937-39	£6,000	£4,000	£2,000
Big Seven	900/4	1938-39	£4,000	£2,500	£1,500
8	900/4	1939-47	£3,000	£2,000	£1,000
28	4016/6	1939	£6,000	£4,000	£2,000

Prices for early Austin models are dependent on body style, landaulette, tourer, etc.

l. **1930 Austin 7 Chummy,** 747cc, restored, mechanically in serviceable order. **£4,750–5,250** *BRIT*

The introduction of the Austin 7 in 1922 changed Britain's whole way of thinking on economy cars. So successful was this little motor car that within a very short space of time the primitive cycle cars of the day became virtually a thing of the past. Also the new model opened up the reality of motor car ownership to the man who had hitherto used a motorcycle combination. Despite the tiny 750cc engine, the little car proved to be so durable that many examples remained in daily use until the 1960s. One of the most popular Austin 7 models was the 4 seater tourer, or Chummy, as it was known. Designed to carry 2 adults and 2 children, this car really was the progenitor of popular family motoring and was effectively Britain's answer to the Model T Ford.

1931 Austin 16/6 Ivor Limousine, with division, blue leather trim to front and Bedford cord to rear, excellent condition. **£12,500–14,000** *AS*

One of Austin's best pre-war models.

1931 Austin 16/6 Ivor Limousine, blue leather upholstery front and grey Bedford cord at rear, excellent condition. **£11,000–13,000** *AS*

r. **1932 Austin 10/4 Saloon,** restored to high standard. **£4,250–5,250** *AS*

1933 Austin 12/6, totally restored.
£6,000–7,000 *DRC*

1933 Austin 10 Four Door Sedan,
older restoration, good condition.
£4,000–4,500 *CGB*

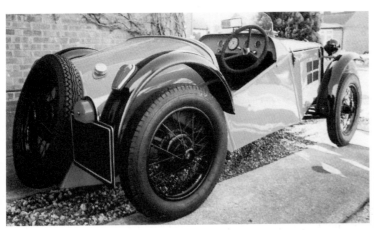

Locate the Source

The source of each illustration in Miller's can be found by checking the code letters below each caption with the Key to Illustrations.

l. **1933 Austin 7 Special,**
4 cylinders, 747cc, aluminium panelled, new tyres, exhaust system and interior trim.
£3,500–4,000 *ADT*

r. **1934 Austin 10/4,** 4 cylinders, 1125cc, coachwork restored and in tidy order, interior re-trimmed.
£2,750–3,500 *ADT*

First appearing in April 1932, the Austin 10/4 successfully filled the gap between the Seven and the recently introduced 12/6 model. Offering excellent value at a price of £168 for the deluxe saloon, the model proved thoroughly reliable and economical. The 10/4 was developed through many variants and a model of this horsepower designation featured in the Austin range until 1947.

1934 Austin 20/6 Limousine, with division, excellent condition.
£14,500–16,500 *AS*

Miller's Starter Marque

Starter Austins: *Austin7; A55/60 Cambridge; A90/95/99/105/110 Westminster; Metropolitan; A30/35/40; 1100 and 1300.*

- From the pre-war period the Austin 7 offers a viable entrée to vintage-style motoring and the friendly competition of The Vintage Sportscar Club. Over 290,000 were made between 1922 and 1939 and that means they are still plentiful today, affordable too and tremendous fun.

- Although post-war Austin models were in general pretty populous not all are in plentiful supply. The ones we've chosen above are blessed with a good survival rate, spares and club support and generally possess those Austin virtues of sturdy and sensible dependability. One of the most engaging Austins of the post-war era is the Austin/Nash Metropolitan. They should really have called it a Neapolitan, for this quaint little dolly-mixture of a car came in a choice of dazzling ice-cream colours – red, yellow and turquoise over white. The Metropolitan, was initially built by Austin for the American Nash Company as a 'sub-compact', or two-thirds scale Yank tank. Available in the UK from 1957.

1934 Austin 7 Ruby Open Road Four Seater Tourer, professionally restored in early 1980s and unused since, very good condition throughout.
£4,500–5,000 *BKS*

The introduction of the Ruby in 1934 marked an important step in the development of Austin's ever-popular light car. The new body styles featured flowing lines, valanced wings and taller, cowled-in radiators, flush fitting self-cancelling trafficators, and with synchromesh on 2nd, 3rd and top gears.

1935 Austin 10 Lichfield, original condition.
£4,000–4,500 *AS*

1936 Austin 7 Nippy Two Door Roadster,
4 cylinder, 747cc, side valve engine, with high-lift camshaft and Zenith downdraught carburettor, 21bhp at 4000rpm, good all-round condition.
£7,500–8,000 *BKS*

Manufactured from 1934 to 1937, the Nippy was one of many sports versions of the Seven and was styled appropriately with streamlined 2 seater bodywork. A development of the almost identical Type 65 which it replaced, the Nippy differed in having steel rather than aluminium body panels.
This example is known to have taken part in competition events in South Africa.

1936 Austin 10/4 Sherborne Saloon,
4 cylinder, 1125cc, side valve engine, rebuilt, good overall condition.
£3,000–3,500 *BKS*

l. **1937 Austin 7 Pearl,**
4 cylinders, 747cc, bodily and mechanically good, new exhaust system, electrics good, interior original with the exception of the front seat bases, some cracking on leather.
£3,750–4,250 *ADT*

The Pearl Cabriolet is a versatile car of distinctive style having the advantage of an open touring model whilst outwardly in profile retaining a similar appearance to the saloon.

1947 Austin 16hp, good condition.
£1,000–1,200 *CC*

1955 Austin Princess Limousine, believed to be
to manufacturer's specification, old style log book.
£3,000–3,500 *S*

r. **1956 Austin A35 Countryman,**
restored to original condition.
£2,200–2,600 *CRE*

AUSTIN Model	ENGINE cc/cyl	DATES	CONDITION 1	2	3
16	2199/4	1945-49	£3,000	£2,000	£1,000
A40 Devon	1200/4	1947-52	£2,000	£1,200	£750
A40 Sports	1200/4	1950-53	£6,000	£4,000	£2,000
A40 Somerset	1200/4	1952-54	£2,000	£1,500	£750
A40 Somerset DHC	1200/4	1954	£5,000	£4,000	£2,500
A40 Dorset 2 door	1200/4	1947-48	£2,000	£1,500	£1,000
A70 Hampshire	2199/4	1948-50	£2,000	£1,500	£1,000
A70 Hereford	2199/4	1950-54	£2,000	£1,500	£1,000
A90 Atlantic DHC	2660/4	1949-52	£8,000	£6,000	£4,000
A90 Atlantic	2660/4	1949-52	£6,000	£4,000	£3,000
A40/A50 Cambridge	1200/4	1954-57	£1,200	£750	£500
A55 Mk I Cambridge	1489/4	1957-59	£1,000	£750	£500
A55 Mk II	1489/4	1959-61	£1,000	£750	£500
A60 Cambridge	1622/4	1961-69	£1,000	£750	£500
A90/95 Westminster	2639/6	1954-59	£2,000	£1,500	£750
A99 Westminster	2912/6	1959-61	£1,500	£1,000	£500
A105 Westminster	2639/6	1956-59	£2,000	£1,500	£750
A110 Mk I/II	2912/6	1961-68	£2,000	£1,500	£750
Nash Metropolitan	1489/4	1957-61	£2,500	£1,500	£750
Nash Metropolitan DHC	1489/4	1957-61	£4,000	£3,000	£1,500
A30	803/4	1952-56	£1,000	£500	-
A30 Countryman	803/4	1954-56	£1,500	£1,000	-
A35	948/4	1956-59	£1,000	£500	-
A35 Countryman	948/4	1956-62	£1,500	£1,000	-
A40 Farina Mk I	948/4	1958-62	£1,250	£750	£200
A40 Mk I Countryman	948/4	1959-62	£1,500	£1,000	£400
A40 Farina Mk II	1098/4	1962-67	£1,000	£750	-
A40 Mk II Countryman	1098/4	1962-67	£1,200	£750	£300
1100	1098/4	1963-73	£1,000	£750	-
1300 Mk I/II	1275/4	1967-74	£750	£500	-
1300GT	1275/4	1969-74	£1,250	£1,000	£750
1800/2200	1800/2200/4	1964-75	£1,500	£900	£600
3 litre	2912/6	1968-71	£3,000	£1,500	£500

Austin Metropolitan (1954–61)

Production: 160,000.
Performance: 0–60mph 23 seconds (1500cc), top speed 75mph.
Price today: Convertible: £1,500–5,500. Hard-top £1,000–3,500.
Pick of the bunch: Convertibles and later cars with 1500cc instead of earlier 1200cc engine. Cars from 1959 onwards even had the luxury of a real opening boot.
For: A miniature period piece with oodles of US retro appeal and styling that is an engaging combination of a Wurlitzer, kitchen blender and a bath tub.
Against: Unfortunately, also handles like a bath tub and with enclosed front wheels has turning circle only slightly tighter than a London bus.
What to watch: Mechanicals are mostly commonplace, but body rot can be a problem as replacement panels and trim can be hard to find. Herringbone seat cloth irreplaceable.
Metropolitan facts: For some time the best-selling British-built car in the US, earning over $35 million. Austin's American partner, Nash-Kelvinator, also built washing machines and fridges; perhaps that's how the Metropolitan got its quirky looks.

1958 Austin Metropolitan 1500, 4 cylinders, 1489cc, refurbished to correct colour scheme. **£2,500–3,000** *ADT*

The distinctive and striking Metropolitan was a Nash design dating back to the early 1950s. At this time Donald Healey, who had in fact been working with Nash on the Nash-Healey sports car, introduced the President of Nash Motors to Leonard Lord of Austins. The outcome was an agreement that the new Metropolitan would be built in Birmingham incorporating Austin components. Although the final assembly was undertaken by Austin, the exclusive marketing rights were actually held by Nash. The car was launched in 1954 in the USA and Canada, and 3 years later it was available in Britain marketed through Austin dealerships.

l. **1958 Austin A35 Countryman,** 4 cylinder, 948cc, engine, 4 speed gearbox, roadworthy sound condition. **£850–1,100** *DB*

Did you know that the late James Hunt, 1976 Formula One World Champion, owned an A35 Countryman for many years. He was a keen budgerigar fancier and used his A35 to transport the budgies to shows.

> *A rebuilt car is not necessarily more valuable than a car in good original condition, even if the restoration has been costly.*

1959 Austin A35, 4 cylinders, 948cc, restored including complete strip of the body shell, removal of glass for repainting in cellulose, optional fresh air heater, period oil pressure gauge and ammeter, all mechanical components overhauled, less than 500 miles since rebuild. **£2,500–2,750** *ADT*

Austin's post-war baby car, the A30 was introduced in 1951 and achieved great success, being very much the right car for its time. An efficient and economical little family car with a top speed of 63mph, powered by an 803cc overhead valve engine, the model remained in production until late 1956 when it was revamped as the A35. This new model was powered by a 948cc engine, giving a considerable increase in power over its predecessor and was distinguished by a larger wrap-around rear window.

1962 Austin A35 Van, Cooper manifold and exhaust, wire wheels, totally restored. **£3,250–3,750** *H&H*

One of the best buys available in today's market.

1964 Austin Princess Hearse, 6 cylinders, 3993cc, generally sound condition, but some re-chroming required.
£3,750–4,750   *ADT*

This hearse was used for the funeral of Sir Winston Churchill in January 1965, carrying the coffin to where the body was to lie in state.

l. **1963 Austin A40 Farina,** requires restoration.
£400–550   *DRC*

This car featured in the TV series Heartbeat.

Cross Reference
For Austin Mini see Mini

1970 Austin 1300GT, 40,000 miles, one previous owner, original condition.
£2,500–3,000   *CRE*

1983 Austin Ambassador, 2 litres, 1994cc, automatic gearbox, one owner from new, 37,000 miles.
£700–900   *H&H*

AUSTIN-HEALEY

The dream that created an enduring piece of sports car magic became reality at the 1952 Earl's Court Motor Show in London. Donald Mitchell Healey, rally driver and engineer, had already sewn up an engine deal with Austin boss Leonard Lord in 1951 for the rugged 4 cylinder engines and transmissions of the Austin A90 Atlantic. Healey's dream of a cheap, true 100mph sports car, the Healey Hundred became the Austin-Healey 100 when Austin's Leonard Lord decided he wanted to build the car everyone was talking about. The Big Healey, as it subsequently became known, slotted in perfectly and in fact about 80 per cent of all production went state-side. Over the years this rugged bruiser became increasingly civilised. In 1956 it received a 6 cylinder engine in place of the 4, but in 1959 the 3000 was born. It became increasingly refined with front disc brakes, then wind-up windows, and ever faster.

1954 Austin-Healey 100/4, overdrive on 3rd and top gears, with tonneau cover. **£8,000–9,000** *HOLL*

r. **1956 Austin-Healey 100/4,** ex-California, completely restored, including rebuilt engine, gearbox and overdrive, full weather equipment. **£15,500–17,500** *PA*

1954 Austin-Healey 100/4, 4 cylinders, 2660cc, thoroughly overhauled, new wiring loom, exterior chrome renovated, new chrome wire wheels, interior, hood and tonneau cover completely re-trimmed. **£15,000–17,000** *COYS*

The 100 was a 100mph sports car for only £750. This was achieved by sourcing well-known components from Austin, among them the Atlantic 90bhp 4 cylinder engine and gearbox.

l. **1957 Austin-Healey 100/6 BN4,** 6 cylinders, 2639cc, 4 speed gearbox with overdrive, bare metal respray, converted to right-hand drive, chrome and wire wheels and interior refurbished. **£12,500–14,000** *H&H*

1958 Austin Healey 100/6, left-hand drive, bare chassis and shell undergone total renovation, mechanical overhaul, new trim, carpets, hood and glass.
£13,000–15,000 *COYS*

It was with an Austin-Healey 100/6 in basic production trim that Tommy Wisdom and Cecil Winby won their class on the 1957 Mille Miglia, while three factory-entered 100/6s went on to take the Manufacturer's Team Prize at the 1958 Sebring 12-hour race. The same year saw the first factory rally team of 100/6s show real potential, including Pat Moss, sister of Stirling Moss, taking her first Coupé de Dames for a penalty-free run.

1959 Austin-Healey Sprite MkI, mechanically good overall condition, engine reconditioned, brakes overhauled, most electrical components new, good condition.
£5,000–5,400 *ADT*

1959 Austin-Healey Sprite MkI, 4 cylinders, 948cc, extensive restoration, sills replaced, floorpan overhauled, full respray, chrome replated, steering overhauled, new rear springs, new brake cylinders, shoes and copper pipes, rebuilt radiator and new wiring loom, interior completely re-trimmed, new black fabric hood, perspex sidescreens replaced.
£8,750–9,750 *ADT*

1959 Austin-Healey Sprite MkI, 4 cylinders, 1275cc, replacement engine, factory hard top, wire wheels, full history of restoration.
£4,000–5,000 *COYS*

AUSTIN HEALEY Model	ENGINE cc/cyl	DATES	CONDITION 1	2	3
100 BN 1/2	2660/4	1953-56	£20,000	£14,000	£8,000
100/6, BN4/BN6	2639/6	1956-59	£18,000	£13,500	£8,000
3000 Mk I	2912/6	1959-61	£20,000	£13,000	£8,500
3000 Mk II	2912/6	1961-62	£22,000	£15,000	£9,000
3000 Mk IIA	2912/6	1962-64	£23,000	£15,000	£11,000
3000 Mk III	2912/6	1964-68	£24,000	£17,000	£11,000
Sprite Mk I	948/4	1958-61	£5,000	£4,000	£2,000
Sprite Mk II	948/4	1961-64	£3,000	£2,000	£1,000
Sprite Mk III	1098/4	1964-66	£3,500	£2,000	£1,000
Sprite Mk IV	1275/4	1966-71	£4,000	£2,000	£1,000

Miller's Starter Marque

Starter Austin-Healeys: *Austin Healey Sprite MkI 'Frog-eye'; Austin-Healey Sprite MkII–V.*

- Few cars have a cuter face than the cheeky little Austin-Healey Sprite MkI that everyone knows as the 'Frog-eye'. Truth be told, it's not very fast. A contemporary road test in *The Motor* quoted a leisurely 0–60mph time of 20.5 seconds. Acceleration petered out altogether at 84mph. But what it lacked in outright pace it more than made up for with true agility and genuine sporting feel.

- It's a viable restore-while-you-drive car, with basic readily available mechanicals – mostly Austin A35 with a bit of Morris Minor. Many of the same virtues apply to the Sprite MkII–V, which is identical to the MG Midget in all but minor detail. With both makes to choose from the Midget and Sprite MkII–V were made in far larger numbers than the 'Frog-eye' and are that much more affordable and readily available.

1959 Austin-Healey 'Frog-eye' Sprite MkI, wood trim steering wheel, tonneau cover and weather equipment, restored, with full history. **£7,000–8,500** *BKS*

1960 Austin-Healey 3000 MkI, left-hand drive, uprated to rally specification, bare shell restoration. **£26,000–30,000** *SC*

1960 Austin-Healey 3000 MkI, rebuilt to 1960 FIA specification with lightweight panels and 160bhp engine, overdrive, works hard-top, split circuit brakes, oil cooler, anti-roll bar and wire wheels. **£14,000–16,000** *H&H*

1963 Austin-Healey 3000 MkIIA, converted to right-hand drive, imported, very good restored condition, including new wheels and tyres, new hood and new tonneau. **£15,000–17,000** *H&H*

1964 Austin-Healey 3000 MkIII, 6 cylinders, 2912cc, converted to right-hand drive, fully restored including new wings all-round and replacement sills, suspension rebuilt, new tyres and new black hood. **£16,000–18,000** *BRIT*

1962 Austin-Healey 3000 MkIIA, left-hand drive, total body restoration, stripped to bare chassis and shell, rebuilt with new floor panels, sills and outriggers, new trim, carpets and hood, new glass and chrome, new chrome wire wheels and new stainless steel exhaust, excellent condition throughout.
£20,000–22,000 *COYS*

The 3000 was launched in March 1959. Like the 100/6, either in 2 seater BN7 or 2+2 BT7 guise, it used a simple but torsionally strong ladder frame chassis with Austin A90 independent coil spring/wishbone front suspension and a live leaf sprung rear axle located by Panhard rod. Front disc brakes were fitted for the first time, the 100/6's 2639cc engine was enlarged to 2912cc and via twin SU carburettors it produced 124bhp at 4600 rpm. With 4 speed gearbox and 0–60mph in 11.4 seconds, the 3000 received much praise for effortless performance and fine handling.

1964 Austin-Healey 3000 MkIII Phase II, right-hand drive, extensive restoration.
£11,500–12,500 *COYS*

1964 Austin-Healey Sprite MkIII, 1098cc engine.
£3,750–4,500 *VIN*

Donald Healey was active in motor sport well before WWII. He drove and designed cars for Triumph from 1934 to 1939, but after the war he decided to go it alone and in 1952 he showed his Healey 100 at the London Motor Show. This used the 4 cylinder, 2.6 litre Austin A90 engine, and by the time the show closed, Healey had signed up a deal for the Austin Motor Co to manufacture the car as the Austin-Healey. The ultimate Healey model came in early 1964 with the introduction of the BJ8, the 3000 MkIII. The car incorporated myriad changes, most notably increased power, twin 2in SUs, revised exhaust system, new dash design and vacuum brake servo. The interior was far more refined, the old steel dash was replaced with wood veneer, the seats covered in real leather and a console placed between the front seats.

1970 Austin-Healey Sprite MkIV, 4 cylinders, 1275cc, fully restored to very good condition.
£5,000–5,500 *ADT*

The 1275cc A series engined MkIV Sprite ran from 1966 until the model's demise in 1971. Running alongside its stable mate, the MG Midget from 1961, the difference between the 2 models was effectively no more than the trim and badging.

l. **1965 Austin-Healey 3000 MkIII,** right-hand drive, ground-up restoration, optional overdrive.
£16,000–19,000 *BKS*

The 3000 MkIII with more powerful 148bhp engine appeared in the spring of 1964 to be followed later in the year by the Phase II version with revised rear suspension. Top speed was now 121mph and the 0–60mph dropped to below 10 seconds.

AUSTRO-DAIMLER

1923 Austro-Daimler AD 617 Sports Two Seater, 6 cylinders, 4426cc engine,
older restoration, excellent condition.
£45,500–47,500 *BKS*

BAYARD

l. **1904 Bayard 9hp Two Seater,**
2 cylinder T-head engine, 3 forward
speeds and reverse gearbox, restored.
£19,500–22,500 *BKS*

*When Adolphe Clément left the
Clément-Gladiator Company in 1903,
which he founded with Alexander
Darracq in 1896, he retained control of
two of his former company's factories
in the Paris suburb of Levallois-Perret
and Charleville-Mézières near the
Belgian border. The vehicles were sold
under the names Talbot in Britain and
Bayard on the continent, the Clément
prefix being dropped from both to avoid
confusion with the cars from Adolphe's
former firm still sold as Cléments. This
car has a provisional date of 1904 from
the Veteran Car Club of Great
Britain and took part in the London
to Brighton centenary run.*

BAYLISS-THOMAS

r. **1925 Bayliss-Thomas 11/22hp Four
Seater Tourer,** 1247cc, overhead valve,
semi-sports engine, dry stored for
25 years and requires recommissioning.
£4,750–5,500 *BKS*

*Like so many of the Midlands car manu-
facturers of the 1920s Bayliss, Thomas & Co
were involved in cycle and then motorcycle
production before venturing into motor car
manufacture. They moved from Coventry
to Tyseley, near Birmingham, where motor
car production commenced just after WWI.
Bayliss-Thomas made a small number of cars
for a mere 7 years, before succumbing to the
pressure of lower cost, mass-produced cars.*

BEAN

Another short-lived British make that took on the majors and lost. John Harper Bean had intended to produce 50,000 cars a year. Production got under way in January 1920, when 100 cars were produced, and by March production stood at 20 cars a day, only a fraction of Bean's target. Bean never had the economies of scale to bring prices down to the level of the Morris Cowley, one of his principal rivals. The company ceased motor car manufacture in 1929.

1928 Bean 14/40 Tourer, fitted with cocktail cabinet, rear trunk and full weather equipment, well restored.
£12,000–13,500 *AS*
A very rare motor car.

1923 Bean 14hp Tourer, 2386cc, good condition.
£12,000–14,000 *CC*

BENTLEY

Vintage Bentleys and those built at Derby when Rolls-Royce took the company over thoroughly deserve their formidable reputation. Walter Owen Bentley founded Bentley Motors in 1919 and over the next twelve years produced just 3,024 cars – but what feats they achieved. The first production Bentley, the 4 cylinder, 3 litre, appeared in 1922; two years later a 3 litre won Le Mans, and again in 1927, 1928, 1929 and 1930. Most imposing of all the Bentleys built at the original Cricklewood site in London were the monstrous 8 litre models, only 100 of which were built before the company succumbed to the financial pressures which had dogged its short life, and the company fell into the hands of Rolls Royce. The next generation of Bentleys produced at Rolls-Royce's Derby plant are now known as the Derby Bentleys. The first new car under new ownership was the 3½ litre, which essentially employed a tuned version of the Rolls-Royce's 20/25, 6 cylinder, 3669cc engine that gave a lusty 105bhp and powered Bentleys to 90mph and sometimes more. The engine was later boosted to 4257cc to become the 4¼ litre, with lighter-bodied cars edging 100mph. It was in this era that Bentleys became dubbed 'the silent sportscars' and British coachbuilders graced the sporting Bentley with some enduringly elegant and stylish bodies.

l. **1924 Bentley
3 Litre Green Label,**
85bhp, restored.
£66,000–76,000 *MAN*

1922 Bentley 3 Litre Open Tourer, coachwork by Cadogan, 4 cylinders, 2996cc, single overhead camshaft, 4 valves and 2 spark plugs per cylinder, Smiths sidedraught carburettor and two-part wet sump lubrication, 80bhp, 4 speed gearbox, top speed of 80mph.
Est. £38,000–42,000 *COYS*

The Bentley 3 litre was a milestone machine and a tribute to the engineering excellence that was to become a hallmark of the marque. Launched in November 1919 at the London Motor Show, it subsequently underwent almost 2 years of competition development including winning its third ever race at Brooklands with Frank Clement in May 1921.

1925 Bentley 3 Litre Red Label, original condition.
£75,000–80,000 *MAN*

1926 Bentley 3/4½ Litre Vanden Plas Sports Tourer, 130bhp, full history, restored.
£120,000–140,000 *MAN*

1927 Bentley 3 Litre Le Mans No. 2 Works Team Car, coachwork by Vanden Plas, No. 1378, British Racing green paintwork, twin SU carburettors, substantial engine restoration including a re-bore, Phoenix balanced crank and shell bearings, new cross-shaft gears, valves and guides, gearbox bearing renewed by Craig Collins, rear bodywork modified, original instrumentation.
£155,000–175,000 *BKS*

This particular car was built in the Bentley Motors racing shop in 1927 as a works entry for the 1927 Le Mans

1928 Bentley 4½ Litre Open Four Seater Tourer,
4 cylinders, in-line, 4398cc, 110bhp at 3500rpm,
4 speed gearbox, right-hand gate change, 4 wheel
drum brakes, semi-elliptic leaf spring suspension,
Vanden Plas open coachwork, restoration started
in 1960s, stripped and rebuilt, with new ash body
frame to original specification, panelled in aluminium
and painted black, interior upholstery replaced,
mechanically rebuilt, 160 miles since restoration.
£105,000–130,000 *C*

1929 Bentley 4½ Litre Sports Saloon,
135bhp, uprated engine, original condition.
£105,000–115,000 *MAN*

*The first series of 4½ litres was launched in 1927
following the success of the prototype at Le Mans,
where it broke the lap record prior to the White
House Corner disaster. Road tests of the day
established it as a very special Bentley and with
its victory at Le Mans in 1928 and Brooklands
competition successes it soon established itself as
the worthy successor to the 3 litre.*

**1930 Bentley Speed Six Dual Cowl Four
Seater Open Tourer,** coachwork by Hooper,
6 cylinders, 6500cc, 140bhp, chassis-up
restoration to original specification,
original rebuilt engine, excellent condition.
£350,000+ *COYS*

1930 Bentley Speed Six Corsica Coupé,
6 cylinders, 6500cc.
£750,000+ *BLK*

*The layout of the Bentley 6½ litre standard six was
conceived in 1924 when it was realised that the
introduction of the long standard 3 litre had not solved
the coachwork problem resulting from customers fitting
bodies for which the 3 litre was not designed. In 1928 the
Speed Six was introduced, W. O. Bentley's favourite car
and, in racing terms, the most successful of the vintage
cars, achieving 5 first places and 4 second places in major
races between 1929 and 1931. The Corsica Company in
London produced only two bodies on Bentley chassis, one
was a sports touring body for a 1931 8 litre on a shortened
chassis, the other was this very imposing coupé.*

*The Speed Sixes rapidly proved their mettle in
competition in the 1929 24-hour Le Mans race.
Bentleys took the first 4 places, the Speed Six
winning at an average speed of 73.62mph. In
the 6-hour Brooklands race the same year the
Speed Six of Barnato and Dunfee won, and a
Speed Six finished second in the 1929 500 mile
Brooklands race, having been ordered to slow
down after a fastest lap of 126.09mph. In the
following year the Speed Six swept the board,
achieving first and second at Le Mans. Indeed
both cars were ordered to reduce speed to a fast
tour, such was their lead. This car is the 26th
from last of the Speed Sixes to be manufactured.*

1929 Bentley 4½ Litre Four Seater Tourer, coachwork by James Pearce in the style of Vanden Plas,
full rebuild to original specification, excellent condition throughout.
£125,000–140,000 *S*

BENTLEY Model	ENGINE cc/cyl	DATES	CONDITION 1	2	3
3 litre	2996/4	1920-27	£100,000	£75,000	£50,000
Speed Six	6597/6	1926-32	£400,000	£250,000	£160,000
4.5 litre	4398/4	1927-31	£175,000	£125,000	£80,000
4.5 litre Supercharged	4398/4	1929-32	£600,000+	£300,000	£200,000
8 litre	7983/6	1930-32	£350,000	£250,000	£100,000
3.5 litre Saloon & DHC	3699/6	1934-37	£70,000	£30,000	£15,000
4.25 litre Saloon & DHC	4257/6	1937-39	£70,000	£35,000	£20,000
Mark V	4257/6	1939-41	£45,000	£25,000	£20,000

Prices are very dependent on engine type, body style and original extras like supercharger, gearbox ratio, racing history and originality.

1931 Bentley 4/8 Litre Sports, 8 litres in a short chassis frame, 300bhp, good condition.
£275,000+ *MAN*

1934 Bentley 3½ Litre William Arnold 'Airflow' Sports Saloon, finished in dark blue, with light blue leather upholstery.
£16,000–19,500 *RCC*

This was a 1934 Olympia show car.

1934 Bentley 3½ Litre Sports Saloon, coachwork by Freestone & Webb, 6 cylinder, 3669cc overhead valve engine, 4 speed gearbox and hypoid final drive, restored in the late 1980s, new exhaust system, sound throughout but could benefit from some cosmetic work.
£20,000–23,000 *BKS*

This model was developed by Rolls-Royce following the takeover of the Bentley company in 1931. It was extremely successful, being in production from 1933 until 1936, and some 1,191 examples found buyers. Dubbed 'the silent sportscar', it earned the admiration of W. O. Bentley himself, who worked for the company for a period before joining Lagonda.

l. **1937 Bentley 4¼ Litre Sports Saloon,** coachwork by Park Ward, original dark blue leather interior, good condition.
£16,500–18,500 *RCC*

1935 Bentley 3½ Litre Sportsmans Coupé, coachwork by Georges Kellner et Fils of Paris, 6 cylinders, 3669cc, fully restored, excellent condition.
£90,000–100,000 *COYS*

l. **1936 Bentley 4¼ Litre Drophead Coupé,** coachwork by James Young, 4257cc, overhead valve engine, carefully maintained by Bentley specialist, finished in black over gold, grey interior trim, good condition, older restoration.
£31,000–34,000 *S*

1937 Bentley 4¼ Litre Roadster, 2–3 seater coupé cabriolet coachwork by Hooper, 4257cc, 126bhp, special features include twin long distance fuel tanks, strengthened chassis and suspension, twin side-mounted spare wheels, instruments calibrated in both metric and imperial measurements, including a barometer, interior windscreen wiper, dashboard and door cappings in ebony, Motorola radio, Lucas air-horns, matching set of Lucas headlamps and spotlamps, comprehensive restoration in 1980s.
£100,000–110,000 *COYS*

In 1936 Rolls-Royce enlarged the 20/25 3½ litre engine to 4257cc. This increased capacity was also being adopted for the Bentley 4¼ litre model. Power rose significantly to 126bhp which allowed a near 100mph maximum speed and notably improved acceleration.

1937 Bentley 4¼ Litre 2+2 Sports Roadster, KU series sports coachwork created in the 1960s, Stephen Grebel headlamps, hand and service books, history file and original log books.
£45,000–47,000 *S*

1937 Bentley 4¼ Litre Sports Saloon, coachwork by Hooper, correct complement of lamps and horns, fitted suitcases in boot, side-mounted spare wheel, in use until recently.
£17,000–19,000 *RCC*

r. **1937 Bentley 4¼ Litre Four Door Sports Saloon,** 6 cylinders, 4257cc, 125bhp at 4500rpm, 4 speed manual gearbox, 4 wheel drum brakes, semi-elliptic leaf spring suspension, right-hand drive, burgundy paintwork and dark leather trim, good condition.
£14,000–17,000 *C*

l. **1937 Bentley 4¼ Litre Saloon,** coachwork by Park Ward, 6 cylinders, 4257cc, partial restoration to original standard specification, finished in black over cream, interior woodwork completely refurbished, brightwork replated, good mechanical condition.
£23,000–26,000 *ADT*

1938 Bentley 4¼ Litre Four Door Sports Saloon, coachwork by Park Ward, finished in black over ivory, interior re-upholstered in grey-blue leather, service records, original chassis card, fine example.
£22,000–24,000 *BKS*

1947 Bentley MkVI Saloon, 6 cylinders, 4257cc, good mechanical condition but coachwork requires attention.
£5,500–7,500 *ADT*

1949 Bentley MkVI Estate Wagon, coachwork by Rippon, 6 cylinders, 4257cc, 135bhp at 4000rpm, 4 speed manual gearbox, 4 wheel drum brakes, right-hand drive, resprayed, with set of tools and accessories, good original condition.
£36,000–40,000 *C*

Upon the return of Rolls-Royce and Bentley motors to car production in 1945, it was decided that all car manufacturing would be transferred from Derby to Crewe. Launched in 1946, the MkVI was, compared to its pre-war counterparts, an entirely new concept in both engineering and design. One of the notable differences between the MkVI and its predecessor was the new 4¼ litre B60 engine which continued in production with refinements until 1959. Featuring an F-type alloy cylinder head and a belt-driven dynamo and water pump, the engine gave a healthy 135bhp at 4000rpm, with a top speed of 100mph. This particular car was exhibited at the Earl's Court Motor Show in London.

1949 Bentley MkVI Saloon, excellent condition.
£12,000–15,000 *CC*

1950 Bentley MkVI Sports Saloon, coachwork by H. J. Mulliner, 6 cylinders, 4257cc, right-hand drive, 3 owners from new, 88,000 miles recorded, original radio and tool roll.
£13,500–15,500 *BKS*

One of only 200 with this body style built by Mulliner, powered by the new F-head 4257cc straight 6 engine introduced after the war, the MkVI Bentley differed from its Rolls-Royce counterpart in having a higher-lift camshaft and twin SU carburettors. Production of this model was approximately 5,000, but only 80 of the cars built carried the 'standard steel' bodywork.

l. **1949 Bentley MkVI Two Door Saloon,** coachwork by James Young, requires cosmetic attention.
£12,500–14,500 *RCC*

An unusually styled car, probably influenced by American designs of the period. An example was exhibited at the 1948 Earl's Court show, and it is believed that only 4 were constructed to this design.

BENTLEY Model	ENGINE cc/cyl	DATES	CONDITION 1	2	3
Abbreviations: HJM = H J Mulliner; PW = Park Ward; M/PW = Mulliner/Park Ward					
Mk VI Standard Steel	4257/ 4566/6	1946-52	£16,000	£11,000	£6,000
Mk VI Coachbuilt	4257/ 4566/6	1946-52	£25,000	£20,000	£12,000
Mk VI Coachbuilt DHC	4566/6	1946-52	£40,000	£30,000	£20,000
R Type Standard Steel	4566/6	1952-55	£12,000	£10,000	£7,000
R Type Coachbuilt	4566/6	1952-55	£25,000	£20,000	£15,000
R Type Coachbuilt DHC	4566/ 4887/6	1952-55	£50,000	£35,000	£25,000
R Type Cont (HJM)	4887/6	1952-55	£80,000	£40,000	£29,000
S1 Standard Steel	4887/6	1955-59	£15,000	£12,000	£7,000
S1 Cont 2 door (PW)	4877/6	1955-59	£30,000	£25,000	£20,000
S1 Cont Drophead	4877/6	1955-59	£80,000	£75,000	£50,000
S1 Cont F'back (HJM)	4877/6	1955-58	£50,000	£35,000	£25,000
S2 Standard Steel	6230/8	1959-62	£15,000	£9,000	£6,000
S2 Cont 2 door (HJM)	6230/8	1959-62	£60,000	£40,000	£30,000
S2 Flying Spur (HJM)	6230/8	1959-62	£45,000	£33,000	£22,000
S2 Conv (PW)	6230/8	1959-62	£60,000	£50,000	£35,000
S3 Standard Steel	6230/8	1962-65	£16,000	£11,000	£9,000
S3 Cont/Flying Spur	6230/8	1962-65	£45,000	£30,000	£25,000
S3 2 door (PW)	6230/8	1962-65	£30,000	£25,000	£18,000
S3 Conv (modern conversion - only made one original)	6230/8	1962-65	£40,000	£28,000	£20,000
T1	6230/6 6750/8	1965-77	£10,000	£8,000	£4,000
T1 2 door (M/PW)	6230/6 6750/8	1965-70	£15,000	£12,000	£9,000
T1 Drophead (M/PW)	6230/6 6750/8	1965-70	£30,000	£20,000	£12,000

1950 Bentley MkVI 'Woody' Estate Car, needs attention.
£13,000–15,000 *RCC*

Of the very few MkVI's bodied as estate cars, this is the only one built by Denby of Belfast, and is therefore unique. Unused for some years, now running and driving nicely.

1951 Bentley MkVI Saloon,
big bore, small boot, totally restored.
£14,000–16,000 *AS*

1951 Bentley MkVI Four Door Lightweight Sports Saloon, lightweight aluminium coachwork by H. J. Mulliner, 6 cylinder B60 engine, 4257cc, 4 speed manual gearbox, 4 wheel drum brakes hydraulically operated to front, mechanical with servo to rear, independent suspension by coil springs and wishbones with lever arm and hydraulic dampers to front, live axle with half-elliptic springs and adjustable lever arm hydraulic dampers to rear, right-hand drive, original interior upholstery, stored for 20 years until recently.
£13,000–15,000 *C*

One of only a dozen fitted with bespoke, lightweight coachwork by H. J. Mulliner.

1952 Bentley MkVI Convertible,
coachwork by Park Ward, totally restored.
£45,000–50,000 *BLE*

1953 Bentley R-Type T Series Standard Steel Saloon, 6 cylinders, 4556cc, good original condition throughout.
£9,500–11,000 *BKS*

1953 Bentley R-Type Saloon, 4566cc, leather trim and chromework in good order, used daily for last 18 months, in need of slight attention to paintwork.
£8,000–10,000 *H&H*

l. **1953 Bentley 4½ Litre R-Type Standard Steel Saloon,** 6 cylinders, 4556cc, completely overhauled in 1991, including electrical system, brake and transmission servos, new tyres and exhaust system, original condition.
£7,000–10,000 *BKS*

The Bentley R-Type or B7 was a more elegant development of the MkVI, the first Bentley with the standard steel bodywork. This was introduced to overcome the shortcomings of the traditional coachbuilt body in the export markets that had become vital – by government dictate – to the survival of the motor industry.

1953 Bentley R-Type Saloon, 6 cylinders, 4500cc, 4 speed manual gearbox, requiring some restoration to body, mechanically sound.
£5,750–6,750 *DB*

1953 Bentley R-Type Sports Saloon, coachwork by Freestone & Webb, right-hand drive, automatic transmission, 39,000 miles recorded.
£27,000–30,000 *BKS*

One of the last cars to be bodied by Freestone & Webb.

1954 Bentley R-Type Hooper Empress Saloon, automatic transmission, original leather upholstery, original condition, including tool kit.
£12,500–14,500 *RCC*

r. **1954 Bentley R-Type Two Door Fixed Head Coupé,** coachwork by Park Ward, automatic transmission, fully restored.
£17,000–22,000 *S*

l. **1954 Bentley
R-Type Continental,**
coachwork by
H. J. Mulliner, restored.
£80,000–100,000 *PJF*

1959 Bentley S1 Continental Prototype,
coachwork by H. J. Mulliner.
£100,000–120,000 *PJF*

1956 Bentley S1 Continental Fastback Coupé,
coachwork by H. J. Mulliner, 6 cylinders, 4887cc,
158bhp, 4 speed automatic transmission,
80,000 miles recorded, top speed of 100mph.
£38,000–42,000 *COYS*

1955 Bentley S1 Convertible Continental,
coachwork by Park Ward, good condition.
£125,000+ *PJF*

1959 Bentley S1 Continental Sports Saloon,
coachwork by Hooper, automatic transmission, power
steering, extensive brake overhaul and service.
£19,000–22,000 *S*

*It is thought that only 5 Hooper bodied saloons
were constructed.*

1955 Bentley S1 Continental Fastback,
coachwork by Mulliner, left-hand drive,
restored to concours winning standard.
£120,000–150,000 *BLK*

1960 Bentley S2 Continental Drophead Coupé, coachwork by Park Ward, S3 power unit, £75,000 restoration, continuous service history.
£59,000–65,000 *BKS*

The S2 Bentley and its Rolls-Royce sibling, the Silver Cloud II, were the first of the Crewe marques to be equipped with the new pushrod ohv 6230cc, V8 power unit. Launched in 1959, the new models came as standard with power steering and automatic transmission, and the Continental version additionally offered a higher than standard 2.92:1 final drive ratio. Just 388 examples of the S2 Continental were built, mostly in closed form. Top speed was in the region of 115mph.

1961 Bentley Continental Four Door Flying Spur, coachwork by Mulliner, includes picnic tables, excellent condition.
£40,000–45,000 *VIC*

1962 Bentley S2 Standard Saloon, V8, overhead valve, single central camshaft, 6230cc, 200bhp at 4500rpm, 4 speed automatic gearbox, left-hand drive, carefully maintained, good condition throughout.
£26,500–27,500 *C*

This particular car has been owned from new by actress Joan Fontaine.

1961 Bentley S2 Four Door Saloon, V8, 6230cc, right-hand drive, re-trimmed in green leather.
£8,500–9,500 *BKS*

Carefully maintained, always chauffeur-driven.

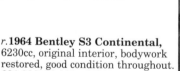

*r.***1964 Bentley S3 Continental,** 6230cc, original interior, bodywork restored, good condition throughout.
£21,000–26,000 *H&H*

1965 Bentley S3 Standard Steel Saloon, 6230cc, V8 engine, 4 speed automatic gearbox, good condition.
£7,500–8,500 *S*

Launched in 1962, the Bentley S3, and its Rolls-Royce equivalent the Silver Cloud III, employed the 6.2 litre aluminium alloy V8 engine introduced on the S2, though with larger carburettors, a new distributor, and raised compression ratio, and it came with a 4 speed automatic transmission as standard equipment. Most obvious among the many changes were the adoption of a 4 headlamp lighting arrangement, the absence of sidelights from the wing tops, and a slightly lower radiator shell. Inside there was revised accommodation with separate front seats and increased room for rear passengers. A total of 1,286 standard S3s were manufactured before the model was superseded by the T-Series in 1965.

1965 Bentley S3 Two Door Coupé, coachwork by H. J. Mulliner/Park Ward, maroon paintwork and brightwork sound, leather upholstery, interior woodwork and carpeting good, requires service and re-commissioning.
£19,000–23,000   *BRIT*

1983 Bentley Mulsanne Turbo Four Door Saloon, 8 cylinder, 6750cc engine, well serviced, warranted 87,000 miles, 3 owners.
£16,000–18,000   *COYS*

1992 Bentley Continental R Two Door Coupé, V8, 6750cc, 4 speed automatic gearbox with overdrive and Sport mode, 30,600 miles recorded, excellent condition throughout.
£90,000–100,000   *BKS*

One of the pitfalls of 'badge engineering' is the inevitable dilution of individual character suffered by the marques concerned. In the case of Rolls-Royce and Bentley, the latter's image as merely a 'cheaper' Rolls had seriously undermined its sales by the end of the 1970s. At the decade's end Bentleys accounted for a mere 3% of Rolls-Royce Motor Cars' production; clearly a situation which could not be tolerated if the once famous marque was to avoid extinction. The solution was to seek to re-establish Bentley's credentials as the purveyor of high performance luxury cars and, in a move calculated to evoke memories of the company's glorious past achievements at Le Mans, the name Mulsanne was chosen for the Silver Spirit's counterpart. Launched at the Geneva Motor Show in March 1982, the Mulsanne Turbo's 6750cc, V8 engine would accelerate to 0–60mph in around 8 seconds, and 135mph would be showing on the clock before the limiter cut in.

Introduced at Geneva in 1985, the Bentley Turbo R continued the theme, but with refined suspension better suited to the car's increased performance. The Bentley Continental R was unveiled 6 years later and its Turbo R engine in the new wind-cheating shape cut the 0–60mph time to under 6 seconds and boosted top speed to in excess of 150mph.

BIZZARINI

1965 Bizzarini 5300GT Strada, 8 cylinders, 5300cc, 365bhp, restored, in excellent condition.
£59,000–64,000   *COYS*

The engine, which produced some 365bhp, was placed far back in the chassis, allowing for a near-ideal weight distribution of 48%/52% front to rear. Combined with a drag co-efficient of only 0.3CD the car was able to achieve the high speeds that would be necessary for competition use (305km/h was claimed). Sadly Giotto Bizzarini left the company he founded and production of the 5300GT ceased after only 134 cars had been built. This particular car is unique in that it was owned by him from new.

BLACKHAWK

1929 Blackhawk Sedan, 6 cylinder, in-line, OHV engine, 241.5cu in, 85bhp, 3 speed manual gearbox, converted to pick-up truck, fair to poor condition throughout.
£3,000–3,500 *C*

1929 Blackhawk Four Door Sedan, 6 cylinder in-line, OHV engine, 241.5cu in, 85bhp, 3 speed manual gearbox, left-hand drive, sound body with some surface rust, interior intact, requires restoration.
£5,500–6,000 *C*

BMW

It is ironic that the first BMW car, built in 1928, was the Dixi, an Austin 7 built under licence. Now Bayerische Motoren Werke owns Rover, the company that the now defunct Austin was absorbed into. From its humble beginnings BMW went on to produce some fine pre-war touring cars. In 1940 a streamlined BMW 328 won Italy's Mille Miglia. After the end of hostilities the company was brought close to oblivion on a number of occasions. The beautiful and extremely expensive 507 of 1956 nearly brought the company to its knees, and the Isetta microcars (see Microcars section), built from 1955 to 1965, created another crisis in the late 1950s. In the early 1960s the company got back on course and began to build its modern reputation as a producer of fine, executive, luxury and sporting machines.

1971 BMW 3.0S, 2985cc, fully Waxoyled and resprayed, excellent condition.
£3,800–4,200 *H&H*

1955 BMW 502, V8, overhead valve, 2562cc, 100bhp, one Solex carburettor, 4 speed manual gearbox, double wishbone front suspension, torsion bars rear, left-hand drive, requires restoration, leather interior in good condition.
£1,250–1,500 *C*

The rounded styling of the body earned the car the nickname 'Baroque Angel' when the shape was first seen on the much less powerful 6 cylinder 501 in 1952, but these large BMWs were beautifully made autobahn cruisers. The new alloy V8 engine lifted the 502 into the 100mph class and put it among the fastest saloon cars available in Germany in the 1950s. With a massively constructed tubular chassis frame the cars handled well and had a true air of refinement, aided by the smoothness of the V8 engine. The car formed the basis of the later 507 sports car which used a shorter version of the same chassis and a more powerful 3.2 litre version of the V8 engine.

1972 BMW 3.0 CSL, 6 cylinders, 3003cc, engine replaced, resprayed, mechanically sound, leather interior in good condition.
£8,000–9,500 *BRIT*

Produced between 1972 and 1975, the CSL was built as a homologation special and was easily distinguishable from the standard model by its distinctive badging and decals. The 3003cc engine produced 206bhp on road-going cars and, with the considerable weight advantage over the standard model by the usage of alloy body panels, performance was excellent. With a production run of only 1,039 cars the model is now highly prized.

> **Miller's is a price GUIDE
> not a price LIST**

BMW Model	ENGINE cc/cyl	DATES	CONDITION 1	2	3
Dixi	747/4	1927-32	£7,000	£3,000	£2,000
303	1175/6	1934-36	£11,000	£8,000	£5,000
309	843/4	1933-34	£6,000	£4,000	£2,000
315	1490/6	1935-36	£9,000	£7,000	£5,000
319	1911/6	1935-37	£10,000	£9,000	£6,000
326	1971/6	1936-37	£12,000	£10,000	£8,000
320 series	1971/6	1937-38	£12,000	£10,000	£8,000
327/328	1971/6	1937-40	£30,000+	£18,000	£10,000
328	1971/6	1937-40	£60,000+	-	-

l. **c1972 BMW 3.0 CS Two Door Coupé,** straight 6, overhead camshaft engine, 4 speed manual gearbox, 4 wheel disc brakes, right-hand drive, engine, electrics, interior and transmission are good, bodywork and paintwork are generally good. **£3,800–4,500** *BKS*

Introduced in 1971 and in production until 1975, the BMW 3.0 CS shared the same wheelbase and style of the 2800 CS with an improved Karmann-built bodyshell, a full 3 litre engine and 4 wheel disc brakes. It provided more power and improved torque, with an output of 180bhp.

1974 BMW 3.0 CSA Coupé, 2985cc, 80,000 miles recorded, dry stored since 1990. **£1,100–1,400** *H&H*

1972 BMW 2002, 4 cylinders, 1990cc, automatic, extensively restored, engine overhaul, complete respray and re-upholstered. **£2,400–2,800** *ADT*

1973 BMW 3.0 CSL 'Batmobile', 206bhp, only produced in left-hand drive. **£30,000–35,000** *MUN*

Available in white or silver.

1974 BMW 2002 Tii Lux, 4 cylinders, 1990cc, restored including front wings, panel and bonnet, interior re-trimmed in black leather, various spares. **£3,500–4,000** *BRIT*

Miller's Starter Marque

Starter BMWs: *1502, 1602, 2002, 2002 Touring.*

- The '02 series two-door saloons made BMW's fortune in the 1960s and established the marque's modern reputation for sporty stylish saloons.

- Today, these spirited machines make good sense as useable everyday classics. All of the '02 series are, in general, re-assuringly solid and robust. All except the 1502 'oil-crisis' model are good for 100mph and the fuel-injected 2002 Tii offered a class-leading 0-60mph time of 8.2 seconds in 1971. This and the twin-carb 2002 Ti are probably the best buys, while the 1602, plain 2002 and 1502 make sensible down-market alternatives.

- Rust problems are no worse than any other steel monocoque saloon, although particular points to watch include the jacking points, which can eventually fall out and leave the sills prone to rotting from the inside out.

- The overhead cam engine uses an alloy cylinder block on a cast-iron block. It is generally long-lived but the more you know about the car's history the better. Regular oil changes will promote long life and all-year-round anti-freeze will help prevent corrosion inside the alloy-head and lessen the chance of it warping through overheating.

- The cabriolet versions of the '02 saloons are a little more exotic but still eminently affordable. However, the rare 2002 Turbo is an enthusiast's car rather than an everyday user. For a start there were only 51 sold in the UK. If you can find one you'll get performance – and, quite possibly, large bills to match.

1974 BMW 2002 Turbo, 170bhp, only produced in left-hand drive, totally rebuilt.
£10,000–15,000 *MUN*

Available in white or silver.

1975 BMW 2002 Tii Lux, 1990cc, 4 speed manual gearbox, some restoration work, original Minilite alloy wheels, factory steel sunroof, wood cappings on the doors and tinted glass, stereo radio cassette.
£1,500–1,800 *H&H*

Cross Reference
For BMW Isettas see Microcars

r. **1975 BMW 2002 Tii Lux Two Door Saloon,** 4 cylinder OHC engine, 1990cc, 130bhp, Lux Turbo wheels, 10 year restoration, correct BMW parts used including factory engine, bodywork and interior good, new transmission and electrics.
£6,800–7,200 *BKS*

BMW Model	ENGINE cc/cyl	DATES	CONDITION 1	2	3
501	2077/6	1952-56	£9,000	£7,000	£3,500
501 V8/502	2580,				
	3168/8	1955-63	£10,000	£8,000	£4,500
503	3168/8	1956-59	£25,000	£20,000	£15,000
507	3168/8	1956-59	£100,000	£70,000	£50,000
Isetta (4 wheels)	247/1	1955-62	£6,000	£3,000	£1,200
Isetta (3 wheels)	298/1	1958-64	£6,500	£2,500	£1,500
Isetta 600	585/2	1958-59	£2,000	£1,000	£500
1500/1800/2000	var/4	1962-68	£1,100	£700	£200
2000CS	1990/4	1966-69	£5,500	£4,000	£1,500
1500/1600/1602	1499/				
	1573/4	1966-75	£2,500	£1,500	£800
1600 Cabriolet	1573/4	1967-71	£6,000	£4,500	£2,000
2800CS	2788/6	1968-71	£5,000	£4,000	£1,500
1602	1990/4	1968-74	£3,000	£1,500	£1,000
2002	1990/4	1968-74	£3,000	£2,000	£1,000
2002 Tii	1990/4	1971-75	£4,500	£2,500	£1,200
2002 Touring	1990/4	1971-74	£3,500	£2,000	£1,000
2002 Cabriolet	1990/4	1971-75	£5,000	£3,000	£2,500
2002 Turbo	1990/4	1973-74	£10,000	£6,000	£4,000
3.0 CSa/CSi	2986/6	1972-75	£8,000	£6,000	£4,000
3.0 CSL	3003/				
	3153/6	1972-75	£16,000	£12,000	£9,500
MI	3500/6	1978-85	£70,000	£50,000	£35,000
633/635 CS/CSI	3210/3453/6	1976-85	£7,000	£3,000	£2,000
M535i	3453/6	1979-81	£4,500	£3,000	£2,500

1930 Alfa Romeo 6C 1750 Gran Sport,
Zagato coachwork, fully restored.
£200,000+ *BC*

Most 6C 1750 roadsters were bodied by Zagato, but a few rival versions were made by Touring and Brianza.

1958 Alfa Romeo 2000 Spider, Superleggera coachwork by Touring, low mileage, very good original condition.
£14,000–17,000 *BC*

Classical Alfa design with 5 bearing twin cam engine of 1975cc, giving 115bhp. From 1958–61, 3,443 Spiders were made.

r. **1964 Alfa Romeo Giulia 1600 Spider,** coachwork by Pininfarina, 4 cylinder in-line, 1570cc twin cam overhead valve engine, 104bhp at 6200rpm, 5 speed synchromesh gearbox, independent wishbones and coil springs suspension, telescopic shock absorbers with anti-roll bar at front, left-hand drive, 21,000 miles recorded, engine overhauled and restored.
£8,000–10,000 *C*

Alfa Romeo introduced the Giulia range in 1962 as an evolution of the earlier Giulietta.

l. **1969 Alfa Romeo 1750 Spider Veloce,** 4 cylinder in-line, twin overhead camshaft, 1779cc engine, 5 speed manual gearbox, 4 wheel disc brakes, independent front suspension with coil springs and double wishbones rear, solid rear axle, coil springs, trailing arms, right-hand drive, fully restored throughout.
£11,000–13,000 *C*

The 2 seater Spider was unveiled at the Geneva Motor Show in March 1966, assuming the name Duetto with boat tail styling at the rear of the car.

r. **1953 Alvis TA21 Two Door Fixed Head Coupé,** coachwork by Graber, 3 litre engine, fully restored including new ash frame, engine uprated to 105bhp TC21 specification and a 3.54:1 final drive ratio, engine overhauled and restored, very good condition.
£22,000–25,000 *BKS*

This oldest surviving Graber Alvis was restored by Alvis specialists Earley Engineering in 1990–1.

l. **1960 Alvis TD21 Two Door Saloon,** coachwork by Park Ward, 6 cylinders, 2993cc engine, manual transmission, right-hand drive, mechanically good, brakes overhauled, electrics all serviceable and chassis sound.
£7,500–9,000 *BKS*

Styled by Graber of Switzerland and introduced in 1955, the TD21 was made in small numbers until 1959 when Park Ward commenced production of the bodywork in steel to the original Graber design.

r. **1929 Aston Martin 1½ Litre International Two Seater,** 4 cylinders, 1498cc, 4 speed gearbox with reverse, mechanical type brakes, semi-elliptic leaf springs suspension, right-hand drive, very good condition throughout. **£40,000–45,000** *C*

The first International was unveiled in the autumn of 1928, an 11.9hp car with a top speed of over 80mph. This car is one of only 6 two seater models produced.

l. **1953 Aston Martin DB2/4 MkI Fixed Head Coupé,** extensively refurbished with complete engine overhaul, competition prepared, excellent condition, full ownership history is known and listed. **£26,000–29,000** *S*

This well-prepared and proven competition Aston has had over £30,000 spent on restoring and maintaining it to date.

1954 Aston Martin DB2/4 MkI Spyder Drophead Coupé, coachwork by Bertone, 6 cylinder, twin overhead camshaft, 2922cc engine, 140bhp at 5000rpm, 4 speed manual gearbox, 4 wheel drum brakes, left-hand drive, fully restored to very good condition throughout. **£180,000+** *C*

1960 Aston Martin DB4GT Coupé, coachwork by Touring of Milan, 6 cylinders, 3670cc, twin plugs per cylinder with twin distributors producing 302bhp, twin plate clutch, close ratio gearbox, Girling brakes and wide Borrani wire wheels. **£90,000+** *COYS*

First shown at the 1959 London Motor Show the DB4GT was Aston Martin's competition answer to the Ferrari 250SWB. The DB4GT was beautifully proportioned and extremely fast with a top speed of 153mph, and was capable of 0–60mph and 0–100mph in 6.1 and 14.1 seconds respectively. Only 100 examples were produced – of which 19 had Zagato coachwork – before production ceased in 1963.

l. **1972 Aston Martin DBS V8 Wills 'Sotheby Special'.** **£32,000–35,000** *BKS*

Conceived by Tom Karen of Ogle Design Ltd as a 'dream car' for the January 1972 Montreal Motor Show, based on an Aston Martin DBS V8 steel platform chassis, suspension and mechanical components. W. D. & H. O. Wills used this car for promotional purposes, and it was used by Graham Hill and Embassy Racing. A unique classic car.

r. **1966 Aston Martin DB6 MkI Vantage Two Door Saloon,** Marek designed straight 6 engine, manual transmission, uprated suspension, engine restored with no modifications from maker's original specification, right-hand drive, very good condition throughout. **£36,000–38,000** *BKS*

Much of the restoration work was carried out by Aston Martin specialists Pugsley & Lewis from 1992–94.

l. **1973 Aston Martin V8 Series III Coupé,** 5.3 litre, V8 engine, 160mph, 70,000 miles recorded, paintwork good apart from 2 small dents and a little bubbling by sunroof. **£13,000–15,000** *BKS*

1932 Auburn 8 Boat Tail Speedster, 8 cylinder, 268.6cu in engine, 98bhp at 4300rpm, completely unrestored condition, last run in 1948, side mount hubcaps and running boards missing. **£32,000–34,000** *C*

r. **1926 Austin 7hp Chummy Tourer,** retrimmed in black with black tonneau cover, very good overall condition to original specification. **£6,000–7,000** *BKS*

The Occasional Four Tourer became known as the Chummy.

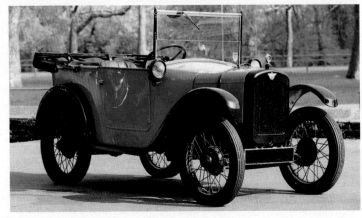

l. **1955 Austin-Healey 100,** 6 cylinders, 2660cc, left-hand drive, fully restored throughout to very good condition. **£14,000–18,000** *COYS*

Launched at the 1952 London Motor Show this model was an instant success and featured in production races on both sides of the Atlantic. Performance was impressive, producing 94bhp at 4000rpm, a top speed of 111mph with the windscreen folded flat and 0–60mph in 10.3 seconds.

1929 Bentley 6½ Litre Barker Sports Torpedo, fully restored, very good condition throughout. **£500,000+** *BLK*

This 'one of a kind' Bentley was displayed at the Olympia Motor Show on the Barker stand. The very exotic coachwork is fully functional and gracefully proportioned, mounted on Bentley's longest wheelbase.

r. **1931 Bentley 8 Litre Sports Tourer,** Vanden Plas style open 4 seater touring body, fully rebuilt and restored. **£200,000+** *BKS*

1931 Bentley 4½ Litre XT Series Four Seater Tourer, original green leather upholstery, matching carpets and Lucas DB Bull's-eye headlamps and Smiths dashboard instruments. **£120,000+** *S*

1937 Bentley 4¼ Litre Coupé Cabriolet De Ville, coachwork by Barker & Co, ground-up restoration, new pistons and liners, concours condition.
£65,000–70,000 *BKS*

This is a very unusual example.

1937 Bentley 4¼ Litre Two Door Fixed Head Coupé, coachwork by Van Vooren, concours condition, fully restored and rebuilt.
£60,000–70,000 *S*

The larger 4¼ litre chassis, introduced as an alternative in 1936, gave better acceleration and the 4257cc overhead valve engine was quickly adopted as standard. Sir Malcolm Campbell, racing driver and speed king, reported: 'The engine, steering, suspension and brakes are absolute perfection. I have never driven a car that holds the road so well.' The Motor magazine, road testing the 4¼, wrote: 'Altogether an extremely satisfactory car, which provides a unique combination of verve with docility, speed with comfort, and performance with silence'. This particular car was delivered in 1937 to the French racing driver Pierre Louis-Dreyfus who raced Alfa Romeos, Talbots and Ferraris.

r. **1953 Bentley R-Type Drophead Coupé,** coachwork by H. J. Mulliner, 4566cc, original hide interior in good condition, all period fittings including, radio, tools and Marchal headlights, bodywork in fair condition.
£35,000–40,000 *H&H*

The rear quarter windows wind down and the hood fully disappears to create a superb line to the car as well as superb visibility. One of only 3 Bentley R-Types made by H. J. Mulliner.

l. **1957 Bentley S1 Continental Fastback,** coachwork by H. J. Mulliner, fully restored to original specification, cosmetic overhaul by Jack Barclay, bare metal respray, interior woodwork restored to original condition.
£65,000–75,000 *S*

This car was displayed at the 1957 Geneva Motor Show.

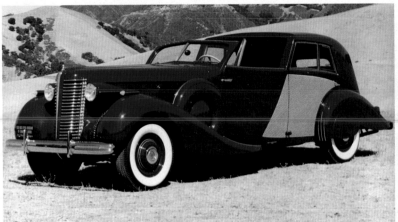

l. **1938 Buick Series 80 Opera Brougham,** coachwork by Fernandez & Darren of Paris, mounted on a Series 80 Roadmaster chassis, 2 vanities and intercom system, fully restored by Fran Roxas to concours condition.
£250,000+ *BLK*

First displayed at the 1938 Paris Auto Salon.

r. **1933 Cadillac 355-C Dual Cowl Sport Phaeton,** V8 engine, coachwork by Fisher, excellent condition.
£180,000+ *BLK*

Standard equipment included a separate cowl for the rear seat passengers and a folding second windscreen. This style tonneau was hinged at the front for passengers entry and exit.

l. **1934 Cadillac Series 452-D (V16) Fleetwood Aerodynamic Coupé,** fully restored.
£300,000+ *BLK*

Designed by Harley Earl and introduced at the 1933 Chicago World's Fair. Between 1934 and 1937 eight of these 5 passenger aerodynamic coupés were built, of which only 3 were built in 1934.

1959 Cadillac Eldorado Biarritz Convertible, V8, 390cu in engine, 325bhp at 4800 rpm, standard power accessories, factory fitted air conditioning and bucket seats, 54,000 miles recorded, fully restored to concours condition.
£40,000–45,000 *C*

The 1959 Cadillac Eldorado Biarritz convertible is one of the greatest icons of the 1950s automotive era.

1954 Chevrolet Corvette Roadster, Blue Flame 6 cylinder, 235.5cu in engine, 150bhp at 4200rpm, 2 speed automatic gearbox.
£16,000–19,000 *C*

In 1953 Chevrolet unveiled their new Corvette, with fibreglass body two seater configuration, which revolutionised the sports car market in America.

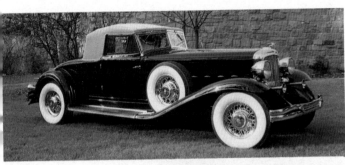

l. **1932 Chrysler Imperial CG Convertible Roadster,** 8 cylinder, 384.84cu in engine, 135bhp at 3200rpm, 96mph top speed, complete body-off restoration to high standard. **£150,000+** *C*

Only 28 examples of the LeBaron Convertible Roadster were produced and only a few genuine examples exist today.

r. **1937 Citroën 11BL Traction Avant Roadster,** 4 cylinder, 1911cc engine, front wheel drive, unitary construction, independent front suspension via wishbone/torsion bar, live rear axle sprung by transverse torsion bars, fully hydraulic brakes. **Est. £20,000–25,000** *COYS*

1941 Chrysler Thunderbolt, designed by Alex Tremulis, built by LeBaron, electrically-operated one-piece retractable roof, headlights behind peek-a-boo lids, electric windows, edge lighted instruments and push-button door handles, anodised aluminium trim around lower body. **£150,000–180,000** *BLK*

Of 6 similar cars built, only 4 remain today.

1936 Cord 810 Supercharged Cabriolet Sportsman, Lycoming V8, side valve, 4729cc engine, 170bhp, 4 speed gearbox with electro-vacuum pre-selector, fully restored. **£65,000–75,000** *C*

This car was designed by Gordon Buehrig and August Duesenberg.

l. **1951 Daimler 2½ Litre Barker Special Sports,** 6 cylinders, 2522cc, 85bhp, replacement engine, pre-selector gearbox reconditioned, steering refurbished, suspension in good order, electrical system functioning except the clock, interior retrimmed and in very good condition. **£7,500–9,000** *BRIT*

r. **1961 Daimler Dart SP250,** B Spec, wire wheels, recent body restoration, black leather interior, chrome wire wheels, tonneau, full history.
£8,000–10,000 *UMC*

The Dart SP250 was Daimler's only true sports car. The unusual glass fibre body failed to appeal and only 2,650 were built between 1959 and 1964.

l. **1969 Daimler 250V8 Saloon,** automatic transmission, 46,000 miles recorded, good condition but interior in need of cosmetic attention, over £12,000 spent on restoration.
£4,000–5,000 *H&H*

Based on the Jaguar MkII body shell, the Daimler 250 V8 saloon offered a traditional Daimler fluted grille and Edward Turner's wonderful 2½ litre, V8 engine.

l. **1973 Daimler 4.2 Litre Limousine,** coachwork by Vanden Plas, 6 cylinder, overhead camshaft engine, automatic transmission, all-independent suspension and disc brakes, 4,140kms recorded, stored since 1979, left-hand drive, flag masts, central division and occasional seats, good condition throughout.
£11,500–13,000 *BKS*

This car was formerly owned by the Shah of Iran.

1977 Daimler Sovereign 4.2 Coupé, 4235cc, 53,400 miles recorded, original wheels.
£3,000–4,000 *H&H*

One of the last pillarless coupés to leave the factory.

1906 Darracq 8/10hp Two Seater Tourer, 1370cc engine, twin cylinder type with long stroke, progressive transmission, unused for several years and dry stored, will require recommissioning prior to use.
£9,500–10,500 *BKS*

1949 Delahaye Type 135M Four Seater Cabriolet, coachwork by Antem, 3227cc, triple downdraught Solex carburettors, 105mph, 0–70mph in under 20 seconds, right-hand drive, Cotal gearbox.
£50,000–60,000 *BKS*

The Type 35 was extremely successful in competition, winning Le Mans in 1938.

1930 Duesenberg Convertible Victoria, coachwork by Hibbard & Darrin, Paris, completely restored.
£750,000+ *BLK*

Hibbard & Darrin built 12 bodies for the Duesenberg Model J chassis between late 1929 and early 1931. European bodied Duesenbergs are extremely rare.

r. 1930 Essex Super Six.
£8,000–10,000 *AS*

In the late 1920s the combined Hudson-Essex operation was 3rd in the US sales league behind Ford and Chevrolet. Hudson dropped the Essex marque in 1932.

l. 1959 Facel Vega HK 500, 8 cylinders, 5910cc, Chrysler V8 engine, manual gearbox, fully restored including bare metal respray, chrome parts replated, period fog and spot lamps, interior refurbished.
£18,000–22,000 *BRIT*

Facel Vegas were large impressive cars which performed as formidably as they looked during the late 1950s and early '60s and appealed to a limited number of wealthy discerning customers.

1951 Ferrari 2.3 Litre 195 Two Door Coupé, special bodywork by Carrozzeria Ghia of Turin, 2.3 litre two cam V12 engine, triple carburettors, right-hand drive, fully restored.
£105,000–120,000   *BKS*

1953 Ferrari 212 Inter Coupé, Ferrari V12, 2562cc engine, 180bhp at 5500rpm, triple 36 DCE3 Weber carburettors, 5 speed manual gearbox, frame-up restoration, 11,000kms recorded.
£110,000–120,000   *C*

l. **1953 Ferrari 3 Litre 250 Europa Coupé,** coachwork by Pininfarina, 2963cc, triple Weber carburettors, 4 speed manual gearbox, 200bhp, maximum speed 134mph, right-hand drive, fully restored to a very high standard.
£110,000–120,000   *BKS*

Introduced at the Paris Show in 1953, the 250 Europa and its stablemate the Ferrari 375 America were the largest Ferraris built up until that time.

r. **1958 Ferrari 250GT Series 1 Cabriolet,** coachwork by Pininfarina, V12, 2953cc engine, 240bhp at 7000rpm, 4 speed manual gearbox, left-hand drive, covered headlights.
£155,000–170,000   *C*

This model sports the very desirable covered headlights, whereas later cars had open headlights and large vertical tail lights.

l. **1959 Ferrari 250 GT Long Wheelbase Spyder California,** coachwork by Scaglietti, V12 engine, single overhead camshaft per bank, 2953cc, carburettor velocity stacks, competition cylinder head with compression ratio of 9.3:1, 250bhp at 7000rpm, factory fitted Dunlop disc brakes, left-hand drive, engine rebuilt, 85,000kms recorded.
£500,000+   *C*

r. **1959 Ferrari 250GT,** 3 litre, V12 engine, 280bhp, Tour de France competition history. **£325,000+** *TALA*

Most Ferrari models took their designation from the approximate capacity of one cylinder in cubic centimetres. This, the V12, 250GT had 12 cylinders of 250cc, making 3 litres. Outputs of up to 290bhp were quoted for the 3 carburettor double overhead camshaft engine. Dunlop disc brakes became standard in 1960. Between 1959 and 1963 just102 examples of the 250GTB with Scaglietti body were built.

l. **1959 Ferrari 4.9 Litre 410 M SuperAmerica Series III Coupé,** coachwork by Carrozzeria Pininfarina, fully restored, maximum speed of 165mph at 6800rpm, 0–60mph in 6.6 seconds and 0–110mph in 14.5 seconds. **£96,000–100,000** *BKS*

The Ferrari 410 SuperAmerica was one of the fastest of all contemporary supercars. This particular 410 SuperAmerica was the 9th of only 12 of these impressive 410SA Series III cars.

r. **1960 Ferrari 250GT Series II Cabriolet,** coachwork by Pininfarina, V12 single overhead camshaft engine, 2953cc, 220bhp at 7000rpm, 4 speed manual gearbox, disc brakes all-round, independent front suspension with helicoidal springs, semi-elliptic springs rear, left-hand drive, 55,550 miles recorded, Borrani wheels with new Michelin MXV tyres, fully restored. **£80,000–95,000** *C*

The new Pininfarina-styled 250GT coupé was first seen at the 1958 Paris Salon.

l. **1963 Ferrari 250GT Lusso Berlinetta Coupé,** coachwork by Scaglietti, styled by Pininfarina, V12, 2953cc engine, overhead valves and camshaft, 4 speed manual all-synchromesh gearbox, 250bhp, top speed 150mph, 0–100mph in 19.5 seconds, right-hand drive, very good condition throughout. **£85,000–90,000** *BKS*

The name Lusso comes from the Italian word for luxury.

r. **1965 Ferrari 330GT 2+2 Coupé,** coachwork by Pininfarina, 60° V12, 3967cc engine, 300+bhp at 6600rpm, right-hand drive, very good condition throughout. **£32,000–34,000** *BKS*

Like its 250GTE predecessor, the all-new 330GT employed a tubular chassis, with a 2in longer wheelbase, making less cramped conditions for the rear passengers. Between 1964 and 1967, 1,080 Ferrari 330GTs were sold.

l. **1973 Ferrari Dino 246GTS,** V6, 2418cc transverse mid engine, 195bhp, well maintained, original condition. **£50,000–55,000** *KHP*

The Dino was named after Enzo Ferrari's son and ushered in a new generation of sports cars with mid-mounted transverse engines.

r. **1966 Ferrari 275 GTB Series II 'Long Nose',** coachwork designed by Pininfarina, built by Scaglietti, V12, single overhead camshaft per bank, 3286cc, 280bhp at 7600rpm, 6 twin choke Weber carburettors, 5 speed gearbox, disc brakes all-round, all aluminium body, left-hand drive, 17,000kms, restored. **£120,000–140,000** *C*

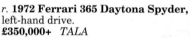

l. **1970 Ferrari 365 GTB/4 Daytona 'Plexiglass',** coachwork by Pininfarina, built by Scaglietti, V12, 4390cc engine, 41,810kms recorded, good original condition. **£70,000–80,000** *C*

The press adopted the nickname Daytona for this new Ferrari after the American 24-hour race.

r. **1972 Ferrari 365 Daytona Spyder,** left-hand drive. **£350,000+** *TALA*

The all-alloy dry sump engine with 6 Weber carburettors pushes out 325bhp. The engine was the awesome 4390cc V12 which powered the Daytona to 174mph. Only 50 Spyders were made.

l. **1973 Ferrari Dino 246GTS Spyder,** 2418cc, Plexiglass headlamp covers, 2 owners from new. **£38,000–40,000** *H&H*

The 246GTS could reach 100mph in 18 seconds with a 150mph top speed. The sheer good looks and fabulous lines ensure that this is a very collectable car.

r. **1975 Ferrari 365 GT/4 Boxer,** coachwork designed by Pininfarina, 4390cc, horizontally opposed 12 cylinder engine, 4 overhead camshafts, 360bhp, right-hand drive, mixed part-tubular, part-monocoque chassis, right-hand drive, in need of major restoration. **£34,000–36,000** *BKS*

1976/77 Ferrari 308GTB, coachwork by Pininfarina, built by Scaglietti, 90° V8, 2926cc, transverse mid engine, 255bhp, glass fibre body, excellent condition and well maintained.
£25,000–30,000 *KHP*

A worthy replacement for the 246 Dino, with same chassis and suspension. Glass fibre bodies were phased out in 1977 and replaced by steel.

1977 Ferrari 512BB, coachwork by Pininfarina, built by Scaglietti, 12 cylinder, 4942cc, horizontally opposed engine, 340bhp, 5 speed synchromesh gearbox, independent front and rear suspension, fully restored, concours condition.
£50,000–55,000 *KHP*

Boxer is the term used to describe the flat opposed cylinder configuration.

1978 Ferrari 308GTS, 90° V8, 2926cc, 4 twin choke Weber carburettors, completely rebuilt and well maintained, excellent condition.
£25,000–27,500 *KHP*

1980 Ferrari 512BB Boxer Berlinetta, coachwork by Pininfarina, 4942cc, mid-mounted engine, 340bhp, 5 speed transaxle package, excellent condition.
£35,000–40,000 *BKS*

l. **1981 Ferrari Mondial 8,** coachwork designed by Pininfarina, built by Scaglietti, 90° V8, 2926cc, Mondial QV engine, 214bhp, good condition and well maintained.
£14,000–16,000   *KHP*

Launched at the Geneva Show in 1980. Since 1969 Fiat had provided support for Ferrari. When Enzo Ferrari died in 1988 Fiat took complete control.

r. **1989 Ferrari Testarossa,** 12 cylinders, 4942cc, horizontally opposed engine, 390bhp, 8,000 miles recorded, excellent condition throughout.
£55,000–60,000   *KHP*

Testarossa means redhead, the colour of the Ferrari's cylinder head covers.

1991 Ferrari F40, 8 cylinders, 2936cc, sports coupé coachwork by Pininfarina, less than 500km recorded, excellent condition.
£140,000–150,000   *COYS*

In 1987 Ferrari celebrated 40 years as a manufacturer and to mark the event Enzo Ferrari wished to introduce a very special car, one which would confirm his company as producing the absolute ultimate sports car that could be used on the road. That car was the F40, drawing heavily on experience gained from the 288GTO. No production car had previously cracked the 200mph barrier but the F40 achieved a maximum speed of 201mph. The F40 was an instant classic and customers clamoured to pay their deposits in order to secure one of the limited number available. The car was in such demand that huge premiums were paid in order to take early delivery, with prices eventually reaching £1,000,000.

1994 Ferrari 456GT 2+2 Coupé, designed by Pininfarina, built by Ferrari, V12, 5474cc, front engine, 6 speed gearbox, independent adjustable suspension, complete with 5 piece luggage set, excellent condition, with full service history.
£95,000–105,000   *KHP*

For many Ferrari fans the 465GT rekindles memories of one of the earlier all-time great front engined Ferraris, the 365GTB/4 Daytona, also endowed with a mighty V12 engine, but a 2 seater rather than a 2+2.

r. **1964 Fiat 600 Jolly,** 633cc, 4 cylinder, in-line, overhead valve engine, 4 speed manual gearbox, front suspension A-arms with transverse leaf springs, A-arms with coil springs rear, 4 wheel drum brakes, left-hand drive, bare metal respray, fully restored and in excellent condition, over £7,000 spent on restoration.
£6,500–8,000 *C*

The Jolly, sometimes referred to as a 'beach buggy', was designed by Ghia in Italy. It had basket weave seats and fully open sides, and was described by Road & Track *magazine as akin to a modern-day 'surrey with the fringe on top'.*

l. **1967 Fiat Dino Spyder,** coachwork by Pininfarina, 6 cylinders, 1987cc, fully restored and in excellent condition throughout.
£15,000–17,000 *COYS*

The Fiat Dino was designed as a result of new FIA rules imposed on the marques competing in the 1967 Formula 2 championship. These stipulated that all F2 engines would have to be built in 500 units at least, something Ferrari could not achieve without Fiat's assistance.

r. **1970 Fiat Abarth 595SS,** race prepared, Weber 50DCOE carburettor, extended wheel arches, wide wheels, 6 point roll cage, rebuilt engine.
£3,500–4,000 *BKS*

Abarth boosted the 499cc air-cooled twin engine to 593cc, and with higher compression pistons, re-worked inlet ports, special camshaft, exhaust system and larger carburettor, raised the power from 22 to 30bhp. Abarth's conversion halved the standard model's acceleration times giving the 595SS (Sprint Speciale) 34bhp and a top speed of 130km/h.
    Carlo Abarth did for the baby Fiat what John Cooper did for the Mini, turning it into a 'pocket rocket'.

l. **1983 Fiat X1/9 Sports Convertible,** designed by Bertone, good condition throughout.
£1,300–1,700 *PA*

The mid-engined X1/9 could reach a modest 105–110mph in 1500cc form, but handling was superb. Among export markets the Fiat X1/9 scored most strongly in the USA. With its mid-engined layout handling was really quite superb. The smaller 1290cc version could only just reach 100mph. Between 1972 and 1989 approximately 180,000 were built.

l. **1928 Ford Model A Roadster Pick-up Truck,** 200.5cu in, 40bhp at 2200rpm, excellent condition.
£8,000–10,000 *C*

The Model A had a high body with a flat vertical windshield, but was more attractive than the antique looking Model T. It was an extremely simple car, and much easier to drive than its predecessor. It had 3 forward speeds and cable-operated 4 wheel brakes. The price was $500 (£315) for the basic Model A Tudor and was available in 3 colourways: grey, green or black.

r. **1936 Ford Model 68 V8 Roadster,** with rumble seat, V8, 3622cc engine, right-hand drive, red paintwork with ivory interior, ex-South Africa, extensive restoration.
£14,500–15,000 *CGB*

This model was available in several body styles, including a 3 window coupé, 2 and 4 door sedans, convertibles and estates.

l. **1929 Hispano-Suiza H6B Torpedo Phaeton,** coachwork by Million et Guiet, Paris, 6 cylinder, in-line, 6597cc engine, 135bhp at 3000rpm, right-hand drive, upholstery replaced.
£90,000–100,000 *C*

The H6B was a favourite car for the wealthy sporting motorist and its success in competitions became legendary. Launched at the 1919 Paris salon, the H6B set the standard for automotive design and engineering that other manufacturers strived to equal. The one model policy provided the highest degree of quality control and at the same time enabled detailed improvements based on experience and customer suggestions.

1932 Invicta 4.5 Litre S-Type, coachwork by Vanden Plas, straight 6 Meadows engine, 115bhp, comprehensive restoration, pre- and post-war competition history.
£150,000–165,000 *COYS*

When the Invicta S-type was unveiled at the 1930 Olympia Motor Show it was the lowest, sleekest car in the world. In fact it was so low that some pundits predicted that it would be uncontrollable and would break away from the driver when driven hard. By the time the S-Type had won the 1931 Monte Carlo Rally, had returned clean sheets in the 1931 and 1932 International Alpine Trials and performed with distinction on tight and twisty hill climbs like Shelsley Walsh and Prescott, the pundits had to eat their words. It was capable of going from 10mph to maximum speed of 95+mph in top gear.

BRISTOL

The Bristol Aeroplane Company branched out into car manufacture in 1947 with an anglicised version of the pre-war BMW 327. Bristol's famed 6 cylinder engine was derived from a pre-war BMW unit. Combined with hand-crafted coachwork and luxury appointments Bristols earned the appellation 'The Businessman's Express'. In the early 1960s Bristol Cars Ltd, as it had become, adopted Chrysler V8 power to endow its luxury sports saloons with extra surge. At their best the V8 Bristols could offer near Jaguar or Ferrari performance but with a most un-Ferrari-like quiet.

1950 Bristol 401 Two Door Saloon, 6 cylinders, 2 litres, 85bhp, comprehensive refurbishment. **£6,000–8,000** *BKS*

Launched in 1949, the Bristol 401 was a more aerodynamic derivative of the mechanically similar 400 model, its bodywork developed in the wind tunnel of the parent Bristol Aeroplane Company.

With aluminium panelling over a tubular steel framing the Bristol 401 weighed a mere 2700lb. The combination of lightweight construction and refined aerodynamics meant that with the standard 85bhp 2 litre, 6 cylinder power unit, the 401 had better top-end acceleration up to 100mph, making it one of the best performing cars of the period.

1958 Bristol 406 Saloon, 2216cc, very good condition throughout. **£8,500–10,500** *H&H*

Originally registered to Mr Tony Crook – the owner of Bristol cars – this was the actual car in which the original road tests were carried out by Autocar *and* Motor *magazines.*

1965 Bristol 408 Two Door Saloon, restored, requires re-assembling and finishing. **£3,000–4,000** *S*

By the early 1960s Bristol had forsaken its long running 5 cylinder engine units in favour of the V8 Chrysler engines. The new engines gave the 407 enhanced performance and the car had a top speed in the order of 120mph. The 408 was announced in 1963 and the light alloy 2 door coachwork had all the luxury features of the earlier model, including quality hide upholstery, polished walnut woodwork and deep pile carpets.

l. **1972 Bristol 411,** 8 cylinders, 6277cc, dry stored for a number of years, recently serviced. **£6,000–8,000** *COYS*

BRISTOL Model	ENGINE cc/cyl	DATES	CONDITION 1	2	3
400	1971/6	1947-50	£18,000	£14,000	£8,000
401	1971/6	1949-53	£18,000	£14,000	£8,000
402	1971/6	1949-50	£22,000	£19,000	£12,000
403	1971/6	1953-55	£20,000	£14,000	£10,000
404 Coupé	1971/6	1953-57	£22,000	£15,000	£12,000
405	1971/6	1954-58	£17,000	£13,000	£10,000
405 Drophead	1971/6	1954-56	£25,000	£22,000	£18,000
406	2216/6	1958-61	£15,000	£11,000	£8,000
407	5130/8	1962-63	£12,000	£8,000	£6,000
408	5130/8	1964-65	£14,000	£10,000	£8,000
409	5211/8	1966-67	£14,000	£11,000	£7,000
410	5211/8	1969	£14,000	£10,000	£6,000
411 Mk 1-3	6277/8	1970-73	£16,000	£11,000	£8,000
411 Mk 4-5	6556/8	1974-76	£12,500	£9,500	£7,000
412	5900/ 6556/8	1975-82	£15,000	£9,000	£6,000
603	5211/ 5900/8	1976-82	£12,000	£8,000	£5,000

BROWN BROTHERS

c1905/6 Brown Brothers 18/20hp 4/5 Seater Side Entrance Tonneau, L-head, 4 cylinder, side valve, 3½ litre engine by Forman, completely restored.
£10,000–12,500 *BKS*

The well-known London-based factors Brown Brothers Ltd offered a variety of cars under their own name between 1901 and 1911, some of which were made for them by Star of Wolverhampton. In 1902 the company was advertising that 'almost any type of engine can be fitted' and both shaft drive and chain drive models were available. The later cars featured Mercedes-like honeycomb radiators from 1904 onwards. This car was unearthed some 40 years ago in a scrapyard, and during WWI it had been rebodied as an ambulance. Now completely restored but needs some detail finishing.

BSA

1934 BSA 10hp Special Saloon, 1185cc engine, Daimler transmission, fully restored retaining the original factory colours, 63,000 recorded mileage, same family ownership since new.
£7,000–8,000 *S*

BUGATTI

1929 Bugatti Type 44 Torpedo Grand Sport, 8 cylinder, 2992cc engine.
£63,000–68,000 *COYS*

The Type 44 was one of the most popular models which Bugatti made, Between 1927–30 1,095 were produced, but its survival rate (a little over 10%) has been unusually low and only 130 are known to exist today.

With an unsupercharged straight 8, 3 litre engine, single overhead camshaft, 9 bearing crankshaft and 3 valves per cylinder, it offered sparkling performance with flexibility. Leaving aside the Royale, the Type 44 had the largest engine Bugatti had made until that time.

l. **1931 Bugatti 37A Grand Prix,** coachwork by Hanni of Zurich, 4 cylinders, overhead camshaft, 1496cc, 90bhp at 4000rpm, 4 speed manual gearbox, complete and unmodified.
£165,000+ *C*

By the mid-1920s a replacement was needed for the successful but outdated Brescia. Bugatti designed an all new 4 cylinder engine and fitted a Type 35A chassis using the same radiator and wheels, this became the Type 37. Some 18 months after the introduction of the Type 37, a supercharged version, the Type 37A, was produced, this was one of Bugatti's more successful Grand Prix cars. Its performance was most impressive – one lapped the Brooklands track at over 122mph. This is the only Type 37A with Hanni coachwork.

BUICK

1923 Buick 30hp Seven Seater Tourer,
6 cylinder engine, Delco coil ignition, 3 speed
gearbox with multi-disc clutch and spiral bevel
final drive, right-hand drive, Canadian built,
'barn discovered' condition.
£4,000–6,000 *BKS*

1927 Buick Master 6 Series 120 Tourer, 6
cylinder, 207cu in, 3392cc, restored to good
standard.
£13,500–15,500 *ADT*

1940 Buick 8 Four Door Sedan, straight 8,
4065cc engine, left-hand drive, roof-mounted
radio antenna, period push-button radio, electric
clock and special Buick battery, excellent order,
restored in the UK.
£7,000–9,000 *S*

1929 Buick Model 25 Open Five Seater Tourer,
6 cylinder in-line engine overhead valve, 239.1cu in,
94bhp at 2800rpm, 3 speed manual gearbox, new
hood, requires some restoration work.
£7,500–9,000 *C*

*David Dunbar Buick was born in Scotland in
1854 and emigrated to the United States with his
parents at the age of 2. The first production Buick
appeared in 1903, a horizontal twin with overhead
valves, followed by 4 cylinder cars and the famous
'square' 20hp of 1908. In October 1908 Buick was
bought by General Motors. By 1915 Buick production
had reached 44,000 cars a year, and made virtually
all its own parts. Apart from the 4 cylinder cars of
1909, all had overhead valve engines. This particular
car has spent the majority of its life in Argentina.*

1938 Buick Series 40 Special Roadster,
engine bay retains majority of original
components, in need of restoration.
£1,400–1,800 *S*

**1948 Buick 8 Super Series 50 Two Door
Sedanette,** coachwork by Fisher Body
Corporation, 8 cylinder, 4.2 litre engine,
manual transmission, right-hand drive.
£9,000–11,000 *BKS*

BUICK Model	ENGINE cc/cyl	DATES	CONDITION 1	2	3
Veteran	various	1903-09	£18,500	£12,000	£8,000
18/20	3881/6	1918-22	£12,000	£5,000	£2,000
Series 22	2587/4	1922-24	£9,000	£5,000	£3,000
Series 24/6	3393/6	1923-30	£9,000	£5,000	£3,000
Light 8	3616/8	1931	£18,000	£14,500	£11,000
Straight 8	4467/8	1931	£22,000	£18,000	£10,000
50 Series	3857/8	1931-39	£18,500	£15,000	£8,000
60 Series	5247/8	1936-39	£19,000	£15,000	£8,000
90 Series	5648/8	1934-35	£20,000	£15,500	£9,000
40 Series	4064/8	1936-39	£19,000	£14,000	£10,000
80/90	5247/8	1936-39	£25,000	£20,000	£15,000
McLaughlin	5247/8	1937-40	£22,000	£15,000	£10,000

Various chassis lengths and bodies will affect value. Buick chassis fitted with English bodies
previous to 1916 were called Bedford-Buicks. Right-hand drive can have an added premium of 25%.

BUICK Model	ENGINE cu in/cyl	DATES	CONDITION 1	2	3
Special/Super 4 Door	248/ 364/8	1950-59	£6,000	£4,000	£2,000
Special/Super Riviera	263/ 332/8	1050-56	£8,000	£6,000	£3,000
Special/Super Convertible	263/ 332/8	1950-56	£7,500	£5,500	£3,000
Roadmaster 4 door	320/ 365/8	1950-58	£11,000	£8,000	£6,000
Roadmaster Riviera	320/ 364/8	1950-58	£9,000	£7,000	£5,000
Roadmaster Convertible	320/ 364/8	1950-58	£14,500	£11,000	£7,000
Special/Super Riviera	364/8	1957-59	£10,750	£7,500	£5,000
Special/Super Convertible	364/8	1957-58	£13,500	£11,000	£6,000

l. **1958 Buick Limited Series Sedan,** 8 cylinders, 5965cc, 364cu in, interior in original condition, mechanically sound, panelwork and paint in good condition. **£8,500–9,500** *ADT*

There were only 5,751 examples of this series produced.

r. **1958 Buick Riviera Limited Sedan,** 8 cylinders, 5933cc, 364cu in, automatic transmission, in original condition except for new paint, air conditioning, heated electric front seat and electric windows, tinted glass, power steering, power brakes, dual exhaust system. **£7,500–8,500** *BRIT*

Finished in opalescent cream metallic paint, this vehicle was imported from the US in 1994.

1958 Buick Roadmaster 75, fully restored, excellent condition. **£17,750–18,750** *CTP*

1961 Buick Invicta, 401cu in, excellent condition. **£5,000–5,500** *CTP*

CADILLAC

Almost from its very beginning the name Cadillac has stood for prestige motoring, and in the luxury car market this General Motors flagship marque has often set the standards for others to follow. In 1912 Cadillac fitted electric lighting as standard on its 5.5 litre/336cu in, 4 cylinder model. In 1914 it introduced its first V8 engine, which has remained a feature of the marque ever since. In 1930 the extravagant V16 arrived, followed closely by the V12 models, in both cases styled by Harley J. Earl who went on to create the ultimate American post-war automotive styling statements with fins, chrome and bullet-shaped bumpers.

1923 Cadillac Type 61 Saloon, mechanical headlamp dipping system, gear lever lock, plush upholstery and mahogany door trims, steering wheel trim and horn button, 15,000 miles recorded, excellent and original condition.
£16,000–19,000   *S*

1933 Cadillac 370 (V12) All-Weather Phaeton, very good condition.
£150,000+   *BLK*
A National CCCA 1st place winner at the 1989 Indiana Annual Meeting.

1955 Cadillac Series 62 Club Coupé, 8 cylinders, 5424cc, 331cu in, white walled tyres, automatic heating system, self seeking radio, power brakes, E–Z eye glass, fog lamps, door guards and Cadillac floor rugs.
£7,000–9,500   *BRIT*

1934 Cadillac V16 Convertible Sedan, V16, overhead valve, 452.8cu in, 180bhp at 3800rpm, 3 speed manual gearbox, semi-elliptic leaf spring suspension, left-hand drive, restored condition.
£110,000–130,000   *C*

Weighing over 6,000lbs, 154in wheelbase and 240in total length, the 1934 V-16s were the longest cars ever built in America. Unfortunately, with the dramatic effects of the Great Depression taking hold, the luxury car market suffered and a mere 54 V16s were produced in 1934. It is capable of 100mph.

CADILLAC (pre-war) Model	ENGINE cc/cyl	DATES	CONDITION 1	2	3
Type 57-61	5153/8	1915-23	£20,000	£14,000	£6,000
Series 314	5153/8	1926-27	£22,000	£15,000	£6,000
Type V63	5153/8	1924-27	£20,000	£13,000	£5,000
Series 341	5578/8	1928-29	£22,000	£15,000	£6,000
Series 353-5	5289/8	1930-31	£32,500	£22,000	£12,000
V16	7406/16	1931-32	£50,000	£32,000	£18,000
V12	6030/12	1932-37	£42,000+	£25,000	£15,000
V8	5790/8	1935-36	£30,000+	£15,000	£6,000
V16	7034/16	1937-40	£50,000+	£30,000	£18,000

CADILLAC Model	ENGINE cu in/cyl	DATES	CONDITION 1	2	3
4 door sedan	331/8	1949	£8,000	£4,500	£3,000
2 door fastback	331/8	1949	£10,000	£8,000	£5,000
Convertible coupé	331/8	1949	£22,000	£12,000	£10,000
Series 62 4 door	331/365/8	1950-55	£7,000	£5,500	£3,000
Sedan de Ville	365/8	1956-58	£8,000	£6,000	£4,000
Coupé de Ville	331/365/8	1950-58	£12,500	£9,500	£3,500
Convertible coupé	331/365/8	1950-58	£25,000	£20,000	£10,000
Eldorado	331/8	1953-55	£35,000	£30,000	£18,000
Eldorado Seville	365/8	1956-58	£11,500	£9,000	£5,500
Eldorado Biarritz	365/8	1956-58	£30,000	£20,000	£15,000
Sedan de Ville	390/8	1959	£12,000	£9,500	£5,000
Coupé de Ville	390/8	1959	£15,000	£9,000	£5,500
Convertible coupé	390/8	1959	£28,000	£20,000	£10,000
Eldorado Seville	390/8	1959	£13,000	£10,000	£6,000
Eldorado Biarritz	390/8	1959	£30,000	£20,000	£14,000
Sedan de Ville	390/8	1960	£10,000	£8,000	£4,500
Convertible coupé	390/8	1960	£27,000	£14,000	£7,500
Eldorado Biarritz	390/8	1960	£25,000	£17,000	£10,000
Sedan de Ville	390/429/8	1961-64	£7,000	£5,000	£3,000
Coupé de Ville	390/429/8	1961-64	£8,000	£6,000	£4,000
Convertible coupé	390/429/8	1961-64	£15,000	£9,000	£7,000
Eldorado Biarritz	390/429/8	1961-64	£19,500	£14,000	£9,000

1959 Cadillac Series 62 Two Door Hard-Top Coupé, fully restored.
£13,000–14,000 *CGB*

1964 Cadillac Fleetwood, very good condition.
£6,500–7,500 *CTP*

1976 Cadillac Eldorado Bicentennial Convertible, V8, overhead valve, 500cu in, 190bhp at 4400rpm, disc and drum brakes, independent front suspension, left-hand drive, turbo Hydra-matic gearbox, 65,000 miles recorded, recent respray.
£11,500–14,500 *C*

The 1976 Cadillac Eldorado Convertible was a collector's item the moment it rolled off the assembly line. It was the only American convertible passenger car in production – American Motors built its last convertible in 1963, Chrysler in 1971, and Ford in 1973. Increasing passenger safety concerns and a new federal rollover standard caused the Detroit automakers to discontinue production of their convertible lines. After sales of the 1975 Cadillac convertibles were down General Motors decided to follow suit and announced that the next year's production would be 'the last of the convertibles'. General Motors decided to produce a very limited edition series and the last 200 cars would be identical – all white, including the top and wheel covers, a white leather interior with red piping, dashboard and carpeting and red and blue striping. This car was purchased with only 5 miles recorded in 1980 from a dealer where it had been stored since its production.

CARTERCAR

1912 Cartercar Model R Roadster, 4 cylinders, 40hp, friction drive transmission, semi-elliptic leaf spring suspension, 2 wheel drum brakes, right-hand drive, fitted with optional Stewart speedometer, brightwork finished in nickel plate, restored.
£7,000–9,500 *C*

Byron J. Carter had been experimenting with horseless carriages since before the turn of the century. He felt that the number of drive speeds should be left up to the driver not his car's transmission. In 1907 the Cartercar Company was born. Initially, all Cartercars were 2 cylinder engines, but by 1910 all were powered by 4 cylinder units.
In 1909 the Cartercar Company became one of almost 30 firms bought by William Durant, head of General Motors. Following a power struggle at General Motors the new board ordered the Cartercar plant to be closed on May 22nd, 1915. Durant had bought the Cartercar for its friction drive, and of all the friction drive cars built in the US, Cartercar was the most famous, the most successful, and the longest lived.

CHENARD-WALCKER

1927 Chenard-Walcker Tourer, restored to the highest standard, finished in maroon with black wings, twin side-mounted spare wheels.
£7,500–8,000 *AS*

Chenard-Walcker of France is best known for winning the first Le Mans race in 1923. The first car was built in 1901, the last in 1946.

CHEVROLET

Following his family's move from France to Canada, Swiss-born Louis Chevrolet worked for, amongst other manufacturers, De Dion Bouton in New York. He also established himself as a successful racing driver and it was his Buick-based special that attracted the attention of General Motors' William C. Durant. When Durant lost control of General Motors, he became interested in Louis' French-inspired designs for 4 and 6 cylinder engined cars. The first prototype, a 4.9 litre, 6 cylinder, appeared in 1911, and in November of that year Durant set up the Chevrolet Motor Car Company. Louis, however, left the business in 1913.

1925 Chevrolet Superior Series K Four Seater Tourer, finished in chocolate and cream, wire wheels, very good condition.
£9,500–10,000 *CGB*

1957 Chevrolet Bel Air Convertible, left-hand drive, restored, very good condition.
£18,000–20,000 *PAL*

1960 Chevrolet El Camino, 350cu in, excellent condition throughout.
£6,000–6,500 *CTP*

l. **1960 Corvette 283,** fuel injection, original, 2 tops, good condition.
£28,000–30,000 *COR*

CHEVROLET Model	ENGINE cc/cyl	DATES	CONDITION 1	2	3
H4/H490 K Series	2801/4	1914-29	£9,000	£5,000	£2,000
FA5	2699/4	1918	£8,000	£5,000	£2,000
D5	5792/8	1918-19	£10,000	£6,000	£3,000
FB50	3660/4	1919-21	£7,000	£4,000	£2,000
AA	2801/4	1928-32	£5,000	£3,000	£1,000
AB/C	3180/6	1929-36	£6,000	£4,000	£2,000
Master	3358/6	1934-37	£9,000	£5,000	£2,000
Master De Luxe	3548/6	1938-41	£9,000	£6,000	£4,000

1963 Chevrolet Corvette Split Window Coupé,
V8 engine, 4 speed transmission, power steering,
fuel injection, restored, very good condition.
£28,000–30,000 *KI*

1963 Chevrolet Corvette Sting Ray, 5359cc,
327cu in, excellent condition throughout.
£13,000–15,000 *H&H*

*This car is finished with red and black leather
interior, which was an expensive option in 1963.*

1963 Chevrolet Corvette Coupé, 5.4 litres,
manual gearbox, split window, full racing history,
good condition.
£18,000–20,000 *COR*

1964 Chevrolet Corvette Coupé, air conditioning,
very good condition.
£11,500–12,500 *COR*

l. **1965 Chevrolet Corvette Sting Ray
Coupé,** replaced 454cu in big block
engine, 465bhp at 5200rpm, 4 speed
manual gearbox, 4 wheel disc brakes, coil
springs, single transverse leaf springs
suspension, left-hand drive, 42,000 miles
recorded, teak steering wheel, side-mounted
exhaust system, excellent condition.
£25,000–27,000 *C*

CHEVROLET Model	ENGINE cu in/cyl	DATES	CONDITION 1	2	3
Stylemaster	216/6	1942-48	£8,000	£4,000	£1,000
Fleetmaster	216/6	1942-48	£8,000	£4,000	£1,000
Fleetline	216/6	1942-51	£8,000	£5,000	£2,000
Styleline	216/6	1949-52	£8,000	£6,000	£2,000
Bel Air 4 door	235/6	1953-54	£6,000	£4,000	£3,000
Bel Air Sports Coupé	235/6	1953-54	£7,000	£4,500	£3,500
Bel Air Convertible	235/6	1953-54	£12,500	£9,500	£6,000
Bel Air 4 door	283/8	1955-57	£8,000	£4,000	£3,000
Bel Air Sports Coupé	283/8	1955-56	£11,000	£7,000	£4,000
Bel Air Convertible	283/8	1955-56	£16,000	£11,000	£7,000
Bel Air Sports Coupé	283/8	1957	£11,000	£7,500	£4,500
Bel Air Convertible	283/8	1957	£14,500	£10,500	£8,000
Impala Sports Sedan	235/6, 348/8	1958	£12,500	£9,000	£5,500
Impala Convertible	235/6, 348/8	1958	£14,500	£11,000	£7,500
Impala Sports Sedan	235/6, 348/8	1959	£8,000	£5,000	£4,000
Impala Convertible	235/6, 348/8	1959	£14,000	£10,000	£5,000
Corvette Roadster	235/6	1953	£18,000	£14,000	£10,000
Corvette Roadster	235/6, 283/8	1954-57	£16,500	£13,000	£9,000
Corvette Roadster	283, 327/8	1958-62	£16,000	£12,000	£9,000
Corvette Sting Ray	327, 427/8	1963-67	£15,500	£12,000	£10,000
Corvette Sting Ray DHC	327, 427/8	1963-66	£22,000	£15,000	£8,000
Corvette Sting Ray DHC	427/8	1967	£16,000	£13,000	£10,000

Value will also be regulated by build options, rare coachbuilding options, and de luxe engine
specifications etc

1965 Chevrolet Corvair Monza Two Door Convertible, 4 speed manual transmission, power-operated hood, 52,000 miles recorded, left-hand drive, excellent overall condition.
£5,250–6,750 *BKS*

The compact, rear-engined Corvair was introduced in late 1959. Powered by an air-cooled 2.3 litre horizontally opposed 6, and featuring independent suspension all-round, the Corvair was highly unconventional by American standards.

1968 Chevrolet Corvette Convertible, V8, 5700cc, automatic gearbox, new interior trim, some British Regulation modifications, excellent condition.
£17,250–19,000 *S*

1970 Corvette CT-1 Convertible, 4 speed gearbox, restored, good condition.
£17,000–19,000 *COR*

1980 Corvette Automatic, glass roofs, GM alloy wheels, good condition.
£10,000–12,000 *COR*

1988 Corvette Coupé Automatic, low mileage, rare 16in wheels, good condition.
£11,000–13,000 *COR*

1966 Chevrolet II Nova Four Door Sedan, 6 cylinders, automatic, power steering, 45,000 miles recorded, left-hand drive, original condition.
£3,000–3,250 *CGB*

1969 Chevrolet Impala Convertible, V8, 327cu in, automatic gearbox, 45,000 miles recorded, good condition.
£2,000–2,500 *WDG*

1980 Corvette 350, 4 speed manual gearbox, glass roofs, low mileage, good condition.
£10,000–12,000 *COR*

CHRYSLER

1929 Chrysler Series 75 Roadster, 6 cylinders, 4078cc, 3 speed manual gearbox, totally restored, very good condition throughout.
£12,500–14,000   *H&H*

1929 Chrysler Type 75 4.1 Litre Four Door Tonneau Phaeton, 6 cylinder, side valve, 4057cc engine, 76bhp, 3 speed sliding mesh gearbox, 4 wheel hydraulic brakes, imported from South America, fully restored, with photographic record.
£14,000–15,500   *C*

Amongst the up-market Chrysler models was the 75, which for 1929 and 1930 featured a distinctive ribbon radiator with thermostatic shutters. In 1929 the most common 75 models, the sedan and coupé, accounted for 32,000 sales, but there were also some limited production models of which the phaetons are the rarest. Only 227 Tonneau phaetons were sold.

1963 Chrysler Crown Imperial Two Door Coupé, V8, 413.2cu in, overhead valve engine, automatic transmission, air-conditioning, auto pilot, power steering, power braking and tinted electric windows, left-hand drive, good condition.
£3,500–5,000   *BKS*

l. **1932 Chrysler CL Imperial Custom Le Baron Convertible Sedan,** fully restored.
£150,000+   *BLK*

It is believed that only 10 original bodied Imperials still exist from the 49 originally built by Le Baron.

CITROEN

l. **1947 Citroën Light 15 Saloon,** 2 owners from new, garage stored.
£6,000–7,000   *S*

Citroën, formed in Paris in 1919, quickly became the most ubiquitous of all French cars. In 1934 a front-wheel driven model, the Super Modern 12, was announced to the public and proved to be one of the classic designs of motoring history, dominating the roads of France between the wars. It was replaced by the 2 litre Light 15, with brisker performance and lighter controls than the early 12s but still retaining a 3 speed gearbox ahead of the final drive assembly, controlled by a gear lever protruding from the fascia. The famous Traction Avant proved very durable and soon attracted a devoted following.

CITROEN Model	ENGINE cc/cyl	DATES	CONDITION 1	2	3
A	1300/4	1919	£4,000	£2,000	£1,000
5CV	856/4	1922-26	£7,000	£4,000	£2,000
11	1453/4	1922-28	£4,000	£2,000	£1,000
12/24	1538/4	1927-29	£5,000	£3,000	£1,000
2½litre	2442/6	1929-31	£5,000	£3,000	£1,500
13/30	1628/4	1929-31	£5,000	£3,000	£1,000
Big 12	1767/4	1932-35	£7,000	£5,000	£2,000
Twenty	2650/6	1932-35	£10,000	£5,000	£3,000
Ten CV	1452/4	1933-34	£5,000	£3,000	£1,000
Ten CV	1495/4	1935-36	£6,000	£3,000	£1,000
11B/Light 15/Big 15/7CV	1911/4	1934-57	£9,000	£5,000	£2,000
Twelve	1628/4	1936-39	£5,000	£3,000	£1,000
F	1766/4	1937-38	£4,000	£2,000	£1,000
15/6 and Big Six	2866/6	1938-56	£7,000	£4,000	£2,000

CITROEN	ENGINE	DATES	CONDITION		
Model	cc/cyl		1	2	3
2CV	375/2	1948-54	£1,000	£500	£250
2CV/Dyane/Bijou	425/2	1954-82	£1,000	£800	£500
DS19/ID19	1911/4	1955-69	£5,000	£3,000	£800
Sahara	900/4	1958-67	£5,000	£4,000	£3,000
2CV6	602/2	1963-	£750	£500	£250
DS Safari	1985/4	1968-75	£6,000	£3,000	£1,000
DS21	1985/4	1969-75	£6,000	£3,000	£1,000
DS23	2347/4	1972-75	£6,000	£4,000	£1,500
SM	2670/				
	2974/6	1970-75	£9,000	£6,000	£4,500

Imported (USA) SM models will be 15% less

1974 Citroën SM Sports Coupé,
left-hand drive, dry stored.
£5,500–7,000 *BKS*

1949 Citroën Light 15, 4 cylinders, 1200cc,
3 speed manual gearbox, Slough built,
concours condition.
£7,500–8,500 *H&H*

*A marriage of Citroën's advanced chassis technology
with Italian engine know-how, the aerodynamic SM
featured DS style hydro-pneumatic self-levelling
suspension, power brakes, self-centring steering and
steered headlamps. Its 2974cc Maserati, 4 cam, V6
power unit was created by chopping 2 cylinders off the
Italian company's Indy 90° V8. Fuel injection was
introduced in 1972, and an automatic transmission
option was offered the following year. The model was
axed in 1975 after Citroën's acquisition by Peugeot.*

1973 Citroën SM, ex-Florida, restored
condition.

CORD

1936 Cord 810 Cabriolet Sportsman,
V8, L-head, 288.6cu in engine, 170bhp, 4 speed
preselector gearbox by Bendix, front-wheel drive.
£25,000–28,000 *C*

*Models 810 and 812 were the most famous for
their incredible design. The brainchild of Gordon
Buehrig, the new Cord was a complete departure
from anything that came before it. In fact the 810
and 812 Cords have one of the most recognised
and highly regarded designs of all time. The Cord
was a futuristic car with elegant pontoon fenders,
distinct coffin nose and wrap-around radiator
louvres. It introduced the first use of retractable
headlights, far ahead of its time. The dashboard
also had a modernistic look with full
instrumentation, including a 150mph
speedometer and tachometer, covered with a
machine-turned plate.*

DAIMLER

A Daimler's elegant fluted radiator grille is much more than a mere badge of automotive distinction; it's the signature of Britain's oldest living make. As the British motor industry celebrated its centenary in 1996 it was the formation of the Daimler Motor Company Ltd on 14 January, 1896 that represented its birth.

In 1900 the Prince of Wales, later King Edward VII, began more than 50 years of royal patronage when he took delivery of a 6hp Daimler with a phaeton body. Ever since then Daimlers have distinguished themselves not as high volume manufacturers, but as quality motor carriages for a discerning clientele. After WWII the company began to lose direction in a changing world and in 1960 was acquired by Jaguar. Today, however, that fluted radiator still stands out as the luxury flagship in the Jaguar hierarchy.

1921 Daimler Light Thirty 5 Seater Tourer, 6 cylinders, 3.3 litres, 4 speed gearbox, worm drive rear axle, new cylinder blocks, clutch relined, new wheel bearings, gearbox overhauled, magneto rebuilt, re-upholstered and repainted.
£10,500–12,000 *BKS*

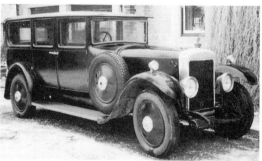

1927 Daimler 25/85hp Six Cylinder Limousine, coachwork by Connaught Motor and Carriage Co Ltd, 7 seater, correct mechanical specification, replaced engine, original engine and a gearbox as spares, restored and re-wired.
£4,000–5,500 *BKS*

1937 Daimler Light 20 Wingham Cabriolet, coachwork by Martin Walter of Folkestone, spring-assisted head mechanism, good overall condition, fixed-head power unit, rebuilt 1995.
£16,500–18,000 *BKS*

1954 Daimler Conquest Century, 6 cylinders, 2433cc, 100bhp, pre-selector transmission unit with fluid flywheel, original brown leather trim, engine in good condition.
£1,500–2,000 *ADT*

1952 Daimler DB18 Special Sports Three Seater Drophead Coupé, coachwork by Barker, 6 cylinders, overhead valves, 2522cc, 85bhp at 4200rpm, 4 speed gearbox, pre-selector, 4 wheel drum brakes, coil spring front suspension, semi-elliptic leaf spring rear, right-hand drive, very good overall condition.
£7,500–8,500 *C*

Mechanically the Special Sports was enhanced by twin carburettors and an overdrive epicyclic gearbox, and produced 85bhp as against the standard 70bhp. Of 608 Special Sports chassis produced, about 500 were given the Barker body, with the remainder having Hooper coachwork.

DAIMLER	ENGINE	DATES	CONDITION		
	Model	cc/cyl	1	2	3
Veteran (Coventry built)	var/4	1897-1904	£75,000	£60,000	£30,000
Veteran	var/4	1905-19	£35,000	£25,000	£15,000
30hp	4962/6	1919-25	£40,000	£25,000	£18,000
45hp	7413/6	1919-25	£45,000	£30,000	£20,000
Double Six 50	7136/12	1927-34	£40,000	£30,000	£20,000
20	2687/6	1934-35	£18,000	£14,000	£12,000
Straight 8	3421/8	1936-38	£20,000	£15,000	£12,000

Value is dependent on body style, coachbuilder and condition of the sleeve valve engine.

1957 Daimler Conquest Century, 6 cylinders, 2433cc, 100bhp, pre-selector transmission unit with fluid flywheel, original red leather interior, bodywork and structure in good condition, overhauled pre-selector gearbox.
£1,700–2,200 *BRIT*

1962 Daimler Dart SP250, 2500cc, 4 speed manual gearbox with no overdrive, engine overhauled, requires restoration, hard-top, not used since 1985.
£6,500–7,500 *H&H*

l. **1966 Daimler 2.5 Litre Saloon,** 26,457 miles recorded, original condition, with handbook and toolbox.
£7,000–8,000 *LF*

r. **1964 Daimler V8 250 Saloon,** automatic gearbox overhauled, new discs, new wire wheels and tyres, carpets, exhaust, radiator and door panels, repainted.
£4,200–4,700 *H&H*

Daimler 250 V8 (1962–69)

Engine: 2548cc, V8.
Transmission: 3 speed automatic (a few manuals).
0–60mph: 14 seconds.
Top speed: 112mph.
Total Production: 17,650.

By the late 1950s Daimler's years of distinction were mostly in the past. Founded in 1893, Daimler was just about the oldest British car manufacturer still in existence, but was in dire straits.

In 1959 it launched the Daimler SP250 glass fibre-bodied sports car as a last ditch effort to remain an independent company, but the quirky-looking grouper-mouthed car that had been dubbed the 'Dart' failed to hit the mark in its intended US market. In 1960 Daimler finally fell into Jaguar's hands and the SP250 lurched on to sell a total of

2,650 before Jaguar gave it the chop in 1964.

The Daimler legacy did, however, give Jaguar the Dart's fabulous V8, 2.5 litre engine and it found a suitable home in Jaguar's first Daimler-badged product, the 250 saloon.

The MkII Jaguar had been introduced in 1960 with 2.4, 3.4 and 3.8 litre engines. Externally, apart from the fluted grille, the Daimler was virtually indistinguishable. It did, however, offer Jaguar a wider marketing platform, appealing to the more traditional driver who considered Jaguars a little brash and valued the traditional upright qualities of Daimler.

In price the Daimler fell between the 3.4 litre MkII and the top-of-the-range 3.8, but more importantly preserved the Daimler name as a marque of distinction that continues to this day.

DAIMLER Model	ENGINE cc/cyl	DATES	CONDITION		
			1	2	3
DB18	2522/6	1946-49	£7,500	£4,000	£1,000
DB18 Conv S/S	2522/6	1948-53	£14,000	£7,000	£2,000
Consort	2522/6	1949-53	£5,000	£3,000	£1,000
Conquest/Con.Century	2433/6	1953-58	£4,000	£2,000	£1,000
Conquest Roadster	2433/6	1953-56	£12,000	£7,000	£4,000
Majestic 3.8	3794/6	1958-62	£5,000	£2,000	£1,000
SP250	2547/8	1959-64	£12,000	£10,000	£4,500
Majestic Major	4561/8	1961-64	£6,000	£4,000	£1,000
2.5 V8	2547/8	1962-67	£8,000	£5,250	£2,500
V8 250	2547/8	1968-69	£8,000	£4,000	£2,000
Sovereign 420	4235/6	1966-69	£5,000	£3,500	£1,500

Daimler/Jaguar

In the 1960s Daimler and Jaguar products converged and in today's market Daimler variants can be significantly cheaper than their Jaguar counterparts. Instead of a MkII Jaguar you might consider a Daimler 250 V8 saloon or a Daimler Sovereign as an alternative to a Jaguar 420.

1966 Daimler V8 250 Saloon, ground-up restoration, bare metal respray, complete mechanical overhaul, original interior renovated, lead-free cylinder heads fitted, 4 owners from new, 75,000 miles. **£5,200–6,000** *S*

1967 Daimler V8 2.5 Litre Sports Saloon, 4 speed manual gearbox, one owner from 1986, rebuilt 1988/89 including mechanical work, new tyres, door skins, cross members, inner and outer sills, wheel spats, valances and bare metal respray, new interior trim, new windscreen and screen and door rubbers, Waxoyled, undersealed, stainless steel exhaust system, only 2,000 miles since restoration. **£7,500–8,000** *BKS*

In 1963 the MkII Jaguar bodyshell formed the basis of a new 2.5 litre Daimler powered by the Edward Turner-designed Daimler V8 engine previously seen in the SP250 Dart sports car.

1968 Daimler 420, restored, very good condition. **£6,300–6,800** *H&H*

A rebuilt car is not necessarily more valuable than a car in good original condition, even if the restoration has been costly.

1968 Daimler V8 250, 90° V8, 2548cc, overhead valve engine, twin SU carburettors, 140bhp at 5800rpm, 3 speed Borg Warner automatic gearbox, 4 wheel Dunlop disc brakes, very clean all-round condition, excellent paintwork, chrome, leather and woodwork. **£6,500–8,000** *C*

1969 Daimler Sovereign, 6 cylinders, 4235cc, very good condition throughout, runs well, stainless steel exhaust, relined roof, 37,000 miles recorded. **£4,500–5,000** *ADT*

1969 Daimler V8 250 Saloon, power-assisted steering, one owner, 61,000 miles recorded, original push button radio, toolkit.
£2,850–3,350 *H&H*

1970 Daimler DS420 Limousine, 4.2 litres, 6 cylinders, good appearance, black and grey leather interior, some refurbishment, chromework good.
£3,000–3,500 *BRIT*

These cars were produced between 1968 and 1992. In all, 4,116 were manufactured, plus 927 which were supplied in chassis form.

1973 Daimler Sovereign 4.2 Litre Four Door Saloon, regulation oil pressure, automatic transmission, front fog lights, period eight-track stereo, new half exhaust system.
£3,800–4,300 *BKS*

The Daimler Sovereign appeared a year after the Jaguar XJ's 1968 launch and was in effect a top-of-the-range model, with most optional extras incorporated as standard. Both XJ6 and Sovereign were built initially in either 2.8 or 4.2 litre versions, with automatic transmission preferred by the vast majority of customers. In total 61,000 were built.

l. **1975 Daimler V12 Coupé,** 5300cc, full bare shell restoration, now in show condition.
£9,000–12,000 *SC*

1983 Daimler DS420, 6 cylinder Jaguar engine, 4200cc, automatic gearbox, excellent condition.
£4,500–5,000 *DB*

DARRACQ

1907 Darracq 20hp, original lamps and fittings, fully restored.
£28,000–35,000 *FHF*

1903 Darracq 8hp Rear Entrance Tonneau, coachwork by La Carrosserie Industrielle, Paris, meticulously restored, totally rebuilt, Lucas side and rear lamps, tonneau covers and some spares.
£32,000–35,000 *BKS*

This car completed London to Brighton Runs between 1960 and 1970, and 1991 and 1996. It languished in a scrapyard from 1908 until the late 1950s, when it was bought and partly restored.

One of the great success stories of the veteran era was the Type 1, single cylinder, 8hp Darracq introduced in 1903. Demand for this popularly priced car in France and abroad took its maker by surprise and by the end of the year there was a waiting list of several months compelling the Darracq factory to produce several batches of the Type 1.

1910 Darracq 14/16hp Four Seater Tourer, body generally sound and complete, well equipped with correct hood and windscreen, restoration project.
£14,000–16,000 *BKS*

This 'barn discovery' came to the UK from Ontario, Canada, some years ago.

DATSUN

l. **1974 Datsun 240 Z Coupé,** 2400cc, original interior, front spoiler, gear knob, seats, steering wheel, period full folding sunroof and wolfrace wheels, rebuilt, very good condition throughout.
£2,500–3,000 *H&H*

DATSUN Model	ENGINE cc/cyl	DATES	CONDITION 1	2	3
240Z	2393/6	1970-71	£6,000	£4,000	£2,000
240Z	2393/6	1971-74	£5,000	£3,250	£1,500
260Z	2565/6	1974-79	£3,000	£2,250	£1,000
260Z 2+2	2565/6	1974-79	£3,200	£2,000	£800

DE DION

r. **1904 De Dion Bouton Model Y 6hp Rear Entrance Tonneau,** new dynostart, battery charging system, new petrol tank, cooling system overhauled, chassis springs repaired, gearbox, steering assembly and engine block reconditioned.
£25,000–27,000 *BKS*

This car has been displayed in the Shuttleworth Collection, and in recent years has been used in several Teuf-Teuf events on the continent. It has continued its UK rally history, notably taking part in every London to Brighton Commemoration Run since 1948, except for 1976.

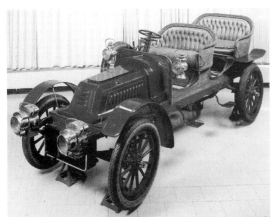

1911 De Dion Bouton Doctor's Coupé.
£11,000–13,000   *H&H*

c1905 De Dion Bouton Wicker Phaeton, 15/24hp
4 cylinder engine, 3 speed manual gearbox, rear
wheel drum brakes, semi-elliptic leaf spring
suspension, right-hand drive.
£30,000–35,000   *C*

*The De Dion Company was the first automobile
company to produce a motor car on both sides of the
Atlantic – Paris, France, and Brooklyn, New York.
The company was formed through the collaboration
of a wealthy aristocrat Compte Albert De Dion and a
talented engineer, Georges Bouton. The latter's most
important contribution to early automobile development
was the introduction of the high speed engine and
using coil ignition with a mechanically-operated
contact breaker. At first they were installed in motor
tricycles, then in quadricycles – not only in the firm's
own vehicles, but in as many as 150 car firms around
the world. Voiturettes followed in 1899, powered by a
single cylinder 3½hp engine centrally mounted in a
tubular steel frame. Shortly afterwards, the petrol car
incorporated De Dion's second remarkable feature,
the now famous De Dion axle principle.*

DELAGE

**1937 Delage D8SS Letourneur & Marchand
Coupé,** one-off 2 door aerodynamic coupé, with
sunroof, short chassis, restored, excellent condition.
£275,000+   *BLK*
This is the only known short chassis 8.120 example.

DELAHAYE

1937 Delahaye 135 Coupé des Alpes Drophead Coupé, coachwork by the Carlton Carriage Company,
4 speed manual transmission, completely restored, 2 owners in the last 37 years.
£60,000–65,000   *BKS*

*The Delahaye 135 was a car equally capable of winning the top concours d'élégance and the most fiercely-
contested races and rallies. It was one of the greatest sporting cars of all time. Testing a Type 135 in 1938,
The Motor enthused: 'There are few cars with such superb roadholding and steering, such performance and
such instantly responsive controls'. When tested by The Autocar in 1936 a Coupé des Alpes Delahaye gave
some 30mph in first gear, 45mph in second and nearly 70mph in third, with a top speed nudging 100mph.
Acceleration was outstanding – the average 0–60mph time recorded was 13.7 seconds.*

DELOREAN

1981 DeLorean, original condition, low mileage, left-hand drive.
£14,000–15,000 *PAL*

DE SOTO

1954 De Soto Firedome,
excellent condition throughout.
£7,000–7,500 *CTP*

DODGE

1915 Dodge Tourer, finished in grey and black with black leather trim, superb condition.
£11,000–12,500 *AS*

1948 Dodge Kingsway Four Door Sedan,
ex-South Africa, dark green with tan interior, right-hand drive, original condition with period extras.
£4,200–4,800 *CGB*

1921 Dodge Tourer, fully restored to a high standard, excellent weather equipment.
£9,000–10,000 *AS*

DURANT

c1923 Durant A22 Five Seater Tourer,
requires total restoration, complete in all major respects.
£750–1,000 *S*

Along with the Eagle, Flint, Locomobile, Princeton, Rugy and Star, the Durant was one of several companies that were to comprise the automobile empire of William C. Durant, a widespread concern with cars produced from plants in California, Michigan and New Jersey amongst others. Durant was perhaps better known as the man who had founded General Motors, and was to lose it twice.

Production of the Durant car was initiated in 1921 with an overhead valve, 4 cylinder engine car. Within one year the company was to reach its height of production – some 55,000 units built – and a few years later it is believed to have had more stockholders (146,000) than any other American company, except for American Telephone and Telegraph.

This car is believed to be a type A22 which could be bought from the company's inception until 1926, and carries simple tourer bodywork for 5 persons. In the present ownership for the last 30 years.

DUESENBERG

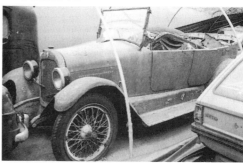

1932 Duesenberg J Franay Convertible Sedan,
extensively restored, excellent condition.
£800,000+ *BLK*

This is one of 2 bodies by Franay that were displayed on the Duesenberg stand at the 1931 Paris Salon. Some time during the later part of the 1930s the car was returned to Franay, where it had the fenders changed from the original clamshell design to its pontoon style. Since restoration, this car was awarded 1st in class at the Louis Vuitton Classic at the Rockefeller Center in New York.

ESSEX

1927 Essex Super Six, outstanding condition.
£9,500–10,500 *AS*

FACEL VEGA

1959 Facel Vega Excellence Four Door Saloon, navy blue with grey/blue interior, left-hand drive, excellent condition.
£13,000–15,000 *BKS*

1928 Essex Super Six Saloon, finished in white and blue, with beige cloth interior.
£10,750–11,750 *AS*

Originally a manufacturer of machine tools for the aircraft industry, Facel turned to the supply of car bodies for Panhard, Simca, and Ford France in the post-war years, before becoming an automobile manufacturer in its own right in 1954 with the launch of the Vega. A luxurious Grand Routier, *the Vega featured elegant coupé bodywork. The chosen power unit was Chrysler's 4.5 litre, 180bhp, V8, and there was a choice of push-button automatic or manual transmission. An improved model with 5.9 litre Chrysler V8 – the HK500 – appeared in 1957, and the following year Facel ventured into the luxury saloon market with the 4 door Excellence. Similar in style and mechanics to the HK500, the 6 seater Excellence featured striking pillarless bodywork on a wheelbase 53cm longer. A top speed of 200km/h was claimed. Developments included a 6.3 litre Chrysler, V8 for 1959 and disc brakes for 1960. Production continued at a rate of around 60 cars per year until 1964. Tested by* Motor Trend *magazine in 1962, the Excellence was reckoned to provide 'exclusivity, blazing performance and dream-car styling on a practical level'.*

1961 Facel Vega HK500 Two Door Coupé, V8, 6286cc, top speed of 140mph, 3 speed automatic gearbox.
£13,000–15,000 *BKS*

The V8 Chrysler-powered Facel Vega HK500 had a modest production run of just 490 examples.

FERRARI

In 1997 Ferrari celebrated its 50th anniversary as a maker of some of the world's most exquisite road and race cars, but the origins of that famous prancing horse emblem date from long before there were any road cars bearing the name. The badge was based on a racing trophy presented to Enzo Ferrari in the 1920s when the young Italian race Alfa Romeos. In 1929 he set up Scuderia Ferrari, racing Alfa Romeos with considerable success through the 1930s. The first true Ferrari car (although it didn't bear the name) was a Fiat-based racer built for the 1940 GP di Brescia. The first Ferrari to bear the name was the V12-engined 1.5 litre 125, which evolved into the 166 (1995cc). A coupé version of the 166 won the 1948 Mille Miglia to usher in a new era of twin accomplishment in racing and on the road. Since 1969 Fiat has been in control of Ferrari, but to this day the passion for the marque from Maranello remains as hot-blooded as the scarlet livery that is still the choice of 70 per cent of Ferrari buyers.

1949 Ferrari 166 Stabilimenti Berlinetta, 2 litre, V12 engine, 125bhp.
£130,000–135,000 *TALA*

1952 Ferrari 2.7 Litre Tipo 225S Spyder, coachwork by Carrozzeria Alfredo Vignale, twin-cam, V12 engine.
£300,000+ *BKS*

This important 2.7 litre two-cam, V12-engined car – the first 225S to carry open bodywork by Alfredo Vignale – was supplied new to Count Vittorio Marzotto's order in time for the round Italy 1,000 mile classic, Mille Miglia. He was accompanied by mechanic Marchetto under start-time race number 625, although he was forced to retire.
Count Vittorio drove this car as race number 94 in the major Monaco Grand Prix. He started from the 5th grid row, and won by a clear 15 seconds. After this historic success, Count Vittorio drove the 225S to 5th place in the Coppa d'Ora delle Dolomiti based upon Cortina d'Ampezzo. This is the only sports Ferrari ever to have won the Monaco Grand Prix.

1953 Ferrari 250 GT Europa, V12, 3 litres, 250bhp.
£120,000–135,000 *TALA*

1954 Ferrari 2 Litre 500 Mondial Spider Corsa, coachwork by Carrozzeria Pininfarina, 4 cylinder, twin overhead camshaft engine, restored to original specification.
£230,000+ *BKS*

Only the third ever Mondial to be manufactured, it is believed to have served the works team as a development and test car.

FERRARI Model	ENGINE cc/cyl	DATES	CONDITION 1	2	3
250 GTE	2953/12	1959-63	£32,000	£22,000	£20,000
250 GT SWB (steel)	2953/12	1959-62	£235,000	£185,000	-
250 GT Lusso	2953/12	1962-64	£85,000	£65,000	£50,000
250 GT 2+2	2953/12	1961-64	£30,000	£21,000	£18,000
275 GTB	3286/12	1964-66	£120,000	£80,000	£70,000
275 GTS	3286/12	1965-67	£90,000	£70,000	£50,000
275 GTB 4-cam	3286/12	1966-68	£150,000	£110,000	£80,000
330 GT 2+2	3967/12	1964-67	£22,000	£18,000	£15,000
330 GTC	3967/12	1966-68	£55,000	£40,000	£25,000
330 GTS	3967/12	1966-68	£80,000	£70,000	£60,000
365 GT 2+2	4390/12	1967-71	£28,000	£20,000	£15,000
365 GTC	4390/12	1967-70	£40,000	£35,000	£30,000
365 GTS	4390/12	1968-69	£110,000	£80,000	£70,000
365 GTB (Daytona)	4390/12	1968-74	£90,000	£70,000	£50,000
365 GTC4	4390/12	1971-74	£45,000	£38,000	£30,000
365 GT4 2+2/400GT	4390/ 4823/12	1972-79	£20,000	£15,000	£10,000
365 BB	4390/12	1974-76	£55,000	£38,000	£30,000
512 BB/BBi	4942/12	1976-81	£50,000	£40,000	£30,000
246 GT Dino	2418/6	1969-74	£35,000	£30,000	£15,000
246 GTS Dino	2418/6	1972-74	£45,000	£32,000	£20,000
308 GT4 2+2	2926/8	1973-80	£15,000	£10,000	£8,000
308 GTB (fibreglass)	2926/8	1975-76	£25,000	£18,000	£15,000
308 GTB	2926/8	1977-81	£22,000	£16,000	£10,000
308 GTS	2926/8	1978-81	£26,000	£18,000	£11,000
308 GTBi/GTSi	2926/8	1981-82	£24,000	£17,000	£10,000
308 GTB/GTS QV	2926/6	1983-85	£21,500	£16,500	£9,500
400i manual	4823/12	1981-85	£12,000	£11,000	£10,000
400i auto	4823/12	1981-85	£12,000	£11,000	£8,000

l. **1957/58 Ferrari 250 GT 3 Litre Tour de France Berlinetta,** coachwork by Pininfarina/Scaglietti, V12, 275bhp at 6750rpm, fully restored. **£350,000+** *BKS*

This long wheelbase Ferrari Berlinetta was supplied new from the Maranello factory in March 1958 to the personal order of their German sports car factory works team driver Wolfgang Seidel. It is believed to be the last built of Ferrari's basically 1957 'three-louvre' fared-headlight 250 GT Tour de France model, with sliding side windows.

1960 Ferrari 250 GT Series II Two Door Cabriolet, coachwork by Pininfarina, V12 engine, 240bhp, restored, very good condition. **£95,000–100,000** *BKS*

The 250 was Ferrari's first volume-produced model. As well as the improvements to brakes and transmission, the Series II cars benefited from an uprated 240bhp, V12 engine. The 250 GT was the most successful Ferrari of its time, production of all types exceeding 900 units, of which 200 were Series II Cabriolets.

1963 Ferrari 250 GT Lusso Berlinetta, coachwork by Carrozzeria Pininfarina, Colombo-designed V12 3 litre engine, 3 twin-choke Weber carburettors, single overhead camshaft, all aluminium unit producing 240bhp at 7500rpm, completely restored with bodywork refurbished by Marazzi of Milan, interior re-trimmed by Luppi, chassis, engine, transmission and electrics overhauled. **£70,000–80,000** *BKS*

The Ferrari 250 GT Lusso Berlinetta made its debut at the Paris Salon in October 1962, combining race track looks with new standards of passenger comfort. The top speed was 150mph with 0–100mph in 19.5 seconds.

l. **1962 Ferrari 250 GTE 2+2 Coupé,** coachwork by Pininfarina, front-mounted, double overhead camshaft V12 engine, 2953cc, 4 speed manual gearbox, 220/240bhp, disc brakes, left-hand drive, restored, paintwork re-finished, interior replaced. **£27,500–32,500** *BKS*

1965 Ferrari 275 GTS, V12, 3.3 litre engine, 260bhp, Borrani wire wheels.
£120,000–125,000 *TALA*

One of only 14 UK right-hand drive cars from a total production of 200 cars.

1965 Ferrari 275 GTB, coachwork by Pininfarina, V12, single overhead camshaft per bank, 3286cc, 280bhp at 7600rpm, 5 speed transaxle gearbox, 4 wheel disc brakes, independent suspension, left-hand drive, extensive service and repair work carried out, complete with tool kit and owner's manual, 20,000 miles recorded.
£125,000–130,000 *C*

At the Paris Salon of 1964, Ferrari chose to launch his new Berlinetta Coupé, the 275 GTB. With an evolutionary design from the preceding Coupés, it was considerably more sporting than the 250 GT Lusso which it replaced.

1968 Ferrari Dino 206 GT Coupé, coachwork by Pininfarina, V6, 1987cc, left-hand drive, French registered, 2 owners from new, totally original.
£45,000–50,000 *BKS*

In production in 1968 and 1969 only, the Ferrari Dino 206 GT (some were simply badged as Ferraris) is the predecessor of the 246 GT Dino, and only 150 were produced. Survivors are therefore rare. The 206 ushered in a new generation of GT Coupés, with its transverse-mounted mid-engine, 5 speed all-syncromesh transaxle and all coil spring independent suspension. Capable of 145mph with super handling and a thirsty 20mpg, the 1987cc V6, 4 overhead camshaft engine was enlarged to 2418cc with the advent of the 246 GT in 1969. It was made for Ferrari by Fiat, and fitted in de-tuned form to Fiat's own front-engined Dino.

1965 Ferrari 500 Superfast, V12, 5 litres, 400bhp.
£85,000–90,000 *TALA*

British comic actor Peter Sellers, star of the Pink Panther *films, was a keen motoring enthusiast. His passions ranged from Minis to Roll-Royces and in 1965 he bought an ultra-rare right-hand drive Ferrari 500 Superfast.*

1965 Ferrari 275 GTB, 3285cc, excellent condition.
£110,000–115,000 *DHAM*

1965 Ferrari 275 GTS 3.3 Litre Two Door Spider, coachwork by Pininfarina, paintwork in fair condition, chromework and bumpers require attention, interior woodwork slightly faded, some mechanical attention required, 75,500kms recorded.
£84,000–88,000 *BKS*

The Ferrari 275 GTS replaced the well-known 250 GT Spider California late in 1964, its convertible coachwork styled by Pininfarina. Production progressed until the end of 1965 without major modification, at which time the torque-tube transmission of the GTB was also applied to the GTS, and light-alloy wheels replaced the original Borrani wire-spoked type. A rare and desirable model of which only 200 were produced.

1969 Ferrari 365 GT 2+2, 60° V12, 4390cc, single overhead camshaft per bank, triple choke Weber carburettors, 320bhp, 5 speed manual gearbox, disc brakes all-round, front wishbone suspension and coil springs rear, power steering and air conditioning, very original car, 84,748kms recorded.
£22,000–26,000 *C*

The 365 2+2 was much more sophisticated than the 4 seater Ferrari coupés that came before it.

1969 Ferrari 365 GTC Two Door Coupé, coachwork by Pininfarina, right-hand drive, resprayed in 1984, interior rerurbished and mechanics thoroughly checked, Borrani wire wheels, excellent condition, radio cassette and tailored cover.
£60,000–65,000 *BKS*

Introduced late in 1968 as a replacement for the 330GTC, the 365GTC was identical in appearance apart from engine cooling vents relocated in the bonnet, though this had been a feature of the last of the 330s. Like so many European sports cars the 365GTC fell victim to increasingly stringent US safety and emissions legislation and production ceased after less than one year during which time fewer than 200 GTC and around 20 GTS models left the factory.

Ferrari 365 GTB/4

Most Ferrari model numbers represented the approximate cubic capacity in cc of one cylinder of the engine. Thus the Ferrari 365 GTB/4 was so called because the capacity of each of its 12 cylinders was approximately 365cc. Overall capacity was 4390cc. One obvious exception is the Ferrari F40 of 1987, so named to celebrate 40 years of the famous prancing horse marque from Maranello.

1973 Ferrari 246 GTS Dino, Campagnolo wheels, professionally restored to high standard, full service history.
£50,000–55,000 *COYS*

This classic Ferrari was named after Enzo Ferrari's son, Alfredino, who died in 1956, aged 24. Enzo Ferrari credits his son with the inspiration for a series of successful small and medium capacity V6 racing engines built by Ferrari from 1956, and in turn the name was given to a new line of mid-engined production Ferrari V6 coupés which first went on sale in 1969 in 2 litre form. The definitive 246 Dino, with its 2.4 litre, V6, appeared in late 1969 and fewer than 4,000 were built (about 1,200 of them with the detachable roof Spyder version). This car was once the property of ex-Beatle George Harrison.

1971 Ferrari 365 GTC/4 Coupé, coachwork by Pininfarina, 12 cylinders, 4390cc, 320bhp at 6200rpm, 6 dual choke Webers, excellent condition.
£30,000–35,000 *COYS*

The 365GTC was unveiled at the 1971 Geneva Salon as a replacement for the 365 GTC and was offered for sale alongside the Daytona as a still very rapid but more civilised road car. As a car for everyday use the 365 GTC/4 was extremely practical for a Ferrari, with both power steering and air conditioning fitted as standard, not to mention independently reclining driver and passenger seats. Only 500 examples of the GTC/4 were produced, all of them coupés. Production only lasted for one year.

1973 Ferrari 246 GTS, V6, 2.4 litres, 195bhp.
£47,000–50,000 *TALA*

1974 Ferrari 365 GT4 2+2, coachwork by Pininfarina, completely original condition.
£23,000–27,000 *BKS*

The Ferrari 365 GT4 2+2 was launched at the Paris Salon in October 1972 and represented the most sophisticated 4 seater model yet to emerge from Maranello. So successful was the basic design and layout of the car that it evolved through various guises – the 400, 400i and 412 – to become one of Ferrari's most enduring ranges ever, remaining in production until the early 1990s.

This car was a present from King Hussein of Jordan to the Shah of Iran. It was used very sparingly with only 1,347kms recorded.

1974 Ferrari Boxer 365 BB, 26,000 miles, full history.
£55,000–65,000 *VIC*

1977 Ferrari 400 Convertible Automatic, finished in blue with light tan interior, excellent condition.
£16,000–18,000 *H&H*

1979 Ferrari 308 GTB, 90° V8, 2926cc, transverse mid engine, 285bp, 4 twin choke Webers, good condition, well maintained.
£25,000–27,000 *KHP*

1979 Ferrari 3 Litre 308 GTS,
V8, 255bhp, good condition.
£28,000–30,000 *TALA*

1979 Ferrari 308 GT4 Sports Coupé,
V8 engine, considerable work on carburettors, in need of restoration and cosmetic work.
£12,500–14,000 *BKS*

Introduced as a larger and more versatile replacement for the 246 Dino, this 2+2 Sports Coupé had a layout similar to its predecessor, but was powered by a brand new V8 power unit mounted transversely behind the seats, and had a longer wheelbase. Styling was by Bertone, never previously associated with Ferrari, and rather more angular than the 246 series Dinos. Introduced in 1973, some 2,826 examples were sold.

> **Cross Reference**
> Colour Review

l. **1980 Ferrari 512 BB LM,**
flat 12.5 litre engine, 400bhp, upgraded LM specification brakes, lowered suspension, larger wheels/tyres, high lift camshaft, larger carburettors.
£60,000–65,000 *TALA*

1982 Ferrari 308 QV, 90° V8, 2926cc, 4 valves per cylinder, 240bhp, Bosch Jetronic fuel injection, excellent condition, well maintained.
£27,000–29,000 *KHP*

1983 Ferrari 512 BB/i, flat 12, 5 litres, 340bhp.
£70,000–75,000 *TALA*

1986 Ferrari 328 GTB, 3185cc, 90° V8 transverse mid engine, 270bhp, Bosch Jetronic fuel injection, excellent condition, well maintained from new.
£35,000–38,000 *KHP*

1982 Ferrari Mondial QV, 8 cylinders, 2926cc, new engine installed by Maranello Concessionaires 9,000 miles ago, service history, good condition,
£14,000–15,500 *ADT*

The Ferrari Mondial made its debut at the 1980 Geneva Motor Show as successor to the 308 GT4. It was close in specification to the fuel injected 308 S but the chassis differed. In mid-1982 came the quattrovalve or QV was introduced, which utilised a 4 valve per cylinder head and considerably boosted power.

1987 Ferrari 412 Automatic, 90° V12, 4924cc, 340bhp, very good condition, well maintained, service history.
£25,000–27,000 *KHP*

A manual version was also available, but was rarer.

1988 Ferrari 3.2 Litre Mondial Cabriolet,
90° V8, 3185cc, 270bhp, right-hand drive,
excellent condition, service history.
£32,000–34,000 *KHP*

1989 Ferrari Mondial T, 90° V8, 3405cc,
300bhp, transverse gearbox, excellent condition,
full service history.
£30,000–32,000 *KHP*

c1990 Ferrari 3 Litre Turbocharged F40 Le Mans Two Seater Mid-Engined Berlinetta,
2936cc, 478bhp at 7000rpm.
£140,000–160,000 *BKS*

This model was conceived to celebrate the 40th anniversary of the wonderful Ferrari marque.

1991 Ferrari 5 Litre Testarossa, flat 12, 390bhp engine.
£60,000–66,000 *TALA*

1994 Ferrari 456 GT, V12, 5.4 litres, 442bhp.
£115,000–120,000 *TALA*

FIAT

1923 Fiat 501 Three Door Saloon, coachwork by James Haworth of Manchester, 4 cylinder, in-line engine, 4 speed gearbox, 3 doors, V-screen and side-mounted spare, all original, right-hand drive, interior requires attention, chassis fair condition.
£2,250–3,000 *S*

1929 Fiat Tipo 509A Weymann Fabric Saloon, grey Bedford cord interior, restored, very good condition.
£4,800–5,300 *BKS*

An early 509 tested by The Autocar *magazine in 1925 was described as 'a silent, vibrationless engine with plenty of power, snappy without being harsh, simple and perfectly accessible; a good clutch and a deliciously sweet gearbox; well sprung and sturdy at speed; possessing good 4 wheel brakes; it was hard to find any points to criticise'. The 'bambina' comfortably accommodated 4 people, cruised at 40–45mph and gave 35mpg economy.*

1961 Fiat-Abarth 1 Litre Bialbero Competition Coupé, coachwork by Carrozzeria Zagato, engine rebuilt by Haferkorn, bodywork in original condition.
£25,500–30,000 *BKS*

Throughout 1962, Abarth claimed no fewer than 222 race successes and their 1000 Bialbero model won the small capacity Manufacturer's GT World Championship in 2 consecutive seasons, 1962 and 1963. Such stars as Jean Guichet (1 litre class winner, 1961 Auvergne 6 hours) and Ludovico Scarfiotti (winner at Lago di Garda, 1962), campaigned Abarth 1000s.

1930 Fiat 514 Berlina, 4 cylinders, 1438cc, Weymann fabric saloon coachwork, recommissioned, good order mechanically, beige cloth interior in serviceable condition.
£3,250–3,750 *ADT*

This car was restored during 1972 and was subsequently stored for 20 years.

FIAT Model	ENGINE cc/cyl	DATES	CONDITION		
			1	2	3
501	1460/4	1920-26	£6,000	£3,500	£1,500
519	4767/6	1923-29	£9,000	£7,000	£3,000
503	1473/4	1927-29	£8,000	£4,000	£2,000
507	2297/4	1927-28	£9,000	£5,500	£3,500
522/4	2516/6	1932-34	£10,000	£8,000	£3,500
508	994/4	1934-37	£5,000	£2,500	£1,500
527 Sports	2516/6	1935-36	£14,000	£8,000	£3,500
1.5 litre Balilla	1498/6	1936-39	£10,000	£7,000	£3,000
500	570/4	1937-55	£6,000	£2,500	£1,000
1100 Balilla	1089/4	1938-40	£4,500	£2,000	£1,000

Fiat 500

Model: Fiat 500D, 1957–77.
Production: 4,000,000+ (all models).
Body Style/s: Saloon, Cabriolet.
Construction: Unitary body/chassis.
Engine: 2 cylinder air-cooled 499.5cc.
Power Output: 17.5bhp at 4400rpm.
Transmission: 4 speed non-synchromesh.
Suspension: Front: Independent, transverse
leaf, wishbones. Rear: Independent,
semi-trailing arms, coil springs.
Brakes: Hydraulic drums.
Maximum Speed: 59mph.
0–40mph: 32.0 seconds.

c1965 Fiat 500D Two Door Saloon, one previous
owner, 60,000 miles recorded, stored for past
20 years, full restoration required.
£100–200 *BKS*

*Introduced in 1960, just one month after the
announcement of the 600D and replacing the 500
Sport model, the Fiat 500D featured a rear-mounted
twin cylinder in-line engine with overhead valves
and an increased capacity of 499.5cc. Between 1960
and 1965, when the production of this model ceased,
some 640,000 found customers.*

1968 Fiat 500 Gamine Vignale Spyder,
good condition, little road use, left-hand drive.
£4,000–4,500 *BKS*

*Alfredo Vignale sold out to de Tomaso on
16 November, 1969, and died in a car crash on
the same day. Gamine production was then wound
down as the Pantera took over.*

1971 Fiat 500, good condition.
£550–650 *H&H*

l. **1971 Fiat 500 Gamine,** 2 cylinders, 499cc,
11,900 miles since new, right-hand drive,
excellent condition throughout.
£3,750–4,500 *ADT*

FIAT Model	ENGINE cc/cyl	DATES	CONDITION 1	2	3
500B Topolino	569/4	1945-55	£5,000	£2,000	£750
500C	569/4	1948-54	£4,000	£1,700	£1,000
500 Nuova	479,499/2	1957-75	£3,000	£1,500	£750
600/600D	633, 767/4	1955-70	£3,000	£2,000	£1,000
500F Giardiniera	479, 499/2	1957-75	£3,000	£1,500	£1,000
2300S	2280/6	1961-68	£3,000	£1,700	£1,000
850	843/4	1964-71	£1,000	£750	-
850 Coupé	843, 903/4	1965-73	£1,500	£1,000	-
850 Spyder	843, 903/4	1965-73	£3,000	£2,000	£1,000
128 Sport Coupé 3P	1116/ 1290/4	1971-78	£2,500	£1,800	£1,000
130 Coupé	3235/6	1971-77	£5,500	£4,000	£2,000
131 Mirafiori Sport	1995/4	1974-84	£1,500	£1,000	£500
124 Sport Coupé	1438/ 1608/4	1966-72	£3,000	£2,000	£1,000
124 Sport Spyder	1438/ 1608/4	1966-72	£4,000	£2,500	£1,500
Dino Coupé	1987/ 2418/6	1967-73	£8,000	£5,500	£2,500
Dino Spyder	1987/ 2418/6	1967-73	£12,000	£7,000	£5,000
X1/9	1290/ 1498/4	1972-89	£4,000	£2,000	£1,500

Miller's Starter Marque

Starter Fiats: *Fiat 500, 1957 onwards; Fiat 600; Fiat X1/9; Fiat 124 Coupé and Spyder.*

- Four-wheeled fun doesn't come in a much smaller package than the Fiat 500 – 9' 9". But forget this baby Fiat if you want to hack down to the country for the weekends. In 1957 *The Motor* magazine tested an early 479cc engined 500 and could only eke out 53mph. Mind you, the fuel consumption was a fantastic 55mpg.

- The best 500 to go for is probably the later and slightly peppier 499cc engined car. In both cases you'll be served by a crash gearbox, which means you'll have to double de-clutch on the way down through the gears. The buzzing, high-revving air-cooled twin-cylinder engines in the back of the car have a good reputation though, and if anything should go wrong they can be removed in under an hour.

- These Fiats do fray though, and the relatively simple monocoque of the 500 is no exception. You'll want to prod any places on the underside and wheel arches where road muck can collect, in particular the structural steel member that runs across the car beneath the front seats. The floors can rust from the inside and outside too; also inspect the welded-on front wings closely and door bottoms.

- With over 4 million 500s made up to 1975, these baby Fiats have a strong network of parts, spares and club support, making them a viable starter classic that's more distinctive – on British roads at least – than a Mini.

- If the 500 is too tight a squeeze, you could always move up – by exactly one foot – to the slightly more commodious 600. It's a fine, well-handling little car, and it will even do 60mph. They don't have quite the cult following of the 500 and that means they're generally slightly cheaper, but harder to find too.

- The Fiat X1/9 offers fresh air, finesse, fine handling and Italian flare in a pint-sized and affordable sporting package.

- Top speed is only just over 100mph, but it will get you there with sure-footed finesse. The Fiat's greatest feature is its mid-mounted engine, which provides the optimum weight distribution to give it superb handling and adhesion normally associated with mega-money sports car thoroughbreds. In short, it's just about the only truly affordable and practical, volume produced, mid-engined sports car.

- Unfortunately, this little Fiat funster tends to reinforce the once-popular notion that when you buy an Italian car of this period you pay for the engine and get the body thrown in for free.

- The only thing that doesn't rust on the Fiat X1/9 is the detachable roof – and that's made of moulded plastic. The rule of thumb is to buy the very best you can afford as body repairs could soon easily outstrip the value of this bargain basement sports car. The electrics are also fragile, but the engine – either 1300 or 1500cc – is a little gem, reliable and long-lasting and generally good for 100,000 miles and more.

- A more substantial sporting Fiat is the 124 Coupé and Spyder. It's got the looks, performance and handling – and an invitingly modest price tag. Unfortunately the 124 Spyder was never officially imported to Britain and that means the car you're looking at is very likely to be a left-hooker. But that's an advantage too, as it may well have come from a rust-free area of the United States. For an MGB alternative with a touch of Italian flare, the 124 Spyder is definitely worth consideration.

1972 Fiat 500, 2 cylinders, 499cc, fully restored throughout, with leopard spot paintwork, excellent condition.
£2,700–3,000 *COYS*

1984 Fiat X1/9 VS 1500cc Sports Coupé, 5 speed gearbox, 64,000 miles recorded, one owner from new, tan leather interior, good condition.
£2,600–3,000 *BKS*

Styled by Bertone, originally as a concept sketch, the Fiat X1/9 earned the nickname 'mini-Ferrari' due to its crisp and elegant styling and was first introduced in 1972. The engine was mounted transversely behind the seats and in front of the rear wheels amidships. The body was a pressed steel monocoque and the 2 seater accommodation was set off with a stylish roll-hoop and removable Targa top panel.

1985 Fiat X1/9 Bertone Sports, one owner, 26,000 miles recorded, as new condition.
£3,000–3,300 *DRC*

1985 Fiat 124 Pininfarina Spyder, 2000cc, fuel injection, leather interior, excellent condition.
£8,000–9,000 *DTR*

Fiat produced the 124 Spyder from 1966 to 1982, when Pininfarina, who had originally designed the car for Fiat, took over production until its demise in 1985. Over 200,000 cars were produced, and were mostly sold in the US.

FORD

Ford may be American but in another sense the Michigan auto maker is as British as roast beef. In 1911 Ford's first manufacturing plant outside the USA was set up at Trafford Park, Manchester, and European Fords have been built in Britain ever since. Over 350,000 Model T Fords were built in Britain and Ireland from 1911 to 1927. In the 1930s Fords built in Britain began to diverge from their American cousins, with new models designed specifically for the UK and European markets, a trend that continued into the 1970s. Now, with the Mondeo, Ford, like many other auto makers, has moved back to 'globalisation', making a model to be sold in all world markets. But it's unlikely that there will ever be another world car to match the remarkable achievement of the Model T Ford, the world's first million seller. The eventual total of model Ts was more than 16 million, a record only overtaken in 1971 by the Volkswagen Beetle.

1907 Ford Roadster, very good condition.
£25,000–30,000 *FHF*

1911 Ford Model T Roadster with Mother-in-Law Seat, totally restored, excellent condition throughout, correct chassis number.
£10,500–12,500 *BKS*

Introduced in 1908 and remaining in production until 1927, the Model T Ford probably did more in its time to put the world on wheels than any other make or model, despite a specification which remained idiosyncratic until the end. High grade vanadium steel was used and the 4 cylinder engine was rated at 22.4hp and incredibly robust. A 2 speed pedal-operated epicyclic transmission with separate reverse pedal and hand throttle made the Model T easy to drive – almost semi-automatic. A variety of body styles were offered.

1921 Ford Model T 3000cc, 4 cylinder side valve engine, 2 speed transmission, good roadworthy condition.
£3,850–4,850 *DB*

> **Miller's is a price GUIDE not a price LIST**

1919 Ford Model T 3000cc, 4 cylinder side valve engine, 2 speed transmission, left-hand drive, excellent condition.
£7,000–8,000 *DB*

FORD Model	ENGINE cc/cyl	DATES	CONDITION 1	2	3
Model T	2892/4	1908-27	£12,000	£7,000	£4,000
Model A	3285/4	1928-32	£8,500	£6,000	£3,500
Models Y and 8	933/4	1933-40	£5,000	£3,000	£1,500
Model C	1172/4	1933-40	£4,000	£2,000	£1,000
Model AB	3285/4	1933-34	£10,000	£8,000	£4,500
Model ABF	2043/4	1933-34	£9,000	£6,000	£4,000
Model V8	3622/8	1932-40	£8,500	£6,000	£4,500
Model V8-60	2227/8	1936-40	£7,000	£5,000	£2,000
Model AF (UK only)	2033/4	1928-32	£9,000	£6,000	£3,500

A right-hand drive vehicle will always command more interest than a left hand drive. Coachbuilt vehicles, and in particular tourers, achieve a premium at auction. Veteran cars (i.e. manufactured before 1919) will often achieve a 20% premium.

1926 Ford Model T Tourer, excellent condition.
£8,500–9,500 *CC*

1928 Ford Model A Four Seater Tourer, finished in white with black trim and black hood, excellent condition.
£9,500–10,500 *AS*

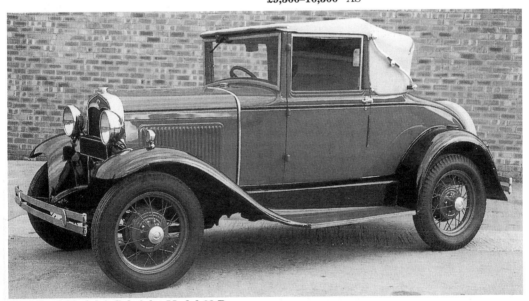

1931 Ford Model A Cabriolet Model 68-B, professionally stored, complete retrim in beige leather by Aston Martin, new cabriolet hood, excellent condition.
£12,000–14,000 *BKS*

'I bought the Model A for £175 in the 1960s with the idea of driving the family down to Brighton at the weekends,' recalled Walter Hayes, the former Fleet Street editor whose glittering 30 year career at Ford Motor Company culminated in his appointment as the Vice Chairman of Ford of Europe and the Chairman of Ford's new acquisition Aston Martin Lagonda. But for Mr Hayes – who became a close friend and confidante of Henry Ford II – the 1960s also saw him playing a pivotal role in such legendary Ford exploits as the world-beating Ford DFV Grand Prix engine programme, the Ford GT40 and the creation of the Lotus-Cortina. For many years his delightful 14.9hp Model A Cabriolet resided at the Ford Trade School, where it was used for promotional purposes.

1936 Ford Fordor Model CX Saloon, well restored to original condition.
£3,750–4,250 *FYC*

1937 Ford Model Y Tudor, professionally restored to a high standard.
£4,000–5,000 *FYC*

1953 Ford Prefect, excellent condition throughout.
£1,750–2,000 *AS*

A good original example of this model.

1939 Ford V8 Deluxe Model 91A Convertible Sedan, 221cu in, 80bhp, 3 speed manual gearbox, 4 wheel hydraulic drum brakes, transverse leaf spring suspension, left-hand drive.
£13,000–15,000 *C*

1953 Ford Prefect, 4 cylinders, 1172cc, original paintwork, good condition.
£1,500–2,000 *BRIT*

1956 Ford Prefect, 4 cylinders, 1172cc, 3 speed gearbox, 49,000 miles, excellent mechanical condition, good original condition overall.
£900–1,200 *ADT*

The Prefect 10hp, when first introduced, was billed 'The Ten at the Head of its Class'. Interestingly, this model was the first Ford of any type to have a name as opposed to a series letter.

l. **1963 Ford Consul MkII,** gearbox with overdrive, whitewall tyres, original chrome boot-rack, finished in ermine white with red trim and hood.
£5,850–6,450 *AS*

FORD (British built) Model	ENGINE cc/cyl	DATES	CONDITION 1	2	3
Anglia E494A	993/4	1948-53	£2,000	£850	£250
Prefect E93A	1172/4	1940-49	£3,500	£1,250	£900
Prefect E493A	1172/4	1948-53	£2,500	£1,000	£300
Popular 103E	1172/4	1953-59	£1,875	£825	£300
Anglia/Prefect 100E	1172/4	1953-59	£1,350	£625	£250
Prefect 107E	997/4	1959-62	£1,150	£600	£200
Escort/Squire 100E	1172/4	1955-61	£1,000	£850	£275
Popular 100E	1172/4	1959-62	£1,250	£600	£180
Anglia 105E	997/4	1959-67	£1,400	£500	£75
Anglia 123E	1198/4	1962-67	£1,550	£575	£150
V8 Pilot	3622/8	1947-51	£7,500	£5,000	£1,500
Consul Mk I	1508/4	1951-56	£2,250	£950	£400
Consul Mk I DHC	1508/4	1953-56	£6,000	£3,500	£1,250
Zephyr Mk I	2262/6	1951-56	£3,000	£1,250	£600
Zephyr Mk I DHC	2262/6	1953-56	£7,000	£4,000	£1,300
Zodiac Mk I	2262/6	1953-56	£3,300	£1,500	£700
Consul Mk II/Deluxe	1703/4	1956-62	£2,900	£1,500	£650
Consul Mk II DHC	1703/4	1956-62	£5,000	£3,300	£1,250
Zephyr Mk II	2553/6	1956-62	£3,800	£1,800	£750
Zephyr Mk II DHC	2553/6	1956-62	£8,000	£4,000	£1,500
Zodiac Mk II	2553/6	1956-62	£4,000	£2,250	£750
Zodiac Mk II DHC	2553/6	1956-62	£8,500	£4,250	£1,800
Zephyr 4 Mk III	1703/4	1962-66	£2,100	£1,200	£400
Zephyr 6 Mk III	2552/6	1962-66	£2,300	£1,300	£450
Zodiac Mk II	2553/6	1962-66	£2,500	£1,500	£500
Zephyr 4 Mk IV	1994/4	1966-72	£1,750	£600	£300
Zephyr 6 Mk IV	2553/6	1966-72	£1,800	£700	£300
Zodiac Mk IV	2994/6	1966-72	£2,000	£800	£300
Zodiac Mk IV Est.	2994/6	1966-72	£2,800	£1,200	£300
Zodiac Mk IV Exec.	2994/6	1966-72	£2,300	£950	£300
Classic 315	1340/ 1498/4	1961-63	£1,400	£800	£500
Consul Capri	1340/ 1498/4	1961-64	£2,100	£1,350	£400
Consul Capri GT	1498/4	1961-64	£2,600	£1,600	£800

1964 Ford Anglia Two Door Saloon, 4 cylinder in-line overhead valve engine, 966.6cc, 5000rpm, one owner, 13,050 miles recorded, new clutch and brakes, excellent original condition.
£3,250-3,750 *S*

r. **1964 Ford Lotus Cortina,** historic rally car.
£14,000-16,000 *MATT*

Miller's Starter Marque

Starter Fords: *Anglia, Prefect, Popular models from 1948 onwards; MkI, II, III Consul, Zephyr and Zodiacs, MkIV Zephyr/Zodiac; Consul Classic 315/Consul Capri; Cortina MkI, II, III; Corsair, Capri, Escort.*

- Fords have been so much a part of our motoring landscape for so long that there can be few people of driving age who don't have fond memories of an early version. Whether it's a humble little 'sit-up-and-beg' model of the immediate post-war period, a glitzy Consul, Zephyr or Zodiac with a touch of transatlantic glamour, or a boy-racer Escort Mexico or Capri, they are all cars that touch our nostalgic sensibilities. Better still, they are all eminently affordable and were made in their millions. Consequently, in most cases there's a ready stock of cars to choose from and a well established network of spares and specialist suppliers. In fact there are more than 30 car clubs in Britain alone that cater for post-war Fords. What's more, Ford's engineering has generally been 'tried and tested' rather than truly leading edge so there aren't many exotic and expensive items and routine maintenance and service is normally within the scope of the ordinary DIY mechanic. Another benefit of the tried and tested formula is longevity and reliability.

- Most exotic and most expensive of the post-war Fords is without doubt the MkII Zodiac convertible. Its styling – as with all MkI, II and III Consuls, Zephyrs and Zodiacs – is very much transatlantic. These cars, in particular, possess some of the flamboyance of true American cars of the period, but are much more affordable in the UK with a ready fund of affordable components and spares.

- From a starter's point of view it is probably best steering clear of performance models like the Lotus Cortina, Escort Mexicos and RS2000s. You'll need to build up a sound familiarity with these models to ensure the one you're buying is really what it claims to be rather than an everyday model with a few extras bolted on.

1967 Ford Lotus Cortina Two Door Saloon, 100km recorded since restoration, left-hand drive, excellent condition throughout.
£9,250–10,000 *BKS*

Ford's extensive programme aimed at raising its sporting profile included recruiting Lotus boss Colin Chapman to give the new Cortina a sporting makeover. Chapman's brief was to develop a Group 2 competition version; Lotus would then build 1,000 cars required for homologation. Launched in 1963, the Lotus Cortina – Cortina Lotus in Ford parlance – featured the Elan's Ford-based twin-overhead camshaft engine in the 2 door saloon bodyshell. The rear leaf springs were replaced by coil spring/damper units, axle location being looked after by twin trailing arms and an A bracket.

1965 Ford Zodiac MkIII, 6 cylinders, overhead valve, 2553cc, 4 speed floor gear change, white-wall tyres, 2 owners, mileage of 17,000, no known modications, excellent overall condition.
£6,500–7,000 *S*

The MkII models were replaced by the MkIII series in 1962. The 6 cylinder, overhead valve, 2553cc Zodiac MkIII was the rarest and most sought-after of the series and remained in production until 1966.

1966 Ford MkI Cortina Estate, 1498cc, overhead valve, 4 cylinders, 4 speed all-synchromesh transmission, rear-wheel drive, drum brakes all-round, maroon livery, black interior, mechanically sound, 38,000 miles recorded, always garaged.
£2,300–2,800 *S*

Ford Cortina MkI, 1962–66

As the 1960s dawned Ford reckoned there was a need for a family car that was larger than the Anglia and smaller than the MkII Consul, Zephyr and Zodiac. The 'missing model', as Ford insiders called it, appeared late in 1962 and soon you couldn't miss the Cortina on Britain's roads as sales soared. Compared with the front-wheel drive Morris 1100 there was nothing revolutionary about the styling or engineering of the Cortina, yet the conventional Cortina scored in two areas: first its mean price tag of just £639, which undercut rivals; and second, the fact the profit had been built in. A lot had been learned from the earlier overweight, over-engineered Consul Classic, and with the Cortina Ford designers set about removing the 'unwanted passenger' to save weight and materials. It all added up to the anatomy of a best-seller, in fact the best-selling British car of its time.

Pick of the Bunch: 1500 GT and Lotus Cortina MkI; the 1500 GT gave a creditable 13 second 0–60mph and 95mph top speed; the Lotus Cortina with 1558cc 105bhp Lotus twin-cam and uprated suspension scorched its way to 108mph. There were only 4,012 genuine MkI Lotus Cortinas. They're highly prized, so watch out for fakes – there are plenty.

Cortina Trivia:

Cortina d'Ampezzo in the Italian Dolomites was the venue of the 1960 winter Olympics; Triumph later adopted the theme with the Dolomite saloon. The MkI Cortina became the first British car to sell more than a million in less than 4 years; total production was 1,010,090. The Cortina was designed under the code name 'Archbishop' and cost just £13 million to develop.

1969 Lotus Cortina MkII, new clutch, gearbox rebuilt, Damask red with Lotus coachline, interior black, bodywork excellent, very good condition throughout.
£2,900–3,400 *H&H*

1968 Ford Cortina Savage, 6 cylinders, 2994cc, 3,300 miles recorded since restoration, engine, gearbox and overdrive rebuilt, new clutch, rebuilt suspension and braking system, original push-button radio, dry stored.
£5,250–5,750 *BRIT*

Developed by Race-Proved Ltd, the Ford Cortina Savage was one of the most formidable sports saloons of the late 1960s. Powered by a modified Ford V6 Essex engine, the car was a sensational performer. Specification included a Laycock overdrive unit and Salisbury limited slip differential with a 3.55 ratio. Approximately 1,100 Cortina Savage's were produced and around 40 are known to have survived. However, only 3 are known to the Register to be of this standard and this is the only Series I.

1971 Ford Escort Mexico, 4 cylinders, 1593cc, fully restored, engine rebuilt.
£2,750–3,250 *ADT*

The Mexico was a 1600cc pushrod engined machine which, despite its high performance, proved very reliable. Throughout the 1970s the Mexico was a regular contender in events and it is still a very sought-after machine today.

FORD (British built) Model	ENGINE cc/cyl	DATES	CONDITION 1	2	3
Cortina Mk I	1198/4	1963-66	£1,550	£600	£150
Cortina Crayford Mk I	1198/4	1963-66	£3,500	£1,800	£950
Cortina GT	1498/4	1963-66	£1,800	£1,000	£650
Lotus Cortina Mk I	1558/4	1963-66	£10,000	£7,500	£4,500
Cortina Mk II	1599/4	1966-70	£1,000	£500	£100
Cortina GT Mk II	1599/4	1966-70	£1,200	£650	£150
Cortina Crayford Mk II DHC	1599/4	1966-70	£4,000	£2,000	£1,500
Lotus Cortina Mk II	1558/4	1966-70	£6,000	£3,500	£1,800
Cortina 1600E	1599/4	1967-70	£2,800	£1,000	£450
Consul Corsair	1500/4	1963-65	£1,100	£500	£250
Consul Corsair GT	1500/4	1963-65	£1,200	£600	£250
Corsair V4	1664/4	1965-70	£1,150	£600	£250
Corsair V4 Est.	1664/4	1965-70	£1,400	£600	£250
Corsair V4GT	1994/4	1965-67	£1,300	£700	£250
CorsairV4GT Est.	1994/4	1965-67	£1,400	£700	£350
Corsair Convertible	1664/ 1994/4	1965-70	£4,300	£2,500	£1,000
Corsair 2000	1994/4	1967-70	£1,350	£500	£250
Corsair 2000E	1994/4	1967-70	£1,500	£800	£350
Escort 1300E	1298/4	1973-74	£1,900	£1,000	£250
Escort Twin Cam	1558/4	1968-71	£8,000	£5,000	£2,000
Escort GT	1298/4	1968-73	£3,000	£1,500	£350
Escort Sport	1298/4	1971-75	£1,750	£925	£250
Escort Mexico	1601/4	1970-74	£4,000	£2,000	£750
RS1600	1601/4	1970-74	£5,000	£2,500	£1,500
RS2000	1998/4	1973-74	£4,500	£2,200	£1,000
Escort RS Mexico	1593/4	1976-78	£3,500	£2,000	£850
Escort RS2000 Mk II	1993/4	1976-80	£6,000	£3,500	£2,000
Capri Mk I 1300/ 1600	1298/ 1599/4	1969-72	£1,500	£1,000	£550
Capri 2000/ 3000GT	1996/4 2994/6	1969-72	£2,000	£1,000	£500
Capri 3000E	2994/6	1970-72	£4,000	£2,000	£1,000
Capri RS3100	3093/6	1973-74	£6,500	£3,500	£2,000
Cortina 2000E	1993/4	1973-76	£2,500	£550	£225
Granada Ghia	1993/4 2994/6	1974-77	£4,000	£900	£350

1971 Ford Cortina 1600XL, 48,000 miles
recorded, full history, original and unrestored.
£1,300–1,600 *H&H*

This is a great example of a third generation Cortina.

1984 Ford Capri 2800, restored, interior converted
to Tickford leather, excellent condition throughout.
£1,700–2,000 *H&H*

*The 2.8 Capris were by far the most potent of
these 'ahead of their time' Ford sports cars. The
restoration on this car included £2,500 spent on
a bare metal respray alone. It has won many
events in the south of England.*

Did You Know?

The Capri, launched in 1968, was Ford's
European interpretation of the American
Mustang 'pony car' theme that had sold a million
in its first year. Early UK adverts billed the Capri
as 'the car you always promised yourself', and by
the end of production in 1987 nearly two million
motorists had treated themselves to a Capri.

1973 Ford Escort RS2000 Two Door Saloon,
new sills, front wings and valance, resprayed,
fully restored.
£2,500–3,000 *BKS*

1958 Ford Edsel Ranger,
low mileage, good condition.
£7,000–8,000 *CTP*

1971 Ford Mustang Coupé, finished in red with
black interior, good condition.
£3,000–3,500 *CTP*

1962 Ford Thunderbird, black Kelsey Hayes
wire wheels, good condition.
£7,000–7,500 *CTP*

FORD (American built) Model	ENGINE cu in/cyl	DATES	CONDITION 1	2	3
Thunderbird	292/ 312/8	1955-57	£18,500	£13,500	£9,000
Edsel Citation	410/8	1958	£9,000	£4,500	£2,500
Edsel Ranger	223/6- 361/8	1959	£6,000	£3,500	£2,000
Edsel Citation Convertible	410/8	1958	£12,000	£6,000	£4,000
Edsel Corsair Convertible	332/ 361/8	1959	£10,500	£7,000	£4,500
Fairlane 2 door	223/6- 352/8	1957-59	£8,000	£4,500	£3,000
Fairlane 500 Sunliner	223/6- 352/8	1957-59	£12,000	£8,000	£6,500
Fairlane 500 Skyliner	223/6- 352/8	1957-59	£14,000	£10,000	£8,000
Mustang 4.7 V8		1964-66	£9,000	£4,000	£2,000
Mustang GT 350		1966-67	£15,000	£10,000	£6,000
Mustang hardtop	260/6- 428/8	1967-68	£6,000	£4,000	£3,000
Mustang GT 500			£20,000	£14,000	£6,000

1968 Ford Mustang Two Door Hard Top Coupé,
6 cylinders, 3.3 litres, automatic transmission,
3 owners, 40,500 miles recorded, resprayed.
£2,750–3,750 *BKS*

*This example of the legendary Mustang 'pony car'
is believed to have had only 3 owners from new, and
was used as daily transport by its current owner until
August 1995.*

1976 Ford Mustang II Mach I, V8, overhead
valve, 4950cc engine, 133bhp at 3600rpm,
3 speed automatic gearbox, vented disc
front brakes, drum rear, coil springs front
suspension, live axle with leaf springs rear,
right-hand drive, electric steel sunroof,
forged aluminium wheels.
£1,300–1,800 *C*

*The 302 V8 engine, despite being in a low state
of tune, gave this car quiet acceleration and
0–60mph in about 10.5 seconds. It is the Ghia
model and, therefore, has a more opulent
interior with cloth seats which were colour co-
ordinated with the exterior.*

FRANKLIN

1934 Franklin 19A Airman Four Door Sedan,
6 cylinder, in-line air-cooled engine, 274cu in,
100bhp, 3 speed manual gearbox, hydraulic brakes
on 4 wheels, semi-elliptic suspension, left-hand
drive, requires some restoration.
£4,500–6,000 *C*

*Representing the final year of Franklin production,
the Airman was given a more contemporary
appearance by sharing styling features of the
Franklin Twelves, including a V-shaped grille,
sloping body style and skirted bumpers.*

GENESTIN

1925 Genestin G6 Four Door Tourer, 4 cylinders,
1200cc, manual gearbox, right-hand drive, restored,
very good condition.
£8,000–8,500 *H&H*

*This unusual right-hand drive car is a very rare
survivor of the small number of cars assembled by
P. Genestin at Fourmies in France during the 1920s.*

HCS

1923 HCS Touring Car, 6 cylinder, in-line, 288cu in
engine, 80bhp, 3 speed manual gearbox, mechanical
internal expanding brakes, semi-elliptic spring
suspension, left-hand drive, suitable for restoration.
£8,500–9,500 *C*

1923 HCS Touring Car, 6 cylinder, in-line,
288cu in engine, 80bhp, 3 speed manual gearbox,
mechanical internal expanding brakes, semi-elliptic
spring suspension, left-hand drive.
£3,000–3,500 *C*

*This is an example of Harry C. Stutz's subsequent
auto-making venture after leaving the Stutz firm.
It is in quite poor condition throughout, and perhaps
would be more suitable as a donar car than a
restoration project.*

HEALEY

l. **1952 Healey Tickford Two Door Saloon,**
engine replaced, new chrome fittings, interior
re-upholstered, tailored car cover, history file,
restored, excellent condition.
£8,000–9,000 *BKS*

*The Donald Healey Motor Company completed its
first car in 1945, going into production in Warwick
the following year. The firm's first offering was a
2.4 litre Riley-powered sports saloon with welded-up
chassis and Healey's own trailing arm independent
front suspension. Coachbuilders such as Abbott,
Duncan, Elliot, Tickford, and Westland supplied
bodies, and for a time the 110mph Healey was
the world's fastest 4 seater production car.
This car became part of the Ellard collection in
1959, and remained there until July 1984.*

HILLMAN

Starting out as a bicycle manufacturer,
Hillman built its first cars in 1907, producing
elegant tourers, then broadening appeal with
up-market small cars and saloons. The cars
were always conventional but quite stylish.
In 1928 the company came under the control
of Humber and the Rootes Group. In the
1930s the Minx stood out as more refined
and luxurious than offerings from rivals.
By 1939 Hillman was ranked fourth largest
car manufacturer in Britain. Immediate
post-war vehicles were equally stylish, but
in the 1950s an epidemic of badge
engineering saw Hillman lose their identity
as there was little more than detail and
different power plants to distinguish the
Minx range from the Singer Vogue and
Sunbeam Rapier. By 1964 Chrysler had
taken control of Rootes, and the Hillman
name vanished for good in 1976.

**1932 Hillman 10hp Burlington Pickford Three
Position Drophead Coupé,** white with black wings
and hood, excellent restored condition.
£7,000–8,000 *AS*

1930 Hillman 14hp Safety Saloon, servo
brakes, triplex glass, excellent condition.
£9,000–9,500 *AS*

r. **1950 Hillman Minx 1200,** 4 cylinder
side-valve engine, running order, unrestored.
£1,150–1,250 *DB*

l. **1947 Hillman Minx
Drophead Coupé,** 4 cylinders,
1184cc, 1,000 miles recorded
since restoration in 1975,
original blue leather interior,
good mechanical condition.
£4,500–5,000 *ADT*

*The first Minx made its
appearance in 1932, and soon
established itself as a worthy
competitor in the popular 10hp
category. The model evolved
through many guises and,
indeed, a Minx appeared in the
Hillman catalogue until 1970.
This car is the first of the post-
war series dating from 1947.*

Miller's Starter Marque

Starter Hillmans: *Californian; Minx models and variants from 1956; Imp; Avenger.*

- One of the most attractive traits of post-war Hillmans is their price. They're affordable and generally reliable and if you're into budget top-down motoring there's a wide choice from a company that persisted with convertibles when lots of other makers didn't bother.

- The 1950s Hillman Californian offers a suggestion of transatlantic glamour with straightforward Rootes underpinnings. The problem is going to be finding one, because as with later Hillmans their low values have lured many a saveable car into the scrapyard.

- The Super Minx convertibles from 1962 to 1966 make an interesting 4 seater fresh air alternative to cars like Triumph Heralds. The Super Minx is more substantially bodied and bigger engined. The Imp was a real might-have-been – if only the Mini hadn't appeared three years before, and if only they were built better. They're redeemed though by a lovely engine, super gearbox and sheer entertainment value when behind the wheel.

- In the 1970s the Hillman Avenger tilted against Morris Marinas, Ford Escorts and Vauxhall Vivas. The GT was surprisingly nimble and offered 100mph performance. The very rare Tiger tipped 110mph and enjoyed a successful rallying career.

1950 Hillman Minx MkVIII, requires restoration. **£1,100–1,250** *DRC*

1965 Hillman Super Minx, 4 cylinders, 1592cc, automatic transmission, very original condition throughout. **1,000–1,200** *ADT*

During 1961 the Hillman range widened considerably, and one new offering was the Super Minx with a slightly larger body. This new model was powered by a 1600cc engine, and remained in production until 1966.

r. **1972 Hillman Avenger GL Saloon,** alloy wheels, JPS steering wheel, radio cassette, new front wings, re-sprayed, good overall condition. **£400–600** *BKS*

A product of the Rootes Group under Chrysler control, the all-new Hillman Avenger was launched in 1970. Aimed at the Escort/Viva/Marina market sector and conventionally engineered, the Avenger featured a 4 cylinder overhead valve engine of either 1250cc or 1500cc (later 1300/1600), McPherson strut front suspension, and a coil-sprung live rear axle. Initially available in a 4 door saloon or estate form, the Avenger range gained a 2 door version in 1973.

HILLMAN Model	ENGINE cc/cyl	DATES	CONDITION 1	2	3
Minx Mk I-II	1184/4	1946-48	£1,750	£800	£250
Minx Mk I-II DHC	1184/4	1946-48	£3,500	£1,500	£250
Minx Mk III-VIIIA	1184/4	1948-56	£1,750	£700	£350
Minx Mk III-VIIIA DHC	1184/4	1948-56	£3,750	£1,500	£350
Californian	1390/4	1953-56	£2,000	£750	£200
Minx SI/II	1390/4	1956-58	£1,250	£450	£200
Minx SI/II DHC	1390/4	1956-58	£3,500	£1,500	£500
Minx Ser III	1494/4	1958-59	£1,000	£500	£200
Minx Ser III DHC	1494/4	1958-59	£3,750	£1,500	£400
Minx Ser IIIA/B	1494/4	1959-61	£1,250	£500	£200
Minx Ser IIIA/B DHC	1494/4	1959-61	£3,750	£1,250	£500
Minx Ser IIIC	1592/4	1961-62	£900	£500	£200
Minx Ser IIIC DHC	1592/4	1961-62	£3,000	£1,500	£500
Minx Ser V	1592/4	1962-63	£1,250	£350	£150
Minx Ser VI	1725/4	1964-67	£1,500	£375	£100
Husky Mk I	1265/4	1954-57	£1,000	£600	£200
Husky SI/II/III	1390/4	1958-65	£1,000	£550	£150
Super Minx	1592/4	1961-66	£1,500	£500	£100
Super Minx DHC	1592/4	1962-64	£3,500	£1,250	£450
Imp	875/4	1963-73	£800	£300	£70
Husky	875/4	1966-71	£800	£450	£100
Avenger	var/4	1970-76	£550	£250	£60
Avenger GT	1500/4	1971-76	£950	£500	£100
Avenger Tiger	1600/4	1972-73	£2,000	£1,000	£500

HISPANO-SUIZA

1933 Hispano-Suiza H6B Four Door Cabriolet, coachwork by Gill & Co, original brown leather interior, Bosch lamps, re-chromed, re-wired, engine overhauled, new exhaust system, excellent condition.
£47,000–52,000 *S*

The legendary Hispano-Suiza, rightly described as one of the world's very great cars, was designed by a versatile genius in the form of Swiss engineer Marc Birkigt. He set the standard for the Vintage years with the entirely French-built H6 model, which created such an overwhelming sensation when announced at the Paris Salon of 1919. A large luxury motor car, magnificently made, superbly proportioned and years ahead of its time, the new model was truly a voiture de prestige. *The H6 remained in production for 15 years and, apart from royalty, numerous Eastern potentates and the nobility, owners of a sporting disposition included 'Bentley Boy' Woolf Barnato, André Dubonnet, Count Zborowski of 'Chitty' fame and speed king Sir Henry Segrave. No other car predominated the premier* Concours d'élégances *of Europe between the wars more than the H6 model, also known as the 32cv, and the common wisdom is that there has never been a car of more regal appearance than Birkigt's masterpiece. The Hispano-Suiza Society believes that only 250 – 300 examples of the H6B survive today.*

HOLDEN

l. **1958 Holden Station Sedan,** 2270cc, re-sprayed, engine reconditioned, excellent condition throughout.
£2,800–3,300 *H&H*

This rare General Motors Australian-built Holden Station Sedan has been in the same ownership since 1973, and has been meticulously maintained.

HORCH

r. **1939 Horch 830 BL V8 3.8 Litre Four Door Cabriolet,** Autobahn-Fernganggetriebe 4 speed gearbox with overdrive on every gear, original specification other than electric fuel pump, excellent condition.
£53,000–58,000 *BKS*

The Horch company became celebrated for luxurious prestige cars available in a variety of body styles and was competitively priced against the other top makes. From 1932 Horch became a member of the Auto Union Group. Horch cars of this period, and particularly the 8 cylinder cars, were impressive in appearance. The chassis approached 2 tons in weight and was built to the highest standards.

HUDSON

1948 Hudson Super Six Four Door Sedan,
manual gearbox, tan leather interior, right-hand
drive, restored, good overall condition.
£5,500–6,000 *CGB*

1928 Hudson Super Six Four Door Sedan,
289cu in, 92bhp, floor-mounted 3 speed sliding
gear transmission, restored, good condition.
£7,500–8,500 *S*

HUMBER

From making bicycles Humber graduated to
motorcycles, forecars, quadricycles and then
cars in the early years of the century. In
the 1930s the imposing 6 cylinder Humber
Pullmans and Super Snipes enjoyed official
patronage and also provided stout service
as staff cars in the war. Since 1928 Humber
had been part of the Rootes Group and
despite some impressive offerings in the
late 1940s and into the 1950s – namely the
Super Snipe and gargantuan Pullman and
Imperial limousines – the marque was
progressively devalued, ending up an
upmarket Hillman, also under Rootes
control. Chrysler took over the Rootes
Group in 1964 and in 1976 the Humber
name died.

1903 Humberette 5hp Two Seater, good running
condition, museum stored for some time.
£14,500–16,000 *S*

*The Coventry-built Humberette featured the reliable
De Dion type vertical single cylinder engine mounted
in a tubular frame with a 2 speed gearbox. The cars
were to prove extremely popular and their quality is
borne out by the number of cars that survive today.*

l. **1920 Humber
15.9hp Tourer,**
re-sprayed,
re-upholstered,
transmission and
gearbox require
recommissioning,
excellent condition.
£8,500–10,000 *H&H*

*This car was used as
an ambulance during
WWII, and comes with
a complete history and
list of its owners.*

HUMBER Model	ENGINE cc/cyl	DATES	CONDITION 1	2	3
Veteran	var	1898			
		1918	£25,000	£20,000	£14,000
10	1592/4	1919	£7,000	£5,000	£3,000
14	2474/4	1919	£8,000	£6,000	£4,000
15.9-5/40	2815/4	1920-27	£9,500	£7,000	£4,000
8	985/4	1923-25	£7,000	£5,000	£2,500
9/20-9/28	1057/4	1926	£7,000	£5,000	£4,000
14/40	2050/4	1927-28	£10,000	£8,000	£5,000
Snipe	3498/6	1930-35	£8,000	£6,000	£4,000
Pullman	3498/6	1930-35	£8,000	£6,000	£4,000
16/50	2110/6	1930-32	£9,000	£7,000	£5,000
12	1669/4	1933-37	£7,000	£5,000	£3,000
Snipe/Pullman	4086/6	1936-40	£7,000	£5,000	£3,000
16	2576/6	1938-40	£7,000	£5,000	£3,000

Pre-1905 or Brighton Run cars are very popular.

Miller's Starter Marque

Starter Humbers: *Hawk and Super Snipe from 1957 onwards; 1965–67 Imperial; 1963–76 Sceptre.*

- The Hawk and Super Snipe make interesting alternatives to P4 and P5 Rovers. In 1957 the styling was considered thoroughly voguish, with American overtones, but by the 1960s the shape had an air of English gentility. The Super Snipe and Imperial, in particular, vied with the P5 Rover for ministerial duties outside No. 10 Downing Street.

- Both Hawk and Super Snipe were of unitary construction, the Super Snipe being the upmarket model and preferred choice, with a larger engine and all the drawing-room appointments one could ask for. For performance go for the 3 litre Super Snipes from 1960 on, which offer a quiet 95–100mph.

- The Sceptre of 1963–67 is a mix of Hillman Super Minx and Sunbeam Rapier, with the typical Humber 'garnish'. From 1968, Sceptres were simply jazzed-up versions of the square-cut three-box Hillman Hunter.

1921 Humber 11.4 Two Seater Tourer with Dickey Seat, 4 cylinders, 1748cc, side-valve engine, re-upholstered, correct instrumentation, fully restored, very good condition.
£9,000–11,000 *ADT*

In 1921 Humber introduced the 11.4, available in Tourer, 2 seater or saloon form. The model became highly regarded and renowned for its strength and reliability.

1931 Humber Pullman 23.8hp Landaulette, 6 cylinders, 3498cc, 4 speed in-unit manual gearbox, right-hand drive, good overall condition.
£10,000–12,000 *BKS*

Introduced for the 1930 season, Humber's Pullman had an 111in wheelbase to accommodate either limousine or landaulette coachwork.

1949 Humber Super Snipe, 2 owners, body-off restoration, excellent condition.
£11,500–12,500 *UMC*

r. **1964 Humber Sceptre Four Door Saloon,** 4 cylinders, overhead valve 1592cc engine, right-hand drive, Laycock overdrive on top and 3rd gears, manual transmission, Motorola push-button radio, 81,000 miles recorded, good overall condition.
£1,800–2,200 *BKS*

The Humber Sceptre was introduced in MkI guise in 1963, and used the Hillman Super Minx bodyshell allied to a Sunbeam Rapier grille. It was replaced in 1965 by the MkII.

HUMBER Model	ENGINE cc/cyl	DATES	CONDITION		
			1	2	3
Hawk Mk I–IV	1944/4	1945-52	£2,750	£1,500	£600
Hawk Mk V–VII	2267/4	1952-57	£2,500	£1,500	£400
Hawk Ser I–IVA	2267/4	1957-67	£2,500	£850	£325
Snipe	2731/6	1945-48	£5,000	£2,600	£850
Super Snipe Mk I–III	4086/6	1948-52	£4,700	£2,400	£600
Super Snipe Mk IV–IVA	4138/6	1952-56	£5,500	£2,300	£550
Super Snipe Ser I–II	2651/6	1958-60	£3,800	£1,800	£475
Super Snipe SIII VA	2965/6	1961-67	£3,500	£1,800	£400
Super Snipe S.III–VA Est.	2965/6	1961-67	£3,950	£1,850	£525
Pullman	4086/6	1946-51	£4,500	£2,350	£800
Pullman Mk IV	4086/6	1952-54	£6,000	£2,850	£1,200
Imperial	2965/6	1965-67	£3,900	£1,600	£450
Sceptre Mk I–II	1592/4	1963-67	£2,200	£1,000	£300
Sceptre Mk III	1725/4	1967-76	£1,600	£600	£200

INTERMECCANICA

One of the first companies which sought to combine the best of Italian and American automotive technology, Intermeccanica was founded in 1959. The company had a hand in various low volume manufacturing ventures before building the first car under its own name in 1965. A stock of bodies left over from the failed Omega project formed the basis of the Intermeccanica Torino, a steel-bodied coupé with a Ford 4.7 litre V8 engine. An open-topped spyder version, the Italia, appeared in 1968. The power unit was now a 5 litre V8, and later versions displaced 5.7 litres. Around 1,000 American V8-engined Intermeccanicas were built.

1968 Intermeccanica Italia Spyder, 5 litres, restored, manual transmission, Borrani wire wheels, excellent condition.
£16,000–18,000 *BKS*

INTERNATIONAL

The highwheeler type automobile grew from a demand in the rural United States for an inexpensive horseless carriage. These buggy-like cars were the result, having tall carriage-style wheels with hard rubber tyres that were well suited for the slow-moving rough road conditions of the time. These vehicles were often designed and used for utilitarian purposes, unlike many of the expensive touring cars in that era. The mass-produced Model T Ford proved far superior in design, reliability and versatility at approximately the same cost. This eventually caused the demise of the highwheeler.

1907 International Highwheeler, 2 cylinders, full-elliptic spring suspension, right-hand drive.
£3,000–4,000 *C*

INVICTA

1933 Invicta 1.5 Litre 12/45 Four Door Open Tourer, completely restored, original parts, engine rebuilt, right-hand drive, excellent overall condition.
£19,000–21,000 *BKS*

1932 Invicta 1.5 Litre 12/45 Four Door Saloon, single overhead camshaft, 1498cc Blackburne engine, 4 speed gearbox, good overall condition.
£9,500–11,500 *BKS*
In 1932 the 1.5 litre model was introduced as the 12/45, which used the same chassis frame as the 4.5 litre type, and in standard form was rather underpowered. The first owner of this car, having owned the car for 16 years by January 1949, simply improved its performance, without any drastic re-engineering, but with careful redesign. He was able to obtain 90mph and 0–50mph in under 18 seconds.

ISO

l. **1974 Iso Rivolta Lele,** Ford V8 engine, 5762cc, metallic grey with cream interior, right-hand drive, air-conditioning, original radio cassette, excellent condition throughout. **£7,000–9,000** *H&H*

ISOTTA

Designed by Giustino Cattaneo, the Isotta Fraschini Tipo 8 announced in August 1919 was the world's first series production straight 8. Some 1,380 examples of this superlative model from Milan's noblest car maker were produced in three series between the launch of the Tipo 8 in 1919 until the last example of the Tipo 8B series was eventually sold around 1935.

The bulk of production was concentrated on the Tipo 8A, of which around 950 were built between 1925 and 1931. For most people the Tipo 8A conjures up a mental image of the magnificent Isotta Fraschini driven by Erich von Stroheim in the film *Sunset Boulevard.* The choice of a Tipo 8A as the car of fading silent movie star Norma Desmond could not have been more apt, for the fortunes of Isotta Fraschini were firmly based on sales in the American luxury market, and the model was the choice of such world-famous film stars as Rudolph Valentino and 'It Girl' Clara Bow. Other Isotta owners included press baron William Randolph Hearst (the real-life model for Citizen Kane) and world heavyweight champion boxer Jack Dempsey.

1929 Isotta Fraschini Tipo 8A Sedanca de Ville, by Carrozzeria Italiana Cesare Sala, excellent condition throughout.
£115,000–120,000 *BKS*

This imposing car has links with a show business legend, as it was owned and restored by Peter Grant, former manager of rock idols Led Zeppelin. Supremely elegant, it is reputed to have belonged at one time to an Indian prince but the factory records show its first owner to have been Franco Paccheti of Milan.

JAGUAR

If ever one man's vision guided the fortunes of a motor company it must surely be William Lyons, for as the marque of the leaping cat prepares to pounce on the next millennium the guiding spirit of Jaguar's creator lives on in the lithe athletic shapes that have characterised these Coventry cats for over 60 years.

In Ford's hands since 1989, Jaguar's recent offerings have rekindled the excitement of earlier glory days. The new XJ series, unveiled in September 1994, revived the muscular grace of Sir William Lyons' original 1968 vision, the last Jaguar on which he exercised his assured styling touch.

When the XK8 sports car was unveiled at the 1995 Geneva Motor Show, Jaguar deliberately invited comparison with the E-type, the 1961 sensation of the same motor show.

So much of the legend is down to the singular vision of William Lyons, born in Blackpool in 1901. Before he ever dabbled with cars the young William Lyons was an enthusiastic motorcyclist who on his 21st birthday formed the Swallow Sidecar Company with partner William Walmsley.

The first 'Jaguar' – although it was many years before the company would adopt the name – was not a car at all but a motorcycle sidecar produced in 1922.

It was in 1927 that William Lyons' specialist coachbuilding company made the transition to four wheels, taking a strengthened Austin 7 chassis and clothing it with a natty two-toned sports jacket. William Lyons had perceived, like others around him, a growing tide of interest in light cars with a little extra. His Austin 7 Swallow didn't go any faster than an ordinary Austin 7 Chummy, but for a little more money it offered a lot more in looks and styling. Alongside the Swallow-bodied Austin, William Lyons also added a little sparkle to other marques with special Swallow versions of Fiats, Wolseleys and Standards.

In 1931 a major development took place with the launch of the SS range of cars. The SS1 was the first Swallow product designed completely by Lyons and his team. By 1935 William Lyons was sole proprietor of the company and at the Olympia Motor Show of 1935 the first true Jaguar range arrived. Most stunning of all was the 2½ litre Jaguar SS100 open two-

seater. It had what were to become the world renowned triple hallmarks of a William Lyons' creation – drop-dead looks and sizzling performance combined with sensational value for money. In 1938 a 3½ litre version of the SS100 appeared and that took top speed just over the ton.

In 1948 at the first post-war Motor Show at Earl's Court, William Lyons stole the show with perhaps the most cat-like of all Jaguars, the XK120. And yes, the 120 in the name really did stand for 120mph. On the road the XK120 evolved into the XK140 and XK150, while the C-type grew into the legendary triple Le Mans winning D-type. For fat cats and cigar-chomping captains of industry there were the gargantuan MkVII, VIII and IX Jaguars. In 1956, the year that William Lyons was knighted, Jaguar had its most complete range of cars ever. It filled the mid-market gap with the new MkI medium-sized saloon, Jaguar's first unitary design. By 1960 the MkI had become the biggest selling Jaguar ever, topping 36,000 and setting standards for aspirational middle-class motoring. In 1960 it evolved into the leaner, cleaner MkII. In 1962 Jaguar launched the mammoth MkX, but for most the story of Jaguar in the swinging sixties is all about that svelte 150mph stunner launched at the 1961 Geneva Motor Show, the E-Type. British motoring magazines produced road tests of pre-production models to coincide with the launch – and yes, the fixed head coupé really could do 150.4mph (149.1 for the roadster).

In 1966, as the British motor industry faced increasing competition worldwide, Sir William Lyons finally relinquished his company's independence to team up with the British Motor Corporation. In 1968 BMC merged with Leyland to form the British Motor Corporation with a bewildering array of competing makes and models.

In 1975 the Labour Government stepped in to nationalise British Leyland. These were the dark times, but by 1984 Jaguar was once again able to stand on its own feet and was privatised. Jaguar went into 1985 with record sales of 33,437 cars the previous year. Sir William Lyons lived to see the company he founded successfully passed back into private ownership but died in early 1985 before the dawning of a new era in 1989 with Ford as custodian of the legendary Coventry car maker.

1954 Jaguar XK120 Drophead Coupé, 3.4 litre twin overhead camshaft, completely restored in 1993. £50,000–55,000   *BKS*

1933 Jaguar SS1 Four Seater Coupé,
6 cylinders, 1608cc, brown leather upholstery,
'sunburst' interior door panels, full complement
of instruments, excellent condition.
£26,500–28,000 *COYS*

*The original SS1 was 'more show than go',
but it was quickly followed by a version which
more completely embodied Lyons' philosophy
and which was an even more remarkable
bargain. With only a small increase in price,
the 1933 SS1 offered improved performance
thanks to new cylinder heads and
manifolding, a much more spacious interior,
and a level of detail finish which then was
normally the preserve of coachbuilders
supplying cars such as Rolls-Royce and
Bentley. The 'sunburst' interior door panels
became an SS hallmark in the 1930s.*

1936 Jaguar SS100 Reproduction, coachwork
by Ashton Keynes Restoration, 3500cc, 5 speed
manual gearbox, engine completely rebuilt with
new standard pistons and liners, new bearings,
valves, clutch and pressure plate, resprayed,
new interior, good condition.
£39,000–44,000 *H&H*

*This was originally an SS saloon dating from
1936 with the reproduction and detailing taken
from 2 genuine SS100s. The chassis was
converted to full SS100 specification by Trac
Engineering of Colchester and 2 SS axles were
fully reconditioned with front twin leading
brakes. The only route taken away from the
original was the fitting of an XJ6 5 speed manual
gearbox with a new propshaft to enhance the
driving abilities of the car – but even this is
undetectable as the correct knob has been fitted.*

1937 Jaguar SS 1½ Litre Saloon, 12hp, steel
cylinder head, toolkit and period badges fitted,
excellent condition throughout.
£18,000–22,000 *H&H*

The Prototype 1937 Jaguar Car Mascot,
8in (20.5cm) long, mounted.
£2,900–3,300 *BKS*

*Frederick Gordon-Crosby, the celebrated artist, was
commissioned by William Lyons to design the leaping cat,
Jaguar mascot in 1937. The Jaguar mascot was certainly
one of his finest inspirations and in various forms has
embellished the bonnets of the marque to this day. If one
compares this model with the large, 1938 production model
of the mascot, there are subtle and interesting differences
although the fundamental image is undoubted.*

JAGUAR Model	ENGINE cc/cyl	DATES	CONDITION 1	2	3
SS1	2054/6	1932-33	£20,000	£16,000	£12,000
SS1	2252/6	1932-33	£22,000	£17,000	£13,500
SS2	1052/4	1932-33	£18,000	£15,000	£11,000
SS1	2663/6	1934	£26,000+	£22,000	£15,000
SS2	1608/4	1934	£18,000+	£15,000	£12,000
SS90	2663/6	1935	£60,000+		
SS100 (3.4)	3485/6	1938-39	£80,000+		
SS100 (2.6)	2663/6	1936-39	£70,000+		

Very dependent on body styles, completeness and originality, particularly original chassis to body.

1939 Jaguar SS100 Sports Two Seater, 2663cc, 3½ litres, engine in excellent condition, new shock absorbers, fitted with Dunlop Racing tyres, black interior trim.
£90,000–100,000 *BKS*

Jaguar SS100

In 1938 a 3½ litre version of the SS100 appeared with a top speed just over the ton, with 0–60mph in just over 10 seconds. By the outbreak of WWII just 309 SS100s had been built when SS Cars Ltd's annual production was topping 5,000 per annum.

1949 Jaguar MkV 3½ Litre Saloon, 6 cylinders, 3485cc, ground-up renovation, brightwork and mechanics in good condition, beige leather interior in original condition, new headlining and carpets fitted to original specification, all instrumentation functioning correctly with exception of temperature gauge and clock.
£14,500–16,000 *ADT*

1959 Jaguar MkIX Four Door Saloon, 6 cylinders, 3.8 litre twin overhead camshaft, power steering, disc brakes front and rear, automatic transmission, right-hand drive, good original condition.
£4,000–6,000 *BKS*

The MkIX Jaguar was the last of the big separate chassis saloons and was powered by a 220bhp version of the 3.8 litre twin overhead camshaft 6 cylinder engine. It featured power-assisted steering and disc brakes front and rear, with a choice of transmission systems.

1954 Jaguar MkVII M, 6 cylinders, 3442cc, good original condition, finished in grey with red leather interior, work has been carried out on brakes and steering, stainless steel exhaust system fitted.
£8,500–9,500 *ADT*

The MkVII achieved first place in the Monte Carlo Rally in 1956.

Jaguar MkVII M

The Queen Mother used a MkVII M as her personal transport from 1955 to 1973, but this big duchess of a saloon had another unexpected side to its character. Under the bonnet was that silky smooth 6 cylinder XK twin-cam and young Stirling Moss used it to good effect on the racetrack, winning the 1952 Daily Express production touring car race at Silverstone. Stirling recalls: 'Although it looked ponderous it was a fabulous car, well balanced and light to drive – powerful enough to pull 110–115mph on the straight and so softly suspended that, through corners, it leant over to the most remarkable degree. In fast, tight corners I had to stretch my leg across to brace myself against the opposite door.'

1955 Jaguar MkVII Saloon, good condition, attention to electrical equipment, upholstery and interior trim required.
£3,500–5,000 *S*

JAGUAR Model	ENGINE cc/cyl	DATES	CONDITION 1	2	3
1½ Litre	1775/4	1945-49	£8,500	£5,500	£2,000
2½ Litre	2663/6	1946-49	£10,000	£7,500	£2,000
2½ Litre DHC	2663/6	1947-48	£17,000	£11,000	£8,000
3½ Litre	3485/6	1947-49	£12,000	£6,000	£4,000
3½ Litre DHC	3485/6	1947-49	£19,000	£13,500	£5,500
MkV 2½ Litre	2663/6	1949-51	£8,000	£5,000	£1,500
MkV 3½ Litre	3485/6	1949-51	£11,000	£7,000	£1,800
MkV 3½ Litre DHC	3485/6	1949-51	£20,000	£17,000	£8,500
MkVII	3442/6	1951-57	£10,000	£7,500	£2,500
MkVIIM	3442/6	1951-57	£12,000	£8,500	£2,500
MkVIII	3442/6	1956-59	£8,500	£5,500	£2,000
MkIX	3781/6	1958-61	£9,000	£7,000	£2,500
MkX 3.8/4.2	3781/6	1961-64	£7,500	£3,500	£1,500
MkX 420G	4235/6	1964-70	£6,000	£3,000	£1,200
MkI 2.4	2438/6	1955-59	£7,000	£5,500	£2,000
MkI 3.4	3442/6	1957-59	£9,000	£6,000	£2,500
MkII 2.4	2483/6	1959-67	£7,000	£5,000	£2,000
MkII 3.4	3442/6	1959-67	£9,000	£6,500	£3,000
MkII 3.8	3781/6	1959-67	£9,850	£6,000	£4,000
S-Type 3.4	3442/6	1963-68	£9,000	£6,500	£2,000
S-Type 3.8	3781/6	1963-68	£10,000	£6,500	£2,000
240	2438/6	1967-68	£9,000	£6,000	£2,500
340	3442/6	1967-68	£8,000	£7,000	£3,000
420	4235/6	1966-68	£6,000	£3,000	£2,000

Manual gearboxes with overdrive are at a premium.
Some concours examples making as much as 50% over Condition 1.

1959 Jaguar 3.4 MkI, 6 cylinders, 3442cc, mainly original, manual/overdrive transmission, wire wheels, full history, approximately 74,000 miles recorded, mechanically and bodily sound, red leather interior and wood veneer in good condition.
£7,500–8,000 *ADT*

Jaguar MkI

In 1956, the year that William Lyons was knighted, Jaguar had its most complete range of cars ever. It filled the middle-market gap with the new MkI medium-sized saloon, Jaguar's first unitary design. Initially powered by a 2483cc version of the 6 cylinder XK engine it stood out in a world of lumpen British porridge as a genuinely sporting saloon with a top-speed close to the ton. In 1957 the MkI received the 3.4 litre XK engine and became a 120mph flyer.

By 1960 the MkI had become the biggest selling Jaguar ever, topping 36,000 and setting standards for aspirational middle-class motoring. In 1960 it evolved into the leaner, cleaner MkII, with slimmer door pillars, more glass, wider rear-track for better handling and disc brakes. Its get-away capabilities are legendary and its thanks to the crooks that many police forces were issued with MkIIs as the only way of catching them.

1960 Jaguar MkII Saloon, 3800cc, manual gearbox with overdrive, total bare shell restoration, mechanically uprated.
£27,500–32,500 *SC*

1963 Jaguar 3.8 Litre MkII Saloon, right-hand drive, manual plus overdrive transmission, initially exported to New Zealand, restored by specialists, electrics converted to negative earth with electronic ignition fitted, excellent overall condition.
£13,000–15,000 *BKS*

The 3.8 litre MkII made its debut in 1959, with some 15,383 produced in right-hand drive, until 1967 when production ended. The engine gave 220bhp at 5500rpm and was capable of 0–60mph in 8.5 seconds, quicker than a modern day VW Golf GTi.

l. **1961 Jaguar MkII 3.4 Litre Four Door Saloon,** complete restoration, right-hand drive, overdrive gearbox, Dunlop disc brakes all-round, good condition.
£25,000–27,000 *BKS*

1964 Jaguar MkII 3.4 Litre Saloon,
6 cylinders, 3442cc, 4 speed gearbox,
overhead camshaft.
£2,000–2,250 *DB*

1964 Jaguar MkII 3.4 Litre Saloon, louvred
bonnet, Coombes-style rear arches, wire
wheels, good condition throughout, history.
£14,000–15,000 *UMC*

1965 Jaguar MkII Four Door Saloon,
3.8 litres, 220bhp at 5500rpm, 0–60mph in
8.5 seconds, ground-up restoration from
1992–96, stainless steel exhaust system,
Avon Turbospeed tyres.
£14,500–16,000 *BKS*

1965 Jaguar 3.4 Litre MkII Saloon,
6 cylinders, 3442cc, structurally sound
with chromework in good condition, original
radio, full toolkit, clutch replaced, interior
woodwork requires reburbishment,
less than 24,000 miles recorded.
£6,000–7,000 *ADT*

Jaguar Milestones

1901:	William Lyons born in Blackpool on 4 September.
1922:	On 4 September William Lyons formed the Swallow Sidecar Company with William Walmsley.
1927:	Austin Seven Swallow was William Lyons' first car.
1928:	Company moved to Coventry, its home ever since.
1933:	The Swallow Sidecar and Coachbuilding Company changed its name to SS Cars Ltd.
1935:	William Lyons now sole proprietor of the business. On 24 September at London's Mayfair Hotel he introduced the Jaguar name for his new range of cars.
1945:	Company changed its name to Jaguar Cars Ltd.
1948:	Sensational new XK120 really did 120mph.
1951:	C-type claimed Jaguar's first Le Mans 24-hour race victory.
1953:	C-type came first, second and fourth at Le Mans. Jaguar's secret weapon was disc brakes.
1955:	D-type won Le Mans.
1956:	D-type won Le Mans.
1956:	William Lyons knighted.
1957:	D-type won Le Mans.
1957:	Fire devastated Jaguar's Browns Lane factory causing an estimated £3,500,000 worth of damage.
1960:	Jaguar bought Daimler.
1961:	E-type was the sensation of the Geneva Motor Show.
1966:	Jaguar merged with British Motor Corporation to form British Motor Holdings.
1968:	British Motor Holdings merged with Leyland Group to form British Leyland.
1972:	Sir William Lyons retired.
1975:	British Leyland, including Jaguar, nationalised.
1984:	Jaguar Cars Ltd privatised.
1985:	Sir William Lyons died at his Warwickshire home on 8 February.
1988:	Jaguar won again at Le Mans with XJR-9.
1988:	Jaguar announced XJ220 supercar.
1989:	Jaguar became wholly owned subsidiary of Ford Great Britain.
1990:	Jaguar won again at Le Mans.
1992:	First production XJ220s.
1994:	XJ220 production ceased at 265.
1995:	Geneva launch of XK8 rekindled excitement of E-type's 1961 launch.
1995:	60th anniversary of the Jaguar name.
1999:	X200 heralded new generation of small Jaguars.

1966 Jaguar MkII Saloon, 3.8 litres, restored, history, uprated brakes, suspension, gearbox, engine, wire wheels.
£14,000–15,000 *UMC*

1967 Jaguar MkII 3.4 Litre Saloon, 3442cc, new radiator, clutch and braking system using stainless steel callipers and stainless steel exhaust, resprayed, fully warranted 46,544 miles recorded, original tool kit, excellent condition throughout.
£9,500–11,000 *H&H*

1963 Jaguar MkX, 6 cylinders, 3781cc, one owner, 47,000 miles recorded, resprayed, mechanically sound, interior trim carefully preserved and instrumentation functioning correctly, good condition.
£4,250–5,000 *BRIT*

**Miller's is a price GUIDE
not a price LIST**

1968 Jaguar 340 Saloon, manual gearbox, wire wheels, excellent original condition.
£8,000–10,000 *VIC*

1968 Jaguar 240 Sports Saloon, 6 cylinders, 2483cc, manual gearbox with overdrive, recently refurbished, new outer sills, new clutch, replaced headlining, chrome wire wheels.
£4,750–5,250 *COYS*

For the car's final production run in 1967, only 2.4 and 3.4 engines were available, at the same time thinner bumpers were fitted and the models renamed 240 and 340 respectively.

1967 Jaguar 420, 6 cylinders, 4235cc, bodywork completely restored, engine overhauled, gearbox and rear axle good, power-assisted steering, suspension and brakes overhauled, reconditioned radiator, manual transmission with overdrive.
£4,000–5,000 *ADT*

1969 Jaguar 420G Four Door Saloon, 4.2 litres, right-hand drive, automatic, good transmission and electrics, excellent condition throughout.
£3,500–4,500 *BKS*

Built at first with the 3.8 litre XK engine, the MkX gained the torquier 4.2 litre unit in October 1964. Other changes during production included improvements to cooling system, fitting of air-blending heater, air conditioning and all-synchromesh gearbox. The 420G introduced in 1966 differed only in minor cosmetic aspects.

Jaguar XK120

In a few short years before the war Jaguar had speedily built up an enviable reputation but even greater glory was to come. In 1948, at the first post-war Motor Show at Earl's Court, William Lyons stole the show with perhaps the most cat-like of all Jaguars, the XK120. The XK120 was hastily developed in time for the show as a short-run prestige sports model.

The ecstatic public reception changed all that though and caught Jaguar on the hop. In 1949 hand-built alloy-bodied cars dribbled out of the factory until production tooling was in place for series production cars in 1950.

The 120 in the name really did stand for 120mph, thanks to the fabulous double overhead-cam engine that went on to power 6 cylinder E-types and Jaguar saloons until 1986. At the time cynical motoring scribes were sceptical and in 1949 William Lyons, by now an accomplished publicist, hired a Dakota aircraft and flew a band of hacks to Belgium to witness the XK120 perform a 132mph run on the unrestricted Jabbeke autoroute. That Jag did have a little aerodynamic tweaking but he'd proved his point: the XK120 was the fastest series production car in the world, no question. In fact the 3.4 litre XK engine pumped out as much power as the 5.4 litre Cadillac engine of the same period. As an encore to the Jabbeke stunt, the XK120 cruised past the hacks at 10mph in fourth gear just to prove the point.

One of the earliest XK120 customers was car connoisseur and actor Clark Gable and he reckoned the XK120 was 'a masterpiece of design and construction'. But the XK120 was more than quick and supremely stylish. It really opened up the export markets for Jaguar, for over its production life of 1949 to 1953, 92 per cent of the 12,000 XK120s built were exported. It was also developed into the XK120C, better known as the C-type, which cleaned up at Le Mans in 1951 and 1953.

1952 Jaguar XK120 Roadster, 6 cylinders, 3442cc, completely restored including bare metal respray, new leather trim, hood, side screens, wiring loom and all chrome work, dry stored since 1981. **£24,000–27,000** *COYS*

The XK120 became a massive success both on the road and the track where it scored numerous victories, the many drivers including Stirling Moss, Peter Walker, Peter Whitehead, Leslie Johnson and Ian Appleyard. In XK120C/C-Type form it won Le Mans in both 1951 and 1953, while its engine was to power 3 more Sarthe winners and a whole host of Jaguars right up to the present day.

1953 Jaguar XK120 Drophead Coupé, 6 cylinders in-line, double overhead camshaft, 3422cc, 160bhp at 5250rpm, 4 speed manual gearbox, left-hand drive, rebuilt engine and bodywork, chassis stripped, repaired and repainted, brakes and wire wheels rebuilt, woodwork reveneered. **£45,000–55,000** *C*

JAGUAR Model	ENGINE cc/cyl	DATES	CONDITION 1	2	3
XK120 roadster aluminum	3442/6	1948-49	£40,000	£20,000	£15,000
XK120 roadster	3442/6	1949-54	£26,000	£20,000	£15,000
XK120 DHC	3442/6	1953-54	£22,000	£17,000	£12,000
XK120 Coupé	3442/6	1951-55	£16,000	£12,000	£10,000
C-type	3442/6	1951	£150,000+		
D-type	3442/6	1955-56	£400,000+		
XKSS (original)	3442/6	1955-57	£400,000+		
XK140 roadster	3442/6	1955-58	£30,000+	£23,000	£16,000
XK140 DHC	3442/6	1955-58	£25,000	£20,500	£15,000
XK140 Coupé	3442/6	1955-58	£15,000	£10,000	£7,500
XK150 roadster	3442/6	1958-60	£28,000++	£22,000	£15,000
XK150 DHC	3442/6	1957-61	£25,000	£18,000	£10,000
XK150 Coupé	3442/6	1957-60	£15,000	£10,000	£6,000
XK150S roadster	3442/ 3781/6	1958-60	£40,000+	£26,000	£20,000
XK150S DHC	3442/ 3781/6	1958-60	£34,000+	£22,000	£18,000
XK150S Coupé	3442/ 3781/6	1958-61	£22,000	£18,000	£14,000

D-Type with competition history considerably more.
Watch out for left-hand to right-hand drive conversions in the XK series of cars.

1954 Jaguar XK120 Drophead Coupé,
6 cylinders, 3442cc, completely restored,
including all mechanical components and
coachwork, chrome wire wheels, new tyres and
stainless steel exhaust system fitted recently.
£29,000–33,000 *ADT*

**1995 Jaguar XK140 Roadster Child's
Electric Car,** scratch-built model built to half
scale of XK140 including steel box section
chassis, steel and aluminium body, finished in
red with black seats, 24volt electric motor with
variable forward and reverse speeds, controlled
by accelerator, wire wheels, pneumatic tyres,
working lights, opening doors, bonnet and boot,
rack-and-pinion steering, independent front
suspension, hand and foot brakes, removable
steering wheel, chrome-plated brightwork.
£7,500–9,000 *C*

1955 Jaguar XK140 MC Roadster, 6 cylinders,
3442cc, 210bhp at 5700rpm, left-hand drive,
equipped to MC specification including wire
wheels, twin exhausts, C-Type cylinder head,
bare metal respray and retrim, well maintained.
£36,500–40,000 *COYS*

r. **1955 Jaguar XK140 Fixed Head Coupé,**
bodywork professionally restored with new
panelling to floor pan, battery boxes, inner and
outer rear wings, sills and door skins,
mechanically sound, interior original.
£14,000–17,000 *S*

l. **1955 Jaguar
XK140 Two Door
Drophead Coupé,**
completely restored,
Moss manual gearbox
with overdrive,
right-hand drive,
very good condition.
£28,000–33,000 *BKS*

1956 Jaguar XK140 MC Drophead Coupé, rebuilt C-Type engine, body restoration, new custom interior and trim with Connolly leather upholstery, 35,000 miles recorded since restoration.
£44,000–48,000 *C*

During the 6 year life span of the fabulous XK120 it became apparent that certain refinements such as more room, standard wire wheels and more power were needed. October 1954 saw the introduction of the XK140, with changes in appearance and engineering. The classic lines were retained but were protected by sturdier bumpers and a tougher grille. A chrome strip ran down the length of the hood, and another on the rear trunk lid drew attention to the medallion in the middle proclaiming the Le Mans wins of the marque. The rear bumper wrapped around the wings and sported overriders.

Inside, the front seat and dashboard remained the same, but with more leg room because the engine block was moved forward on the chassis. There was also space behind the front seat. Moving the engine forward led to better straight line stability, and with the adoption of the Alford and Alder rack-and-pinion steering came a much more direct response to the wheel. On the Special Equipment models (MC) were wire wheels and Lucas FT576 foglamps, mounted above the front bumper. With the C-Type head, developed for the C-Type Le Mans race car, the bhp was raised to 210 at 5750rpm. Also with the C-Type head came a dual exhaust system which used 2 separate silencers, with pipes running through holes in the chassis cross members and emerging below the rear overrider.

1958 Jaguar XK150S 3.4 Litre Drophead Coupé, 6 cylinders, special equipment model with high compression cylinder head, overdrive gearbox, unused for some years, requires batteries and clutch hydraulics easing.
£21,000–25,000 *BKS*

On the road the XK120 evolved into the XK140 and XK150 while the C-type grew into the legendary triple Le Mans winning D-type.

l. **1956 Jaguar XK140 Roadster,** left-hand drive, manual gearbox with no overdrive, high ratio differential, excellent condition.
£21,000–25,000 *H&H*

1958 Jaguar XK150 Fixed Head Coupé, good order throughout, original factory specifications.
£16,000–18,000 *S*

The XK150 was introduced in May 1957 and featured a higher scuttle and door line than its predecessor, enlarged wrap-around bumpers, a curved windscreen and a wider radiator grille. Dunlop disc brakes were fitted all-round. The competitively priced XK150 proved a best-seller with about 9,400 examples produced by the Coventry works before the series was replaced by the E-Type in March 1961.

r. **1959 Jaguar XK150 Two Door Roadster,** 3.4 litres, right-hand drive, meticulously restored, 6,000 miles recorded since, very good condition.
£50,000–55,000 *BKS*

This car was a winner at Jaguar Drivers' Club concours events and was owned by Tony Vandervell.

Jaguar E-Type

In 1962 Jaguar launched the mammoth MkX, but for most the story of Jaguar in the swinging 1960s is all about that svelte 150mph stunner launched at the 1961 Geneva Motor Show, the E-type. British motoring magazines had produced road tests of pre-production models to coincide with the launch – and yes, the fixed head coupé really could do 150.4mph (149.1 for the roadster). OK, so the road-test cars were perhaps tweaked a little and early owners found 145mph a more realistic maximum, but the legend was born. It wasn't just a stunning, svelte sports´car though; it was a trademark Jaguar sporting package, once again marrying sensational performance with superb value for money. Contemporary

Astons and Ferraris, for example, were more than double the money.

The liquid lines of the E-type displayed a direct lineage from the D-type and that's no surprise as the C-, D- and E-type were penned by aerodynamicist Malcolm Sayer. In fact the E-type was the first Jaguar road car not drafted by William Lyons, although his guiding influence is clearly visible. In 1964 the 4.2 litre engine supplanted the original 3.8 and in 1971, as US emission regs were increasingly strangling the cat's performance, the Series III emerged with a 5.3 litre V12. By the end of production in 1974, 72,520 E-types had been built and two-thirds of them had been exported, mostly to the USA.

1961 Jaguar E-Type Flat Floor Coupé, 3.8 litres, right-hand drive, 68,000 miles recorded, excellent condition, bodywork clean and rust-free, interior in good condition with original Moss gearbox.
£22,500–25,000 *BKS*

1961 Jaguar E-Type Roadster, 6 cylinders, 3781cc, restored in 1984, good overall condition, black double duck hood, spare set of wheels and tyres.
£17,000–20,000 *ADT*

l. **1962 Jaguar E-Type Fixed Head Coupé,** 3781cc, fully restored to include complete engine rebuild, rebuilt back axle, new shock absorbers and springs, new wire wheels and chromework, period radio, new tyres, stainless steel exhaust and brake disc calipers, excellent condition.
£15,000–17,000 *H&H*

1962 Jaguar E-Type Fixed Head Coupé, 3781cc, restoration work includes new doors, sills and rear arches, wheels shotblasted and powder coated, rubber seals and most of chromework replaced, full history, 57,000 recorded miles.
£15,500–17,000 *H&H*

r. **1963 Jaguar E-Type Roadster,** 6 cylinders, 3781cc, bare metal respray, mechanically sound, red leather interior renewed to original, fair condition.
£16,500–20,000 *ADT*

1963 Jaguar E-Type Fixed Head Coupé,
3.8 litres.
£12,000–14,000 *H&H*

**1964 Jaguar E-Type 3.8 Litre Fixed Head
Coupé,** 3781cc, completely restored, correct
crossply tyres fitted, 6,000 miles recorded
since restoration, full history, good condition.
£21,500–23,000 *H&H*

**1965 Jaguar E-Type SI Fixed Head
Coupé,** 4.2 litres, mechanically serviceable,
good condition.
£17,000–19,500 *EAE*

1965 Jaguar E-Type 4.2 Litre SI Roadster,
6 cylinder in-line, 4,235cc, 265bhp at 5400rpm,
4 speed manual gearbox, 4 wheel Dunlop disc
brakes, independent suspension, left-hand
drive, 56,000 miles recorded, original example.
£22,000–25,000 *C*

*This E-Type is the 10th Series I 4.2 litre made.
A delightful, original and unrestored example.*

1966 Jaguar E-Type Roadster, completely
restored including bare metal respray, all new
chromework and components as required, new
wheels and tyres, new exhaust system and
electrics, interior retrimmed in correct material.
£25,500–28,000 *ADT*

JAGUAR Model	ENGINE cc/cyl	DATES	CONDITION 1	2	3
E-type 3.8 flat floor roadster (RHD)		1961	£40,000	£30,000	£22,000
E-type SI 3.8 roadster	3781/6	1961-64	£30,000	£19,000	£15,000
E-type 3.8 FHC	3781/6	1961-64	£18,000	£13,000	£10,000
E-type SI 4.2 roadster	4235/6	1964-67	£26,000	£18,000	£14,000
E-type 2+2 manual FHC	4235/6	1966-67	£16,000	£11,000	£9,000
E-type SI 2+2 auto FHC	4235/6	1966-68	£14,000	£10,000	£9,000
E-type SII roadster	4235/6	1968-70	£25,000	£19,000	£14,000
E-type SII FHC	4235/6	1968-70	£18,000	£12,000	£10,000
E-type SII 2+2 manual FHC	4235/6	1968-70	£15,000	£10,000	£8,000
E-type SIII roadster	5343/12	1971-75	£35,000	£24,000	£15,000
E-type SIII 2+2 manual FHC	5343/12	1971-75	£19,000	£14,000	£10,000
E-type SIII 2+2 auto FHC	5343/12	1971-75	£17,000	£12,000	£9,000
XJ6 2.8 Ser I	2793/6	1968-73	£3,000	£1,500	£1,000
XJ6 4.2 Ser I	4235/6	1968-73	£3,500	£2,000	£1,000
XJ6 Coupé	4235/6	1974-78	£7,000	£4,000	£2,500
XJ6 Ser II	4235/6	1973-79	£3,500	£2,000	£750
XJ12 Ser I	5343/12	1972-73	£3,500	£2,250	£1,500
XJ12 Coupé	5343/12	1973-77	£9,000	£5,000	£3,000
XJ12 Ser II	5343/12	1973-79	£2,000	£1,500	-
XJS manual	5343/12	1975-78	£6,000	£4,500	£2,500
XJS auto	5343/12	1975-81	£4,500	£3,000	£2,000

Jaguar E-Type Series III Commemorative Roadsters fetch more than SIII Roadster – 50 limited editions only.

1967 Jaguar E-Type Series 1½ Roadster, 4.2 litres, fully rebuilt mechanically, excellent condition, restoration work carried out 10 years ago. **£34,000–36,000** *EAE*

l. **1967 Jaguar E-Type Series 1½ Drophead Coupé,** 4235cc, bare shell restoration to show standard. **£30,000–35,000** *SC*

r. **1968 Jaguar E-Type 4.2 Litre SII Fixed Head Coupé,** excellent condition throughout, fully restored in 1989. **£30,000–32,500** *EAE*

l. **1968 Jaguar E-Type Two Door Sports Coupé,** 4.2 litres, right-hand drive, 3 owners from new, generally good condition, chrome and paintwork good, wire wheels recently refurbished. **£18,500–20,000** *BKS*

Some 7,770 examples of the Series 1½ were sold.

1968 Jaguar E-Type 2+2, excellent condition. **£11,000–12,000** *PAL*

1968 Jaguar E-Type 4.2 Litre SII, British Racing green, manual gearbox, fully restored. **£18,000–22,000** *VIC*

1969 Jaguar E-Type 4.2 Litre 2+2, 3 owners from new, well maintained with new brakes, steering, tyres, recent back axle work, always been garaged, original radio, wire wheels and sliding sunroof. **£9,500–10,500** *H&H*

l. **1970 Jaguar E-Type Series II Fixed Head Coupé,** 4.2 litres, fully rebuilt, excellent condition.
£30,000–32,500 *EAE*

r. **1970 Jaguar E-Type Fixed Head Coupé,** 6 cylinders, 4235cc, fully restored, bare metal respray, original specification, 70,000 miles recorded, very good condition throughout.
£14,000–16,000 *ADT*

1970 Jaguar E-Type 2+2 Fixed Head Coupé, Webasto sunroof, power steering, chrome wire wheels, new engine and gearbox, very good condition.
£6,500–7,500 *PA*

1971 Jaguar E-Type Series III Fixed Head Coupé, V12, overhead camshafts, 5343cc, 4 speed manual gearbox, wire wheels, 71,000 miles recorded, good condition.
£9,500–11,000 *C*

In 1971 the V12 5.3 litre engine became available, Jaguar's first whollynew engine since the debut of the XK engine introduced in 1948.

1971 Jaguar E-Type Series II Roadster, 6 cylinders, 4235cc, new body shell, restored, excellent condition throughout.
£24,000–27,000 *BRIT*

r. **1972 Jaguar E-Type V12 Roadster,** 5343cc, manual gearbox, completely overhauled and repainted, very good condition.
£26,000–28,000 *H&H*

l. **1973 Jaguar E-Type Series III V12 Roadster,** manual transmission, right-hand drive, good overall condition.
£19,000–22,000 *BKS*

The Series III came with transistorised ignition and a power output of 272bhp from its twin overhead camshaft V12. Distinguished by flared wheel arches and a grille in the front air intake, wire wheels were an option and are fitted to this example. The 4 Zenith Stromberg carburettors helped performance to nearly 150mph with 0–100mph in 15 seconds. The model continued production until 1975.

1973 Jaguar E-Type Series III Two Seater Sports Roadster, imported from Australia, refurbished, new walnut dashboard, 38,000 miles recorded, chrome wire-spoked wheels, excellent condition.
£29,000–33,000 *BKS*
Formerly the property of the Hon Marquis of Bristol.

1973 Jaguar E-Type V12 Roadster, 5343cc, restored, retrimmed, new chrome work, 62,000 miles recorded, right-hand drive.
£23,500–26,000 *H&H*

r. **1973 Jaguar E-Type Series III Roadster,** 12 cylinders, 5343cc, manual gearbox, chrome wire wheels, right-hand drive, professionally restored, 83,200 miles recorded.
£26,000–28,000 *COYS*

l. **1974 Jaguar E-Type V12 Series III Roadster,** air conditioning, carburettors overhauled, battery cut-off switch installed, 56,000 miles recorded, very good condition.
£25,500–27,500 *C*

Jaguar XJ6

Initially Jaguar's fortunes seemed set fair with the excellent XJ6 saloon, the last Jaguar on which Sir William Lyons exercised his assured and confident styling skills. The company's founder retired in 1972 and the first Jaguar produced without his input was the XJS of 1975 which, although initially controversial, has mellowed over 20 years to become an established classic. Inflation and the fuel crisis hit Jaguar hard as the luxury car market contracted. Exports to the USA withered and British Leyland was beset with problems, not least poor quality control, that undermined Jaguar's reputation.

1971 Jaguar XJ6, 6 cylinders, 4235cc, professionally converted to left-hand drive, resprayed, 46,500 miles recorded.
£3,500–4,000 *BRIT*

1972 Jaguar XJ6 Short Wheelbase, 4200cc, bare shell restoration to show standard.
£8,000–10,000 *SC*

1975 Jaguar XJ6 Coupé, 6 cylinders, 4235cc, repainted, original leather trim, good condition throughout.
£5,000–6,000 *BRIT*

1977 Jaguar XJ6 3.4, 6 cylinders, 3442cc, sunroof, 52,000 miles recorded, excellent condition throughout.
£2,750–3,250 *ADT*

l. **1976 Jaguar XJ6 Coupé,** 6 cylinders, 4235cc, replaced automatic transmission and torque converter, new front wings, door skins, rear wheel arches, rear quarter panels, exhaust system, floorpan and sills, repainted, good condition.
£3,250–3,750 *ADT*

> *A rebuilt car is not necessarily more valuable than a car in good original condition, even if the restoration has been costly.*

1977 Jaguar XJ6 4.2 Litre Saloon, automatic transmission, very good condition throughout.
£1,200–1,800 *BKS*

This car was an export model, assembled under licence in South Africa. It was chauffeur maintained until imported to the UK in 1986.

1987 Jaguar Sovereign Four Door Saloon, automatic transmission, right-hand drive, good condition throughout.
£2,500–3,500 *JNic*

1973 Jaguar XJ12 Series I, 5343cc, replaced outer sills, rear wheel arches, rear panel, quarter panels, door bottoms and front wings, bare metal respray, long wheelbase, excellent condition throughout.
£8,500–9,500 *LF*

1977 Jaguar XJS 5.3 Coupé, 5343cc, completely restored, manual gearbox, right-hand drive, excellent condition.
£3,500–4,000 *H&H*

1980 Jaguar XJS 5.3 Coupé, 5343cc, lowered suspension, alloy wheels, full leather interior, rear spoiler, sunroof, full T.W.R. body kit, very good condition throughout.
£2,500–3,000 *H&H*

1985 Jaguar XJS HE Cabriolet, 5343cc, 57,000 miles recorded, cruise control, rear seats fitted, full service history, very good condition.
£8,500–10,000 *H&H*

This car was purchased new by the actor Ben Cross, best known for his role in the film Chariots of Fire. His filming commitments meant that the car spent long periods in storage, particularly between 1988 and 1991.

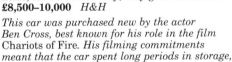

1986 Jaguar XJS V12 Cabriolet, excellent condition.
£6,500–7,000 *H&H*

1987 Jaguar XJS, V12, 5.3 litres, excellent condition throughout.
£7,000–8,000 *PAL*

Forgotten Jaguars – Buying Suggestions

Virtually all Jaguars are collectable, but there are a couple of neglected Jaguar models that make interesting alternatives. The MkII Jaguar, associated in the 1960s with colourful cockney twins in tonic-toned suits and most recently with TV's Inspector Morse, has enjoyed enduring appeal. Top recent auction price for a MkII was £26,000, but the majority fell into the £5,000 to £15,000 range.

Less obvious is the S-Type saloon, in effect a MkII with a stretched boot, and actually a better handler with its independent rear end. Top auction price in 1996 was a mere £5,100. Buying privately or from a dealer you'd have a tough time spending more than £12,000. Car for car an S-Type should set you back between two-thirds and three-quarters of the price of a MkII.

Another orphan is the Jaguar 420, an S-Type with a MkX quad-headlamp nose. Because they look even less like MkIIs they can be a tad cheaper than the S-Type. Probably the least loved Jag of all is the gargantuan MkX/420G, a bloated bollard scraper with a girth of 6ft 4in (194cm) and nearly 17ft (500cm) long. Anti-social, true, but this barrel-sided behemoth is a barrel of laughs at seriously funny money. Yours again for less than MkII money and pretty much on a par with the 420 and S-Type.

The other Jag worth considering is a Daimler 250 V8 saloon, a MkII with a fluted Daimler grille and a lovely 2.5 litre V8, again about two-thirds to three-quarters the price of a MkII.

1968 Jaguar 420 Four Door Saloon, 62,000 miles recorded, right-hand drive, no modifications from original specification, excellent condition.
£5,500–6,000   *BKS*

The 420 Jaguar was powered by a 245bhp version of the 4.2 litre twin overhead camshaft 6 cylinder engine, and this example has the standard 8:1 compression ratio. The 420 was similar in appearance to the S-Type saloon of 1964–68, but with quad headlamps as previously seen on the MkX.

1970 Jaguar 420G, very good condition.
£7,000–7,650   *PAL*

Competition Jaguars

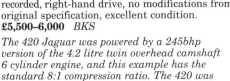

1954 Jaguar MkVII Historic Rally Competition Saloon, 6 cylinders, 3.4 litres, twin camshaft, Spax adjustable dampers, radial tyres, manual gearbox with electric Laycock de Normanville overdrive, sunroof, excellent condition throughout.
£8,000–9,000   *BKS*

1953 Jaguar C-Type, a scale model of the car which won Le Mans, and was the first to do 100mph average lap, produced 1980–95, 4in (10cm) long.
£125–150   *PC*

r. **1956 Jaguar D-Type,** unrestored, ex-Ecurie-Ecosse team.
£650,000–700,000   *DHAM*

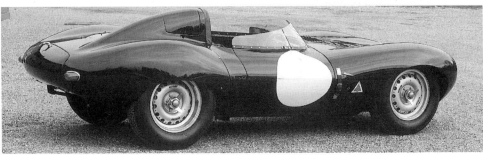

1956 Jaguar D-Type, 3½ litres, excellent condition.
£475,000+   *DHAM*

1956 Jaguar SK SS 3.4 Litre, excellent condition.
£400,000+ *DHAM*

1984 Jaguar XJS Group A Race Car,
6 litres, excellent condition.
£70,000–75,000 *DHAM*

1986 Jaguar XJR6, excellent condition.
£300,000+ *DHAM*
This car won the 1986 1,000km race at Silverstone.

Roy Nockolds, the C-Type of Whitehead and
Walker on its way to victory in the 1951
Le Mans race, hand-coloured silk screen print,
22 x 30in (56 x 76cm).
£115–130 *BKS*

*The original painting was commissioned by
William Lyons, later Sir William Lyons, after
the event.*

Jaguars for Restoration

1958 Jaguar XK150 Roadster, dismantled, some work carried out, original registration mark, requires total restoration.
£12,000–13,000 *BKS*

Miller's is a price GUIDE not a price LIST

1934 Jaguar SSI Two Door Saloon, 'barn discovery' from the north west of England, for restoration or spare parts.
£5,500–6,000 *BKS*

Described by The Autocar as 'long, low and rakishly sporting, the general effect being that of a powerful sports coupé costing £1,000 new, although the actual price is less than a third of that figure,' the SSI, although unspectacular in performance, established the pattern for Lyons' future Jaguars. The chassis was revised with a wider track for 1934, and larger Standard engines coupled to synchromesh gearboxes introduced. Top speed of the 20hp model was now in the region of 80mph.

l. **1970 Jaguar E-Type 4.2 Litre Series III 2+2 Prototype,** V12 body shell and running gear, manual transmission, restoration project following fire damage.
£1,500–1,800 *BKS*

This former Jaguar Cars Ltd experimental vehicle represents a significant landmark in the development of Jaguar's world-beating E-Type.

Jaguar Replicas

1968/69 Jaguar C-Type Replica by Heritage, 6 cylinders, 3.8 litres, 3781cc, fibreglass body, triple Weber carburettors, 300bhp, full racing exhaust, 72-spoke wire wheels, running gear from a 1968 S-Type, excellent condition.
£13,000–15,000 *ADT*

This C-Type Replica, constructed by Heritage Engineering, was built in 1989 at a cost of £46,000 and is finished in the Ecurie-Ecosse racing colour of dark blue with a grey hide interior.

r. **1964 Jaguar D-Type Replica by RAM,** spring ratings adjusted, electric cut-out fitted, radial tyres, repainted in British Racing Green, green leather upholstery, in good running condition.
£19,000–22,000 *S*

This example is based on 1964 3.8 litre MkX running gear and is bodied in glass fibre by the makers, L & R. It features the 'long nose' type body, and has been extensively improved.

1990 Challenger E-Type Roadster, 6 cylinders, 3781cc, 220bhp, fully rebuilt 3.8 litre MkX engine, 2,000 miles recorded, new all-synchromesh gearbox, excellent condition.
£11,500–13,000 *COYS*

This modern interpretation of the Jaguar E-Type by Challenger was built by marque specialist DJB Performance. Under a high quality fibreglass bodyshell moulded from a genuine E-Type 3.8 Roadster, the car uses Challenger's own steel semi-monocoque chassis allied to completely refurbished components from a Series II XJ6 donor saloon.

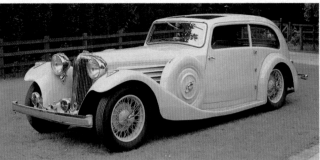

l. **1934 Jaguar SS1 Four Seater Airline Coupé**, 6 cylinders, 1608cc, synchromesh gearbox, high compression cylinder head, new camshaft, restored, maintained to highest standards.
£32,000–36,000 *COYS*

Apart from the distinctive new body line of the Airline Coupé, there was a new chassis frame with the cross-bracing moved forward to give larger footwells, and the front track was 2in (5cm) wider. The result of these small changes was a big increase in refinement.

r. **1936 SS2 Jaguar Four Seater Coupé**, 4 cylinders, 1608cc, 4 speed gearbox with synchromesh, servo-assisted brakes, 104in wheelbase, one owner for many years, excellent condition, maintained to highest standards.
£13,500–15,000 *COYS*

The longer wheelbase enhanced the model's reputation for good handling and steering, and improved the cars lines. In a little over 2 years 1,247 SS2 units were sold, but it has always been among the rarest of the SS Jaguar models.

1938 Jaguar SS100 Sports Two Seater, 3½ litres, restored, very good condition mechanically, spare parts including Luvax shock absorbers.
£93,000–100,000 *BKS*

Only 118 examples of this larger-engined SS100 were built before war ended production.

1947 Jaguar 1½ Litre, 4 cylinders, 1776cc, mechanically sound, instrumentation functioning with exception of rev counter, 88 miles since 1982, good overall condition.
£5,000–6,500 *ADT*

The advertising slogan of 'Grace–Space–Pace' was true of Jaguars in the immediate pre- and post-war periods.

r. **1950 Jaguar MkV 3½ Litre Drophead Coupé**, 6 cylinders, push-rod operated overhead valves, 3485cc, 125bhp at 4500rpm, 4 speed manual gearbox with synchromesh, chassis-up restoration, top speed of 90mph, original engine, body and transmission, left-hand drive, good condition.
£40,000–45,000 *C*

This model proved to have extraordinary longevity, and was used by the British Police forces. Only around 500 left-hand drive drophead coupés were made.

l. **1950 Jaguar XK120 Two Door Roadster**, 6 cylinders, 3442cc, twin overhead camshaft, bare metal respray, maximum speed 132mph, engine in good condition, interior good, original right-hand drive.
£25,000–30,000 *BKS*

The XK120's comfort and performance set new standards for sporting cars worldwide. After 240 Roadster models had been produced with aluminium body panelling, they were replaced with a steel-bodied variant.

l. **1953 Jaguar XK120 Fixed Head Coupé,** C-Type engine, racing carburettors, 9:1 pistons, quick release fuel filler, requires cosmetic attention, full history, good condition.
£16,000–18,000 *BKS*

It is understood that this car was works-prepared to compete in the 1953 Le Mans 24-hour Race. However, an accident in preparing for that race severely damaged the car, and it did not take part.

r. **1954 Jaguar XK120 Drophead Coupé,** 6 cylinder in-line engine, double overhead camshaft, 3422cc, 160bhp at 5250rpm, 4 speed manual gearbox, hydraulic drum brakes all-round, V screen, walnut-veneered fascia panel and cappings, comprehensive ground-up restoration, left-hand drive, excellent condition.
£35,000–40,000 *C*

This model is the rarest of all XK120s. The production run was short-lived and only 1,767 were built.

l. **1955 Jaguar XK140 3.4 Litre Drophead Coupé,** twin spot lamps, Kenlowe fan, 4 speed manual transmission, rack-and-pinion steering, dry-stored, fully restored, excellent condition.
£43,000–46,000 *BKS*

Only 479 examples of this sought-after model were made.

r. **1956 Jaguar XK140 Fixed Head Coupé,** 6 cylinder in-line engine, double overhead camshaft, 3442cc, twin SU carburettors, 190bhp, automatic gearbox, 4 wheel drum brakes, left-hand drive, totally restored, excellent condition throughout.
£35,000–40,000 *C*

The XK140 was exceptionally good value for money – it was well under half the price of the rival Mercedes 300SL, yet could almost match its performance, with a top speed of nearly 130mph.

l. **1958 Jaguar MkVIII,** 6 cylinders, twin overhead camshaft, 3442cc, 4 speed manual gearbox with overdrive, Girling hydraulic brakes with servo-assistance, sliding steel sunroof, folding picnic tables to rear of front seats, stainless steel exhaust, completely restored, right-hand drive, excellent condition.
£21,000–25,000 *C*

r. **1958 Jaguar XK150S Two Door Roadster,** straight 6 overhead camshaft engine, 3.4 litres, manual transmission with overdrive, wind-up windows, dics brakes, wire wheels, 73,000 miles recorded from new, engine and gearbox overhauled, electrical equipment replaced, original toolset, right-hand drive, restored, good condition throughout.
£30,000–35,000 *BKS*

The XK150S is a most sought-after and very rare car, due to its small and exclusive production run.

r. **1959 Jaguar XK150 Drophead Coupé,** 6 cylinders, double overhead camshaft, 3442cc, 190bhp at 5600rpm, 4 speed gearbox, servo-assisted 4 wheel disc brakes, new top, chrome wire wheels and tyres, 20,000 miles recorded from new, left-hand drive, very good condition. **£30,000–35,000** *C*

The XK150, launched in 1957, had various styling developments over the XK140 including a wrap-around windscreen and a new 'hip line'. It had a wider body and slimmer doors, providing more interior room, and Dunlop disc brakes.

l. **1963 Jaguar MkII 3.8 Litre Four Door Saloon,** 4 speed manual gearbox with overdrive, independent front suspension by wishbones and coil springs, leaf-sprung live rear axle, Dunlop servo-assisted disc brakes on all 4 wheels, ground-up restoration, only 2,000 miles recorded in past 6 years, excellent condition throughout. **£26,500–28,000** *BKS*

The MkII made its debut in October 1959 and had a wider rear track than the MkI, providing better roll-resistance and stability.

r. **1962 Jaguar E-Type Series I 3.8 Litre Roadster,** 6 cylinders, 3781cc, 150mph top speed, 0–60mph in 6.9 seconds, fully restored, fitted with superior cooling fan and larger brake calipers, excellent condition. **£44,500–48,000** *COYS*

One of the greatest post-war sports cars, Jaguar's E-Type caused a sensation on its Geneva Show debut. It combined speed with superb road-holding and remarkable docility.

l. **1964 Jaguar E-Type 3.8 Litre Fixed Head Coupé,** one owner from new, stored for past 17 years, 36,737km recorded, modification to exhaust tail pipes, spare-wheel, brace and tool-box remain unused, left-hand drive, very good original condition throughout. **£17,250–19,500** *S*

This car was stored underground in a paris apartment garage, and used infrequently only in dry conditions.

r. **1966 Jaguar MkII 3.4 Sports Saloon,** 6 cylinders, 3442cc, manual gearbox with overdrive, chrome wire wheels, factory power steering, reclining seats, fully restored, excellent condition throughout. **£16,000–18,000** *COYS*

The MkII was launched in October 1959, and had a larger glass area than the MkI, wider rear track and minor front suspension changes.

l. **1950 Jaguar MkV 3½ Litre Drophead Coupé,** engine rebuilt, low mileage since, sand coloured hood, tan interior, comprehensive history, well maintained, good condition throughout.
£20,250–22,000 *S*

In October 1948 an elegant new range of open and closed cars was announced by Jaguar Cars Ltd. The MkV 3½ litre Drophead Coupé bore all the hallmarks of William Lyons' styling flair, and was an advanced development of the pre-war cars.

r. **1966 Jaguar S-Type Saloon,** 6 cylinders, 3400cc, interior excellent, original tool-kit and handbook, requires minor restoration and recommissioning, very good condition.
£3,200–3,500 *COYS*

This car was 4 years old when purchased from its original owner, used for 3 years and then stored. The engine was carefully prepared for storage, with cylinders and valves well lubricated. The car is a unique example and requires only superficial restoration.

l. **1967 Jaguar Model 420 Saloon,** 6 cylinders, 4235cc, double overhead camshaft, 255bhp at 5400rpm, automatic gearbox, 4 wheel disc brakes, independent front and rear suspension, 40,000 miles recorded, chrome wire wheels rebuilt, power steering, factory fitted air conditioning, left-hand drive, very good condition.
£5,700–6,500 *C*

r. **1963 Jaguar E-Type Fixed Head Coupé,** 3.8 litres, fully restored, very good condition throughout.
£28,000–30,000 *EAE*

The impact the E-type made at its launch on March 15, 1961, at the Geneva Motor Show is now the stuff of Jaguar lore. The very first E-type roadsters and fixed head coupés produced until June 1962, are now referred to as 'flat floor' models and they are the most prized of all.

l. **1968 Jaguar E-Type SI Roadster,** 4.2 litres, excellent condition throughout.
£34,500–36,500 *EAE*

The 4.2 litre engine, introduced in 1964, supplanted the 3.8 litre. It was slightly more torquey and now had an all-synchromesh gearbox.

r. **1968 Jaguar XJ6,** 6 cylinders, 2792cc, stored in private museum, full history, excellent condition throughout. **£5,000–6,500** *BRIT*

This is the first UK registered XJ6, and was Jaguar Cars' press and publicity vehicle. It was a milestone in Jaguar's history, and this car heralded the successful launch of the series. The Jaguar XJ6 was the last Jaguar on which Sir William Lyons exercised his assured styling touch. It is a great tribute to the enduring appeal of this fabulous design that the re-styled XJ series of 1995 re-introduced the elegant curves of the original that had been flat-ironed out through the 1980s.

l. **1973 Jaguar E-Type Series III 2+2 Coupé,** V12, 5343cc, 4 Zenith-Stromberg carburettors, 272bhp, manual transmission, maximum speed 150mph, 0–100mph in 15 seconds, 51,000 miles recorded, right-hand drive, excellent condition throughout. **£10,000–12,000** *BKS*

Between 1971 and 1975 7,297 examples of the 2+2 were sold, when production of the E-Type ceased.

r. **1973 Jaguar E-Type Series III Roadster,** 12 cylinders, 5343cc, only 330 miles recorded, dry stored, right-hand drive, excellent overall condition throughout. **£42,000–46,000** *COYS*

This car has never been road registered, and overall appearance is as new.
   The Series III had wider wheels and tyres, anti-dive front suspension, ventilated front disc brakes, and an 18 gallon fuel tank. The bonnet had a spoiler and larger grille.

l. **1974 Jaguar E-Type Series III Roadster,** V12, 5343cc, 272bhp, manual transmission, power steering, black factory hard top, top speed 142mph, very good condition. **£21,000–24,000** *BKS*

The V12 E-Type was aimed strongly at the export market, and during its 4 year production run approximately 16,000 were built.

r. **1974 Jaguar E-Type X12 Roadster,** manual gearbox, chrome wire wheels, 36,000 miles recorded, excellent original condition throughout. **£32,000–35,000** *VIC*

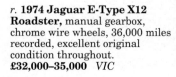

1956 Jensen 541 Two Door Coupé,
3993cc, overdrive, new interior trim,
fully restored, excellent condition.
£6,500–7,000 *H&H*

*This car has been stored for the past
6 years.*

1975 Jensen Interceptor Series III Convertible, 7.2 litres, 3
speed Chrysler Torqueflite automatic gearbox, power-operated
hood, top speed 126mph, 0–60mph in 7.6 seconds, original
specification, good condition, requires cosmetic attention.
£18,000–22,000 *BKS*

*Approximately 476 Series III Convertibles were sold in 2 years.
Many of these found a market abroad, as fewer manufacturers
were now making convertibles, owing to the US safety laws.*

1973 Jensen Interceptor,
full mechanical and body restoration,
air conditioning, power-assisted
steering, excellent condition.
£12,000–15,000 *VIC*

1973 Jensen Interceptor III,
8 cylinders, 7212cc, new floor pan,
sills, front valance and bonnet,
engine reconditioned, dry stored,
fully restored, excellent condition.
£5,500–6,000 *ADT*

*This car represents excellent value
for money in today's market.*

1952 Jowett Jupiter, restored, whitewall tyres,
modifications include indicators, door lock on passenger
side, and headlamps to US specification, fully restored,
excellent condition.
£11,000–13,000 *S*

*Brothers Benjamin and William Jowett from Yorkshire
started manufacturing cars in 1910, building practical
light cars at an affordable price.*

l. **1934 Lagonda M45 T7 Sports Four
Seater Tourer,** non-standard driver's
door, water pump, radiator and cooling
system overhauled, gearbox input shaft
replaced, replaced hood, sidescreens,
upholstery and carpets, good condition.
£45,000–50,000 *BKS*

*First seen in 1933 and powered by the
4.5 litre Meadows 6 cylinder engine, the
M45 Lagonda was the biggest and most
powerful car to leave the Staines factory
since the early 1900s.*

r. **1938 Lagonda V12 Drophead Coupé,**
60° V12 engine, 4.5 litres, 180bhp at
5500rpm, factory coachwork by Lagonda,
chrome wire wheels, whitewall tyres,
interior requires attention.
£40,000–45,000 *BKS*

*The launch of this model was aimed at
demonstrating that the revitalised
Lagonda company was back in business
following the original firm's brief spell in
receivership. However, the outbreak of
WWII in 1939 ended production after just
189 examples had left the factory.*

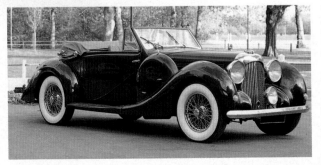

l. **1969 Lamborghini Espada,** coachwork by Bertone, V12 4 camshaft engine, 3929cc, 6,975km, excellent condition. **£22,000–25,000** *BKS*

The Espada was one of Lamborghini's greatest achievements, and was unveiled at the 1968 Geneva Salon. This early example was delivered to His Imperial Highness the late Shah of Iran.

r. **1969–70 Lamborghini P400S Miura 4 Litre Two Door Mid-engined Coupé,** coachwork by Bertone, paintwork good, interior and chromework in fair condition. **£56,500–60,000** *BKS*

The initial production run of the mid-engine Miura amounted to some 475 examples by the time the Miura S emerged in 1968–9. Sant'Agata production then proceeded to turn out some 140 examples of the model S, as pictured here.

l. **1924 Lancia Lambda Third Series Short Chassis Tourer,** V4 engine, back axle and brakes rebuilt, original exhaust cut-out system, original engraved headlight glasses with dash-operated dipping shields, enamelled radiator badge, Montevideo star and special brass three-part rear light, original wheels with beaded-edged Michelin tyres, twin rear-mounted spares, very good condition. **£55,000–60,000** *BKS*

This vehicle was delivered new in 1924 to Montevideo, Uruguay.

r. **1931 Lancia Dilambda Cabriolet,** coachwork by Carrozzeria Castagna, V8, 4 litres, 100bhp, sliding pillar front suspension, servo-assisted brakes, 4 speed gearbox, low mounted hypoid differential, left-hand drive, excellent working condition. **£70,000–75,000** *BKS*

The Dilambda was Lancia's answer to the early 1930s market for big powerful touring cars. It could do 80mph without gear-changing, starting in top gear.

l. **1954 Lancia Aurelia B20GT,** Berlinetta coachwork by Pininfarina, 6 cylinders, 2451cc, 118bhp, De Dion rear axle, restored to concours standard. **£32,000–35,000** *COYS*

r. **1955 Lancia B56S Florida Aurelia,** coachwork by Pininfarina, V6 overhead valve, 2266cc engine, 87bhp at 5000rpm, 4 speed manual gearbox, 4 wheel drum brakes, sliding pillar suspension with solid axle and coil springs rear, De Dion axle with leaf spring to front, left-hand drive, excellent original condition, replaced tyres, battery, temperature gauge and new fuel pump, original upholstery.
£22,000–25,000 *C*

l. **1957 Lancia Aurelia B24S Two Door Convertible,** coachwork by Carrozzeria Pininfarina, 2415cc, restored, finished in Azure blue with black leather upholstery, toolkit, owners manual, full history, excellent condition throughout.
£37,500–42,500 *BKS*

Lancia's classic Aurelia was launched at the 1950 Turin Motor Show and was joined the following year by the B20 Coupé. An enlarged 1991cc engine was used on the 1951 Aurelia Saloon, increased to 2451cc in 1953 for the B20 2500GT and adopted for the B24 Spider and Convertible models launched in 1955. These open-topped models differed only in the degree of weather protection offered.

r. **1963 Lancia Flaminia 3C Convertible,** coachwork by Carrozzeria Touring, 2.8 litre, V6 engine, triple twin choke Weber carburettors, 150bhp, coil spring and wishbone front suspension, stainless steel exhaust, well maintained, 135,000kms recorded, good condition.
£18,000–19,500 *BKS*

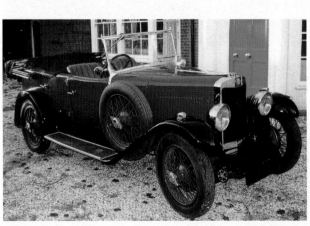

1976 Lancia Stratos Two Door Mid-Engined Coupé, V6, 4 camshaft engine, triple-Weber carburettors, 190bhp at 7000rpm, extensive engine and gearbox work, resprayed, interior in good condition.
£32,000–35,000 *BKS*

1981 Lancia Monte Carlo II, coachwork by Pininfarina, 4 cylinders, 1995cc Fiat/Lancia twin camshaft engine, 120bhp at 6000rpm, 42,000 miles recorded, finished in silver with grey cloth interior, good condition throughout.
£4,000–4,500 *ADT*

In 1973 and 1974 a great deal of rumour circulated regarding Fiat's plans to add a larger mid-engined sports car to their range to complement the new X1/9. It therefore was to come as quite a shock when, at the 1975 Geneva Motor Show, the new car was badged as a Lancia.

l. **1930 Lea-Francis P-Type 12/40 Open Tourer,** coachwork by Avon Bodies, 4 cylinders, 1496cc, bare metal respray, rechromed, rewired, full history, good condition throughout.
£14,500–16,000 *COYS*

1938 Lincoln K Brunn Two Door Convertible Victoria, V windscreen, finished in blue with beige top, white-walled tyres, restored to concours condition.
£200,000+ *BLK*

This was the only Brunn V windscreen Convertible Victoria built in 1938 on a 145in chassis.

1983 Marcos 3 Litre Coupé,
6 cylinders, 3400cc, alloy wheels, mechanically rebuilt, Ford 5 speed gearbox, new clutch assembly, steering, suspension and brakes uprated, Cosworth cooling fans, good condition.
£7,000–8,000 *ADT*

1970 Maserati Ghibli Coupé, coachwork by Ghia, 8 cylinders, 4719cc, power-assisted steering, restored, bare metal respray, retrimmed and rechromed, 6,000kms recorded, good condition.
£22,000–24,000 *COYS*

l. **1970 Lotus Elan S4SE Drophead Coupé,** stage III big valve competition engine, 5 speed close-ratio gearbox, tubular manifold and stainless steel exhaust system, solid drive shafts, dual circuit, twin servo disc brakes, alloy wheels, finished in metallic sea-blue livery with gold bumper, black interior, full history, good condition.
£11,000–12,000 *S*

r. **1962 Maserati 3500GT Spyder,** coachwork by Vignale, twin-ignition straight 6 engine, top speed of 130mph, Borrani wheels, front disc brakes, Weber carburettors, restored, 500kms recorded since restoration, finished in silver with black interior trim and hood, excellent condition throughout.
£35,000–40,000 *BKS*

l. **1971 Maserati Ghibli SS Spyder,** 8 cylinders, 4930cc, manual gearbox, chrome wire wheels, power steering, air conditioning, completely restored, right-hand drive, very good condition.
£40,000–50,000 *COYS*

This is one of only 7 right-hand drive Spyders ever built.

1973 Maserati Merak Two Door Sports Coupé, V6, 4 overhead camshafts, manual transmission, 12,000 miles recorded, left-hand drive.
£9,000–11,000 *BKS*

Maserati produced more Meraks than any other model in the 1970s.

1922-24 Mercedes Targa Florio 1.5 Litre Two Seater Competition Torpedo, 4 cylinder, 1500cc, twin overhead camshaft 16 valve supercharged engine, restored, museum stored.
£225,000+ *BKS*

This car can be traced back to the 1922 Targa Florio race in Sicily, when it finished 3rd in its category.

1937 Mercedes-Benz 540K Supercharged Cabriolet B, coachwork by Sindelfingen, 8 cylinders, 5401cc, 180bhp with blower engaged, 115bhp without it, totally restored, left-hand drive, excellent condition.
£160,000–180,000 *BKS*

1935 Mercedes-Benz 170H Saloon, 4 cylinders, 1697cc, 38hp at 3200rpm, top speed 110km/h, 4 wheel independent suspension, 3 speed gearbox with semi-automatic overdrive, requires restoration.
£6,500–7,500 *BKS*

This rear-engined saloon is an example of the largest of the rear-engined Mercedes models of the mid-1930s.

1938 Mercedes-Benz 320 Two Door Cabriolet B, 3.4 litres, 2 panel V windscreen, twin spare wheels, hood re-covered, original condition, requires recommissioning.
£25,000–30,000 *BKS*

1952 Mercedes-Benz 220 Cabriolet A, coachwork by Sindelfingen, 6 cylinders, 2200cc, 80bhp at 4600rpm, 90mph top speed, fully restored, excellent condition.
£20,000–23,000 *COYS*

l. **1956 Mercedes-Benz 300SL Gullwing Coupé,** 6 cylinders in-line, 2996cc overhead camshaft fuel injection engine, independent suspension, 215bhp at 5800rpm, 4 speed manual gearbox, 0–60mph in 8.8 seconds, top speed of 129mph, body restored, mechanically overhauled, full history, good condition. **£120,000–140,000** *BKS*

Initial versions of the 300SL racer were open topped. Unusually high sills were a feature and while access was not a problem of the open car, the adoption of coupé bodywork required innovative thinking – hence the gullwing doors.

r. **1957 Mercedes-Benz 300SL Roadster,** 6 cylinders in-line, 2996cc, 240bhp, 4 speed manual gearbox, hydraulic drum brakes, independent suspension, left-hand drive, completely restored, engine rebuilt, gearbox overhauled, good conditon. **£85,000–100,000** *C*

The first 300 SL roadsters exported to America were successful in racing. In contrast to the Gullwing coupé it had the 'low pivot' rear suspension, making it more predictable in its handling.

l. **1961 Mercedes-Benz 190SL Sports Roadster,** 4 cylinders, 1.8 litres, twin carburettors, independent suspension, totally restored, bare metal respray, new chromework, Connolly hide interior trim and mohair hood, engine rebuilt, electrics overhauled, right-hand drive, good condition. **£25,000–28,000** *BKS*

1965 Mercedes-Benz 230SL Roadster, 6 cylinders, 2300cc, 150bhp at 5500rpm, 4 speed manual gearbox, front disc brakes, independent front suspension, single joint swing axle coil springs rear, left-hand drive, top speed of 125mph, resprayed, 13,000 miles recorded, good condition. **£18,000–20,000** *C*

1968 Mercedes-Benz 280 SE Cabriolet, 6 cylinders in-line, 2778cc, overhead camshaft engine, Bosch fuel injection, 160bhp at 5500rpm, left-hand drive, one owner, well maintained, 40,000 miles recorded, good condition. **£28,000–32,000** *C*

r. **1969 Mercedes-Benz 300SEL 6.3 Litre Sedan,** V8, single overhead camshaft per bank, Bosch fuel injection, 6332cc, 250bhp at 4000rpm, 4 speed manual gearbox, 4 wheel disc brakes, independent suspension, left-hand drive, good condition. **£16,500–18,000** *C*

r. **1971 Mercedes-Benz 600 Pullman Four Door Limousine,** V8, single overhead camshaft, fuel injected, 6332cc, 150bhp, 4 speed automatic gearbox, servo-assisted twin circuit disc brakes, self-levelling air-independent suspension, left-hand drive, 69,000 miles recorded, good overall condition. **£30,000–35,000** *C*

l. **1930 MG 18/80 MkII Speed Model,** totally restored, optional extras include fan, sports radiator grille, servo brake, excellent condition.
£26,000–30,000 *BKS*

Described as the first production MG, the MG Sports Six, as it was originally named, was first seen at the 1928 Motor Show. The MkII appeared a year later with a sturdier chassis, stronger axles, larger brake drums and 4 speed lockable gearbox. Only 6 MkII Speed Models were built, and this is one of the best examples.

r. **1934 MG KN/K3 Open Sports-Racing,** 6 cylinders, 1087cc, pre-selector gearbox, half-elliptic front and rear spring suspension, engine modified, totally restored, replica coachwork, excellent condition.
£60,000–70,000 *COYS*

This is an original 6 cylinder car, and has been subject to careful and substantial restoration with invoices totalling more than £93,000. During its restoration it has been extensively modified and uprated to K3 specification.

l. **1936 MG NB Magnette Four Seater Tourer,** overhead camshaft, Bluemels steering wheel, twin spotlamps, fold-flat screen, cut-away doors, wire knock-on wheels, full history, restored, very good condition.
£15,500–18,000 *BKS*

This car was in the hands of its last owner for 43 years, and has been continuously maintained.

r. **1949 MG TC Two Seater Sports,** 4 cylinder, overhead valve, 1250cc engine, twin SU carburettors, 54bhp at 5200rpm, maximum speed of 73mph, extensively restored, very good condition.
£16,000–17,500 *VIN*

Between 1947 and 1949, 10,000 MG TC Midgets were produced.

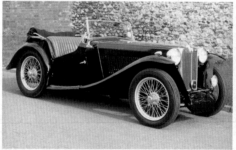

l. **1953 MG TD Roadster,** 1250cc, fully restored, new exhaust and radiator, manual transmission, right-hand drive, very good condition throughout.
£10,000–12,000 *LF*

The post-war MG sports car progressed through the TC range to the TD, which was built from 1950 to 1953. The TD derived its style from the TC, but with a more modern concept. It had a wider track and independent front suspension.

l. **1954 MG TF 1500 Open Sports,** 4 cylinders, 1466cc, left-hand drive, well maintained, very good condition. **Est. £12,000–14,000** *COYS*

The MG TF first appeared at the 1953 Motor Show and was the ideal successor to the TD. A more refined car than the TD, it featured a sloping bonnet line and radiator, headlights grafted into the wings, sharply raked tail and individual bucket seats to replace the previous bench type fitted to the TD.

r. **1956 MG TD Arnolt Two Door Cabriolet,** coachwork by Bertone, restored, excellent condition. **£19,000–24,000** *BKS*

This Arnolt cabriolet on the TD MkII chassis was first sold in Canada. Mechanically, the MG TD owed much to the Y-type saloon, using a narrowed and modified version of the latter's chassis, with a roomier body than before. The inevitable weight gain resulted in a performance inferior to the smaller and lighter TCs.

1968 MGB GT, 4 cylinders, 1798cc, twin SU carburettors, overdrive, front disc brakes. drums rear, wire wheels, red leather interior, excellent condition. **£7,000–8,000** *VIN*

1956 MGA Roadster Works Rally Two Seater, 1.5 litres, body-off restoration, right-hand drive, excellent condition. **£33,000–38,000** *BKS*

This car is one of only 5 works rally specification MGAs prepared at Abingdon in 1956.

1971 MG Midget MkIII, 4 cylinders, 1275cc, stainless steel exhaust, replaced hood, 26,000 miles recorded, very good original condition. **£3,500–4,000** *ADT*

The MkIII Midget had a top speed approaching the then magic 'ton', together with brisk acceleration and predictable road holding.

1965 MGB Roadster, chrome bumpers, wire wheels, restored, excellent condition. **£7,000–7,500** *PAL*

This is an early example of the popular Roadster. The original specification MGB cost £834.6s 3d when launched in 1962. Top speed was 105mph with 0–60mph in 12.2 seconds.

l. **1966 Austin Mini Cooper S,** 4 cylinders, 1275cc, 100bhp, restored, finished in correct works colours of red with white roof, excellent condition.
£35,000–40,000 *COYS*

The Mini Cooper S had many rally successes during the 1960s. In January 1966 the works Mini Cooper S caused a furore when all 3 cars entered in the RAC Rally finished an impressive 1st, 2nd and 3rd only to be disqualified on highly spurious grounds to the benefit of the French. The car that should have been 3rd was this example, driven by Paddy Hopkirk.

1928 Morgan Three Wheeler Aero, water-cooled, V twin JAP KT, 999cc side valve engine, 2 speed chain driven gearbox, 3 wheel drum brakes, independent front suspension, quarter-elliptic springs rear, right-hand drive, considerable amount of restoration, very good condition throughout.
£12,500–14,000 *C*

1936 Morgan 4/4 Series I, 1122cc, mechanically sound, resprayed, retrimmed, less than 10,000 miles recorded, excellent condition.
£17,000–20,000 *RUT*

1937 Morris 8 Two Seater Tourer, 8hp, totally restored, mechanically sound, concours condition.
£6,500–7,500 *SW*

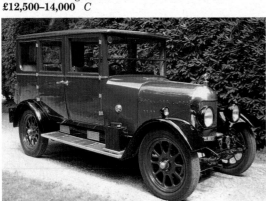

1925 Morris Oxford 14/28hp Bullnose Four Door Saloon, completely restored, finished in Claret livery with black wings and fabric roof, full history, excellent condition throughout.
£14,000–16,000 *S*

r. **1953 Morris Minor Four Door Saloon,** 803cc, split windscreen, 25,000 miles recorded, finished in black with red trim, immaculate throughout, bodywork totally original, interior in good original condition, 3 owners from new, full history.
£3,500–5,000 *H&H*

1928 Packard Model 533 Roadster,
6 cylinders, 288.6cu in, 81bhp at 3200rpm,
3 speed manual gearbox, 4 wheel drum
brakes, semi-elliptic leaf spring suspension,
left-hand drive, restored, very good condition.
£65,000–70,000 *C*

1939 Packard Twelve 1707 Convertible Victoria, V12,
473.31cu in, 175bhp at 3200rpm, 3 speed manual gearbox,
4 wheel drum brakes, semi-elliptic leaf spring suspension,
left-hand drive, excellent overall condition.
£55,000–65,000 *C*

l. **1958 Porsche 356A Cabriolet,**
4 cylinders, 1582cc, engine rebuilt,
bodywork refurbished, new hood,
right-hand drive, well maintained,
very good condition.
£12,000–15,000 *COYS*

*Porsche has always manufactured
rewarding cars, beautifully made
and totally individual, arguably the
modern equivalent to the pre-war
Bugatti. The 365A series was
considered by many to be the purest
and most attractive of the 356 family.
This car was acquired in 1967 for
just £250!*

r. **1963 Porsche 356B Coupé,**
1600cc, horizontally opposed flat
4 cylinder overhead valve engine,
air-cooled, rear-mounted, manual
gearbox, left-hand drive, coachwork
and interior in fair condition,
well maintained.
£5,000–7,000 *BKS*

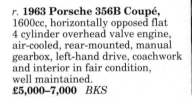

l. **1973 Porsche Carrera RS 2.7
Lightweight Coupé,** 6 cylinders,
2687cc, 2.7 litres, 210bhp, top speed
158mph, 0–60mph in 5 seconds,
rebuilt, very good condition.
£42,500–50,000 *COYS*

*This rare original Lightweight was
supplied to racing driver Peter Schetty,
who raced the car in several events
including the famous Nürburgring
1,000km race.*

1975 Porsche 911S Targa 2.7, 2700cc,
Carrera spoiler and rear arches, fully restored
including leather interior, good condition.
£7,000–9,000 *SC*

1989 Porsche 911 Turbo Coupé, 3.3 litres,
5 speed gearbox, leather trim, 41,000 miles
recorded, full service history, excellent condition.
£32,000–35,000 *PARA*

1949 Riley RMC 2½ Litre Roadster, 4 cylinders, 2443cc, restored, excellent condition throughout.
£17,000–20,000 *ADT*

Despite the fact that Riley had been acquired by the Nuffield Group in 1938, the post-war RM Series remained essentially the 'true Riley'. The third year of production saw the introduction of a drophead version of the 2½ litre, and a most attractive 2/3 seater Roadster.

1909 Rolls-Royce Silver Ghost Three-Quarter Landaulette, coachwork by Barker, 6 cylinders, 7428cc, side valves, 48bhp at 1000rpm, 3 speed manual gearbox, 2 wheel drum brakes, semi-elliptic leaf spring suspension, Westinghouse Air shock absorbers, right-hand drive, original interior and coachwork in good condition.
£200,000+ *C*

1923 Rolls-Royce 20hp Landaulette, coachwork by Hamshaw, 6 cylinders, 3127cc, finished in yellow with black trim, good condition.
£55,000–60,000 *COYS*

Introduced in 1922 and quickly named the 'Baby Rolls', the 20hp soon became popular. Production ceased in 1929 after a total of 2,940 20hp models had been manufactured.

1912 Rolls-Royce 40/50hp Silver Ghost London-Edinburgh Style Tourer, coachwork by Wilkinson, nickel chassis, 5 seater, Rudge-Whitworth wire wheels, finished in dove grey livery, blue hide interior, black duck hood, sound mechanical condition, CAV head and sidelights, running board, klaxon horn, stored for a number of years, good condition.
£160,000–200,000 *S*

1938 Rolls-Royce Wraith Limousine, coachwork by Park Ward, 6 cylinder in-line, 4257cc, 4 speed manual gearbox, servo-assisted brakes, independent enclosed coil spring front suspension, semi-elliptic rear, right-hand drive, older restoration, electric division, occasional tables, rear ashtrays, interior and woodwork in good condition.
£18,000–22,000 *C*

1938 Rolls-Royce Phantom III Six Light Limousine, coachwork by Hooper, 7.3 litre V12 engine, independent front suspension, offside spare wheel and shutters to bonnet, comprehensive restoration including engine rebuild, chrome renewed, roof panel replaced, finished in Vauxhall Royal Red, original interior, occasional seats fitted, original blinds and microphone, Lucas horns, full history.
£20,000–25,000 *S*

l. **1939 Rolls-Royce Phantom III Sports Sedanca De Ville,** coachwork by James Young, V12 overhead valve, 4 speed manual gearbox, 4 wheel drum brakes, semi-elliptic leaf spring suspension, right-hand drive, older restoration, finished in claret and black, good condition.
£30,000–35,000 *C*

JENSEN

Brothers Richard and Alan Jensen started out as coachbuilders before producing their own cars from 1936 onwards. The original Interceptor of 1950 to 1957 used an Austin 4 litre engine, which was also employed in the dramatic glass fibre-bodied 541 of 1954. From 1962, with the launch of the CV8, Jensen adopted Chrysler V8 power. With the 1967 Interceptor, Jensen mated the massive American V8 engine with elegant Italian coachwork to create a formidable high-performance GT with a ferocious thirst for fuel – 10mpg if you enjoyed yourself. After driving into two oil crises and a worldwide recession, as well as suffering serious losses with the Jensen-Healey project, the company closed its doors in 1976. Since then there have been several short-lived attempts to revive manufacturing.

1956 Jensen 541, fully restored, R-type bonnet fitted.
£9,500–10,500 *H&H*

1959 Jensen 541R, major overhaul and bare metal respray, very good condition.
£21,000–23,000 *H&H*

A very rare car, No. 118 of 193 built.

l. **1963 Jensen CV8 MkI,** fibreglass body in sound condition, paintwork good.
£7,500–8,000 *BRIT*

The CV8 replaced the 541S in 1962. Built on an entirely new chassis and powered by a Chrysler V8 engine, this new sports saloon had front end styling which was especially distinctive, if somewhat controversial. The car was particularly well equipped and specification included a Salisbury Powr-Lok differential, reclining front seats and radio. Performance was sensational with a top speed of approximately 140mph. This vehicle was the 4th of 68 CV8s built and it is believed to be the oldest surviving MkI.

1968 Jensen Interceptor 6.3 Litre MkI, automatic transmission, power-assisted steering, electric windows, 2 owners from new, 13,500 miles recorded, unrestored, correct toolkit and Jensen first-aid pack.
£18,500–20,000 *BKS*

The Touring of Milan-inspired Jensen Interceptor was one of the classic shapes of the late 1960s luxury performance car market. It offered 140mph, combined with up-to-the-minute styling, competing with Aston Martin and their new DBS. Unlike the V8 Aston Martin, the Jensen relied on a tried and tested combination of Chrysler engine and automatic transmission. Test figures of 0–60mph in 7.3 seconds and 0–100mph in 19 seconds made these cars among the fastest Jensens built.

JENSEN Model	ENGINE cc/cyl	DATES	CONDITION 1	2	3
541/541R/541S	3993/6	1954-63	£13,000	£7,000	£4,500
CV8 Mk I-III	5916/				
	6276/8	1962-66	£14,000	£7,000	£6,000
Interceptor SI-SIII	6276/8	1967-76	£11,000	£8,000	£6,000
Interceptor DHC	6276/8	1973-76	£23,000	£13,000	£10,000
Interceptor SP	7212/8	1971-76	£11,000	£9,000	£7,000
FF	6766/8	1967-71	£14,000	£11,000	£9,000
Healey	1973/4	1972-76	£5,000	£3,000	£1,500
Healey GT	1973/4	1975-76	£6,000	£3,000	£2,000

1969 Jensen Interceptor MkI, good condition.
£6,000–7,000 *PAL*

1973 Jensen Interceptor, 7 litres, 8 cylinders,
3 speed automatic transmission.
£5,000–6,000 *H&H*

1974 Jensen Interceptor, concours condition.
£23,000–25,000 *BLE*

1969 Jensen Interceptor, 8 cylinders,
6276cc, carefully maintained, original handbook.
£5,000–5,750 *ADT*

1972 Jensen Interceptor III, 8 cylinders, 7212cc,
engine good condition but requires slight attention,
sills replaced and resprayed.
£4,500–5,000 *ADT*

*Alan and Richard Jensen commenced their activities
by re-bodying an Austin 7 with attractive sporting
coachwork. They offered varying styles of coachwork
on a number of popular makes and by 1936 a car
bearing the name of Jensen appeared, using a
modified version of the Ford V8 engine. Austin 4 litre
engines and later Chrysler V8 units were also adopted.*

l. **1976 Jensen
Interceptor Convertible,**
new hydraulic and electric
black mohair hood,
air conditioning,
70,000 miles recorded,
complete history.
£20,000–23,000 *H&H*

*Jensen produced very few
of these Interceptors and
this is the last right-hand
drive 7212cc convertible
ever made.*

JOWETT

After experimenting with flat twin-engined cars from 1906, Benjamin and William Jowett started production in 1913. A flat 4 joined the line-up in 1936, but Jowett's most distinguished cars came after the WWII in the shape of the advanced and innovative Javelin saloon and Jupiter roadster, both powered by the 1486cc flat 4. The Yorkshire company finally disappeared in 1954.

1928 Jowett 7 Two Seater with Dickey, dry stored, engine turns freely, bodywork sound, requires restoration.
£3,000–3,500 *S*

1948 Jowett Javelin, 4 cylinders, 1486cc, fully restored throughout.
£4,000–5,000 *ADT*

The Javelin saloon was introduced in 1946 and is regarded today as a true milestone in original car design. Certainly, performance stands comparison with many 1½ litre cars 30 years its junior and indeed, the Javelin was the best performing 1½ litre saloon of its day. The 4 cylinder horizontally-opposed engine gave a top speed in excess of 80mph, with fuel consumption of 32mpg.

1953 Jowett Jupiter MkIA, 8 cylinders, 1485cc, fully restored throughout.
£10,750–12,000 *BRIT*

The Jupiter roadster utilised a tubular space frame and the mechanics from the Javelin saloon. A memorable feature of this model was the one piece lift-up bonnet/wing assembly which gave easy access to the engine. The Jupiter ran from 1950–54, with a production run of approximately 900 cars.

LAGONDA

1937 Lagonda LG45 Drophead Coupé, 6 cylinders, 4453cc, Sanction III engine, side change gearbox, requires restoration.
£30,000–33,000 *COYS*

The original firm of Lagonda Ltd was replaced in 1935 by LG Motors, a new company with Alan Good as Chairman and W. O. Bentley as technical director and designer. There were 2 immediate tasks – to get the M45 model back into production and to build the best car in the world. Only 2 years were to be allowed for the latter exercise, and the result was the great 12 cylinder car. The M45 received some cosmetic treatment and was then replaced by the LG45.

1936 Lagonda Rapier Four Seater Drophead Coupé.
£15,000–16,000 *AS*

LAGONDA Model	ENGINE cc/cyl	DATES	CONDITION 1	2	3
12/24	1421/4	1923-26	£14,000	£10,000	£8,000
2 litre	1954/4	1928-32	£28,000	£25,000	£19,000
3 litre	2931/6	1928-34	£35,000	£30,000	£22,000
Rapier	1104/4	1934-35	£13,000	£6,500	£5,000
M45	4429/6	1934-36	£40,000	£30,000	£20,000
LG45	4429/6	1936-37	£45,000	£32,000	£22,000
LG6	4453/6	1937-39	£40,000	£28,000	£20,000
V12	4480/V12	1937-39	£75,000+	£50,000	£40,000

Prices are very dependent upon body type, originality and competition history.

l. **1938 Lagonda LG6,** 6 cylinder, in-line, overhead valves, 4453cc engine, 4 speed manual gearbox, 4 wheel drum brakes, independent front suspension with coil springs, live rear axle with semi-elliptic leaf springs, right-hand drive, some restoration work carried out, bodywork modified to open tourer, further work required.
£12,500–14,000 *C*

1953 Lagonda Two Door Drophead Coupé, up-rated 3 litre engine, engine rebuilt, rewired, well maintained.
£18,000–20,000 *BKS*

The David Brown takeover of Lagonda in 1947 allowed production of W. O. Bentley-designed, all-new model to commence the following year, and at the same time made Lagonda's 2.6 litre twin-cam 6 available for the new Aston-Martins. An advanced design employing a cruciform-braced chassis with independent suspension all-round, the Lagonda was available in saloon and coupé versions, both with coachbuilt bodies. The interior with its leather upholstery, plentiful walnut and quality fittings stood comparison with the very best of the luxury car class. This first pre-production model was used by David Brown himself.

1964 Lagonda 4 Litre Rapide, 6 cylinder overhead camshaft, automatic transmission, stored for many years, good condition.
£8,000–8,950 *DB*

There were only 54 cars of this type built.

LAGONDA (post-war) Model	ENGINE cc/cyl	DATES	CONDITION 1	2	3
3 litre	2922/6	1953-58	£10,500	£7,000	£4,500
3 litre DHC	2922/6	1953-56	£15,000	£11,000	£9,000
Rapide	3995/6	1961-64	£11,000	£7,000	£4,500

LAMBORGHINI

Ferrucio Lamborghini's fortune, made from tractors and air-conditioning, fuelled his ambition to out-Ferrari Ferrari. The charging bull insignia was taken from his star sign, Taurus the bull. Undoubtedly the company's most stunning 1960s creation was the impossibly beautiful 175mph Miura, named after a Spanish fighting bull. In the 1970s the Countach once again stunned the motoring world into slack-jawed amazement.

1971 Lamborghini Miura SV, coachwork by Carrozzeria Bertone, resprayed in original yellow, new starter motor and tyres, 57,700km recorded.
£110,000–120,000 *BKS*

The original Miura boasted 350bhp, a top speed of over 170mph (281km/h) and an actual 0–60mph in 6.5 seconds, delivering shattering performance and drop-dead looks in a single package. Mid-1969 saw the arrival of the Miura S, followed by the swansong Miura SV, 2 years later. Each development reflected gradual improvements to the engineering as well as stylistic changes, and the SV incorporated numerous modifications to make it the most powerful and best handling Miura. Sadly production ended in 1972, by which time just 150 of these fabulous supercars had been built. It is not surprising that today they are highly sought-after collectors items.

1969–70 Lamborghini Jarama 400 GT Sport Two Door Coupé, coachwork by Carrozzeria Bertone, experimental one-off modified version of the Jarama, lightweight panels, Perspex windows, completely rebuilt.
£31,000–36,000 *BKS*

The Jarama model itself was first introduced at the Geneva Salon of 1969 as a replacement for the Islero, and the lines of the front-engined new car were penned by Marcello Gandini of the Bertone styling house – later to become famous as creator of the amazing Countach. Early version Jaramas used the 3929cc, 4 cam V12 engine, delivering around 350bhp at 7500rpm to provide a top speed of around 160mph. This 'Bob Wallace Special', christened after the company's senior development engineer and test driver, is claimed to develop closer to 400bhp, and is the only remaining Lamborghini built in their short-lived competition shop by Bob Wallace.

1971 Lamborghini Miura SVJ, coachwork by Carrozzeria Bertone, modified to incorporate brake vents behind front and rear wheels, upright fixed headlights behind Plexiglass covers, racing type fuel filler cap, front oil cooler, chin spoiler, altered suspension settings, single pantograph windscreen wiper, bonnet and door slates removed, straight-through exhaust, seldom used, recorded mileage of 3,035km, original road tyres.
£300,000+ *BKS*

Formerly the property of His Imperial Highness the late Shah of Iran who 'wanted something special and was willing to pay for it'. The car was delivered complete with special Pirelli studded snow tyres to the Shah in St Moritz in December 1971. Subsequently 3 further cars were similarly modified and upgraded. These 4 cars are considered by aficionados to be the only true SVJs.

LAMBORGHINI Model	ENGINE cc/cyl	DATES	CONDITION 1	2	3
350 GT fhc	3500/12	1964-67	£80,000	£50,000	£30,000
400 GT	4000/12	1966-68	£60,000	£50,000	£30,000
Miura LP400	4000/12	1966-69	£60,000	£50,000	£30,000
Miura S	4000/12	1969-71	£80,000+	£60,000+	£40,000
Espada	4000/12	1969-78	£18,000	£14,000	£10,000
Jarama	4000/12	1970-78	£22,000	£15,000	£13,000
Urraco	2500/8	1972-76	£18,000	£11,000	£8,000
Countach	4000/12	1974-82	£60,000+	£40,000	£30,000

Countach limited editions are sought-after.

LANCHESTER

1929 Lanchester 30hp Straight Eight Model Southport Weymann Saloon, completely restored, full history.
£26,000–28,000 *BKS*

Fred, George and Frank Lanchester were 19thC pioneers of the development of the British motor car industry. Creative and original thinkers, their early models were noted for their wick carburettors, leaf valve springs, tiller steering and unsurpassed cantilever suspension.

The luxury 40hp model announced in 1919 featured a single overhead camshaft engine undoubtedly influenced by aero-engine design. In 1921 a Lanchester, driven by S. F. Edge, was to lap the Brooklands Circuit at 100mph.

Eager to maintain a prominent position in the luxury car market in the difficult times at the end of the 1920s, Lanchester developed the 30hp model, essentially the existing 6 cylinder engined 21hp car with 2 extra cylinders. The road test reporter for Automotor Journal *wrote: 'I have never sat behind a silkier, stealthier motor, and the rest of the car is pure, unadulterated and therefore impeccable Lanchester'. It is believed that only 126 examples of the 30hp were built and this is one of just 2 Southports known to survive.*

LANCHESTER Model	ENGINE cc/cyl	DATES	CONDITION		
			1	2	3
LD10	1287/4	1946-49	£2,500	£1,500	£750
LD10 (Barker bodies)	1287/4	1950-51	£2,800	£1,500	£700

LANCIA

From its foundation in 1906, Vincenzo Lancia's company produced cars that soon earned a reputation for inspired innovation and technical excellence, often married to stunning shapes. The Lambda of 1922 was tremendously advanced, with a monocoque structure, independent front suspension and a compact narrow V4 engine with overhead camshaft. At the lower end of the market, the Aprilia of the late 1930s was a little jewel. In the 1950s Lancia made some able and beautiful machines but could never offer a line-up that was comprehensive enough to compete with Alfa Romeo or Fiat. In 1969, mounting debts forced a sell-out to Fiat.

l. **1924 Lancia Lambda Torpedo Tourer,** V4 overhead camshaft engine, 2120cc, 49bhp at 3250rpm, 3 speed manual gearbox, 4 wheel drum brakes, independent front suspension, semi-elliptic rear suspension, right-hand drive, disc wheels, dual windscreen, all instrumentation appears original and correct.
£16,500–18,000 *C*

When announced in 1922, the Lancia Lambda was without doubt the most advanced motor car design of its day. It incorporated design features which are still modern, including a rigid monocoque hull structure instead of a conventional flexible chassis frame, independent front suspension and a compact narrow V engine with aluminium cylinder block and single overhead camshaft. The excellent ride, handling characteristics and performance, together with very high manufacturing quality, ensured the success of the Lambda during its 9 year production run.

LANCIA Model	ENGINE cc/cyl	DATES	CONDITION		
			1	2	3
Theta	4940/4	1913-19	£24,000	£16,500	£8,000
Kappa	4940/4	1919-22	£24,000	£16,000	£8,000
Dikappa	4940/4	1921-22	£24,000	£16,000	£8,000
Trikappa	4590/4	1922-26	£25,000	£18,000	£10,000
Lambda	2120/4	1923-28	£40,000	£20,000	£12,000
Dilambda	3960/8	1928-32	£35,000	£16,000	£10,000
Astura	2604/8	1931-39	£30,000	£20,000	£10,000
Artena	1925/4	1931-36	£9,000	£5,000	£2,000
Augusta	1196/4	1933-36	£9,000	£4,000	£2,000
Aprilia 238	1352/4	1937-39	£10,000	£5,000	£3,000

1935 Lancia Augusta, V4, 4 cylinder, 1194cc engine, staggered cylinders, single overhead camshaft, 35bhp at 4000rpm, pillarless saloon coachwork, bare metal respray, engine, gearbox, suspension and rear axle in good condition, original grey cord interior.
£4,500–6,000 *ADT*

1934 Lancia Dilambda Four Door Saloon, coachwork by H. J. Mulliner, restored, SU electric fuel pumps fitted, low mileage, used only occasionally, requires tuning.
£20,000–23,000 *BKS*

Designed with the lucrative American market in mind, Lancia's Dilambda, with its 24° V8, 3960cc engine developed some 100bhp, giving the Dilambda a top speed of around 75mph.

1951 Lancia Aurelia Coupé, coachwork by Vignale, 6 cylinders, 1754cc, completely restored, limited use since.
£18,000–20,000 *COYS*

The Lancia Aurelia was designed by Vittorio Jano who was responsible for all the great Alfa Romeos including the Monza and the P3. Year after year Jano produced classics for Alfa Romeo but that did not protect him when, in late 1937, company and national politics caused him to be dismissed. Alfa Romeo's loss was Lancia's gain and when the Aurelia was introduced in 1949 it was the most advanced production car in the world – by a considerable margin.

1951 Lancia 2 Litre First Series Aurelia Coupé, restored, rebuilt engine, transmission, brakes and suspension, body stripped and resprayed, retrimmed, 2 Ferrari type large Veglia instruments, floor gear change, Nardi wood-rimmed wheels, original features including aluminium bumpers, Lancia radiator badge.
£29,000–33,000 *BKS*

LANCIA Model	ENGINE cc/cyl	DATES	CONDITION 1	2	3
Aprilia 438	1486/4	1939-50	£11,000	£6,000	£3,000
Ardea	903/4	1939-53	£10,000	£5,000	£3,000
Aurelia B10	1754/6	1950-53	£9,000	£6,000	£3,000
Aurelia B15-20-22	1991/6	1951-53	£11,000	£7,000	£3,500
Aurelia B24-B24S	2451/6	1955-58	£35,000	£17,000	£12,000
Aurelia GT	2451/6	1953-59	£16,000	£11,000	£9,000
Appia C10-C105	1090/4	1953-62	£6,000	£3,000	£2,000
Aurelia Ser II	2266/6	1954-59	£11,000	£6,000	£4,000
Flaminia Zagato	2458/6	1957-63	£18,000	£10,000	£7,000
Flaminia Ser	2458/6	1957-63	£15,000	£10,000	£5,000
Flavia 1500	1500/4	1960-75	£6,000	£4,000	£2,000
Fulvia	1091/4	1963-70	£3,000	£2,000	£1,000
Fulvia S	1216/4	1964-70	£5,000	£3,000	£1,500
Fulvia 1.3	1298/4	1967-75	£6,000	£4,000	£2,000
Stratos	2418/6	1969-71	£45,000	£20,000	£10,000
Flavia 2000	1991/4	1969-75	£3,000	£2,000	£1,000
Fulvia HF/1.6	1584/4	1969-75	£7,000	£3,000	£2,000
Beta HPE	1585/4	1976-82	£3,000	£1,500	£500
Beta Spyder	1995/4	1977-82	£4,000	£1,500	£800
Monte Carlo	1995/4	1976-81	£6,000	£3,000	£1,000
Gamma Coupé	2484/4	1977-84	£2,500	£1,500	£500
Gamma Berlina	2484/4	1977-84	£2,000	£1,000	£300

Competition history and convertible coachwork could cause prices to vary.

1958 Lancia Aurelia B20 6th Series Two Door Coupé, V6, 2451cc engine, 118bhp at 5000rpm, top speed of 115mph, 2 owners from new, restored, excellent condition.
£28,000–32,000 *BKS*

A year after launching its revolutionary V6 engined Aurelia saloon in 1950, Lancia followed with the Pininfarina-styled B20 coupé, a shorter wheelbase fastback 2+2 GT. With its combination of sportscar performance and saloon car practicality, it can be said to have introduced the Grand Turismo concept to the world.

1960 Lancia Flaminia 2.5 GT Coupé, coachwork by Touring of Milan, V6 engine with twin choke carburettor, completely restored, new tyres, black leather interior trim and carpets.
£13,000–15,000 *BKS*

The first new model to be introduced after the wealthy enthusiast Carlo Pesenti acquired Lancia from Gianni Lancia. The launch gave the opportunity for the renewal of the association between Lancia and Carrozzeria Touring. The first Flaminia GT coupé appeared in 1959, followed a year later by a convertible.

r. **1960 Lancia Flaminia Coupé,** coachwork by Pininfarina, 60° V6 engine, 2458cc, left-hand drive, one owner, repainted, excellent condition.
£3,750–5,000 *ADT*

l. **1962 Lancia Flaminia Two Door Convertible,** coachwork by Touring, V6 overhead valve engine, 2458cc, manual transmission, 3 carburettors producing 140bhp, left-hand drive, totally restored.
£22,500–25,000 *BKS*

1964 Lancia Flavia Sports Coupé, by Zagato, 4 cylinders, 1800cc, electric windows, new shock absorbers, clutch and overhauled brakes, new sills, resprayed, good working order.
£7,000–9,000 *COYS*

In 1960 Lancia introduced the Flavia with many advanced features, notably a flat 4 engine, front-wheel drive and all wheel disc brakes. The 1500cc engined saloon proved a popular choice on the domestic market, even before the introduction of an 1800cc engine, with consequent increased performance. An even greater performance increase was made when the Sport version was introduced.

1975 Lancia Fulvia S3 Sports Coupé, restored, bodywork, engine and transmission all in good condition.
£2,150–2,650 *S*

The specification included a narrow V formation 4 cylinder engine of 1298cc, 5 speed transmission and disc brakes all-round. The car was no mean performer and achieved a top speed of over 100mph with acceleration to match.

1977 Lancia Monte Carlo, interior recently retrimmed, instrumentation all in working order, new Firestone tyres, twin headlight conversion, rear spoiler, primoflow exhaust system, new suspension.
£2,750–3,250 *PA*

1980 Lancia Beta Spyder, 4 cylinders, 1995cc, interior trimmed in black leather, 28,000 miles recorded, good original condition.
£2,500–3,500 *ADT*

1985 Lancia Gamma Coupé, less than 34,000 miles recorded, resprayed to correct specification, good condition throughout.
£2,750–3,250 *BRIT*

LAND ROVER

Undoubtedly inspired by the success of the American Jeep, the Wilkes brothers at Rover decided soon after WWII that there was a demand for a rugged utility vehicle and thus the Land Rover was born. Described by *The Autocar* as a 'mobile power station', few British vehicles have achieved the outstanding export record of the Land Rover, and fewer still can claim the record of continuous production in 6 decades. Designed initially for agricultural use, the vehicle was quickly adopted for military service and has proved equally at home on the battlefield, drawing a trailer at the cattle market or arriving for cocktails before the hunt ball. The Land Rover's importance to Rover's balance sheet can be seen by the production figures for 1955, where cars accounted for 13,436 units while 28,882 Land Rovers rolled off the production line.

1955 Land Rover Series S Short Wheelbase, original specification, finished in traditional green livery.
£1,200–1,500 *BKS*

LAND ROVER Model	ENGINE cc/cyl	DATES	CONDITION 1	2	3
Ser 1	1595/4	1948-51	£6,000	£3,000	£1,500
Ser 1	1995/4	1951-53	£4,500	£2,500	£1,000
Ser 1	1995/4	1953-58	£4,000	£2,000	£500
Ser 1	1995/4	1953-58	£3,000	£1,800	£800
Ser 2	1995/4	1958-59	£2,000	£950	£500
Ser 2	1995/4	1958-59	£2,800	£1,200	£500
Ser 2	2286/4	1959-71	£2,000	£950	£500
Ser 2	2286/4	1959-71	£2,500	£1,200	£500
Range Rover	3528/V8	1970-	£5,000	£1,200	£600

Series 1 Land Rovers are now very sought after.

LEA-FRANCIS

1928 Lea-Francis P Type Two Seater Sports with Dickey, recently refurbished, good condition.
£12,000–13,000 *AS*

1949/50 Lea Francis Monaco Shooting Brake, completely restored, including treating and replacing woodwork, new carpets and trim, instruments re-calibrated, engine, gearbox and transmission overhauled, electrical equipment and HMV radio renewed, 60,000 miles recorded, full history.
£15,000–17,000 *S*

The Shooting Brake was requisitioned in 1991 by the BBC for Strath Blair, *a drama series filmed in the Scottish Highlands.*

l. **1928 Lea-Francis Weymann Sports Saloon.**
£11,000–12,000 *FHF*

LEA-FRANCIS Model	ENGINE cc/cyl	DATES	CONDITION 1	2	3
12HP	1944/4	1923-24	£10,000	£5,000	£3,000
14HP	2297/4	1923-24	£10,000	£5,000	£3,000
9HP	1074/4	1923-24	£7,000	£4,000	£2,000
10HP	1247/4	1947-54	£10,000	£5,500	£3,000
12HP	1496/4	1926-34	£11,000	£6,000	£4,000
Various 6 cylinder models	1696/6	1927-29	£13,500	£9,500	£5,000
Various 6 cylinder models	1991/6	1928-36	£10,500	£8,750	£5,000
14HP	1767/4	1946-54	£6,000	£4,000	£2,000
1.5 litre	1499/4	1949-51	£10,000	£5,000	£2,500
2.5 litre	2496/4	1950-52	£13,000	£8,000	£4,000

LINCOLN

1933 Lincoln KB Convertible Sedan,
V12 overhead valve engine, 448cu in,
150bhp at 3400rpm, 3 speed manual gearbox,
4 wheel drum brakes, semi-elliptic leaf spring
suspension, left-hand drive, restored.
£135,000–150,000 *C*

*In late 1931 Lincoln announced that it would be
introducing a V12 designated the KB, to compete
with the high standards set by Duesenberg, Cadillac
and Marmon. At the direction of Edsel Ford,
Lincoln's chief engineer Frank Johnson came up
with one of the greatest powerplants of the classic
era. The KB's impressive 448cu in (7.2 litre) engine
developed a conservative 150bhp at 3400rpm with
a peak torque of 292lbs/ft at 1200rpm.*

1946 Lincoln Continental Two Door Coupé,
5 litre side valve engine, 130bhp, 3 speed manual
gearbox with overdrive, left-hand drive, partially
restored, rebuilt engine, bare metal respray,
brightwork re-chromed, new electrics and
overhauled brakes, excellent condition.
£6,750–8,000 *BKS*

*Just 466 Lincoln Continentals were produced by
the end of 1946. Of the total built, 201 were
Convertibles and 265 Club Coupés.*

l. **1933 Lincoln KB Brunn
Semi-Collapsible Cabriolet,**
restored, excellent condition.
£150,000–170,000 *BLK*

*One of 8 Brunn Semi-Collapsible
Cabriolets built in 1933. This
stunning town car was originally
owned by Bishop Hickey of New
York. The car's original colour
was green, but the Bishop had
it painted cardinal maroon and
fanfare red. A beautiful restoration
that resulted in a National
CCCA Senior 1st place at the
1990 Florida annual meeting.*

LINCOLN Model	ENGINE cu in/cyl	DATES	CONDITION 1	2	3
Première Coupé	368/8	1956-57	£6,000	£4,000	£2,000
Première Convertible	368/8	1956-57	£14,000	£8,000	£5,000
Continental Mk II	368/8	1956-57	£10,000	£6,000	£4,000
Continental 2 door	430/8	1958-60	£6,000	£4,000	£2,000
Continental Convertible	430/8	1958-60	£18,000	£10,000	£7,000

LINON

The Linon Company, founded in
1897, made a number of cars to a
Gauthier-Wehrlé design prior to
building their own belt-driven
voiturette, using a 3hp De Dion
engine, at Ensival-Verviers in 1900.
   By 1902 the Belgian concern was
selling voiturettes fitted with 3.5,
4.5 and 6hp De Dion engines,
alongside larger models driven by
8, 10 and 16hp Linon engines.
Fafnir, Fondu, Ballot and Vautour
also supplied engines to Ateliers
Linon, and in the years up to 1914
models from 9 to 40hp capacity
were available. The firm, one of the
earliest of Belgian manufacturers,
did not survive beyond WWII.

r. **1901 Linon 4½hp Vis-à-Vis,**
single cylinder overhead valve,
4½hp belt-driven De Dion
engine, original condition.
£25,000–28,000 *S*

LOTUS

From the humblest beginnings – an Austin 7-based trials special created in a north London lock-up – Colin Chapman's Lotus has collected a remarkable motor-racing trophy cabinet and produced a string of road cars that at their very least were always innovative and sometimes quite brilliant. The Lotus Super 7 lives on today as the Caterham.

1956 Lotus MkVI Two Seater Sports, coachwork by Williams & Pritchard, 1172cc Ford engine, fitted with Elva overhead valve conversion, twin SU carburettors, right-hand drive, fully restored, 100 recorded miles since restoration.
£16,000–18,000 *BKS*

Available surviving records would appear to indicate that this was the 17th Lotus manufactured. The MkVI was the first production Lotus, and featured a multi-tube frame weighing just 55lbs.

Lotus Elite

The Elite – the ultimate marque landmark – was the first Lotus designed for road use rather than out-and-out racing, paving the way for a string of stunning sports and GT cars that, at the least, were always innovative. But the first Elite was much more than that. Its all glass fibre construction – chassis as well as body – was a bold departure which, coupled with many other innovations, marked the Elite as truly exceptional, and all the more so considering the small scale operation that created it. What's more, its built-in Lotus race-breeding gave it phenomenal handling and this, together with an unparalleled power-to-weight ratio, brought an almost unbroken run of racing successes. It also happens to be one of the prettiest cars of its era – in short, a superb GT in miniature.

1960 Lotus Elite 1.3 Litre Two Door Competition Coupé, recently restored with new paintwork, new electrics and fittings, interior in excellent condition.
£29,000–33,000 *BKS*

Colin Chapman's lovely Lotus Elite was created in 1956 as the world's first moulded glass fibre monocoque GT car. This particular example started as a 1960 Team Lotus entry in the Le Mans 24 hour race due to be driven by Sir John Whitmore, it was taken over pre-race by Sir Gawaine Baillie/Michael Parkes and their race ended in retirement.

It was later cannibalised for parts before being restored and sold, more extensive restoration was recently required.

Lotus Elite

Model: Lotus Elite, 1957–63.
Production: 988.
Body Style: 2 door 2 seater Sports Coupé.
Construction: Glass fibre monocoque.
Engine: 4 cylinder single overhead camshaft Coventry Climax, 1216cc.
Power Output: 75–105bhp at 6100–6800rpm.
Transmission: 4 speed MG or ZF gearbox.
Suspension: Independent all-round by wishbones and coil springs at front and MacPherson-type 'Chapman strut' at rear.
Maximum Speed: 118mph.
0–60mph: 11.1 seconds.
Average Fuel Consumption: 35mpg.

1962 Lotus Elite Super 95, 1216cc, 4 speed gearbox, 0–60mph in 7.9 seconds with a top speed of around 125mph, totally stripped and restored to race standard, excellent condition.
£25,000–28,000 *H&H*

A rare Super 95 model of which only approximately 25 were built.

1968 Lotus Elan+2, superb restoration.
£8,750–9,750 *MATT*

1970 Lotus Europa, 1565cc, bodywork and trim in good condition, alloy wheels, electric windows.
£2,800–3,400 *H&H*

l. **1971 Lotus Elan Sprint Fixed Head Coupé,** rebuilt mechanically, good condition.
£18,500–19,750 *MATT*

A lot of Fixed Head Coupés have now been converted to Drop Head Coupés.

1972 Lotus Elan Sprint Fixed Head Coupé, 1558cc, engine and steering rack rebuilt, resprayed, rebuilt gearbox and suspension, replacement fuel tank, fuel lines, dynamo and starter motor, front discs, callipers and brake pipes, new larger higher capacity radiator, good condition.
£7,500–8,000 *H&H*

1973 Lotus Europa JPS Special, 1558cc, good condition.
£12,000–13,500 *MATT*

Rare in the UK, most examples have been exported to Japan.

LOTUS Model	ENGINE cc/cyl	DATES	CONDITION 1	2	3
Six		1953-56	£13,000	£7,000	£5,000
Seven S1 Sports	1172/4	1957-64	£12,000	£9,000	£5,000
Seven S2 Sports	1498/4	1961-66	£10,000	£8,000	£5,000
Seven S3 Sports	1558/4	1961-66	£10,000	£8,000	£5,000
Seven S4	1598/4	1969-72	£7,000	£5,000	£2,500
Elan S1 Convertible	1558/4	1962-64	£12,000+	£8,000	£4,500
Elan S2 Convertible	1558/4	1964-66	£11,000+	£7,000	£4,000
Elan S3 Convertible	1558/4	1966-69	£12,000+	£8,000	£5,000
Elan S3 FHC	1558/4	1966-69	£11,000	£6,000	£4,000
Elan S4 Convertible	1558/4	1968-71	£11,000+	£9,000	£6,000
Elan S4 FHC	1558/4	1968-71	£10,000	£7,500	£5,000
Elan Sprint Convertible	1558/4	1971-73	£12,000+	£8,000	£6,000
Elan Sprint FHC	1558/4	1971-73	£10,000	£7,000	£5,000
Europa S1 FHC	1470/4	1966-69	£4,000	£3,500	£2,000
Europa S2 FHC	1470/4	1969-71	£5,500	£3,000	£2,000
Europa Twin Cam	1558/4	1971-75	£8,000	£6,000	£4,000
Elan +2S 130	1558/4	1971-74	£8,000	£5,000	£4,000
Elite S1 FHC	1261/4	1974-80	£3,000	£2,500	£1,500
Eclat S1	1973/4	1975-82	£3,500	£3,000	£1,500
Esprit 1	1973/4	1977-81	£6,500	£5,000	£3,000
Esprit 2	1973/4	1976-81	£7,000	£4,000	£2,500
Esprit S2.2	2174/4	1980-81	£7,000	£5,500	£3,000
Esprit Turbo	2174/4	1980-90	£9,000	£7,000	£4,000
Excel	2174/4	1983-85	£5,000	£2,500	£1,800

Prices vary with some limited edition Lotus models.

1973 Lotus Elan Sprint, good condition, recently serviced, used daily.
£9,000–10,000 *COYS*

MARCOS

1970 Marcos 3 Litre Two Door Sports Coupé, V6 Ford engine, 2997cc, manual transmission, right-hand drive, rebuilt to include a reconditioned engine, 5,000 miles since, bodywork and interior in good condition.
£6,500–7,500 *BKS*

MARMON

The first Marmon was built and tested in 1902 by Howard C. Marmon, a master engineer. They were advanced cars in their period and in these early days featured air-cooled V4 engines with mechanically-operated overhead valves and pressure lubrication. Marmons did well in competition, achieving 54 first places between 1909 and 1912, Harroun winning the first ever Indianapolis 500 in 1911 with a specially built 6 cylinder car named 'The Wasp'. Production continued into the 1920s, with 6 cylinder overhead valve models featuring coil ignition and front wheel brakes after 1923.

In 1927 the first straight 8 engine model was introduced, with the option of a cheaper side valve engine or a higher performance overhead valve unit. This overhead valve engine had a capacity of 3.1 litres and was available with a number of body styles, from a 4 door saloon to an open 5 seater tourer. The 1930 model featured an increased engine capacity of 3300cc.

r. **1930 Marmon,**
8 cylinders, 3300cc,
3 speed manual gearbox,
4 wheel drum brakes,
left-hand drive, finished
in red with black wings
and brown leather interior,
older restoration, dry
stored in recent years,
requires re-commissioning.
£7,500–9,000 *C*

MASERATI

Founded by five brothers, Maserati's racing cars enjoyed an awesome reputation from the 1930s through to the 1950s. A string of world-beating racers were driven by some of the all-time greats including Stirling Moss, Juan Manuel Fangio and Mike Hawthorn. In the late 1950s the company withdrew from competition and concentrated on producing stunning luxury GT and sports cars, yet always struggled to keep abreast of Ferrari. Many reckon the peak of Maserati's art is represented by the gorgeous Ghibli, penned by Giorgetto Giugiaro at Ghia, a car that really tilted at Ferrari's Daytona. Despite producing sensational machines the company struggled to make money. In 1969 Citroën stepped in with finance and when Citroën pulled out in 1975 Alejandro de Tomaso stepped into the rescue. The famous Maserati trident is the symbol of the city of Bologna where the brothers started production.

1956 Maserati A6G/2000 2 Litre Berlinetta, coachwork by Carrozzeria Zagato, 6 cylinder twin overhead camshaft, extensively restored and rebuilt, good condition.
£165,000+ *BKS*

This attractive Maserati was first owned by enthusiastic competitor Eugenio Lubich in April 1956.
Total production of the A6G/2000 appears to have run to 56, amongst which only 20 carried Zagato's muscular bodyshape.

l. **1956 Maserati A6G/2000 Coupé,** partially dismantled, 6 cylinders in-line, twin overhead camshaft, 3 twin-choke Weber carburettors, 150bhp at 6000rpm, left-hand drive, requires restoration.
£14,000–17,000 *BKS*

1960 Maserati 3500GT, 6 cylinder, twin overhead camshafts, good condition.
£14,000–15,000 *DB*

1962 Maserati 3500GT Coupé, 3500cc, left-hand drive, Borrani wire wheels, imported to UK from Monte Carlo, good condition throughout.
£14,000–17,000   *H&H*

1965 Maserati Sebring MkII, 3700cc, all bodywork, chassis, engine and interior restored, right-hand drive, original Borrani wire wheels and Lucas injection system.
£10,000–14,000   *H&H*

This is one of only 6 right-hand drive examples made and was the most expensive car of its time.

l. **1960 Maserati 3500GT Two Door Vignale Spyder,** restored, well maintained.
£29,000–33,000   *BKS*

Two Maserati 3500 Spyder Vignale cars were produced in 1959, followed by 88 more in 1960. The Spyder had a 4in shorter wheelbase than the closed 3500s which greatly improved their handling and produced a better balanced and more agile car. In 1961, 49 of these Spyders left the Maserati factory in Modena, and thereafter production declined to just 5 cars in 1964 as the series reached closure. This example is thought to be one of just 6 long bonnet models built.

1966 Maserati 3700 GTI Sebring Series II Coupé, coachwork by Vignale, completely renovated, optional carburettors fitted, original twin exhausts, very good condition, unused since restoration.
£31,000–35,000   *BKS*

Maserati's first production road car, the 3500GT, made its debut at the 1957 Geneva Salon. The twin camshaft 6 cylinder engine was derived from the 350S sports racer and, via triple Weber carburettors and twin ignition it produced a healthy 240bhp, enough to power the 3500GT to 144mph and 0–60mph in under 8 seconds.

In 1960 front disc brakes were introduced, rear discs being added in 1962, the same year that Lucas fuel injection became an option, and the model was renamed the 3500GTi – the first ever to use such a suffix. The final evolution, the Series II, appeared in 1965 featuring various improvements including a larger engine, more efficient lighting and a better equipped interior.

MASERATI Model	ENGINE cc/cyl	DATES	CONDITION 1	2	3
AG-1500	1488/6	1946-50	£30,000	£20,000	£10,000
A6G	1954/6	1951-53	£50,000	£35,000	£22,000
A6G-2000	1985/6	1954-57	£45,000	£35,000	£20,000
3500GT fhc	3485/6	1957-64	£25,000	£15,000	£12,000
3500GT Spyder	3485/6	1957-64	£35,000	£22,000	£15,000
5000GT	4935/6	1960-65	£60,000	£20,000	£15,000
Sebring	3694/6	1962-66	£25,000+	£18,000	£10,000
Quattroporte	4136/8	1963-74	£12,000	£10,000	£7,000
Mistral	4014/6	1964-70	£15,000	£11,000	£9,000
Mistral Spyder	4014/6	1964–70	£30,000	£18,000	£12,000
Mexico	4719/8	1965-68	£15,000	£12,000	£9,000
Ghibli	4719/8	1967-73	£20,000	£15,000	£12,000
Ghibli-Spyder/SS	4136/8	1969-74	£50,000	£40,000	£25,000
Indy	4136/8	1969-74	£18,000	£13,000	£10,000
Bora	4719/8	1971-80	£25,000	£18,000	£11,000
Merak	2965/6	1972-81	£16,000	£14,000	£9,000
Khamsin	4930/8	1974-81	£16,000	£11,000	£9,000

1972 Maserati Ghibli SS, 4.9 litres, V8, manual transmission, left-hand drive, bare metal respray, good condition.
£23,000–25,000 *KHP*

1970 Maserati Ghibli Coupé, by Ghia, V7, 4719cc, manual gearbox, 13,000 recorded miles, good condition.
£26,000–29,000 *COYS*

Introduced at the Turin show of 1966 the Ghibli displayed dramatic, purposeful lines, drawn by none other than Giorgietto Giugiaro whilst still at Ghia's design studio.

Under the bonnet was Maserati's magnificent all alloy 4.7 litre, 4 cam, V8 engine. Top speed was 174mph.

1967 Maserati Mistral Spyder, straight 6 double overhead camshaft, 4014cc, 3 Weber carburettors, 255bhp, 5 speed ZF manual gearbox, disc brakes, wishbone and coil spring front suspension, live axle with semi-elliptic leaf springs at rear, left-hand drive, stored from 1980–95, engine overhauled, chromework in fair condition, interior in good original condition, Borrani chrome wire wheels, excellent condition.
£26,000–31,000 *C*

The Mistral was the swansong of the straight 6 Maserati engine (with its twin overhead camshafts and twin spark plug per cylinder ignition system) which had first seen service in the 3500GT launched in 1957. After the Mistral, all front-engined Maseratis used a larger 4 camshaft, V8 engine.

Top speed was over 140mph and Maserati claimed almost 160mph. The Mistral Spyder was mechanically identical to the Coupé but with a conventional trunk lid and a retractable fabric top. A total of 120 were built compared to the 800 Mistral Coupés making the convertible more desirable.

1971 Maserati Indy 4.7 Coupé, 4700cc, 5 speed gearbox, power-assisted steering, stainless steel exhaust system, right-hand drive, work carried out to electrics and radio, good condition.
£15,000–17,000 *H&H*

1975 Maserati Khamsin Coupé, coachwork by Bertone, quad camshaft V8 engine, 4930cc, 320bhp at 5500rpm, regularly maintained, electrics, air conditioning and rear suspension, well maintained, 2 owners from new, cosmetic detailing required, good condition.
£13,000–15,000 *COYS*
Limited production ran from 1974 until 1978, with a total of only 352 cars being produced.

1981 Maserati Merak SS Coupé, coachwork by Ital Design, 90° V6 engine, 2965cc, 190bhp, maximum speed of 240km/h, right-hand drive, just over 6,000 miles recorded, good condition.
£15,000–17,000   *COYS*

The Geneva Salon of 1975 saw the debut of the most desirable Merak, the SS. Improvements included a reduction in overall weight of 153kg, an increase in power of 30bhp.

Only 250 SS versions of the Merak were made before the production ceased, as opposed to 1,309 of the normal 3000 and 102 of the Merak 2000. This car was one of the last 6 right-hand drive examples to be sold in the UK.

1984 Maserati B1 Turbo, V6 twin turbo, 2.5 litre engine, 5 speed manual gearbox, left-hand drive, imported from USA, good condition.
£3,000–3,500   *DB*

l. **1986 Maserati Quattroporte III Four Door Saloon,** V8, 4930cc, double overhead camshaft engine, 4 double choke Weber carburettors, automatic transmission, 0–60mph in 9.1 seconds, capable of 122mph, good condition.
£8,500–9,500   *BKS*

Based on the floor pan of the Kyalami, and using the 4930cc (originally 4136cc) V8, double overhead camshaft engine and suspension from that model, the Quattroporte is best described as a sporting limousine.

MASS

l. **1905 Mass 8hp Two Seater,** restored during the 1950s, excellent condition, full history.
£9,000–11,000   *S*

Mass cars were built in Courbevoie on the Seine from 1903–23 for the British market, taking their name from the British concessionaire's name, Mr Masser-Horniman. From 1912 the cars were also available on the French market as the Pierron. This example, typical of the single cylinder De Dion engined cars with Lacoste et Battmann chassis, was found in the 1950s, having been left in a lock-up garage in Highgate by its original owner since before the 1914–18 war. This is the sole surviving example of the marque known to exist.

MERCEDES-BENZ

Mercedes-Benz motor cars have only truly existed since 1926, following the merger of the separate Daimler (Mercedes) and Benz companies, although both can claim to have fathered the motor car. Working independently, both Karl Benz and Gottleib Daimler produced petrol-engined road vehicles in 1886. In 1894 Benz's Velo became the world's true production automobile. The name Mercedes was first used on a Daimler in 1899. When Benz, an early pace-setter in volume production, merged with the dynamic Daimler, the combination proved formidable. In the 1930s the range of road cars was thoroughly comprehensive, and from 1934 to the outbreak of WWII Mercedes-Benz signalled to the world that it was back on top with the gorgeous 300SL Gullwing, the forerunner of modern supercars. Since then the company has concentrated on producing up-market executive saloons, sporting coupés and cabriolets, all formidably engineered. In most cases Mercedes-Benz has shunned the merely voguish to produce some long-lived models whose designs have remained modern while other manufacturers adopted and dropped the latest styling fads. Superb build quality and thoughtful engineering are just two more reasons why the company is still Germany's largest industrial concern.

1895 Roger-Benz Velo, 1850cc, 2.75hp, 3 speed belt-and-chain drive, restored, good overall condition.
£31,000–36,000 *BKS*

Parisian businessman, Emile Roger, who was the first customer for a Benz automobile, soon acquired his own works and issued a catalogue advertising Benz horseless carriages, which he assembled from components to avoid import duty.

Formerly the property of the celebrated Schlumpf Collection in Mulhouse, France, and one of the very few cars ever disposed of by the Schlumpf brothers, this delightful little veteran was acquired by Daimler-Benz in 1965 and restored the following year.

1918 Benz 27/70 Six Seater Town Car, by Kruck, Frankfurt, 6 cylinders, 5340cc, 70hp, right-hand drive, fair overall condition.
£29,000–34,000 *BKS*

l. **1911 Benz 8/20 Limousine,** excellent condition.
£30,000–33,000 *BKS*

Launched in 1911, the 8/18hp Benz, sold in Britain as the 12/20, was in many respects a scaled-down version of the successful 14/30hp model of 1909, with a thoroughly modern monobloc L-head, 4 cylinder engine, with bore and stroke of 90 x 140mm, giving a swept volume of 1792cc. The 'Benz Baby', the smallest model in the Benz range, was a powerful hill climber, and drivers asserted that the steering was 'particularly good, being very light and quite irreversible'.

1934 Mercedes-Benz Type 130 Cabriolet,
1299cc, 3 speed gearbox with overdrive,
right-hand drive, only 2,000 miles recorded since
restoration, excellent condition.
£8,500–10,000 *H&H*

1934 Mercedes 130H Four Seater, 4 cylinders,
1.3 litres, 3 speed and direct drive transmission,
requires restoration.
£4,000–5,000 *BKS*

*The 130H (the H stood for 'Heckmotor', or rear
engine') was Mercedes' first venture into the light
car class, with a top speed of 57.5mph. The 1.3 litre
unit was rubber-mounted at the rear of a tubular
backbone frame, driving the rear wheels through
an unorthodox gearbox incorporating 3 direct
ratios plus a semi-automatic overdrive. Beautifully
made but expensive, it only remained in production
until 1936.*

**1938 Mercedes-Benz 320 Pullman Six Seater
Limousine,** 6 cylinders, 3185cc, 75hp, maximum
speed 80mph, restored, good overall condition.
£28,500–32,500 *BKS*

*As the largest of the naturally-aspirated Mercedes
models, the 320 was a comfortable and practical
fast tourer.*

1937 Mercedes-Benz 320 Two Door Cabriolet 'B',
2 panel V windscreen, engine overhauled,
new brakes, restored to concours condition.
£60,000–70,000 *BKS*

*Mercedes-Benz' luxurious 320 series was
introduced in 1936 as a replacement for the 290
series. Its 6 cylinder side valve engine started out
at 3208cc, before being bored out to a capacity of
3405cc towards the end of production. Hydraulic
brakes were a very necessary refinement in a car
which, in saloon form, weighed almost 2,000kgs.*

1938 Mercedes-Benz 540K W29 Cabriolet 'B',
straight 8, 5.4 litres, 115/180hp, 4 speed gearbox,
top speed 110mph, servo-assisted hydraulic brakes,
restored, requires recommissioning.
£105,000–120,000 *BKS*

*This impressive supercharged cabriolet was
originally delivered to the Oberkommandeur of
the Wehrmacht, the highest-ranking officer in the
Army of the Third Reich. It was used throughout
WWII, but was then confiscated by the US army and
sent to the USA.*

*The manufacturing record of the 540K revealed its
exclusive nature: in 1936 Mercedes produced 97 cars,
in 1937 output was 145, in 1938 the total was 95,
and 69 were built in 1939 before the war ended
series production.*

1954 Mercedes-Benz 300SL Gullwing, 6 cylinder, in-line engine, 2996cc, 4 speed manual gearbox, hydraulic drum brakes, independent suspension, left-hand drive, 80,000 miles recorded, new exhaust system, good condition.
£95,000–110,000 *C*

1954 Mercedes-Benz 170SV W136 VIII Four Door Saloon, 4 cylinders, 1.7 litre side valve engine, light alloy cylinder head, 52hp, 4 speed manual transmission, top speed 75mph, electrics require attention, restored, good condition.
£7,500–9,000 *BKS*

1955 Mercedes-Benz 300SL Gullwing, 6 cylinder in-line engine, 2996cc, 240bhp, 4 speed manual gearbox, hydraulic drum brakes, independent suspension, left-hand drive, restored, good condition.
£85,000–95,000 *C*

The Flight of the Gullwing

In 1952 Mercedes stormed back into motorsport with a space-framed chassised car that didn't allow for conventional doors. Its engine was a development of the 3 litre engine of the 300 Series saloons. This aluminium-bodied car was called the 300SL – SL stood for Super Leicht – and it was straight out of the box. In its first race, the 1952 Mille Miglia, it finished second, snatched victory at the Berne Grand Prix, took a 1 and 2 at Le Mans, won at the Nürburgring, and finished the year with 1 and 2 in the ultra-gruelling Carrera Panamericana Mexican road race. Mercedes proved its point and in 1954 concentrated once more on Grand Prix goals.

But the 300SL Gullwing was about to enter a new life and New York sports car importer Max Hoffman was instrumental in Mercedes' decision to unleash the 300SL Gullwing as undoubtedly the fastest and most glamorous production car of its era.

Hoffman was so convinced of the 300SL's appeal that he was willing to back up his word with a large firm order – up to 1,000 – if Mercedes would build them. The road-going 300SL was still clearly based on the racer, although it was kitted out with a host of luxury refinements and its suspension was derived from the 330 saloons. Most importantly it shared the spaceframe chassis of the racer and that meant it retained its Gullwing doors.

1955 Mercedes-Benz 300SL Gullwing, 3,500 miles recorded, original tools, manuals, service books, excellent overall condition.
£200,000+ *BLK*

Between 1954 and 1957, 1,400 Gullwings were built, of which 146 were built in 1954. This particular car is thought to be the lowest mileage Gullwing in existence.

Mercedes-Benz 300SL Gullwing (1954–7)

Production: 1,400
Body style: 2 door, 2 seater coupé.
Construction: Multi-tubular spaceframe with steel and alloy body.
Engine: In-line 6 cylinder overhead camshaft, 2996cc.
Power output: 240bhp at 6100rpm.
Transmission: 4 speed all-synchromesh gearbox.
Suspension: Coil springs all-round, with double wishbones at front, swinging half-axles at rear.
Brakes: Finned alloy drums.
Maximum speed: 135–165mph, depending on gearing.
0–60mph: 8.8 seconds.
Average fuel consumption: 18mpg.

1955 Mercedes-Benz 220 Cabriolet, coachwork by Sindelfingen, single overhead camshaft, 80bhp at 4600rpm, top speed of 90mph, very good condition.
£40,000–45,000 *BKS*

1955 Mercedes 300SL Gullwing, 'knock-off' Rudge wheels, factory undertrays, restored, 10,800 miles recorded, left-hand drive.
£145,000–160,000 *S*

1957 Mercedes-Benz 300Sc 3 Litre Coupé, Bosch fuel injection system, compression ratio of 8.5:1, 200bhp, power-assisted brakes, restored in USA, excellent condition.
£120,000–125,000 *BKS*

1956 Mercedes-Benz 300SL Gullwing Coupé, completely overhauled, bare metal respray, brightwork rechromed, Tracker anti-theft system, Waso GR2000 car alarm, excellent condition.
£90,000–105,000 *BKS*

It appears that only 97 Coupé 300Sc models were produced from a total of 197 Scs, this figure including Cabriolet and Roadster-bodied versions which were manufactured from December 1955 to March 1958.

1958 Mercedes-Benz 220S Two Door Cabriolet, 6 cylinders, 2195cc, overhead camshaft, 100bhp, manual transmission, unitary construction bodyshells, independent suspension all-round, drum brakes, good condition throughout.
£14,500–17,000 *BKS*

MERCEDES-BENZ Model	ENGINE cc/cyl	DATES	CONDITION		
			1	2	3
300ABCD	2996/6	1951-62	£15,000	£10,000	£8,000
220A/S/SE Ponton	2195/6	1952-60	£10,000	£5,000	£3,000
220S/SEB Coupé	2915/6	1956-59	£11,000	£7,000	£5,000
220S/SEB Cabriolet	2195/6	1958-59	£22,000	£18,000	£7,000
190SL	1897/4	1955-63	£20,000	£15,000	£10,000
300SL 'Gullwing'	2996/6	1954-57	£120,000+	£100,000	£70,000
300SL Roadster	2996/6	1957-63	£110,000	£90,000	£70,000
230/250SL	2306/ 2496/6	1963-68	£13,000	£9,000	£7,000
280SL	2778/6	1961-71	£14,000	£10,000	£8,000
220/250SE	2195/ 2496/6	1960-68	£9,000	£7,000	£3,000
300SE	2996/6	1961-65	£11,000	£8,000	£6,000
280SE Convertible	2778/6	1965-69	£20,000	£16,000	£12,000
280SE V8 Convertible	3499/8	1969-71	£25,000	£18,000	£15,000
280SE Coupé	2496/6	1965-72	£12,000	£7,000	£4,000
300SEL 6.3	6330/8	1968-72	£12,000	£7,000	£3,500
600 & 600 Pullman	6332/8	1964-81	£40,000+	£15,000	£8,000

1958 Mercedes-Benz 190SL Roadster, 1897cc, matching hard-top, manual gearbox, right-hand drive, excellent condition.
£21,000–24,000 *H&H*

1959 Mercedes-Benz 220S Four Door Saloon, 6 cylinders, single overhead camshaft, 2195cc, 80bhp at 4500rpm, maximum speed 90mph, all independent suspension, 0–60mph in 19.5 seconds, left-hand drive, excellent original condition throughout.
£5,750–6,750 *S*

r. **1960 Mercedes-Benz 220SE Cabriolet,** fuel injection, ground-up restoration, fitted luggage, good condition.
£30,000–35,000 *KI*

1959 Mercedes-Benz 300D Four Door Saloon, 160bhp, fuel injection, 3 speed automatic transmission, very original condition.
£8,500–10,000 *BKS*

The 300 saloon was capable of carrying 6 passengers in comfort at sustained high speeds. Initially developing 115bhp, the 3 litre overhead camshaft, 6 cylinder engine was boosted in power for the 300B and 300C models. Finally it gained fuel injection in the re-styled 300D of 1957, by which time output had risen to 160bhp and the car's top speed to around 170km/h.

1961 Mercedes-Benz 220SEb Two Door Coupé, 2195cc, 120bhp, top speed 170km/h, 100km/h in 14 seconds, 4 speed automatic transmission, front disc brakes, unitary construction bodyshell, all-round independent suspension, good original condition.
£5,000–6,000 *BKS*

l. **1962 Mercedes-Benz 300SE Saloon,** fuel-injected light-alloy engine, all-round disc brakes, power steering, self-levelling air suspension, 4 speed automatic transmission, good condition.
£3,500–5,000 *BKS*

1964 Mercedes 230SL, automatic transmission, hard-top, 'side saddle' rear seat, restored, good condition.
£16,000–17,000 *UMC*

1964 Mercedes-Benz 300SE Convertible,
6 cylinders, 2996cc, 160bhp at 5000rpm, 4 speed manual gearbox, 4 wheel disc brakes, independent front and rear suspension, air suspension at the rear, 60,000 miles recorded, left-hand drive.
£15,000–18,000 *C*

l. **1966 Mercedes-Benz 300SE Convertible,** by Sindelfingen, resprayed, right-hand drive, mechanically good, excellent condition.
£13,000–15,000 *COYS*

1967 Mercedes-Benz 250SL Two Door Roadster, automatic transmission, detachable hard-top and tailored cover, right-hand drive, very good condition throughout.
£16,500–18,000 *BKS*

1967 Mercedes Benz 200 Saloon, 1988cc, some spare parts including 2 bumper sections, clutch plate, front fog flasher light units and quarter lights, good condition.
£2,000–2,500 *H&H*

r. **1967 Mercedes-Benz 250SE Two Door Cabriolet,** overhead camshaft 7 bearing 6, 2496cc, 150bhp at 5600rpm, engine rebuilt, body repainted, original interior, restored, excellent condition.
£26,500–30,000 *BKS*

1969 Mercedes-Benz 280SL Roadster, 5 speed manual transmission, detachable hard-top and folding hood, good overall condition.
£16,000–18,000 *BKS*

The ultimate version of the celebrated 'pagoda-roof' line of sporting 2 seaters of the 1960s, the 280SL was launched late in 1967 as part of a complete revision of the company's range of luxury and sports cars. The larger engine brought an increase of some 11 per cent in torque compared with the earlier 230SL and 250SL models. The car was an effortless 100mph cruiser, with a top speed of over 120mph.

1969 Mercedes-Benz 250 Saloon, 170bhp, original interior, manual gearbox, right-hand drive, imported from Australia, very good condition throughout.
£2,500–3,500 *S*

1969 Mercedes-Benz 280SL, 6 cylinders, 2778cc, 2.8 litre straight 6 engine, restored to high standard.
£14,000–16,000 *ADT*

l. **1970 Mercedes-Benz 300SEL Saloon,** 6.3 Litres, 90° V8 lightweight engine, power-assisted steering, self-levelling air suspension, anti-locking brakes with ventilated discs front and rear, quartz iodine headlamps, electric windows, central locking, automatic transmission, very good condition.
£2,500–3,250 *BKS*

1970 Mercedes-Benz 280SE 3.5 Cabriolet, V8 single overhead camshaft engine, 3499cc, 230bhp at 6000rpm, automatic gearbox, servo-assisted disc brakes all-round, independent suspension with coil springs, wishbones and anti-roll bar all-round, right-hand drive, manual hood, electric windows, excellent condition.
£34,500–37,000 *C*

r. **1971 Mercedes-Benz 280SE 3.5 Two Door Coupé,** V8 engine, top speed of 130mph, factory air conditioning, electric sunroof, automatic transmission, left-hand drive, very good condition.
£9,000–11,000 *BKS*

1972 Mercedes-Benz 380SL, 105,000 miles recorded, full service history, good condition.
£14,000–16,000 *VIC*

1972 Mercedes-Benz 280SE Saloon, one owner, 100,000 miles recorded, fully restored, good condition.
£6,000–7,000 *VIC*

1973 Mercedes-Benz 450SLC, 4520cc, automatic transmission, electric sunroof, alloy wheels, 88,000 miles recorded, dry stored, very good condition throughout.
£5,000–6,000 *H&H*

1977 Mercedes-Benz 450SEL Automatic Saloon, power-assisted steering, cruise control, central locking, electric windows, tinted glass, electric sunroof, air-conditioning, 26,780 miles recorded, excellent overall condition.
£8,000–9,000 *S*

1972 Mercedes-Benz 350SLC, 8 cylinders, 3499cc, automatic transmission, bare metal respray, sills replaced, concours condition.
£6,500–8,000 *ADT*

1974 Mercedes-Benz 289CE, 6 cylinders, 2746cc, engine rebuilt, new rear brake discs and pads, good condition.
£1,850–2,350 *ADT*

1976 Mercedes-Benz 450SEL 6.9 Automatic Saloon, V8, 6384cc, Bosch fuel injection, 280bhp, long wheelbase 450SEL bodyshell, constant levelling suspension, tinted glass, electric windows, front and rear head-rests, central locking, air conditioning, power-assisted steering, cruise control, left-hand drive, very good condition.
£5,300–5,800 *S*

The 450SEL 6.9 litre saloon was launched in 1974, and was described as 'the fastest, best sedan in the world'. James Hunt, owner of 2 examples, famously remarked 'they looked like a taxi but performed like a Ferrari in terms of speed'.

1979 Mercedes-Benz 350SL, full service history, well maintained.
£12,000–13,000 *SJR*

1979 Mercedes-Benz 350SE, 8 cylinders, 3499cc, automatic transmission, repainted, good condition.
£2,000–2,750 *ADT*

1980 Mercedes-Benz 450SEL, alloy wheels, cosmetically and mechanically in good condition.
£2,000–3,000 *PA*

1981 Mercedes-Benz 280CE, 2746cc, good condition throughout, paintwork requires attention, cruise control, electric windows, factory fitted sunroof, good condition.
£2,500–3,000 *H&H*

1994 Mercedes-Benz 500E, 1,851 miles recorded, good condition.
£30,000–35,000 *LHA*

1984 Mercedes-Benz 500SEC, very good condition.
£5,000–6,000 *PA*

MERCURY

1956 Mercury Montclair Two Door Hard-Top 312 V8 Automatic, ivory and red with matching trim and interior, excellent condition.
£8,500–9,000 *CGB*

MG

It's great to see MG back on top today in the fresh-air funster field with the accomplished MGF, which continues a sporting tradition that started in the 1920s. That was when Cecil Kimber, general manager of Morris Garages in Oxford, attached a stylish two-seater sporting body to a standard Morris chassis and 4 cylinder engine to create the first MG in 1923. The two letters were nothing more than the initials of the garage which produced them, but they have come to represent an exceptional and long-lived tradition of affordable and enjoyable sports cars. Pre-war sporting products were always entertaining and occasionally

exceptional, like the first of the M-type Midgets of 1929. That started a lineage that lasted until the stylish MGA brought MG up to date with its delightful styling. In 1962 the MGB broke the mould again in MG terms and lasted until 1980 to become Britain's best-selling sports car with over 500,000 sales. Unfortunately the MG badge was devalued in the hands of British Leyland in the 1970s. The MGB never received the development it deserved and the famous MG name was finally reduced to little more than a go-faster tag on hum-drum saloons. Fortunately, the magic of the MG marque has enjoyed a fitting revival in the 1990s.

1933 MG Magna L2, 6 cylinders, 1087cc, complete restoration including alloy body, rebuilt engine, chassis restored, rebuilt supercharger, very good condition.
£25,000–27,000 *COYS*

In late 1932 the 1087cc Magnette K Type was announced, destined to become one of the most famous of all MG models and culminating in the immortal supercharged K3. Although its engine had less capacity than the F-Types, it boasted an extra 4bhp and was very susceptible to further tuning. It was March 1932 that the Magna L-Type succeeded the F-Type and a version of the K2's 1087cc engine producing 41bhp at 5500rpm – enough for 75mph via a 4 speed gearbox. In total 576 Magna L-Types were produced before production ceased in 1934, of which just 90 were the desirable L2 model.

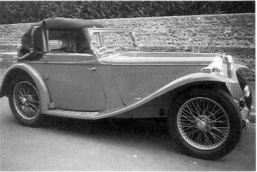

1933 MG J2 Midget, 847cc overhead camshaft engine, twin SU carburettors, 35bhp, maximum speed of 80mph, 30mpg, stored since 1987, original condition.
£13,000–15,000 *LF*

In 1932 a new Midget, the J2, was introduced with distinctive styling which was to become a hallmark of British sports car styling for the next 20 years or so. Just over 2,000 of these cars were built.

1938 MG TA Tickford, 3 position folding hood with 'pram irons', original condition, restored.
£19,000–20,000 *BBo*

Only 130 of these cars were made but just 29 exist today. This car was with its last owner for 38 years. It was restored 25 years ago and hardly used since.

1951 MG TD, 1250cc, newly restored, converted to right-hand drive, good condition.
£12,000–12,500 *VIN*

1953 MG TD MkII, restored, excellent condition, genuine UK vehicle.
£12,000–12,500 *SJR*

1954 MG TF 1250, excellent condition throughout, recently refurbished mechanically and cosmetically.
£13,500–14,500 *PA*

1957 MG Magnette ZA, recently restored, good condition, full history.
£3,000–3,500 *CRE*

MG Model	ENGINE cc/cyl	DATES	CONDITION 1	2	3
14/28	1802/4	1924-27	£26,000	£18,000	£10,000
14/40	1802/4	1927-29	£25,000	£18,000	£10,000
18/80 Mk I/Mk II/Mk III	2468/6	1927-33	£40,000	£28,000	£20,000
M-Type Midget	847/4	1928-32	£11,000	£9,000	£7,000
J-Type Midget	847/4	1932-34	£14,000	£12,000	£10,000
J3 Midget	847/4	1932-33	£18,000	£14,000	£12,000
PA Midget	847/4	1934-36	£13,000	£10,000	£8,000
PB Midget	936/4	1935-36	£15,000	£10,000	£8,000
F-Type Magna	1271/6	1931-33	£22,000	£18,000	£12,000
L-Type Magna	1087/6	1933-34	£22,000	£16,000	£12,000
K1/K2 Magnette	1087/6	1932-33	£45,000	£40,000	£35,000
N Series Magnette	1271/6	1934-36	£35,000	£30,000	£20,000
TA Midget	1292/4	1936-39	£13,000	£12,000	£9,000
SA 2 litre	2288/6	1936-39	£22,000+	£18,000	£15,000
VA	1548/4	1936-39	£12,000	£8,000	£5,000
TB	1250/4	1939-40	£15,000	£11,000	£9,000

Value will depend on body style, history, completeness, racing history, the addition of a supercharger and originality.

l. **1957 MGA 1500,** totally rebuilt, concours condition. £15,000–16,500 *SJR*

1958 MGA 1500 Coupé, 1500cc, restored, new interior fitted, excellent condition throughout. £7,000–8,000 *H&H*

MGA

This is the separate chassised fore-runner to the MGB. It wasn't made in anything like the numbers of the MGB; 101,000 MGAs were built between 1956 and 1962 and a staggering 81,000 of those were exported to America. Although that makes it rare compared with the MGB, the MGA is still eminently practical and useable. One good reason is that so many parts – the unburstable BMC B-Series engine – were shared with other vehicles under the Morris/BMC/Nuffield banner.

1959 MGA Roadster MkI, fully reconditioned engine, black/grey leather interior, wire wheels, fully documented restoration. £11,000–12,000 *VIN*

1959 MGA Twin Cam Two Door Roadster, comprehensively restored, finished in aqua blue with black leather interior, left-hand drive. £14,000–16,500 *BKS*

Popular though it was, the MGA faced stiff competition from the bigger engined Triumph TR3 and Austin-Healey 100/6. Coaxing more power from the standard engine was becoming increasingly difficult, so development concentrated on a twin overhead camshaft head for the B Series block. Introduced in 1958, the new engine did not disappoint, producing an impressive 108bhp at 6700rpm.

Considerably faster than the stock MGA, the twin camshaft could comfortably exceed 175km/h, and to cope with the increased performance, Dunlop disc brakes were fitted front and rear and Dunlop centre-lock steel wheels adopted. A high price did little for sales, however, and the model was dropped after 2 years. Production totalled 2,111 cars, and today the twin camshaft is one of the most sought-after of post-war MGs.

1960 MGA 1600 Two Seater Sports Roadster, 1588cc pushrod overhead valve engine, twin carburettors, 80bhp, 4 speed manual gearbox, front disc brakes, right-hand drive, totally restored, 750 miles recorded since, good condition, full history. £13,500–15,000 *BKS*

MGA 1955–62

Production: 101,081.
Body styles: Two seater roadster and fixed-head coupé; aluminium bonnet, doors and boot lid; separate steel chassis.
Engine: 4 cylinder, overhead valve, 1489cc, 1588cc and 1622cc.
Transmission: 4 speed manual.
Power output: 72-108bhp.
Steering: Rack-and-pinion.
Suspension: Front independent by coil and wishbone; rear semi-elliptic leaf springs.
Brakes: 4 wheel drums; front discs from 1958; 4 wheel discs on twin cam, (1958-60).
0–60mph: 13–15.5 seconds.
Maximum speed: 99–114mph.
Average fuel consumption: 20–30mpg.

1961 MG Model A MkI Roadster, 1500cc, US car restored in UK, left-hand drive, good condition. £9,000–9,500 *CGB*

1962 MGA MkII Fixed Head Coupé, rebuilt 10 years ago, excellent condition.
£10,000–10,500 *SJR*

MG Milestones

1923: Cecil Kimber, general manager of Morris Garages in Oxford, introduced his first special bodies on standard Morris chassis.
1928: MG Car Company formed.
1935: Lord Nuffield sells his privately held shares in MG to Morris Motors Limited.
1955: MGA roadster launched.
1961: MGA production topped 100,000.
1962: MGB roadster launched.
1967: MGB GT fixed-head coupé launched.
1968: MG, with the rest of BMC, becomes part of British Leyland.
1980: BL discontinued MG sports cars, continued on saloons.
1992: Return of MG sports cars with RV8.
1995: MGF launched at Geneva Motor Show in March, first deliveries in August.
1996: MGF voted import car of the year.
1996: 10,000th MGF built in July.

1961 MG Midget MkI, 948cc, bare shell restoration to show standard.
£6,500–8,500 *SC*

1964 MGB Roadster, 4 cylinders, 1798cc, restored, wire wheels, mechanically sound, good condition.
£6,500–7,500 *BRIT*

1965 MGB Roadster, completely restored, engine rebuilt, gearbox and overdrive overhauled, new clutch and hydraulic cylinders, suspension and brakes rebuilt, new radiator, water pump and hoses, new stainless steel exhaust system, Dunlop tyres and chromed wire wheels, rewired electrical system, wood rim steering wheel, re-upholstered, good condition.
£10,000–11,000 *ADT*

1965 MG Magnette Four Door Saloon, manual transmission, 4,717 miles recorded, chromework replaced, excellent condition.
£4,750–5,250 *BKS*

Built at Cowley rather than at MG's Abingdon home, the Pininfarina-styled MG Magnette MkIII replaced the popular ZB in 1959. A comfortable, roomy, and well-appointed family saloon, the new 1.5 litre Magnette was considered lacking in performance by some, though the introduction of the 1622cc MkIV in 1961 went some way towards appeasing the critics. Perhaps most notable as the first MG offered with an automatic gearbox and the last to bear the Magnette name, the MkIV ceased production in 1968.

1966 MGB Sports Roadster, 4 speed manual transmission with overdrive, reconditioned gearbox, new clutch assembly, work to suspension, new rear springs, engine overhauled, new leather-faced trim, hood and tonneau cover, good condition.
£4,750–5,250 *BKS*

l. **1967 MG Midget Roadster,** complete restoration, finished in Tartan Red with red and black interior, immobiliser, excellent condition.
£3,500–4,000 *BKS*

The Midget first appeared in July 1961. Powered initially by BMC's 948cc A series engine, the Midget gained a 1098cc unit for 1963, disc brakes, improved synchromesh, and a larger clutch being introduced at the same time. The MkII Midget/MkIII Sprite benefited from an improved 59bhp version of the 1098 motor from 1964, the power increase boosting top speed to over 90mph. At the same time, the quarter-elliptic rear springs, a feature of Healey's original design, at last gave way to half-elliptics, and wind-up windows became standard.

l. **1967 MGB Roadster,** super original condition.
£9,000–10,000 *SJR*

1968 MGB GT, 4 cylinders, 1798cc, comprehensive rebuild in 1990, mechanically sound, stainless steel exhaust system, new Britax sunshine roof, good condition.
£3,500–3,750 *ADT*

1969 MGB MkII Roadster, fully rebuilt with Heritage bodyshell and Goldseal engine, new interior trim in black vinyl, wire wheels, brightwork renewed, good condition.
£4,750–5,250 *S*

r. **1966 MGB GT,** 4 cylinders, 1798cc, restored, many extras including Minilite style alloy wheels, overdrive and sunroof, engine well maintained.
£4,000–4,500 *BRIT*

l. **1946 Rolls-Royce Silver Wraith Hearse,** engine restored, requires refit for use as a hearse, good condition.
£6,500–8,000 *RCC*

Originally a Park Ward saloon, this car was re-bodied as a hearse later in life. It was one of the very first Silver Wraiths produced.

r. **1949 Rolls-Royce Silver Wraith Touring Limousine,** coachwork by H. J. Mulliner, 6 cylinder in-line, 4257cc, 125bhp at 4000rpm, 4 speed automatic gearbox, independent front suspension with coil springs and wishbones, rear semi-elliptic leaf spring suspension, 4 wheel brakes, mechanical at rear, hydraulic at front, right-hand drive, air conditioning, partial set of original tools.
£17,000–20,000 *C*

1954 Rolls-Royce Silver Dawn Saloon,
4½ litres, 'big boot' manual gearbox, original leather interior, good overall condition.
£18,000–19,500 *RCC*

Only 57 examples of this configuration were built.

1952 Rolls-Royce Silver Wraith Drophead Coupé, coachwork by Park Ward, 6 cylinder in-line, 4566cc, 150bhp at 4000rpm, 4 speed manual gearbox, repainted, good condition.
£36,000–40,000 *C*

1955 Rolls-Royce Silver Dawn Standard Steel Saloon, automatic gearbox, paintwork good, original leather upholstery, good overall condition.
£16,000–17,000 *RCC*

This is a very late example of the model.

1957 Rolls-Royce Silver Wraith Touring Limousine, coachwork by James Young, 6 cylinders, 4887cc, 133in wheelbase, pushrod inlet over exhaust, electric division and windows, walnut cocktail cabinet, foldaway footrests.
£20,000–22,000 *BKS*

1955 Rolls-Royce Silver Dawn,
standard coachwork, very good condition.
£35,000–39,000 *PJF*

1961 Rolls-Royce Silver Cloud Convertible II, coachwork by H. J. Mulliner, very good condition.
£95,000–125,000 *PJF*

1962 Rolls-Royce Silver Cloud II, V8, 6230cc, twin SU carburettors, 4 speed automatic gearbox, coil springs and wishbone front suspension, rear rigid axle with semi-elliptic leaf springs, drum brakes all-round, top speed up to 115mph, left-hand drive, excellent condition.
£16,000–19,000 *C*

Silver Clouds are rarely seen in such beautiful condition as this restored example.

r. **1963 Rolls-Royce Phantom V Limousine,** coachwork by Park Ward, V8, 6230cc, 4 speed automatic transmission, new engine, new leather in front, original Bedford cloth to rear, interior veneered in burr walnut, Cartier clock on dual-control division, radio and magazine rack to rear, tinted rear window, restored, excellent condition.
£49,000–54,000 *S*

This car was once owned by HRH the Duke of Kent.

l. **1964 Rolls-Royce Silver Cloud III Flying Spur Saloon,** coachwork by Mulliner Park Ward, 6.2 litres, aluminium alloy V8 engine, 4 speed automatic transmission, right-hand drive, interior in good condition, 95,000 miles recorded, excellent condition.
£32,000–35,000 *BKS*

Virtually all Flying Spur bodywork was built on the Bentley chassis, and only about 15 or 20 were made for the Rolls-Royce chassis.

r. **1965 Rolls-Royce Silver Cloud III Two Door Coupé,** coachwork by H. J. Mulliner, V8, 6230cc, overhead valve, 4 speed automatic gearbox, exterior restored, interior in good condition, 37,000 miles recorded, top speed 115mph, 0–60mph in 10.8 seconds, left-hand drive, excellent overall condition.
£21,000–24,000 *C*

The Cloud III is considered to be one of the most reliable Rolls-Royce models ever made.

1964 Rolls-Royce Cloud III Continental Convertible, very good original condition, only 2 owners from new.
£37,000–40,000 *BLE*

l. **1969 Rolls-Royce Shadow,** fair condition.
£6,000–7,000 *PAL*

l. **1970 Rolls-Royce Drophead Coupé,**
coachwork by Mulliner Park Ward, 6750cc,
special features including flag masts to
front wings, Marchal Route Nationale
horns and flashing Police lamps in place of
the customary fog lights, 20,388km
recorded, excellent condition.
£27,000–30,000 *BKS*

*This car was built for His Excellency
A. Zahedi, the Shah of Iran's son-in-law
and Iranian ambassador to Washington,
and has not been driven since 1979.*

r. **1971 Rolls-Royce Silver Shadow,**
long wheelbase with division, finished in
Astrakhan with light tan leather, left-hand
drive, excellent overall condition.
£15,000–16,500 *RCC*

*This example has none of the usual rust
problems that are frequently encountered
on these cars.*

1973 Rolls-Royce Corniche Convertible,
80,000 miles recorded,
rack-and-pinion steering, split-level air
conditioning, very well maintained.
£23,000–25,000 *VIC*

1976 Rolls-Royce Camargue Two Door Saloon,
all-aluminium 6.75 litre pushrod V8 engine,
air conditioning, repainted, 20,000 miles recorded,
excellent overall condition.
£28,000–33,000 *BKS*

1976 Rolls-Royce Shadow I, finished
in original gold with brown Everflex roof,
Magnolia hide interior.
£7,000–7,500 *AS*

*The Silver Shadow was the first monocoque
Rolls-Royce with an integral body/chassis.*

1976 Rolls-Royce Silver Shadow I,
67,000 miles, full service history,
excellent condition.
£9,000–11,000 *VIC*

1984 Rolls-Royce Camargue, excellent condition.
£55,000–60,000 *BLE*

*The Carmargue was the result of a unique
partnership between Rolls-Royce and Italy's
Pininfarina design studio. It was built on the
Silver Shadow's floor pan and running gear.*

1967 Rover P5 3.5 Litre Coupé,
3528cc, repainted, original toolkit,
rare factory sliding sunroof,
very good overall condition.
£4,750–5,250 *H&H*

1933 Singer Nine Sports Two Door Tourer,
4 cylinders, overhead camshaft, 972cc, 26.5bhp,
4 speed freewheel gearbox, good condition.
£6,500–8,000 *BKS*

*The Singer Nine was particularly effective
in trials events, successfully challenging
the previously dominant MGs.*

r. **1922 Stutz Series K Touring Car,**
4 cylinders, in-line, T-head, 360.8cu in, 80bhp,
3 speed manual gearbox, old amateur repaint, body
in good condition, interior fair, right-hand drive.
£17,500–20,500 *C*

1954 Sunbeam Alpine Two Door Roadster,
4 cylinders, 2267cc, 4 speed column gearchange,
original tonneau and sidescreens, new leather
seats, right-hand drive, good condition.
£10,500–12,500 *BKS*

l. **1949 Triumph 2000 Roadster,** 4 cylinders,
2088cc, 68bhp at 4200rpm, 3 speed column
gearchange, restored, excellent condition.
£10,500–12,500 *C*

1954 Triumph TR2 Sports Two Seater,
4 cylinders, 1991cc, 90bhp at 4800rpm, 4 speed
manual gearbox with overdrive, 20,177 miles
recorded, repainted, rewired, new exhaust system,
front fog and spot lights, very good condition.
£10,000–12,000 *C*

**1920 Vauxhall 30-98 E Type Two Seater Sports
Coupé,** coachwork by Grosvenor, 4 cylinders, 100bhp,
4.5 litres, 4 speed gearbox with reverse, footbrake to
propeller shaft, right-hand drive, very good condition.
£90,000–100,000 *C*

1965 Triumph TR4A IRS, 2138cc,
Surrey top and soft top, well maintained,
very good condition throughout.
£6,000–7,000 *H&H*

These cars are now very sought-after.

1972 Volkswagen Beetle Two Door Cabriolet,
manual transmission, 4 stud Empi spring star wheels,
left-hand drive, good condition.
£4,500–5,000 *BKS*

This car comes with Monaco registration documents.

l. **1929 Stutz Blackhawk Sports Racer,** 32 valves, 5 litres, rare high compression head, 4 speed gearbox, Marchal lamps, double aero screens, 45 gallon bolster tank, top speed over 100mph, very good condition. **£40,000–50,000** *S*

The fast touring AA Vertical Eight, in appearance more European than American, was produced for the 1926 model season. In 1927 the engine was enlarged to 4.9 litres, and a speedster model, the Blackhawk, established itself as America's fastest production car.

r. **1934/35 4.5 Litre Lagonda LG45R Fox & Nicholl Team Car,** 6 cylinder Meadows engine in high specification alloy, 122bhp at 3600rpm, very good condition. **£155,000+** *BKS*

This car is one of the 3 built by the Fox & Nicholl team to compete in the 1934 RAC Tourist Trophy race classic at Ards in Ulster. It was selected as the team's number one car, to be driven by its fastest driver, The Hon Brian Lewis, later Lord Essendon.

1956/59 2.5 Litre Maserati 250F Formula 1 Grand Prix Single Seater, 6 cylinders, originally with an additional 3 litre unit for Formule Libre races, very good condition. **£380,000+** *BKS*

This car was built as a private customer car to the order of Australian owner/driver Stan Jones. The photographic record of Maserati's Formula 1 history reveals that it was first used by the factory team before being shipped 'brand new' to Jones in Australia. Its first race was actually the 1956 Argentine Grand Prix, in which it was driven by Jose Froilan Gonzalez.

1955 Elva MkI, 1100cc, Climax FWA engine, recently restored, excellent condition. **£18,000–20,000** *Car*

1935 Lagonda Rapier Two Seater Road/Racing Special, 4 cylinders, 1500cc, double overhead camshaft Rapier engine, 4 speed manual gearbox, rebuilt using different Rapier chassis. **£17,000–22,000** *C*

This car was used extensively in VSCC events.

l. **1956 Maserati 250F Recreation,** 2.5 litres, very good condition. **£220,000+** *DHAM*

1958 Austin Healey 100/6 Competition, 6 cylinders, 2912cc, 3 litre engine with 6 port head and triple Weber carburettors, completely rebuilt to full race specification, alloy body panels, good overall condition. **£23,500–27,500** *COYS*

This is probably one of the quickest 3 litre Austin Healeys in the UK. It won at Brands Hatch in May 1991.

1958 Lotus Eleven Series 2, coachwork by Williams & Pritchard, 4 cylinders, 1500cc, Coventry-Climax FWB engine, MG 4 speed manual gearbox, independent front and rear suspension, 4 wheel disc brakes, right-hand drive, excellent overall condition. **£33,000–38,000** *C*

1960 Bandini Formula Junior, Fiat 1100cc engine, ex-Monza museum, very good condition, restored by Alan Baillie. **£14,000–15,000** *Car*

This is the only rear-engined Bandini Formula Junior. Chassis FJ21-61 was originally raced in France by R. Bouharde, and raced in FIA historic events by Ken Booth.

l. **1960 Walker Formula 1,** Climax engine, 2.5 litres, 5 speed Colotti gearbox, requires restoration. **£28,000–30,000** *Car*

This is a unique car, built by Alf Francis for Stirling Moss.

r. **1960/61 BRM P48 Formula 1 Single Seater,** 2.5 litres, engine and gearbox require restoration. **£60,000–70,000** *BKS*

This was Swedish works driver Joakim Bonnier's regular team car during the 1960 season. For 1961 this chassis was updated and Graham Hill drove it in British InterContinental Formula events. It eventually went back to its original manufacturers at Bourne in Lincolnshire, as part of the BRM Collection.

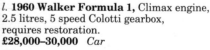

l. **1961 Cooper T56 Formula Junior,** 1100cc, Ford MAE engine, VW gearbox, restored. **£20,000–22,000** *Car*

John Cooper had a huge influence on competition with a string of immensely successful single seaters and world championships in many categories. On the road he worked his magic on the Mini to turn it into a pocket rocket, a kind of hot hatch before the idiom was born.

r. **1962 Triumph TR4 Rally,** 4 cylinders, 2250cc, body off restoration, specially tuned engine with hot camshaft and twin DCO 45 Weber carburettors, special exhaust manifold, uprated radiator, new HD overdrive by Laycock, limited slip differential, alloy safety fuel tank, twin electric fuel pumps, twin classic Lucas fog lights, oversized alloy filler cap, Sparco seats with 4 point harnesses, rebuilt instruments, extra oil temperature gauge, Halda Speedpilot and Tripmaster, 6,000 miles recorded since rebuild, excellent condition. **£14,000–18,000** *COYS*

l. **1964 Lotus Elan 26R,** 4 cylinders, 1588cc, 172bhp, completely restored using genuine parts on original chassis, fully rose-jointed suspension, excellent condition. **£26,000–32,000** *COYS*

Although Colin Chapman was adamant that the Elan was a road car, people insisted on racing the Elan, so they produced a competition model, the 26R. Even in kit form, the 26R cost £2,450, which was more than double the price for the standard car.

1964 Sunbeam Tiger, road modified, high specification, full history, concours condition. **£17,500–19,500** *UMC*

r. **1965 Gerhardt Indy Car,** Ford V8 4 camshaft engine, 500bhp, 4200cc, requires restoration. **£25,000–27,500** *Car*

This car was driven by Carl Williams in the 1965 Indy.

l. **1966 Brabham BT18 Cosworth,** 4 cylinders, 997cc. **£26,000–30,000** *COYS*

This ex-Roy Winkelmann Brabham was raced by Jochen Rindt, the king of Formula 2 in the late 1960s, and used by him in one of his most successful drives. Roy Winkelmann Racing set the standard for preparation and presentation. At Brands Hatch in September 1966, in the last race for the formula, Rindt engaged in a formidable battle with Brabham, with Rindt finally winning by 0.2 seconds. It was the highlight of Jochen Rindt's season, although he had won the Eifelrennen at the Nürburgring with the same car.

r. **1965 Shelby Mustang GT350 Competition,** 8 cylinders, 4727cc, 358bhp, 350lb ft, top speed 125mph, 0–60mph in 7 seconds, right-hand drive. **£16,000–20,000** *COYS*

This is one of just 4 right-hand drive cars converted by Ford Advanced Vehicles in Slough, and was once owned by Viscount Cranborne. It was then fitted with a competition engine, and is arguably the quickest GT350 in the UK.

1971 Brabham BT 36 Formula 2, Richardson BDA 240bhp engine, 1600cc, restored, excellent ready-to-race condition. **£40,000–42,500** *Car*

This was the last space frame Brabham made.

1971 Martin BM8 Group Six, Richardson BDG engine, 2000cc, Hewland FT 200 gearbox, excellent ready-to-race condition, prepared by Racing Fabrications. **£43,000–45,000** *Car*

l. **1971 Matra-Simca MS120B Formula 1 Single Seater,** 3 litres, stored for many years, complete and original, ready for restoration. **£35,000–40,000** *BKS*

The first 2 MS120Bs with re-profiled monocoques were built new for 1971. This car was used by team leader Jean-Pierre Beltoise in the Spanish Grand Prix, where he finished 6th.

r. **1975 McLaren M-23 Grand Prix Car,** 3 litres, excellent condition.
£145,000+ *DHAM*

Bruce McLaren was a quiet New Zealander and although his name is best-known as a constructor, he was a leading driver in the 1960s. He died in a test accident at Goodwood in 1970.

l. **1976 Brabham BT-45,** 3 litres, excellent condition.
£100,000–110,000 *DHAM*

As a driver, Australian Sir Jack Brabham scored 3 world championships. In 1966 he became the first driver to win a world championship race in a car bearing his name.

r. **1983 Ferrari 126C2B Racing Formula 1 Turbocharged Single Seater,** 1.5 litres, 120° quad-cam V6 engine, 620bhp at 11,500rpm, excellent condition.
£140,000–160,000 *BKS*

This is Patrick Tambay's victorious machine, in which he won the 1983 San Marino Grand Prix at Imola. It is one of only 2 aluminium honeycomb hulled interim model 126C2B machines built new for the 1983 season.

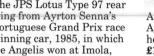

A Camel Lotus Honda 99T wing end plate from Ayrton Senna's Monaco Grand Prix race winning car, signed 'Ayrton Senna Monaco 87' in blue pen.
£4,500–5,000 *BKS*

The JPS Lotus Type 97 rear wing from Ayrton Senna's Portuguese Grand Prix race winning car, 1985, in which De Angelis won at Imola, also in 1985.
£5,200–5,500 *S*

A limited edition of Ayrton Senna's racing helmet for 1994 season.
£1,500–1,700 *BKS*

A pair of Ayrton Senna's race-worn gloves from 1987, signed in black.
£2,500–2,700 *BKS*

A Nacional cap, signed by Ayrton Senna, 1993.
£450–550 *GPT*

The set of overalls worn by Ayrton Senna in his first Formula 1 race at Monaco for the Toleman team, in race condition.
£25,000–28,000 *BKS*

Senna was given 2nd position after the race was stopped due to rain. These are probably the most used of all his Formula 1 overalls.

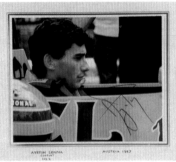

A Stand 21 Nomex race suit, used by Ayrton Senna during the 1985 season with Lotus.
£17,500–20,000 *S*

An autographed photograph of Ayrton Senna at the 1987 Austrian Grand Prix, driving the Camel Lotus, signed 'Ayrton', 10 x 8in (25.5 x 20.5cm).
£400–500 *GPCC*

An autographed photograph of Ayrton Senna at Silverstone, when driving for McLaren, signed 'Ayrton', 10 x 8in (25.5 x 20.5cm).
£400–500 *GPCC*

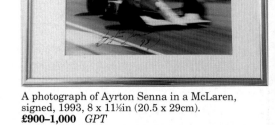

A photograph of Ayrton Senna talking with McLaren team chief Ron Dennis in 1993, signed in 1994.
£1,600–1,800 *BKS*

A photograph of Ayrton Senna in a McLaren, signed, 1993, 8 x 11½in (20.5 x 29cm).
£900–1,000 *GPT*

Graham Hill's race-worn BUCO safety race helmet, with leather interior, foam crown, chin-strap and rubber edging, the exterior with London Rowing Club style white strips, dated '1962'.
£17,500–19,000 *BKS*

Jody Scheckter's race-worn Bell helmet, with South African colours with Goodyear logo and Hermes motifs, c1974/75.
£6,500–7,000 *BKS*

Mario Andretti's race-worn Bell helmet, with Goodyear stickers, worn when he won the 1976 Japanese Grand Prix.
£13,000–14,500 *C*

Mario Andretti was the winner of 12 Grands Prix.

Nigel Mansell's Union Jack Bell helmet, worn by him during 1978 Formula 3 race season, marked 'Nigel'.
£3,700–4,000 *BKS*

James Hunt's Bell helmet, with Wellington school colours and RAC sticker, last used at Monaco 1979.
£11,000–13,000 *C*

Alan Jones' race-worn Formula 1 Bell helmet, used when he raced for Saudia-Williams Ford.
£1,500–1,750 *BKS*

This helmet was displayed at the Hilton Hotel, Adelaide until 1993.

Nigel Mansell's race-worn Arai helmet, in which he won the 1989 Brazilian Grand Prix.
£5,800–6,400 *BKS*

Jonathan Palmer's race-worn Arai Formula 1 Grand Prix helmet, with visor, intercom and microphone, and stylised JP motif, 1989.
£600–650 *BKS*

Gerhardt Berger's Ferrari helmet, 1995.
£2,500–3,000 *GPT*

Jean Alesi's Shoei race helmet, with Troy Lee paint design and Elf, Renault, Mild Seven and Persol logos, used in the 1996 Monaco Grand Prix, signed.
£12,700–13,500 *BKS*

Emerson Fittipaldi's race-worn Bell Short-Oval helmet and visor, used in the 1994 IndyCar season, tinted visor signed.
£6,600–7,400 *BKS*

Jean Alesi's visor, with Renault logo, signed, 1996.
£175–225 *GPT*

A Dunlop two-piece waterproof racing suit, worn by Stirling Moss, with additional stormproof over-layer to chest, minor acid burn holes and evidence of wear, c1957.
£7,500–9,000 *C*

A set of overalls by Faramaz Creation Sport, with Ford badge and other insignias, worn by Jackie Stewart in the 1971 Monaco Grand Prix.
£22,500–24,500 *BKS*

A set of Sparco racing overalls, with logos from Benetton, Camel, Ford, Denim, and Mobil, worn by Nelson Piquet, 1980s.
£1,400–1,500 *BKS*

A Stand 21 race suit, worn by Mika Hakkinen during the 1992 World Championship season, when he finished 8th overall, driving for Team Lotus.
£1,200–1,300 *BKS*

A Jordan team refuelling suit, 1995, with Peugeot and Total logos.
£200–300 *GPT*

A Williams team jacket, with Canon, Renault, Labatt's, Elf and Camel logos, 1992.
£45–55 *GPT*

A Camel Team Lotus jacket, 1987.
£25–35 *GPT*

A Marlboro team cap, signed by Eddie Irvine, 1996.
£95–145 *GPT*

A pair of Stand 21 racing boots, worn by Damon Hill during 1993 Australian Grand Prix, signed.
£950–1,150 *BKS*

These boots are stained by the champagne sprayed whilst on the podium.

A Ferrari race suit, worn by Eddie Irvine, with Ferrari, Shell, Goodyear and Momo logos, signed on the back, 1996.
£1,200–1,500 *GPT*

The Momo steering wheel, with Ferrari logo, from the Ferrari 312T in which Niki Lauda crashed at the Nürburgring in 1976, still bearing signs of the accident.
£14,000–16,000 *BKS*

Nigel Mansell's Momo black felt covered steering wheel, from his Lotus Type 95 racing car which he drove in the 1984 Portuguese Grand Prix, signed, mounted on chromium-plated cogs.
£3,250–3,300 *BKS*

A Jordan Formula 1 nose cone, 1996, 31in (78.5cm) high.
£800–1,200 *GPT*

Nigel Mansell's Momo steering wheel, from his Formula 1 Lotus Type 94T, in which he was 3rd at the 1984 Grand Prix of Europe, Brands Hatch.
£1,500–1,750 *BKS*

Johnny Herbert's Momo steering wheel, from his Lotus, 1994, 10in (25.5cm) diam.
£800–850 *GPT*

A Williams wheel and tyre, 1996, 25in (63.5cm) diam.
£200–300 *GPT*

A Benetton carbon fibre front wing end plate, 1995, 47in (119.5cm) long.
£95–125 *GPT*

Johnny Herbert's race-worn Momo steering wheel, from his Lotus Ford 107B, signed in gold pen, 1993.
£600–700 *BKS*

r. A jeroboam of Formula 1 Moët et Chandon champagne, from 1993 British Grand Prix, signed by every driver.
£9,000–9,500 *BKS*

A reproduction model of Alfa Romeo 159 Grand Prix car, with alloy body and wheels, Pirelli tyres, 16in (40.5cm) long.
£240–250 *JAR*

The chequered flag which Alain Prost paraded on his victory lap after coming 2nd in 1993 Portuguese Grand Prix.
£650–750 *BKS*

l. A glass ashtray, featuring Jackie Stewart, 1974, 7in (18cm) wide.
£8–12 *COB*

An Onyx model of 196A Jordan 194 Sasol, signed by Eddie Irvine, 1993, display case 4¼in (11cm) square.
£45–65 *GPT*

A model of a helmet, signed by Eddie Irvine, 1995, display case 3in (7.5cm) wide.
£35–65 *GPT*

A limited edition leather-bound album of 21 photographs, with one signed by Fangio and one by Stirling Moss, 14 x 18in (35.5 x 45.5cm).
£1,500–1,650 *JAR*

An autographed photograph of John Surtees in a Ferrari at the British Grand Prix, 1963, by Colin Waldeck, 9 x 11½in (23 x 29cm).
£65–70 *JAR*

An autographed photograph of John Surtees at Le Mans 24-hour race, 1964, by Colin Waldeck, 9 x 11½in (23 x 29cm).
£65–70 *JAR*

A photograph of Gilles Villeneuve in a Ferrari, winning the Monaco Grand Prix, 1981, by Nigel Snowden, 22 x 28in (56 x 71cm).
£180–190 *JAR*

An autographed photograph of Niki Lauda at Estoril in 1986, by David Hayhoe, 10 x 8in (25.5 x 20.5cm).
£100–150 *GPCC*

An autographed photograph of Nelson Piquet at the 1987 Hungarian Grand Prix when driving for Williams, by David Hayhoe, 10 x 8in (25.5 x 20.5cm).
£100–150 *GPCC*

A photograph of Michael Schumacher, signed, 1995, 12 x 8in (30.5 x 20.5cm).
£75–100 *GPT*

A photograph of Jean Alesi, signed, 1996, 8 x 11½in (20.5 x 29cm).
£75–90 *GPT*

A photograph of Damon Hill, signed, 1996, 5 x 7in (12.5 x 18cm).
£75–100 *GPT*

Michael Wright, Count Gaston Brilli-Peri in a 1926
Grand Prix Talbot-Darracq, in the Mugello race
in the Etruscan Appenines, on 9th June 1929,
watercolour and gouache, mounted, framed and
glazed, 27 x 32in (68.5 x 81.5cm).
£2,000–2,300 *BKS*

Pat Nevin, Tazio Nuvolari passing Kaye Don's
burning Alfa Romeo, depicting an incident
during the 1930 RAC Tourist Trophy at Ards,
signed Frederick Nevin, 17 x 21in (43 x 53.5cm),
with smaller working sketch.
£500–700 *BKS*

Roy Nockolds, Raymond Mays ERA R4D, 1947,
Shelsley Walsh Hill Climb, hand-coloured silk
screen print, 18 x 26in (45.5 x 66cm).
£180–220 *BKS*

Roy Nockolds, Bugatti T35 at Speed, oil on canvas,
signed and dated '1935', 25½ x 19½in (65 x 49.5cm).
£1,300–1,500 *CSK*

Roy Nockolds, the Hamilton/Rolt Jaguar
D-Type passes the stalled Ferrari of Gonzales/
Trintignant in a dramatic bid for a debut victory
in the 1954 Le Mans race, hand-coloured
lithograph, 25½ x 36in (65 x 91cm).
£200–250 *BKS*

Terence Cuneo, Hillman Imp in Monte Carlo Rally,
signed, c1964, oil on canvas, 25 x 30in (63.5 x 76cm).
£1,800–2,000 *CSK*

r. Michael Turner, an Austin-Healey 3000 climbing the
Moistracco Pass during the 1961 Liège rally, watercolour.
£500–700 *BKS*

Lawrence Klonaris, James Hunt and Niki Lauda at the Spanish Grand Prix at Jarama in 1976, oil on canvas, signed and framed, 36 x 42in (91.5 x 106.5cm).
£1,500–1,800 *BKS*

Phil May, Another Bentley Boy, watercolour of a 4½ litre Bentley at speed, framed and glazed, 7½ x 12in (19 x 30.5cm).
£250–300 *BKS*

Michael Turner, Jackie Stewart in the 1973 Italian Grand Prix at Monza, Tyrrell-Ford 006/2, watercolour, signed and inscribed, 1983, mounted, framed and glazed, 14 x 20in (51 x 35.5cm).
£4,200–4,500 *BKS*

Dexter Brown, Jackie Stewart driving a 2 litre VR8 BRM at the British Grand Prix, Silverstone, 1966, acrylic on board, 16 x 24in (40.5 x 61cm).
£1,500–2,000 *LE*

Randy Owens, a Serigraph picture entitled 'Monaco', signed by Ayrton Senna, Jean Alesi, Gerhardt Berger, Thierry Boutsen and the artist, famed and glazed, 25 x 40in (63.5 x 101.5cm).
£4,800–5,200 *BKS*

Roy Nockolds, Aintree, '200' International Car Racing, Saturday April 22nd and organised by the BARC, signed artwork, slight damage.
£275–325 *BKS*

Jim Bamber, an artistic impression of Nigel Mansell in his Indianapolis car, acrylic on board, signed on frame, 24 x 30in (61 x 76cm).
£900–1,100 *BKS*

1970 MGB Roadster, 4 cylinders, 1798cc, left-hand drive, finished in blue with black cloth interior trim, new carpets, hood replaced, imported from Colorado, rust free and original, new exhaust system, starter motor and battery.
£5,250–5,750 *ADT*

1971 MGB Roadster, 1798cc, manual transmission with overdrive, recently restored including body panels, floor and sill sections, carpets, bumpers, hood, petrol tank and some brightwork, good condition.
£4,750–5,250 *LF*

1971 MGB GT, 4 cylinders, 1798cc, overdrive, refurbished to include new black upholstery, Webasto sunroof.
£2,750–3,250 *BRIT*

1971 MGB GT, 1998cc, restored, finished in white, full history.
£1,750–2,000 *H&H*

1971 MGB Roadster, 1798cc, totally restored from bare shell, good condition.
£8,000–10,000 *SC*

Miller's Starter Marque

Starter MGs: *MGA, MGB, MGB GT, MG Midget 1961 onwards.*

- The MGB has got to be one of the most practical, affordable and enjoyable classic sporting packages around. For a start, it's the most popular British sports car ever made, a winning formula based on rugged reliability, simple clean lines, fine road manners and adequate performance.

- For sheer classic credentials, models before the 1974 introduction of rubber bumper cars with higher ride height are favoured, but later models can be even more affordable. They're also a great way to make 50,000 friends, for that's how many members there are in the MG Owners' Club, the world's largest one-make car club. There is also a superb parts and specialist network, even down to brand-new body shells made on original tooling.

- The fixed-head MGB GT is cheaper than the open roadster yet offers additional practicality and comfort.

- **What to watch:** Few worries with engines and mechanicals but MGBs can rot and because of unitary construction pay particular attention to sills and other structural aspects.

1972 MG Midget MkIII, 4 cylinders, 1275cc, recent bare metal respray, good condition, full history.
£3,300–3,800 *ADT*

l. **1972 MGB Roadster,** 4 cylinders, 1798cc, concours restoration project, bare metal respray, engine overhauled, new radiator and exhaust system, new hood and chrome wire wheels, new tyres, good condition.
£11,500–12,500 *ADT*

1973 MGB GT V8, 8 cylinders, 3528cc, overdrive, restored, mechanically sound, new exhaust system and radiator.
£5,750–6,250 *ADT*

1973 MG Midget MkIII, 4 cylinders, 1275cc, reconditioned engine, braking system overhauled, new exhaust system, new hood with period hard-top, new kingpins, good condition.
£2,500–2,750 *BRIT*

l. **1973 MGB GT Sports Coupé,** 1950cc, fully restored, walnut dashboard, centre console, door cappings and door pulls, Britax folding sunroof, wood-rimmed steering wheel, Minilite alloy wheels, anti-roll bar, transmission restored, less than 3,000 miles recorded since rebuild, good condition.
£8,500–9,500 *BKS*

1973 MG Midget, 1275cc, reconditioned gearbox, new front wings, new bonnet, good all-round condition.
£2,250–2,750 *H&H*

1973 MGB GT, recently restored, good condition.
£6,000–6,500 *SJR*

MG Midget

When it comes to breezy budget motoring about the only thing that matches the MG Midget is the Austin-Healey Sprite, for apart from badging, trim and instruments they're the same thing (the earlier MkI 'Frog-eye' Sprite though, was only produced as an Austin-Healey).

The Midget is a compelling classic cocktail for the cost conscious – in fact about the only cheaper way of enjoying fresh-air on four wheels is probably to buy a skateboard. Midgets have a massive following, with more than 200,000 built up to 1979 and that means there's tremendous club support, a well-established and competitive spares and re-manufacturing industry and a mature network of established marque specialists and restorers.

Better still, the Spridget, as the Midget/Sprite models are often called, is a BMC parts-bin special based on the mechanicals and running gear from the likes of the million-selling Morris Minor and Austin A35. If the body's riddled with rust you can also get a complete new body shell from Rover subsidiary British Motor Heritage.

What to watch: Particular points include the inner and outer sills. Be wary of ill-fitted replacement sills and check the closing action of the doors. If they bind or snag, someone may have welded new sills without supporting the car in the middle to ensure the frame maintains its correct shape. Another trouble area is the door pillar. You should shake each door firmly in this area to reveal any flexing. The engines are generally reliable and long lasting, but check for fluid leaks. Gearboxes can be noisy, but are similarly robust, and the rear axle – similar to the Morris Minor – rarely gives trouble.

Pick of the Bunch: For classic credibility the Sprite MkIV and Midget MkIII (1966–70) are probably the best bet, with better performance from the 1275cc engines than earlier cars. They are still chrome-era classics, however, with all the visual appeal of the older versions. If performance matters more the 1500cc Triumph Spitfire-engined Midgets from 1974 will touch 100mph, but they have the vast black plastic bumpers that some people loathe.

1974 MGB GT V8 Two Door Coupé, mechanical service and respray, excellent condition throughout, 80,000 miles recorded, full history.
£6,750-7,250 *BKS*

MG enthusiasts have Kent-based engineer Ken Costello to thank for the existence of the V8-engined MGBGT. In 1970 Costello began selling cars converted to take the 3.5 litre Rover V8, and their favourable reception prompted British Leyland to follow suit. As the aluminium alloy engine weighed only a few pounds more than the cast-iron 4 cylinder it replaced, little re-engineering of the existing suspension was called for. Both transmission and brakes were up-rated though, the original gearbox being swapped for a modified MGC manual-plus-overdrive unit, and thicker, larger diameter front discs being fitted. A Lockheed servo was now standard equipment. Considerably quicker than the 4 cylinder B, the V8 could reach 60mph in around 8 seconds, and had a top speed of 125mph – respectable figures even today. It was supplied only to the UK market. Only 2,591 cars were manufactured before the model was withdrawn in 1976, making the MGBGT V8 one of the rarest and most sought-after of post-war MGs.

MG Model	ENGINE cc/cyl	DATES	CONDITION 1	CONDITION 2	CONDITION 3
TC	1250/4	1946-49	£13,000	£11,000	£7,000
TD	1250/4	1950-52	£13,000	£9,000	£5,000
TF	1250/4	1953-55	£15,000	£13,000	£8,000
TF 1500	1466/4	1954-55	£16,000	£14,000	£9,000
YA/YB	1250/4	1947-53	£5,500	£2,750	£1,500
Magnette ZA/ZB	1489/4	1953-58	£3,000	£2,000	£500
Magnette Mk III/IV	1489/4	1958-68	£2,500	£850	£350
MGA 1500 Roadster	1489/4	1955-59	£10,000	£7,000	£4,000
MGA 1500 FHC	1489/4	1956-59	£7,000	£5,000	£3,000
MGA 1600 Roadster	1588/4	1959-61	£11,000	£9,000	£4,500
MGA 1600 FHC	1588/4	1959-61	£7,000	£5,000	£3,000
MGA Twin Cam Roadster	1588/4	1958-60	£18,000	£12,000	£9,000
MGA Twin Cam FHC	1588/4	1958-60	£14,000	£9,000	£7,000
MGA 1600 Mk II Roadster	1622/4	1961-62	£12,000	£10,000	£4,000
MGA 1600 Mk II FHC	1622/4	1961-62	£9,000	£7,000	£3,000
MGB Mk I	1798/4	1962-67	£7,000	£4,000	£1,200
MGB GT Mk I	1798/4	1965-67	£5,000	£3,500	£1,000
MGB Mk II	1798/4	1967-69	£7,500	£4,000	£1,500
MGB GT Mk II	1798/4	1969	£4,500	£2,500	£850
MGB Mk III	1798/4	1969-74	£6,500	£4,000	£1,100
MGB GT Mk III	1798/4	1969-74	£4,500	£2,500	£1,000
MGB Roadster (rubber bumper)	1798/4	1975-80	£6,000	£4,500	£1,200
MGB GT	1798/4	1975-80	£5,000	£3,000	£1,000
MGB Jubilee	1798/4	1975	£5,000	£3,000	£1,200
MGB LE	1798/4	1980	£8,500	£4,750	£2,250
MGB GT LE	1798/4	1980	£6,000	£3,750	£2,000
MGC	2912/6	1967-69	£8,000	£6,500	£4,000
MGC GT	2912/6	1967-69	£7,000	£5,000	£2,000
MGB GT V8	3528/8	1973-76	£9,000	£6,000	£3,000
Midget Mk I	948/4	1961-62	£4,000	£2,000	£850
Midget Mk II	1098/4	1962-66	£3,000	£2,000	£850
Midget Mk III	1275/4	1966-74	£3,200	£2,000	£850
Midget 1500	1491/4	1975-79	£3,000	£2,000	£850

All prices are for British right hand drive cars. Deduct 10-15% for left hand drive varieties, even if converted to right-hand drive.

1974 MG Midget Two Seater Sports,
reconditioned engine and body shell, all parts
overhauled, resprayed in maroon livery, good condition.
£5,500–6,000 *S*

1975 MGB Roadster, good condition,
78,000 recorded miles, full history.
£5,500–6,500 *VIC*

1975 MGB GT Jubilee Edition, 4 cylinders,
1798cc, restored to original specification, overdrive
transmission, sunroof, very good condition.
£2,750–3,500 *ADT*

*In 1975, in celebration of the Golden Jubilee of MG,
British Leyland announced a limited run of the GT
model finished in dark racing green with distinctive
gold side stripes and gold finished alloy wheels. As
with any limited production MG, the model has
become highly sought-after over the years.*

1978 MGB Roadster, 1798cc, 8,000 miles recorded,
finished in vermilion with black trim, one owner
with maintenance history.
£4,000–4,400 *VIN*

1980 MGB GT, 1798cc, rubber bumpers, finished in black, Rostyle wheels with chrome rim trims,
stainless body trim, good condition.
£3,350–3,850 *VIN*

1980/81 MGB Limited Edition Roadster,
finished in metallic bronze with special sill decals,
good condition.
£6,000–8,000 *CARS*

*This model is one of 500 final limited edition
vehicles produced, half of these being GT, the
remainder in Roadster form.*

1995 MG RV8 Sports Roadster Limited Edition,
finished in black with tan leather tonneau cover,
sheepskin over-rugs, luggage rack, good condition.
£20,000–23,000 *CARS*

*Limited edition of only 2,000 produced, most of
which went to the Far East.*

MINERVA

Minerva – the 'Goddess of Automobiles' – was the finest make produced by Belgium's once vibrant motor industry. One of the select aristocracy of motoring that included such patrician marques as Rolls-Royce, Hispano-Suiza, Isotta-Fraschini and Cadillac, the Minerva originated with the cycle business run by the energetic Sylvain de Jong, a Dutchman living in Antwerp. The first Minerva car appeared in Britain in 1899 and was soon an amazing success in its principal export market, Britain, thanks to its enterprising London agent David Citroën (cousin of car maker André), who joined de Jong on the board of a recapitalised Minerva company in 1903.

Minerva soon became known for its luxury cars and in 1908 took out a licence for the Knight sleeve-valve engine in the interests of silent running. By 1910, its entire range was powered by Knight engines and, with 1,600 workers, its factory was the biggest car plant in the country.

1912 Minerva 26hp Torpedo Tourer, coachwork by Carrosserie Vanden Plas, 4.1 litres, 26hp, totally rebuilt, finished in red with new black upholstery, good condition.
£35,000–38,000 *BKS*

MINI

A commuter runabout, a racing and rallying giant killer and living legend, the Mini is all of these things.

Alec Arnold Constantine Issigonis, creator of the Morris Minor and Mini, would have made a great end-of-pier gypsy clairvoyant. For this Greek-born son of an itinerant marine engineer once showed an uncanny prophetic talent when he quipped to Italian automobile couturier Sergio Farina: 'Look at your cars, they're like women's clothes – they're out of date in two years. My cars will still be in fashion after I've gone.'

It's a prophecy tinged with sadness as Sir Alec Issigonis died in 1988 when the Mini was poised for a renaissance as a fully catalysed enviro-friendly car for the 1990s and beyond.

The revolutionary, front-wheel-drive Mini with its east-west engine layout and brilliant compact packaging, was launched in 1959. Offered originally as an Austin 7 Mini or Morris Mini Minor, this pocket-sized wonder car achieved its own identity by 1970, becoming simply the Mini. The amazing thing about the Mini is that it's still going strong, particularly in overseas markets like Japan. The Austin Metro of 1980 was supposed to replace the Mini but wasn't up to the task. The Mini was so right at its launch that it's actually benefited from being left pretty much alone. Five million-plus customers can't be wrong.

1961 Austin Mini Cooper, 4 cylinders, 1275cc, 45 side draft Weber carburettors, 4 speed manual gearbox, disc and drum brakes, left-hand drive, overhauled to racing specification, spax shock absorbers, dry independent suspension, steel braded brake lines, Austin America master brake system, racing seat, 3 point harness and cage, many spares, good condition.
£7,800–9,300 *C*

Miller's Starter Marque

Starter Minis: *All models.*

- Whether yours is a 1959 car with sliding windows, cord door pulls and external hinges, or a 1995 model, all Minis are classics. Even though modern Minis are still closely related to the 1959 original, the early cars have an extra, subtle charm. Parts are rarely a problem, but the Mini's major enemy is rust, and here are a few guides to buying a sound older example.

- Before looking underneath, inspect the roof panel, guttering and pillars supporting the roof. If they are rusted or show signs of filler it suggests that the rest of the structure may be in similar or worse shape.

- Examine floorpans from above and below, joints with the inner sill, front and rear bulkheads, crossmember and jacking points. If the subframe has welded plates, check they've been properly attached. Look inside the parcel compartment on either side of the rear seat, beneath the rear seat, all corners of the boot, spare wheel well and battery container. These are all common rust spots.

- Clicking from beneath the front of the car indicates wear in the driveshaft constant velocity joints – not easy or cheap to rectify.

- Rear radius arm support bearings deteriorate rapidly unless regularly lubricated; check the grease points ahead of each rear wheel for signs of recent attention.

- The A-Series engine is generally reliable and long-lived. However, expect timing chain rattle on older units; exhaust valve burning can be evident on higher mileage examples, as can exhaust smoke under hard acceleration, indicating cylinder/piston wear.

- Mini Cooper: What to watch: Is it a Cooper? Mini Coopers can be worth more than double the price of an ordinary classic Mini and consequently fakes abound. It's not just a question of checking the uprated specification, twin carbs, disc brakes, badges and the like, but unravelling engine and chassis numbers and subtle tell-tale signs that you'll only learn about from club and professional experts. First join the club, then go shopping (see our Directory of Car Clubs on page 336).

- **Pick of the bunch:** Of the original generation of Coopers the best all-round performer is the 1275S with 60mph coming up in 10.9 seconds and puff running out just shy of the ton. As usual the aficionados prefer first-of-breed purity of earlier cars with sliding windows, cord door pulls and external hinges.

1966 Morris Mini Cooper S, 1275cc, completely reconditioned including rebuilt engine, resprayed and re-upholstered, finished in red and black, good condition.
£3,750–4,250 *H&H*

1967 Morris Mini Cooper MkI, 4 cylinders, 998cc, complete rebuild including reconditioned engine and gearbox to original specification, finished in Island Blue, Old English white roof and grey interior, wider rimmed wheels, good condition.
£2,750–3,500 *ADT*

1968 Austin Mini Cooper Works Replica, 4 cylinders, 1275cc, seam-welded body, nitrided crankshank, Weber carburettor, full roll cage, competition seat, finished in correct tartan red and white livery, Minilite type wheels.
£3,500–4,000 *ADT*

Mini Cooper works cars are nowadays highly prized and valuable possessions. As a direct result of this, a number of works replica cars have been created, and this particular vehicle was built by Don Pither, the President of the Historic Rally Car Register.

l. **1968 Morris Mini,** good condition.
£1,150–1,300 *H&H*

1970 Austin Mini Cooper S MkII, 4 cylinders, 1275cc, restored, engine rebuilt, Hydrolastic suspension, Webasto sunroof, Minilite wheels, finished in Snowberry white, black roof, original black PVC interior, extras include rev counter, sports style steering wheel, modified cylinder head, good condition.
£4,000–5,000 *ADT*

1970 Austin Mini 1000 MkII Automatic, 997cc, one owner, 23,000 miles recorded, automatic gearbox.
£1,100–1,300 *H&H*

Mini Cooper

Mini designer Alec Issigonis didn't approve when John Cooper approached him with plans for a hot Mini. The creator of the miniature marvel car stuck steadfastly to his vision of a car that would provide 'everyman transport'. But Cooper went over his head, got the go-ahead to breathe magic on the Mini and created an unlikely sporting legend. The Mini's engine was bored out to 997cc and fitted with twin SU carburettors, gear ratios altered, a remote gear change installed in place of the waggly wand, and to stop this pocket rocket he challenged Lockheed to produce 7in front disc brakes. The result was a rallying world beater that was so invincible that when Coopers came home one-two-three in the infamous 1966 Monte Carlo Rally, the miffed Monegasque organisers disqualified them on trumped up technicalities.

Mini Cooper fact: What did John Cooper get from the original Mini Cooper? A £2 royalty for each one built. But he's not complaining. He recalls: 'Harriman [then BMC chairman George Harriman] said we had to make 1,000 – but we eventually made 150,000.' That translates into £300,000 commission.

1970 Mini Special, 4 cylinder in-line, 1380cc, uprated with S head and mild Kent S44 camshaft, 100bhp, Jack Knight 5 speed Helical manual gearbox, Cooper S front disc brakes, standard S rear super Minifin drums, independent suspension all-round, adjustable shock absorbers, right-hand drive, Recaro front seats with black Connolly hide, walnut dashboard, black glass windows, air conditioned, 5,000 miles recorded since restoration.
£7,500–9,000 *C*

This Mini Special has been built to an extremely high standard of both craftsmanship and workmanship. The original plan was to recreate the well known 'Omar Sharif' car of the 1960s, a Mini with Mercedes front wings and lights that was specially prepared for the famous actor.

1971 Mini Cooper S, 4 cylinders, overhead valve, 1275cc, Downton No. 5 Touring conversion, new 4 speed manual gearbox, disc front brakes, drums rear, independent suspension, right-hand drive, engine modified for extra performance, new body shell, excellent condition.
£2,850–3,350 *C*

MINI Model	ENGINE cc/cyl	DATES	CONDITION 1	2	3
Mini	848/4	1959-67	£3,500	£1,200	-
Mini Countryman	848/4	1961-67	£2,500	£1,200	-
Cooper Mk I	997/4	1961-67	£7,000	£4,000	£1,500
Cooper Mk II	998/4	1967-69	£6,000	£4,000	£1,500
Cooper S Mk I	var/4	1963-67	£7,000	£5,000	£2,000
Cooper S Mk II	1275/4	1967-71	£6,000	£5,000	£2,000
Innocenti Mini Cooper	998/4	1966-75	£4,500	£2,000	£1,000

l. **1978 Mini Moke,** 4 cylinders, 998cc, genuine 5,900 miles recorded, mechanically sound, weather equipment serviceable, blue vinyl interior in good condition.
£2,850–3,350 *ADT*

Making its first appearance in 1964 as the Mini Moke, this little vehicle was originally developed with an eye to military and agricultural usage. However, because it was deemed to be subject to purchase tax in Britain, the vast majority were sold overseas and from 1969 the Moke was only produced abroad, initially in Australia and finally in Portugal.

1978 Morris Mini 1000 Automatic, 998cc, dry stored for 15 years, complete reassembly including full engine and gearbox overhaul, warranted 16,800 miles, one owner, very good condition.
£1,850–2,350 *H&H*

1979 Mini 1100LE Two Door Saloon, 1100cc, stored from new, 120 miles recorded, unregistered, finished in metallic rose and tan check trim, ex-factory condition.
£4,500–5,500 *H&H*

This Limited Edition car was made for the 20th anniversary of the Mini and has been stored in a car showroom ever since.

1979 Mini Special 1000LE, 1000cc, finished in metallic rose with white vinyl roof, tan tartan striped interior, 3 dial dashboard instruments, good condition.
£2,500–3,500 *CARS*

1984 Mini 25 Saloon, rev counter, leather-bound steering wheel, twin door mirrors, finished in silver, grey interior trim, grey and red interior, tinted glass, unregistered, delivery mileage only.
£5,300–5,800 *BKS*

One of a host of Mini special editions which commenced with the Limited Edition 1000 of 1976, the 25 marked the 25th anniversary of the Mini.

MORGAN

For most of its life Morgan has spurned fashion and modern practices to produce timewarp machines that have somehow remained enduringly fashionable. Founded in 1910 by H. F. S. Morgan, the Malvern company initially produced motorcycle-engined three-wheelers, which remained the mainstay until the first four-wheeler was introduced in 1935. By then the three-wheelers were on their last legs and no longer able to challenge more conventional cars on performance and price. The first four-wheeler, the 4/4, soon earned a fine reputation and today's products still display a direct lineage back to that original pre-war four-wheeler.

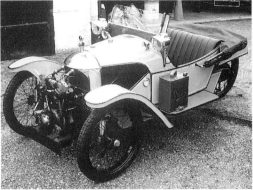

c1920 Morgan Grand Prix, very good condition. **£18,000–20,000** *FHD*

1951 Morgan 4/4 Four Seater Sports, good condition. **£12,000–12,500** *AS*

1959 Morgan 4/4, 1200cc Ford engine, totally restored, excellent mechanically, concours condition. **£13,500–14,500** *SW*

1973 Morgan 4/4 Four Seater, 1600cc Ford engine and gearbox, good condition. **£9,000–9,750** *DB*

Three-wheeled Morgans were powered by a variety of proprietary engines including JAP and Anzani. In 1936 a 4 wheel sports car was introduced with power courtesy of Ford's 10hp side valve unit or Coventry Climax, whilst other models were to use Triumph and Ford engines, and the powerful Morgan Plus Eight, introduced in 1969, utilised the Rover V8 3.5 litre unit. Today, Morgans are still produced in very much the same way as 60 years ago at the same factory and its production techniques have been largely untouched by time.

1976 Morgan +8, lightweight model. **£22,500–25,000** *FHD*

Only 19 all-aluminium bodied cars were made.

1983 Morgan 4/4 Four Seater, 4 cylinders, 1600cc Ford engine recently uprated to CVH-type, factory-fitted wire wheels, exterior door handles, radio and tonneau cover, luggage rack, stainless steel exhaust system, rust proofed, good order throughout.
£10,500–12,000 *ADT*

c1990 Morgan Plus 8, 3.9 litres, twin exhaust, aluminium body and wings.
£22,500–25,000 *FHD*

1993 Morgan Plus 4, 2 litres, 34,000 miles recorded, good condition.
£18,500–20,000 *WYK*

1995 Morgan 4/4 Two Seater, 1800cc, all original as new condition, 1,740 miles recorded.
£20,000–21,000 *RUT*

1996 Morgan Plus 8, 3.9 litres, 1,800 miles recorded, good condition.
£31,000–33,000 *WYK*

MORRIS

Morris may be no more – the name disappeared from the Austin-Rover inventory in 1984 – but for 70 years the marque founded by William Morris in 1913 stood out as a byword for stout middle-class motoring. The firm's early reputation was built on the sturdy and reliable 'bullnose' Morris Oxford and Cowley models. In fact in 1924 Morris was Britain's number one car manufacturer, ahead of Ford, and in 1929 Morris produced 51 per cent of all new cars built in Britain that year. During the 1930s Morris' market share dwindled and in 1952 William Morris, by now Viscount Nuffield, agreed to merge with Austin to form the British Motor Corporation. Thereafter the Morris marque struggled for prominence, but one car that was conceived before the merger, the miraculous Morris Minor, went on to become Britain's first million-selling car. In the 1960s and 1970s other Morris offerings were little more than alternatively badged Austins.

1928 Morris Oxford 14/28hp Saloon De Luxe, fully restored, mechanically rebuilt, coachwork restored, original interior, garage stored for over a year, requires recommissioning, excellent condition.
£8,600–9,300 *S*

> **Cross Reference**
> Restoration Projects

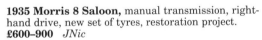
1935 Morris 8 Saloon, manual transmission, right-hand drive, new set of tyres, restoration project.
£600–900 *JNic*

MORRIS Model	ENGINE cc/cyl	DATES	CONDITION 1	2	3
Prices given are for saloons					
Cowley (Bullnose)	1550/4	1913-26	£12,000	£8,000	£6,000
Cowley	1550/4	1927-39	£10,000	£6,000	£4,000
Oxford (Bullnose)	1803/4	1924-27	£14,000	£10,000	£6,000
Oxford	1803/4	1927-33	£10,000	£8,000	£6,000
16/40	2513/4	1928-33	£8,000	£7,000	£6,000
18	2468/6	1928-35	£9,000	£7,000	£5,000
8 Minor	847/4	1929-34	£5,500	£4,000	£2,000
10/4	1292/4	1933-35	£5,000	£3,000	£1,500
25	3485/6	1933-39	£10,000	£8,000	£5,000
Eight	918/4	1935-39	£4,000	£3,000	£1,500
10HP	1140/4	1939-47	£4,500	£3,000	£1,500
16HP	2062/6	1936-38	£5,000	£3,500	£2,000
18HP	2288/6	1935-37	£5,000	£3,500	£2,500
21HP	2916/6	1935-36	£6,000	£4,000	£2,500

A touring version of the above is worth approximately 30% more and value is very dependent on body type and has an increased value if coachbuilt.

MORRIS Model	ENGINE cc/cyl	DATES	CONDITION		
			1	2	3
Minor Series MM	918/4	1948-52	£2,000	£1,200	£500
Minor Series MM Conv	918/4	1948-52	£4,000	£1,800	£800
Minor Series II	803/4	1953-56	£2,000	£1,000	£500
Minor Series II Conv	803/4	1953-56	£5,500	£3,500	£1,500
Minor Series II Est	803/4	1953-56	£3,000	£1,250	£800
Minor 1000	948/4	1956-63	£1,750	£925	£250
Minor 1000 Conv	948/4	1956-63	£3,000	£2,000	£750
Minor 1000 Est	948/4	1956-63	£4,000	£2,200	£1,200
Minor 1000	1098/4	1963-71	£2,000	£950	£250
Minor 1000 Conv	1098/4	1963-71	£4,500	£3,000	£1,500
Minor 1000 Est	1098/4	1963-71	£3,500	£2,200	£1,000
Cowley 1200	1200/4	1954-56	£1,675	£1,000	£300
Cowley 1500	1489/4	1956-59	£1,750	£950	£350
Oxford MO	1476/4	1948-54	£2,000	£850	£250
Oxford MO Est	1476/4	1952-54	£3,000	£1,500	£350
Series II/III	1489/4	1954-59	£2,000	£1,200	£300
Series II/III/IV Est	1489/4	1954-60	£2,250	£1,350	£250
Oxford Series V Farina	1489/4	1959-61	£1,800	£800	£250
Oxford Series VI Farina	1622/4	1961-71	£1,750	£750	£200
Six Series MS	2215/6	1948-54	£2,500	£1,500	£500
Isis Series I/II	2639/6	1955-58	£2,500	£1,300	£450
Isis Series I/II Est	2639/6	1956-57	£2,600	£1,350	£500

1936 Morris 8 Two Seater Tourer, 3 speed gearbox with synchromesh, single dry plate clutch, right-hand drive, restored in 1992 to include radiator rebuild, rewired, finished in maroon and black, 16,500 miles recorded, good condition.
£3,500–4,000 *BKS*

Having established themselves as leaders in the sales race in the 1920s, Morris dropped behind Austin in the early 1930s. The arrival of Leonard Lord, however, arrested the decline, and in 1935 the 918cc side valve Series I Eight proved to be a best-seller and helped Morris to achieve their first million car output by the summer of 1939.

1946 Morris 8 Series E, 4 cylinders, 918cc, unrestored, panelwork, floorpan and interior in fair condition, correct headlamp lenses.
£1,000–1,300 *ADT*

> **Don't Forget!**
>
> *If in doubt please refer to the 'How to Use' section at the beginning of this book.*

1950 Morris Oxford Saloon, 1409cc, 4 speed manual gearbox, 40,300 miles recorded, original condition.
£1,300–1,700 *H&H*

1953 Morris Minor SII Four Door Saloon de Luxe, 4 cylinders, later 1098cc engine, full history.
£2,200–2,500 *ADT*

1956 Morris Minor Two Door Saloon, 803cc, split windscreen, fitted flashers and seat belts, good condition, full history.
£1,700–1,850 *UMC*

1956 Morris Minor Series II, replacement 1967 1100cc engine and gearbox, split windscreen, new battery, good condition.
£900–1,100 *H&H*

1956 Morris Minor 1000, split windscreen, good condition.
£1,900–2,200 *H&H*

1957 Morris Minor Convertible, 4 cylinders, 948cc, manual transmission, rebuilt, generally good condition throughout.
£3,200–3,600 *JNic*

1964 Morris Minor Convertible, 1098cc, underbody restored, new wings, doors and quarter panels, new hood, frame and carpets, new copper brake pipes, slave cylinders, battery, dynamo and petrol pump, finished in black with red and white trim, good condition.
£2,800–3,300 *H&H*

Miller's Starter Marque

Starter Morris: *Minor, 1948–71.*

- The Minor's a motoring milestone, Britain's first million seller, our very own people's car and, in its day, staple transport for everyone from midwives to builders merchants. The Jaguar XK120 was the undoubted star of the 1948 London Motor Show, the car that everybody wanted, but the Series MM Morris Minor was the car that ordinary people needed. Designed by Alec Issigonis, the genius who later went on to pen the Mini, the Minor featured the then novel unitary chassis-body construction and its famed handling finesse and ride comfort more than made up for the lack of power. In fact in 1950 a Minor even tempted the young Stirling Moss into high-speed cornering antics that lost him his licence for a month.

- Today, the Minor has undeniable classic credentials. Any model is eminently affordable and almost as practical to own now as when in production, owing to ready availability and a blossoming cottage industry that provides everything you need to keep your Minor in fine fettle. The Minor is also generally long-lived and one of the easiest cars for DIY maintenance. The wide engine bay provides plenty of room to work; cylinder head overhauls and even more major work, such as removing the sump and big ends, can be carried out without removing the engine. The major problem is likely to be rust. Front and rear wings are bolt-on items and sound wings can conceal horrors underneath. On Travellers the wood framing is structural and should be checked very carefully.

- Convertibles should be given especially close scrutiny. Convertibles are more prized and although there's a legitimate industry converting saloons to open tops, there are also fast-buck cowboys and inept DIY bodgers. These 'rogue rag-tops' are potential killers – literally – so contact the Morris Minor Owner's Club (see club directory) to check out a prospective buy. The club is so concerned about this unfortunate phenomenon that it has produced a fact sheet on convertibles.

1964 Morris 1100 MkI Four Door Saloon, 2 owners, 46,000 miles recorded, very good condition. **£1,700–1,900** *S*

1970 Morris Minor 1000 Two Door Saloon, right-hand drive, engine, gearbox and axle overhauled, all chromework renewed, new trim, full history, excellent condition. **£1,700–2,000** *PA*

1968 Morris Minor 1000 Traveller, 4 cylinders, 1098cc, well maintained, vinyl interior in good condition, woodwork in good order, largely original. **£2,100–2,500** *ADT*

1970 Morris Minor 1000 Saloon, mechanically sound, finished in almond green with matching interior, good condition. **£1,800–2,000** *VIN*

NAPIER

1911 Napier 15hp Colonial Model Four Seater Tourer, 4 cylinders, 2863cc, 4 speed gearbox, reupholstered in black leather, excellent condition.
£28,000–30,000 *BKS*

This is an example of the special Colonial model built for the export trade. It had increased ground clearance enabling it to ford fairly deep streams and to avoid all but the most formidable obstacles on unmade roads. Powered by a 2863cc, 4 cylinder engine built in unit with a 4 speed gearbox and 3 point suspended in an unusually robust chassis, the '15hp Noiseless Napier Touring Car' was hailed by The Autocar *magazine as a magnificent example of automobile engineering. Its appearance coincided with the best years that Napier ever had in the motor trade, with production of Napier cars peaking at 801 in 1911.*

It was developed from an earlier 15hp model launched in 1907 as a more affordable foil to the huge 6 cylinder models that had established Napier's reputation in the luxury car trade. The 15hp was the company's most successful model.

NASH

1921 Nash Six Litre, 6 cylinder overhead valve, unrestored, in working road-going condition.
£4,500–5,000 *DB*

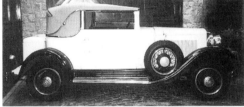

1932 Nash Advanced 8 Three-Position Drophead Coupé, 8 cylinders, in-line, overhead valves, twin plugs per cylinder, 115bhp at 3600rpm, 3 speed manual gearbox, 4 wheel drum brakes, semi-elliptic leaf spring suspension, right-hand drive, good condition throughout, imported from South America, stored for past few years, requires recommissioning.
£10,500–11,500 *C*

l. **1927 Nash Two Door Coupé,** 3600cc, left-hand drive, imported from North America in 1980, 76,500 miles recorded.
£8,000–9,000 *S*

NAYLOR

l. **1985 Naylor TF-1700,** 1.7 litres, 4 speed gearbox, front disc brakes, rear drums, steel chassis, all-steel panels on an ash frame, walnut dashboard and leather upholstery.
£12,000–14,000 *NCC*

OLDSMOBILE

1956 Oldsmobile Super 88 Convertible, V8, 350cu in, automatic transmission, needs a new hood, good condition.
£18,000–20,000 *PARA*

OLDSMOBILE Model	ENGINE cc/cyl	DATES	CONDITION 1	2	3
Curved Dash	1600/1	1901-04	£16,000	£14,000	£12,000
30	2771/6	1925-26	£9,000	£7,000	£4,000
Straight Eight	4213/8	1937-38	£14,000	£9,000	£5,000

OPEL

1931 Opel Tourer, 10hp, built in South Africa, right-hand drive, restored, good condition.
£7,000–7,800 *CRE*

1972 Opel GT, 1900cc, left-hand drive, imported, good condition.
£6,000–8,000 *CRE*

r. **1973 Opel GT,** 1900cc, good condition.
£5,500–6,000 *PC*

Of 106,000 Opel GTs produced, only 163 were officially imported into the UK. Engine sizes were either 1.1 litre or 1.9 litre with twin choke Solex carburettor. This car was previously owned by K. J. Hause and is illustrated extensively in his book Nur Fliegen ist Schöner.

OSCA

1954 OSCA Maserati 2000S, Maserati 6 cylinder engine, twin overhead camshafts, twin plugs per cylinder, 1985cc, 160bhp, 4 speed manual gearbox, 4 wheel drum brakes, restored, good condition.
£70,000–80,000 *C*

The history of Maserati is world renowned, but the early post-war years of the Maserati brothers is less familiar. The 3 remarkable brothers, Ernesto, Ettore and Bindo, had sold their successful racing car business to wealthy industrialist Adolfo Orsi in 1938. Orsi retained the brothers on a 10 year contract, at the end of which they started a similar business in Bologna as Officine Specializzate per la Construzione di Automobile-Fratelli Maserati SpA, abbreviated to OSCA.

OSCAs scored a large number of class successes in Continental events, including Le Mans and the Mille Miglia. Their greatest success, however, was achieved by Stirling Moss and Bill Lloyd in the 1954 Sebring 12 hour Race, which they won with a Briggs Cunningham car at an average speed of 73.65mph. In his book, Moss sums up the car: 'I was incredibly impressed by what turned out to be a real little thoroughbred of a car. It was powerful and well-balanced and very nimble... you could drive it as hard as you liked, slinging it sideways was no trouble.'

This 2000S is one of only 5 produced and one of only 3 fitted with all enveloping barchetta bodywork by Morelli, the other two being originally supplied in monoposto form.

> **Cross Reference**
> Restoration Projects

1964 OSCA 1600GTS Zagato Berlinetta, coachwork by Carrozzeria Zagato, 4 cylinder Fiat engine, 1568cc, 95bhp at 6000rpm, dismantled, partly restored, with gearbox, radiator and oil cooler, suspension, wheels, steering column, box and wheel, exhaust manifold, differential, half-shafts and dash panel ready for completion.
£10,000–14,000 *BKS*

This particular car was one of a total production run of only 128 of which 98 wore the Berlinetta body by Carrozzeria Zagato.

1909 Overland Model 30 Touring, 4 cylinders, L head, 30hp, 2 speed plantetary gearbox, rear wheel brakes only, full elliptic leaf spring suspension rear, semi-elliptic front, right-hand drive, special Roi Des Belges-style tonneau body, full mechanical and body restoration in the 1980s, engine/axles and transmission rebuilt, full history, good condition.
£19,000–23,000 *C*

The Overland first appeared in 1903. In 1907, the company was in serious difficulties until John North Willys, a car dealer from Elmira, New York, took over. In 1908, before Willys could secure factory premises, he built 465 Overlands in a circus tent. In 1909, 4,907 cars were produced. The same year Willys took over the Marion Motor Car Company and purchased the former Pope-Toledo factory in Toledo, Ohio, from where all future Overlands were made. He renamed his new organisation the Willys-Overland Company. This particular car was a show car for Overland.

OVERLAND

1914 Overland Runabout Speedster, 4 cylinders, complete mechanical overhaul, new tyres and overdrive, good condition.
£8,000–10,000 *KI*

PACKARD

Founded by James Ward Packard in Ohio, the company produced its first motor cars in 1899 and went on to build an envied reputation in the luxury car field. In 1915 the company produced the world's first production V12 engine and in the 1920s built some magnificent cost-no-object machines. In the following decade, with a dwindling luxury market, Packard's salvation came with a move into the middle market with the 120 series cars. After the war Cadillac made severe inroads into Packard's traditional luxury market, and even though Packard bought Studebaker in 1954, the Packard name disappeared in 1958.

1929 Packard Model 645 De Luxe 8 Phaeton, straight 8, 384.8cu in, 120bhp at 3200rpm, 4 speed manual gearbox, 4 wheel drum brakes, semi-elliptic leaf spring brakes, left-hand drive, fully restored, mechanical brakes uprated to a hydraulic system, good condition.
£44,000–48,000   *C*

l. **1930 Packard 740 Roadster,** 8 cylinders, chrome wire wheels, twin spotlights, finished in orange with brown fenders, tan upholstery, white wall tyres, side mounts, good condition.
£45,000–50,000   *KI*

1934 Packard Eleventh Series Twelve Model 1107 Five Seater Custom Coupé Type 737/21, V12, 7.3 litres, 0–60mph in 20.4 seconds, 22,000 miles recorded, good original condition.
£67,000–73,000   *BKS*

With its proud slogan 'ask the man who owns one', the Packard was always among America's finest automobiles during its long production life.

The Packard company had pioneered the V12 configuration with their Twin Six of 1915–24, and when they brought out a new V12 in 1932 as a counter to multi-cylinder models from makers like Cadillac, they initially revived the old nomenclature, though from 1933 it became simply the Twelve.

One of just 960 Eleventh Series of all kinds to be built. It is believed that only 2 or 3 of these 5 passenger coupés were constructed by the factory.

c1931 Packard Standard 8 Sedanca Town Car, 8 cylinders, 6300cc, 110bhp, engine overhauled, requires recommissioning following a period of storage, good condition.
£11,000–15,000   *BKS*

Inspired to build their first car in 1899, having tried an 1898 Winton and found it wanting, brothers J. W. and W. D. Packard progressed rapidly from building a primitive single cylinder buggy into the grand touring car market. A twin cylinder car appeared in 1902 followed in 1903 by a 4 cylinder, a 6 cylinder car in 1911 and the company achieved a major landmark in 1915 with the introduction of the world's first production V12 engine.

This car may be one of a kind, possibly by a European coachbuilder such as Le Baron.

PACKARD Model	ENGINE cc/cyl	DATES	CONDITION		
			1	2	3
Twin Six	6946/12	1916-23	£30,000	£20,000	£15,000
6	3973/6	1921-24	£20,000	£15,000	£12,000
6, 7, 8 Series	5231/8	1929-39	£35,000	£25,000	£14,000
12	7300/12	1936-39	£50,000+	£30,000	£18,000

1934 Packard 8 Model 1101 Two Seater Roadster, 5.2 litres, 319.2cu in, 120bhp at 3200rpm, right-hand drive, chassis and running gear restored, rebuild including replica 2 seater boat-tailed body, 42,000 miles recorded, stored since 1959, good condition.
£22,000–27,000 *BKS*

1934 Packard Golfer's Coupé, left-hand drive, totally restored by Packard specialists, good condition.
£85,000–87,500 *PAL*

1936 Packard 8 Convertible Victoria, straight 8, L-head, 320cu in, 130bhp at 3200rpm, 3 speed manual gearbox, 4 wheel drum brakes, semi-elliptic leaf spring suspension, left-hand drive, engine recently rebuilt, leather upholstery in good condition, paintwork requires attention, new top required.
£24,500–25,500 *C*

l. **1938 Packard V12 Touring Cabriolet,** V12, 473.31cu in, 175bhp at 3200rpm, 3 speed manual gearbox, independent coil spring front suspension, semi-elliptic leaf spring rear, 4 wheel drum brakes, left-hand drive, recent mechanical restoration, accessories include dual sidemounts with metal covers, walnut interior wood trim, good condition.
£53,000–58,000 *C*

This Packard is from the Sixteenth Series. A total of 157 were built during one year from September 1937.

PANHARD-LEVASSOR

l. **1902 Panhard-Levassor Type A2 Twin Cylinder Rear Entrance Tonneau,** coachwork by Labourdette, 7hp, 3 speed type KA transmission, chain drive to the rear wheels, Bleriot headlamps, good original condition.
£37,000–40,000 *S*

This car left the Paris works in 1902 and has been in Spain ever since.

PANTHER

1978/79 Panther Lima, completely restored, right-hand drive, mechanically sound, concours condition, full history.
£5,300–5,800 *PA*

1986 Panther Kallista, V6, 2.8 litre Ford engine, 5 speed gearbox, recently restored, 23,000 miles recorded, excellent condition.
£7,450–8,450 *VIN*

1987 Panther Kallista, good condition.
£5,000–5,500 *H&H*

PEGASO

A Spanish truck manufacturer with supercar aspirations, in 1951 Pegaso produced a stunning-looking and complex V8-engined high-performance sports car. In its most potent form, with 3178cc and twin blowers, power output was reckoned to be 285bhp. However, between 1951 and 1958 only 125 Pegasos were built.

1954 Pegaso Z-102 Coupé, coachwork by Saoutchik, quad cam 2822cc V8 engine, 5 speed constant mesh transaxle, restored, fully restored, good condition.
£73,500–76,000 *BKS*

This car was the first of 7 with this particular body style. Built in the former Hispano-Suiza factory in Barcelona by the state truck company ENASA, the Pegaso was designed by the gifted Wilfredo Ricart y Perez, a former chief engineer of Alfa Romeo, and was intended as a showcase of Spanish technical expertise. Virtually every part was made in-house, and only 100 or so cars were built before the success of the company's commercial vehicles forced the end of its prestigious but uneconomical car line. In 1953 a 2.8 litre Pegaso recorded a flying mile figure of 151mph on the Jabbeke Highway in Belgium.

PEUGEOT

1899 Peugeot 8hp Double Phaeton with Surrey Top, rear-mounted twin cylinder 8hp engine, mechanically restored, including new main and big end bearings, overhaul of brakes, clutch, gearbox and transmission, king pins and steering, stored since 1975, good condition.
£22,500–27,500 *BKS*

1913 Peugeot Bébé Type BPI Two Seater, 856cc, engine rebuilt, reversed quarter-elliptic leaf spring rear suspension, finished in French blue livery, folding windscreen, hood, klaxon horn and Mondia fork-mounted acetylene headlamps.
£8,000–10,000 *BKS*

Ettore Bugatti was responsible for the design of the Bébé Peugeot at a time when production of Bugatti cars at the Molsheim works was slowly getting off the ground. The sale of the T-head lateral valve engine design to Peugeot generated a useful injection of capital for Bugatti's operation, at the time providing Peugeot with a design which put them at the forefront of French light car design.

PEUGEOT Model	ENGINE cc/cyl	DATES	CONDITION 1	2	3
Bebe	856/4	1912-14	£18,000	£12,000	£8,000
153	2951/4	1913-26	£9,000	£5,000	£3,000
163	1490/4	1920-24	£5,000	£4,000	£2,000
Bebe	676/4	1920-25	£7,000	£6,000	£3,000
156	5700/6	1922-24	£7,000	£5,000	£3,000
174	3828/4	1922-28	£7,500	£5,000	£2,000
172	714/4	1926-28	£4,000	£3,000	£1,500
183	1990/6	1929-30	£5,000	£3,000	£1,500
201	996/4	1930-36	£4,500	£3,000	£1,500
402	2140/4	1938-40	£4,500	£3,000	£1,000

Right-hand drive cars and tourers will always achieve more interest than left-hand drive. Good solid cars.

PIERCE-ARROW

1929 Pierce-Arrow Model 133 Golfing Coupé, straight 8, 5998cc, 125bhp, wood-spoked artillery wheels, finished in blue and black livery.
£21,000–25,000 *BKS*

This car was built during the honeymoon year of the ill-fated merger between Pierce-Arrow and Studebaker. Though economies of scale led to Pierce-Arrow cylinder blocks being cast in the Studebaker foundries at South Bend, Indiana, there was no compromising on Pierce-Arrow's legendary high standards. The blocks were cast from harder material than the contemporary Studebaker units, each one bearing a code that detailed the day and hour of casting so that the Pierce-Arrow metallurgists could monitor production quality.

1904 Pierce-Arrow Stanhope Model 8M Transformable Motorette, one cylinder, 8hp, 2 speed planetary gearbox, full elliptic leaf spring suspension, right-hand drive, repainted, original interior intact.
£24,000–27,000 *C*

r. **1930 Pierce-Arrow Model B Four Door Sedan,** 9 bearing, 5997cc, straight 8 engine, factory-designed bodywork, 139in wheelbase, finished in blue and black, wire wheels, good condition.
£17,000–19,000 *BKS*

1936 Pierce-Arrow Model 1603 Derham Town Car, 12 cylinders, restored in 1990, good condition.
£140,000+ *BLK*

PIPER

1972 Piper P2 Sports, 4 cylinder, Ford 1700cc BDA, 16 valve engine, 162bhp, 4 speed gearbox, competition clutch, twin Weber carburettors, magnesium wheels with Pirelli P6 tyres, Connolly hide trim, 2,100 miles recorded, as new condition.
£5,750–7,250 *S*

PLYMOUTH

The Chrysler Corporation's new car for 1928 was called the Plymouth in recognition of the strength and endurance of the first American colonists, the Pilgrims, who had landed there in 1620. It was clearly aimed at the market cornered by Henry Ford's Model A. By 1931 some 100,000 or so Plymouths left the factory each year and by 1933 production figures saw the Plymouth firmly behind Chevrolet and Ford.

1953 Plymouth Cranbrook Four Door Sedan, 6 cylinder in-line, 3569cc, 100bhp, 3 speed manual gearbox, left-hand drive, finished in maroon with grey fabric trim, fully restored, good condition.
£2,500–3,000 *C*

1931 Plymouth Model 3OU Two Door Coupé, restored, 32,700 miles recorded from new, resprayed.
£13,000–15,000 *S*

This car was first registered to a minister in Pennsylvania and kept by him until his death. It was then bought by a collector who, as a boy had cleaned the car for the minister.

1971 Plymouth Duster, 340cu in, requires a respray.
£4,000–4,500 *CTP*

PONTIAC

Although the name Pontiac had been attached to several early American automobile ventures, it wasn't until 1926 that the marque as we know it today really got under way as a new General Motors brand produced by GM's Oakland Motor Company. In the General Motors hierarchy the early Pontiacs slotted in just above Chevrolet and enjoyed immediate success, outselling the more expensive Oaklands. Consequently in 1932 General Motors dropped the Oakland brand and renamed the division the Pontiac Motor Company. The Pontiac name derives from the native American Indian tribe and is one of the few subsidiary US marques to have been created rather than acquired. Pontiac is also distinguished as the only companion car in the GM line-up to have eclipsed its parent in sales volume.

1954 Pontiac Chieftain Convertible, straight 8, left-hand drive, automatic transmission, finished in light blue with white interior, new white hood, good condition throughout.
£11,500–12,000 *CGB*

> **Miller's is a price GUIDE not a price LIST**

1959 Pontiac Bonneville Two Door Hard Top, automatic transmission, 17,000 miles recorded, finished in peach pink with cream top, original interior.
£7,500–8,500 *CGB*

1968 Pontiac Le Mans, good condition.
£6,000–6,750 *CTP*

r. **1987 Pontiac Firebird,** 5 litres, good condition.
£6,000–8,000 *VIC*

| PONTIAC | ENGINE | DATES | CONDITION | | |
Model	cc/cyl		1	2	3
Six-27	3048/6	1926-29	£9,000	£7,000	£4,000
Silver Streak	3654/8	1935-37	£12,000	£9,000	£5,500
6	3638/6	1937-49	£7,000	£4,000	£3,500
8	4078/8	1937-49	£7,000	£4,000	£3,500

PORSCHE

Volkswagen Beetle designer Ferdinand Porsche may have given the world the people's car, but it was his son Ferry who, with long-time associate Karl Rabe, created a car that people all over the world would prize from the day the first Porsche rolled off the production line. These days a Porsche – virtually any Porsche – stands for precision, performance, purity and perfection, and the 356 is the first chapter in that story. Well, not quite. The 356 was so named because it was actually the 356th project from the Porsche design office since it had been set up in 1930. It was also the first car to bear the Porsche name. Post-war expediency forced a make-do reliance on VW Beetle underpinnings, but the 356 is much more than a bug in

butterfly's clothes. Its concept, rear-engined layout and design descended directly from the father car, but in the handsome athletic son the genes were mutated miraculously into a true sporting machine. Some aficionados adore the first-of-the-breed purity of the earliest 'jelly mould' cars, but with each successive modification the Porsche detached itself further from its humble roots. A pert, nimble, tail-happy treat the 356 is still the prettiest production Porsche there's ever been, the foundation stone of a proud sporting tradition. And if you squint at more modern Porsches, like the 911 and today's current models, you can still identify the genetic inheritance passed down from a true original.

1964 Porsche 356 Carrera 2 Cabriolet, 2 litres, 4 cylinders, flat, horizontally opposed air-cooled engine, 4 overhead camshafts driven by bevel gear and upshafts, 5 speed manual gearbox, 4 wheel disc brakes, independent suspension, left-hand drive, fully restored, finished in ivory with black top, plus a hard top, black leather upholstery, good condition.
£85,000–95,000 C

Ferry Porsche and Karl Rabe began work on the Type 356 project in June 1947. The concept was to put a mildly tuned version of the 4 cylinder Volkswagen engine and its gearbox in a tubular space frame. Volkswagen components such as suspension units, steering and brakes were used for economy and reliability. The VW engine, mounted first ahead of the rear axle and then behind it, produced a paltry 25hp in standard form but was improved by englarging the ports and raising the compression ratio from 5.8:1 to 7.0:1. The roadster bodywork was designed by Erwin Komenda.

This is the rare Cabriolet version of the later 356 Carreras. It is believed that less than 50 Carrera two Cabriolets were built.

PORSCHE Model	ENGINE cc/cyl	DATES	CONDITION 1	2	3
356	var/4	1949-53	£15,000	£8,000	£5,000
356 Cabriolet	var/4	1951-53	£20,000	£14,000	£10,000
356A	1582/4	1955-59	£13,000	£9,000	£5,000
356A Cabriolet	1582/4	1956-59	£16,000	£10,000	£7,000
356A Speedster	1582/4	1955-58	£25,000	£19,000	£14,000
356 Carrera	1582/ 1966/4	1960-65	£35,000	£25,000	£18,000
356C	1582/4	1963-65	£14,000	£10,000	£5,000
356C Cabriolet	1582/4	1963-64	£22,000	£16,000	£10,000
911/911L/T/E	1991/6	1964-68	£10,000	£7,000	£5,000
912	1582/4	1965-68	£6,500	£5,000	£2,000
911S	1991/6	1966-69	£12,000	£8,000	£5,500
911S	2195/6	1969-71	£13,000	£9,000	£6,000
911T	2341/6	1971-73	£13,000	£8,000	£6,000
911E	2341/6	1971-73	£12,000	£8,000	£6,000
914/4	1679/4	1969-75	£4,000	£3,000	£1,000
914/6	1991/6	1969-71	£6,000	£3,500	£1,500
911S	2341/6	1971-73	£16,000	£10,000	£8,500
Carrera RS lightweight	2687/6	1973	£35,000	£28,000	£16,000
Carrera RS Touring	2687/6	1973	£30,000	£26,000	£17,000
Carrera 3	2994/6	1976-77	£14,000	£9,000	£7,000
924 Turbo	1984/4	1978-83	£5,000	£4,000	£2,000
928/928S	4474/4664/V8	1977-86	£10,000	£7,000	£4,000
911SC	2993/6	1977-83	£12,000	£8,000	£6,000

Sportomatic cars are less desirable.

1972 Porsche 914, good condition.
£2,400–2,800 *H&H*

1973 Porsche 911 Carrera, 2.7 litre engine,
very good condition.
£16,000–17,000 *FHF*

1974 Porsche 911S Carrera Coupé, 2.7 litres,
210bhp at 6300rpm, air conditioning, 41,000km
recorded from new, well maintained, good condition.
£13,000–15,000 *BKS*

**1973 Porsche 911 Carrera RS Touring Sports
Coupé,** manual transmission, left-hand drive, full
restoration, good condition.
£20,000–24,000 *BKS*

1977 Porsche 911 Carrera Sportmatic, 3 litres,
100,000 miles recorded, service history, electric
sunroof, very good condition.
£9,000–12,000 *VIC*

1979 Porsche 911SC Sport, 3 litres, 100,000 miles
recorded, full service history, very good condition.
£15,000–16,500 *PARA*

1979 Porsche 928 Coupé, 4500cc, stored for the last 3 years, Series II wheels, new rear section to exhaust fitted, good condition.
£4,500–5,000   *H&H*

1980 Porsche 911SC Targa, 6 cylinders, 3000cc, removable roof panel, left-hand drive, well maintained, overhauled braking system, good condition.
£10,400–11,400   *ADT*

1984 Porsche 911 Targa Carrera, 3.2 litres, mechanically sound, 79,000 miles recorded, one owner, interior needs some attention.
£17,000–18,000   *PARA*

1987 Porsche 944 Turbo, 54,000 miles recorded, full service history, good condition.
£8,000–10,000   *VIC*

1990 Porsche 911 Turbo 2 Coupé, finished in Guards red, air conditioning, 17in cup alloy wheels, anti-lock brakes, 51,000 miles recorded, full service history, good condition.
£40,000–45,000   *PARA*

1997 Porsche Boxster, finished in black with tan leather interior, sports pack, 17in cup alloy wheels, twin air bags, 500 miles recorded, excellent condition.
£40,000–41,500   *PARA*

RAILTON

1934 Railton Drophead Coupé, excellent condition.
£14,000–16,500 *FHF*

RELIANT

It's ironic that the Reliant's humble and often ridiculed glass-fibre utility three-wheelers born in the 1950s should outlast the dramatic sports cars that joined Reliant's range in the next decade. Reliant's sporting products started off quirkily with the ugly Sabre of 1961–3, which grew into the far more harmonious Sabre Six of 1962–4, then the ground-breaking Ogle-designed Scimitar. Although there was nothing revolutionary in the production of its glass-fibre-moulded body, the shape and styling of the Scimitar GTE created a new class of car, the sports estate. This cross-country carry-all with sports appeal appeared three years before Volvo leapt on the sports-wagon bandwagon with the P1800ES. Today this plastic classic still cuts it as one of that rare breed of sensible sports cars. It's a mark of how enduring the design was that the Scimitar GTE lasted from 1968 to 1986 and still looked fresh even at the end of the 16,000 production run.

1967 Reliant Scimitar Coupé SE4, V6, 3 litres, excellent condition.
£4,000–4,250 *GW*

1972 Reliant Scimitar GTE, 6 cylinders,
2994cc, manual transmission with overdrive,
mechanically good overall, black interior,
good condition.
£1,900–2,400 *BRIT*

1975 Reliant Scimitar SE5A, 3 litres, restored,
excellent condition.
£6,000–6,500 *GW*

1973 Reliant Scimitar GTE, 2994cc,
manual transmission with overdrive,
resprayed, good overall condition.
£2,200–2,500 *VIN*

1979 Reliant Scimitar SE6A, 3 litres, full
restoration including reconditioned engine,
suspension, repaint, retrim, very good condition.
£9,000–10,000 *GW*

1979 Reliant Scimitar GTC, 2792cc, Ford V6,
2.8 litre engine, automatic transmission.
£6,300–7,000 *LF*

*Fewer than 450 GTCs were built. Reliant called
upon Ogle to design an open convertible on the GTE
base and this very attractive car was the result. It is
a genuine 4 seater convertible, capable of 120mph.*

RELIANT Model	ENGINE cc/cyl	DATES	CONDITION		
			1	2	3
Sabre 4 Coupé & Drophead	1703/4	1961-63	£4,500	£2,750	£1,000
Sabre 6 " "	2553/6	1962-64	£5,000	£3,250	£1,000
Scimitar GT Coupé SE4	2553/6, 2994 V6	1964-70	£4,500	£2,500	£1,000
Scimitar GTE Sports Estate SE5/5A	2994/V6	1968-75	£4,500	£2,000	£750
Scimitar GTE Sports Estate SE6/6A	2994/V6	1976-80	£6,000	£3,500	£1,250
Scimitar GTE Sports Estate SE6B	2792/V6	1980-86	£8,000	£5,000	£2,000
Scimitar GTC Convertible SE8B	2792/V6	1980-86	£9,000	£8,000	£5,500

RENAULT

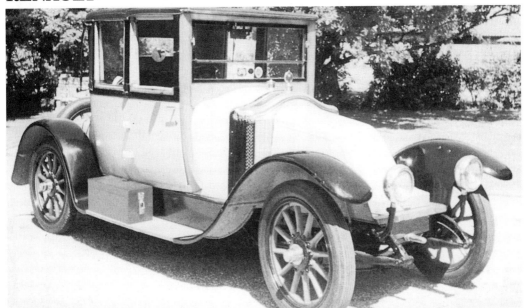

1919 Renault Type EU 15.8hp Drophead Coupé, 4 cylinders, 2800cc, aluminium coachwork by Hayes & Miller, New York, electric lighting and dynastart, electric screen wiper, 4 speed gearbox, ready to rally.
£10,500–12,000 *BKS*

1930 Renault Monastella, imported into UK in 1930, finished in cream and black with beige interior, excellent restoration.
£7,500–8,000 *AS*

1962 Renault Caravelle Roadster, bare metal respray, full engine rebuild, completely restored in France in 1993, excellent condition.
£2,250–2,750 *S*

The successor to the Dauphine and Floride models, the rear-engined Caravelle featured a Gordini 4 cylinder unit of 956cc, and carried elegant sports bodywork. A car with more presence than those which preceded it, it was well equipped and had 4 wheel disc brakes, amongst other rare features as standard.

RENAULT Model	ENGINE cc/cyl	DATES	CONDITION 1	2	3
40hp	7540/6	1919-21	£30,000	£20,000	£10,000
SR	4537/4	1919-22	£10,000	£7,000	£5,000
EU-15.8HP	2815/4	1919-23	£5,000	£3,000	£2,000
GS-IG	2121/4	1920-23	£5,000	£3,000	£2,000
JP	9123/6	1922-29	£25,000	£20,000	£15,000
KJ	951/4	1923-29	£6,000	£4,000	£2,000
Mona Six	1474/6	1928-31	£7,000	£5,000	£3,000
Reinastella	7128/8	1929-32	£25,000	£20,000	£15,000
Viva Six	3181/6	1929-34	£10,000	£7,000	£3,000
14/45	2120/4	1929-35	£7,000	£5,000	£2,000
Nervahuit	4240/8	1931	£12,000	£10,000	£7,000
UY	1300/4	1932-34	£7,000	£5,000	£2,000
ZC/ZD2	4825/8	1934-35	£12,000	£10,000	£7,000
YN2	1463/4	1934-39	£7,000	£5,000	£2,000
Airline Super and Big 6	3620/6	1935	£10,000	£8,000	£5,000
18	2383/4	1936-39	£9,000	£5,000	£3,000
26	4085/6	1936-39	£12,000	£8,000	£5,000

Veteran pre-war models like the 2 cylinder AX, AG and BB are very popular, with values ranging between £6,000 and £15,000. The larger 4 cylinder cars like the AM, AZ, XB and VB are very reliable and coachbuilt examples command £30,000+, with 6 cylinder coachbuilt cars commanding a premium.

RENAULT Model	ENGINE cc/cyl	DATES	CONDITION		
			1	2	3
4CV	747/ 760/4	1947-61	£3,500	£2,000	£850
Fregate	1997/4	1952-60	£3,000	£2,000	£1,000
Dauphine	845/4	1956-66	£1,500	£1,000	£350
Dauphine Gordini	845/4	1961-66	£2,000	£1,000	£450
Floride	845/4	1959-62	£3,000	£2,000	£600
Caravelle	956/ 1108/4	1962-68	£4,500	£2,800	£750
R4	747/ 845/4	1961-86	£2,000	£1,500	£350
R8/R10	1108/4	1962-71	£1,800	£750	£200
R8 Gordini	1108/4	1965-66	£8,000	£5,000	£2,000
R8 Gordini	1255/4	1966-70	£8,000	£5,500	£2,500
R8S	1108/4	1968-71	£2,000	£1,200	£400

1981 Renault 5 Turbo, 4 cylinders, 1397cc, imported from Germany, converted to 210bhp, reconditioned turbocharger fitted, new clutch, brake discs and dampers, bodywork refurbished and repainted at a cost of £830, very good condition.
£9,500–12,000   *COYS*

The Renault 5 Turbo was born from a casual conversation between 2 like-minded engineers. As both of them, Jean Terramorsi and Henry Lherm, worked for Renault, they were in a position to persuade the company of the merits of a road-burner that could double as an image-enhancer and a competition machine. The Project 822 evolved in the spring of 1977, assisted by Michel Tetu (who later designed both Renault and Ligier Grand Prix cars), and the unassuming hatchback was transformed into a powerful mid-engined 2 seater. Powered by a turbocharged 1397cc, 4 cylinder engine, it produced 160bhp at 6000rpm, and 155lb.ft at 3250rpm. With a 5 speed transaxle, the now rear wheel drive 5 could achieve 0–60mph in 7.7 seconds, and 125mph.

RICKENBACKER

1926 Rickenbacker Super Sport, torpedo-shaped rear deck, aerofoil bumpers, laminated mahogany cycle wings, brass-bound with wood inlay, bullet-shaped headlamps, safety glass all-round, totally restored, excellent condition.
£170,000–190,000   *BLK*

Captain and Squadron Commander Edward Vernon Rickenbacker was an American WWI hero, and a driving ace with a record of wins. The Rickenbacker Motor Company officially came into being in July 1921, with the first car being produced in 1922. The Super Sport was introduced at the New York Show in 1926, and was thought to be America's fastest stock car, and guaranteed to do 90mph. This particular example is the only known surviving example of the Super Sport model.

REO

1923 Reo T6 Four Door Saloon, 1300cc, repainted, rewired, new interior, period fittings, excellent condition throughout.
£9,500–10,000   *H&H*

1925 Reo T6 Flying Cloud Roadster, 4000cc, 3 speed manual gearbox, dickey seat, right-hand drive, restored, stored for some time in dry conditions, excellent condition throughout.
£6,500–7,000   *H&H*

RGS

1954 RGS Atalanta, 2.6 litres, restored Aston Martin DB2/4 Vantage engine, fully restored, excellent condition.
£40,000–45,000   *PC*

Raced in the 1950s, and with a full race history, this was the first RGS Atalanta produced.

RILEY

The small firm of Riley was right at the forefront of the early British motor car industry, producing its first car in 1898. In the 1920s and 1930s the Coventry firm produced some very appealing and highly regarded small sporting cars, with elegant bodies and excellent power units, all of which used twin low-set cams operating pushrods and overhead valves. In the late 1930s the company spread itself too thinly with too many models and not enough capital and was forced to sell out to Morris in 1938. The immediate post-war products, the RM series cars, were hallmark Riley sporting saloons, still much appreciated by enthusiasts today for their looks, long-legged cruising ability and assured handling. For many fans the RMs also rate as the last real Rileys. Sadly later Rileys were rather ill-served under the BMC banner, which spawned a series of dull badge-engineered look-alikes. About the only intriguing off-spring was the Elf. It's really only a Mini with a boot – or a bustle, if you like – a fancier grille and a smattering of wood veneer, but they can make a distinctive budget classic. The Riley name eventually faded away for good in 1969.

1930 Riley Nine Monaco, 4 cylinders, 1087cc, MkIV chassis, Weymann fabric saloon body, unused for several years, requires restoration, complete except for rear seat squab.
£4,500–5,000 *ADT*

1932/3 Riley March Special Four Seater Tourer, coachwork by John Charles & Son, Kew, right-hand drive, red paintwork and upholstery, fully restored to high standard, excellent condition.
£7,000–9,000 *BKS*

The basis of the March Special was the rolling chassis of the basic Riley Nine 106½in wheelbase, with bolt-on wire wheels. It was developed by Kevill-Davies and March Ltd of London, the 'March' being Freddie March, who was already a well-known racing driver, and who created the Goodwood racing circuit. Only about 60 examples of the Riley March Specials were built.

1933 Riley Nine Falcon Four Door Saloon, 1087cc high camshaft engine, black factory paintwork, ash body framing in good condition, 44,000 miles recorded, original wiring, good original condition.
£8,000–9,000 *BKS*

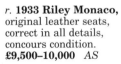

r. **1933 Riley Monaco,** original leather seats, correct in all details, concours condition.
£9,500–10,000 *AS*

RILEY Model	ENGINE cc/cyl	DATES	CONDITION 1	2	3
9hp	1034/2	1906-07	£9,000	£6,000	£3,000
Speed 10	1390/2	1909-10	£10,000	£6,000	£3,000
11	1498/4	1922-27	£7,000	£4,000	£2,000
9	1075/4	1927-32	£10,000	£7,000	£4,000
9 Gamecock	1098/4	1932-33	£14,000	£10,000	£6,000
Lincock 12hp	1458/6	1933-36	£9,000	£7,000	£5,000
Imp 9hp	1089/4	1934-35	£35,000	£28,000	£20,000
Kestrel 12hp	1496/4	1936-38	£8,000	£5,000	£2,000
Sprite 12hp	1496/4	1936-38	£40,000	£35,000	£20,000
Many Riley 9hp 'Specials' available ideal for VSCC and club events.					

1936 Riley Merlin Special, black fibreglass body, aluminium bonnet and restraining straps, aeroscreens, cycle wings, Lucas lamps, red knock-on wire wheels, pre-selector gearbox, twin SU carburettors, side exit exhaust, good condition.
£5,750–6,250 *S*

1937 Riley Monaco 9hp Saloon, 4 speed pre-selector gearbox, fully restored, new carpets, roof lining, leather trim, tyres and respoked wire wheels, low mileage since rebuild, excellent condition.
£7,350–8,000 *H&H*

1936 Riley Merlin 9hp Four Door Saloon, unused and in dry storage for several years, requires careful recommissioning, same ownership since new.
£4,200–4,800 *BKS*

r. **1951 Riley RME 2½ Litre Saloon,** 2443cc, original green leather interior, restored, ash frame at rear replaced, brightwork renewed, engine fully reconditioned, very good condition.
£5,000–5,500 *H&H*

RILEY Model	ENGINE cc/cyl	DATES	CONDITION 1	2	3
1½ litre RMA	1496/4	1945-52	£6,000	£3,500	£1,500
1½ litre RME	1496/4	1952-55	£6,000	£3,500	£1,500
2½ litre RMB/F	2443/4	1946-53	£9,000	£7,000	£3,000
2½ litre Roadster	2443/4	1948-50	£13,000	£11,000	£9,000
2½ litre Drophead	2443/4	1948-51	£20,000	£18,000	£10,000
Pathfinder	2443/4	1953-57	£3,500	£2,000	£750
2.6	2639/6	1957-59	£3,000	£1,800	£750
1.5	1489/4	1957-65	£3,000	£2,000	£850
4/68	1489/4	1959-61	£1,500	£700	£300
4/72	1622/4	1961-69	£1,600	£800	£300
Elf I/II/III	848/4	1961-66	£1,500	£850	£400
Kestrel I/II	1098/4	1965-67	£1,500	£850	£400

1954 Riley RME 1½ Litre, 4 cylinders, 1496cc, twin camshafts, original beige leather seats, new headlining and carpets, interior woodwork and chromework in good condition.
£3,200–3,700 *ADT*

The Riley RME first appeared in 1946, and was the first all-new Riley for some years. Although retaining many of the original Coventry designs, it had modern features such as torsion bar front suspension and rack-and-pinion steering. Power was supplied by a slightly modified version of the Riley 12/4 engine, which was in fact an enlarged version of the original 9hp design from 1926, with twin high set camshafts. This model remained in production until 1955.

1954 Riley RME Saloon, 1496cc, drives well, good condition throughout.
£1,800–2,200 *H&H*

1954 Riley RME, painted in French grey, original burgundy leather interior, restored at great expense, good condition.
£6,500–7,000 *DH*

1968 Riley Elf MkII Saloon, 998cc, 38,000 miles recorded since new, engine, electrical equipment, transmission, chassis and tyres in very good condition.
£1,650–1,850 *S*

'As old as the industry, as modern as the hour' was the slogan of the famous Riley. The diminutive Elf, with distinctive built-out boot and 998cc engine which replaced the standard 848cc type employed by Austin and Morris, was Riley's version of the Mini.

1968 Riley Elf MkIII, fully restored, very good condition.
£2,000–2,500 *CARS*

ROLLS-ROYCE

Henry Royce was a Manchester electrical engineer who built three experimental 10hp 2 cylinder cars in 1903. The Honourable Charles Rolls was an entrepreneur selling foreign cars in London. They teamed up in 1904 to form Rolls-Royce, a name that ever since has represented excellence with elegance and supreme luxury. From the beginning of their partnership they established Rolls-Royce's credentials as an exclusive producer of very expensive and superb motor cars of the highest quality. The 40/50, which became known universally as the Silver Ghost, really could make a plausible claim to being the 'best car in the world', although in the 1930s, for example, such an extravagant claim was harder to justify against rival luxury contenders at home and abroad. The Silver Ghost was continually developed through the years until it was replaced in 1925 by the New Phantom, later referred to as the Phantom I. This continued the Rolls-Royce policy of evolution rather than revolution – it was in essence a Ghost chassis with a new overhead valve engine. Earlier in 1922 Rolls-Royce had added the smaller 3127cc 20 model, which evolved in 1929 into the 3669cc 20/25 and later into the 25/30. In 1931 Rolls-Royce bought Bentley – some suggest the main motive was to stifle competition from the magnificent 8 litre Bentley. In 1949 Rolls-Royce entered a new era with the Silver Dawn, the first Rolls-Royce offered complete by the factory rather than as a chassis to be fitted with bespoke coachwork of the owner's choosing. Rolls-Royce continued to offer chassis to coachbuilders alongside its own factory-bodied cars until 1965 with the launch of the Silver Shadow. This new Rolls-Royce was the first to feature monocoque construction with an integral body and chassis which, at a stroke, removed the scope for coachbuilt bodies, although the Phantom V Limousine still retained a separate chassis. In 1971 Rolls-Royce Limited became bankrupt after trouble with the RB211 aircraft engine, and the car division was separated out and floated as a public company. In recent years Rolls-Royce has recovered strongly and injected new energy into the Bentley marque.

1921 Rolls-Royce 40/50 Silver Ghost Alpine Eagle, 6 cylinder, side valves, 7428cc, 4 speed manual gearbox, well maintained, original engine recently overhauled, new correct pattern exhaust system.
£65,000–75,000 *C*

The Alpine Eagle Silver Ghost was a development of the highly successful London to Edinburgh model. In 1912 James Radleigh, driving a London to Edinburgh Rolls-Royce Silver Ghost, took part in the Austrian Alpine Trial. The car he used was fitted with a 3 speed gearbox and suffered failure on one or two of the very severest gradients. Following this unfortunate episode, and as a result of ongoing works trials, new features were introduced on the London to Edinburgh type chassis, the most significant being a 4 speed gearbox option and a larger volume radiator matrix. Following these modifications a team of cars competed with huge success on the 1913 Alpine Trials and as a result the model name 'London to Edinburgh' became supplanted by 'Alpine Eagle' for this specification. This particular car was rescued in 1959 in Derbyshire where it was being used as a glider launching tug.

l. **1921 Rolls-Royce 40/50 Silver Ghost Sedanca De Ville,** coachwork by Hibbard & Darrin, 4 wheel brakes, SU electric fuel pump, later Lucas headlamps, two-tone green paintwork and brightwork in good condition, green leather interior trim to chauffeur's compartment, Bedford cord trim to rear passenger compartment with veneered cabinet.
£45,000–50,000 *BKS*

1925 Rolls-Royce Phantom I Barker Sports Torpedo, meticulously restored.
£225,000+ *BLK*

This unique car was built for the Maharajah of Bekanar, Ganga Singh for use as a hunting car on his 23,000 square miles of property. He later gave the car to the Maharajah of Jodhpur who, in turn, gave it to the Maharajah of Idan.

1929 Rolls-Royce 20/25 Foursome Sports Coupé, coachwork by Hooper, 3669cc, panelled top, integral luggage boot, semaphore indicators, rear mounted spare wheel, extensive mechanical and electrical overhaul.
£23,000–25,000 *BKS*

The 20/25hp model of 1929 was a direct development of the 20hp with an enhanced and enlarged engine, now 3669cc. This offered the bespoke coachbuilder more scope to fit a larger and heavier body without adverse effect on performance.

1930 Rolls-Royce 20/25 Four Door Open Tourer, barrel-sided body, twin-side mounted spares, spoke wheels, rear trunk, rebuilt engine, new head fitted and valve seats hardened, 500 miles recorded since rebuild, good condition overall, attention to electrical equipment required.
£21,000–25,000 *S*

The popularity created by the smaller 3.2 litre 6 cylinder Rolls-Royce 20 which appeared in 1922 was maintained by its lineal successors. The 20/25 with an increased bore of 82.5mm producing an additional half-litre capacity was announced in 1929. A faster car with engine suitably modified formed the basis of the Derby-built Bentleys of 1934 onwards.

1926 Rolls-Royce 20hp Maythorn Four Door Four Seater Open Tourer, full weather equipment including sidescreens, original artillery wheels, twin sidemounts, correct lamps, klaxon horn, good condition.
£27,000–30,000 *RCC*

1929 Rolls-Royce Phantom II Sports Tourer, boat tail tourer with cut-away wings, torpedo side-mounted tool boxes, twin windscreens, possibly a Brockman body, new stainless steel exhaust system, good overall condition.
£30,000–35,000 *RCC*

1931 Rolls-Royce Phantom II 40/50 Sedanca De Ville, coachwork by Barker & Co, chassis, running gear, bodyframe and coachwork in good condition, some exhaust system parts replaced, new Bedford cord upholstery, new carpets and new leather front door trims, would benefit from some cosmetic attention to paintwork and exterior chrome, careful recommissioning and polishing required, well maintained.
£25,500–28,500 *BKS*

1932 Rolls-Royce 20/25 Sports Saloon, coachwork by Thrupp & Maberly, side and rear-mounted spare wheels, louvred bonnet, new tyres, quiet engine, requires cosmetic attention.
£13,000–15,000 *RCC*

1933 Rolls-Royce 20/25, coachwork by William Arnold, good original car.
£23,000–25,000 *BLE*

1934 Rolls-Royce 20/25 Sports Saloon, coachwork by James Young, sunroof, excellent original vehicle.
£26,500–27,500 *BA*

1933 Rolls-Royce Phantom I.
£60,000–65,000 *BLE*

ROLLS-ROYCE Model	ENGINE cc/cyl	DATES	CONDITION		
			1	2	3
Silver Ghost 40/50	7035/6	pre-WWI	£350,000+	£120,000	£80,000
Silver Ghost 40/50	7428/6	post-WWI	£110,000+	£70,000	£40,000
20hp (3 speed)	3127/6	1922-25	£29,000+	£23,000	£15,000
20hp	3127/6	1925-29	£30,000+	£24,000	£15,000
Phantom I	7668/6	1925-29	£50,000+	£28,000	£22,000
20/25	3669/6	1925-26	£30,000+	£18,000	£13,000
Phantom II	7668/6	1929-35	£40,000+	£30,000	£20,000
Phantom II Continental	7668/6	1930-35	£60,000+	£40,000	£28,000
25/30	4257/6	1936-38	£24,000+	£18,000	£12,000
Phantom III	7340/12	1936-39	£38,000	£28,000	£14,000
Wraith	4257/6	1938-39	£38,000	£32,000	£25,000

Prices will vary considerably depending on heritage, originality, coachbuilder, completeness and body style. A poor reproduction body can often mean the value is dependent only upon a rolling chassis and engine.

1934 Rolls-Royce 20/25 Shooting Brake,
coachwork converted by Charlesworth from a saloon,
restored paintwork, chromework, ash panels, engine,
suspension and wiring, original leather interior.
£65,000–70,000 *S*

1934 Rolls-Royce Phantom II,
coachwork by Hooper.
£140,000–150,000 *PJF*

A one-off gentleman's golfing coupé.

**1935 Rolls-Royce Phantom II Long Chassis
Saloon,** restored in North America, carefully
maintained, 8,000 miles recorded, good working
order throughout.
£41,000–45,000 *S*

*One of only 4 Continentals built on the longer 150in
chassis – the model was generally designed around a
shorter 144in chassis – and fitted with 19in wheels.*

**1936 Rolls-Royce Phantom III Hooper
Limousine,** black paintwork, leather and cloth
interior trim in good original condition,
structurally sound.
£23,000–25,000 *RCC*

1937 Rolls-Royce 25/30 Sports Saloon,
coachwork by Hooper, finished in grey with grey
interior, good condition.
£28,000–29,500 *BA*

1937 Rolls-Royce Phantom III Barker Tourer, 11,000 miles recorded, excellent condition.
£300,000+ *BLK*

One of the very few convertible PIIIs originally built, this rare example of the 12 cylinder series was ordered by and shipped to his Highness the Maharajah Saheb Bahadur of Kolhapur, India. The factory-built sheets indicate that the specified colour inside and out was ivory. Presumably this was to attract even more attention to this spectacular car in the ongoing automotive competition amongst heads of state in that country.

1937 Rolls-Royce 25/30 Hooper Sports Saloon,
requires small amount of cosmetic work, dark blue
and light grey paintwork in good order, original
leather to front seats, replaced fawn cloth to rear,
correct lamps, horns and mascot, good condition.
£15,000–17,500 *RCC*

1959 Rolls-Royce Silver Cloud I, 4887cc,
full history, resprayed, finished in Velvet Green
with Magnolia trim, good condition.
£22,000–25,000 *H&H*

ROLLS-ROYCE Model	ENGINE cc/cyl	DATES	CONDITION 1	2	3
Silver Wraith LWB	4566/ 4887/6	1951-59	£25,000	£17,000	£10,000
Silver Wraith SWB	4257/ 4566/6	1947-59	£20,000	£13,000	£10,000
Silver Wraith Drophead	4257/ 4566/6	1947-59	£50,000	£35,000	£25,000
Silver Dawn St'd Steel	4257/ 4566/6	1949-52	£25,000+	£15,000	£10,000
Silver Dawn St'd Steel	4257/ 4566/6	1952-55	£30,000+	£20,000	£15,000
Silver Dawn Coachbuilt	4257/ 4566/6	1949-55	£35,000+	£25,000	£18,000
Silver Dawn Drophead	4257/ 4566/6	1949-55	£60,000	£50,000	£30,000
Silver Cloud I	4887/6	1955-59	£18,000	£10,000	£8,000
SCI Coupé Coachbuilt	4887/6	1955-59	£30,000	£20,000	£15,000
SCI Conv (HJM)	4887/6	1955-59	£80,000	£60,000	£40,000
Silver Cloud II	6230/8	1959-62	£19,000	£10,000	£8,000
SCII Conv (HJM)	6230/8	1959-62	£80,000	£75,000	£40,000
SCII Conv (MPW)	6230/8	1959-62	£60,000	£40,000	£32,000
Silver Cloud III	6230/8	1962-65	£25,000	£12,000	£10,000
SCIII Conv (MPW)	6230/8	1962-65	£70,000	£45,000	£35,000
Silver Shadow	6230/ 6750/8	1965-76	£14,000	£9,000	£7,000
S Shadow I Coupé (MPW)	6230/ 6750/8	1965-70	£15,000	£10,000	£8,000
SSI Drophead (MPW)	6230/ 6750/8	1965-70	£33,000	£25,000	£18,000
Corniche fhc	6750/8	1971-77	£15,000	£11,000	£8,000
Corniche Convertible	6750/8	1971-77	£28,000	£22,000	£18,000
Camargue	6750/8	1975-85	£35,000	£25,000	£18,000

1960 Rolls-Royce Silver Cloud II Four Door Saloon, one owner, original toolkit, maintenance manuals, spare parts, special equipment includes a foot-operated wind-tone horn, right-hand drive, good condition.
£15,000–18,000 *BKS*

Introduced in 1959, the Rolls-Royce Silver Cloud II and Bentley S2 appeared externally unchanged from their Silver Cloud and S-type predecessors, though their performance was considerably enhanced by the new 6230cc aluminium-alloy power unit. They were both superseded by the re-styled Silver Cloud III and Bentley S3 in 1962.

1965 Rolls-Royce Silver Cloud III Flying Spur Saloon, coachwork by Mulliner Park Ward, 4 speed automatic transmission, 41,720 recorded miles, very good condition throughout, well maintained.
£47,000–52,000 *BKS*

Virtually all Flying Spur bodywork was built on the Bentley chassis, and only 15 to 20 were made for the Rolls-Royce chassis.

1967 Rolls-Royce Silver Shadow Two Door Saloon, 6230cc V8 engine, disc brakes, self-levelling suspension, power steering, repainted, new tyres, brakes and automatic transmission, good overall condition.
£10,000–12,000 *BKS*

One of only 35 of a limited edition from the last year that the coachmakers James Young of Bromley produced special bodywork.

1965 Rolls-Royce Silver Cloud III, 8 cylinders, 6230cc, coachwork and structure are both very good, mechanically all components are excellent, original leather trim, Wilton carpeting and interior woodwork in good order.
£21,000–24,000 *ADT*

1969 Rolls-Royce Silver Shadow, 6.2 litre, V8 engine, 31,481kms recorded, stored since 1979.
£12,000–14,000 *BKS*

This car was built for His Highness Prince Charam of Iran.

1975 Rolls-Royce Silver Shadow, V8 overhead valve, cast aluminium alloy crank case and cylinder heads, 6750cc, 3 speed automatic gearbox with torque converter, disc brakes, mechanically well maintained, resprayed, good condition.
£7,000–9,000 *C*

1975 Rolls-Royce Camargue, coachwork by Pininfarina, 2,442km recorded, excellent condition. **£38,000–43,000** *BKS*

1976 Rolls-Royce Camargue, coachwork by Pininfarina, 3,482km recorded, excellent conditon. **£38,000–40,000** *BKS*

Launched in 1975, the Camargue was an ideal marriage between the design flair of Pininfarina in Italy and the coachbuilding experience of Mulliner Park Ward. The renowned Italian studio had been given the brief to create the ultimate owner-driver coupé, and the large, lush Camargue was the outcome of their endeavours. It was always an exclusive model, even by Rolls-Royce standards, and just 531 Camargues were delivered during the 10 year production run. These very special Camargues were made for His Imperial Highness the late Shah of Iran. The Shah must have been very taken with Rolls-Royce's plans for the new Camargue, because he ordered not one but 2 of them, despite the fact that it was the most expensive car on the market.

1979 Rolls-Royce Silver Shadow II, 6750cc, excellent condition. **£9,000–10,000** *H&H*

1977 Rolls-Royce Silver Shadow II, 6750cc, 80,300 recorded miles, woodwork and chromium plating in good condition, large and small toolkits, full history. **£10,000–12,000** *H&H*

r. **1984 Rolls-Royce Silver Spirit,** 6750cc, warranted 81,000 miles, original handbooks, service book. **£14,500–16,500** *H&H*

1985 Rolls-Royce Silver Spur, V8, 6750cc, 4 speed automatic gearbox, left-hand drive, 10,000 miles recorded, service records. **£40,000–45,000** *C*

ROVER

Like so many of Britain's motor manufacturers, Rover's roots were in the booming bicycle industry of the last decades of the 19th century. The first Rover car appeared in 1904. In its early years Rover had never been a high volume car producer and in the mid-1920s it concentrated on the solid middle-class territory that to this day is Rover's home ground. As Rover emerged from the war it made do with the P3, an updated pre-war design, until the now much loved and so-called 'Auntie' Rover, the P4, was ready in 1950. Today the P5 and P6 saloons of the 1960s and 1970s are much admired and enjoyed in enthusiastic everyday use.

But while Rover models remained distinguished, Britain's motor industry was in turmoil with merger mania. Rover could no longer remain independent against this tide and in 1967 merged into the Leyland Motor Corporation. In this environment Rover could have slithered into oblivion, but it managed to produce one great vehicle: the Range Rover of 1970 which is without doubt a living classic. Somehow Rover weathered the BL years and emerged on top as the group was named Rover Group in 1986. Now, as part of BMW, Rover produces a wider range of cars than at any time in its history.

1913 Rover 12hp Drophead Coupé with Dickey Seat, 12 volt lighting, detachable wheels, side-mounted spare, 2 panel windscreen, toolkit, finished in original beige Bedford cord, with brass fittings, used regularly until 1993.
£14,500–16,000 *S*

Motor *magazine reported in July 1914 on the Rover 12: 'There is nothing phenomenally remarkable in the design anywhere. On the contrary, it is chiefly noticeable for its general all-round excellence'.*

1937 Rover 12 Saloon, generally good condition.
£4,750–5,750 *BKS*

The 12/4 was introduced in 1934 and the 4 cylinder engine was a new development with coachwork that was both elegant and practical. Although a heavy car, the Twelve was fast enough to satisfy Rover buyers who were more interested in quality and comfort than speed.

1927 Rover 10/25hp Riviera Folding Top Saloon, coachwork by Weymann, 1185cc, overhead valves, worm drive rear axle, restored, good condition, requires recommissioning following period of museum display.
£6,000–7,000 *BKS*

The post-WWI 8hp V twin was perhaps not the success that Rover would have liked, but the 10/25hp model of 1927 helped Rover to re-establish their share of the lower middle market.

This car was a regular prize winner when rallied in the 1970s and featured in Chariots of Fire, Brideshead Revisited, Agatha *and* When The Boat Comes In.

1930 Rover 10/25 Sportsman's Coupé, 1185cc, fully restored, excellent condition.
£5,300–6,000 *H&H*

ROVER Model	ENGINE cc/cyl	DATES	CONDITION		
			1	2	3
10hp	998/2	1920-25	£5,000	£3,000	£1,500
9/20	1074/4	1925-27	£6,000	£4,000	£2,000
10/25	1185/4	1928-33	£6,000	£4,000	£2,500
14hp	1577/6	1933-39	£6,000	£4,250	£2,000
12	1496/4	1934-37	£7,000	£4,000	£1,500
20 Sports	2512/6	1937-39	£7,000	£4,500	£2,500

1939 Rover 14, 6 cylinders, 1900cc, 4 speed gearbox, good condition.
£3,000–3,500 *DB*

1947 Rover 14 Saloon, fully restored, excellent condition.
£5,000–5,500 *AS*

1939 Rover 12hp Four Door Saloon, sound mechanical order, good original body, coachwork and interior, new floor and carpets, 69,485 miles recorded.
£3,750–4,250 *BKS*

Previously a Six, Rover's 12hp model was relaunched in 1934 with an entirely new 4 cylinder engine. The 1½ litre overhead valve unit gave a good account of itself when the Twelve was tested by The Autocar *magazine, proving capable of propelling the attractively-styled all-steel saloon to more than 70mph. The 4 speed gearbox incorporated Rover's traditional freewheel mechanism. Restyled for 1937, the Twelve became lower and more streamlined, and by 1939 had gained Luvax-Bijur chassis lubrication, synchromesh gears, and hydraulic piston-type shock absorbers. The car re-appeared after the war, continuing in production until 1948.*

1949 Rover 75 14hp Saloon, 6 cylinders, major restoration including engine overhaul, interior retrimmed in burgundy leather, resprayed, good condition.
£9,000–10,000 *Bro*

r. **1948 Rover 12hp Tourer,** 1600cc, restored, excellent condition throughout.
£14,500–15,500 *SW*

This is a very rare car.

1949 Rover 75, requires restoration.
£2,500–3,000 *DRC*

1953 Rover 75, good condition.
£1,100–1,400 *H&H*

l. **1963 Rover 95,** 2625cc, 6 cylinder inlet over exhaust valve engine, manual transmission, mechanically sound, bodywork and interior in good condition, original log book, handbook and dealer workshop manual.
£1,000–1,500 *LF*

Last of the 'Auntie' Rovers, the 95 was built, as was the 110, from 1962 to 1964, her young sister, the P5 eventually usurping her. Previously the numbering system of Rovers related to the bhp, thus the 90 produced 90bhp. The 95 was slightly different and was indeed modest as the power produced was 102bhp.

ROVER Model	ENGINE cc/cyl	DATES	CONDITION 1	2	3
P2 10	1389/4	1946-47	£3,200	£2,500	£1,000
P2 12	1496/4	1946-47	£3,500	£2,800	£1,200
P2 12 Tour	1496/4	1947	£7,500	£3,500	£1,500
P2 14/16	1901/6	1946-47	£4,200	£3,000	£1,000
P2 14/16 Sal	1901/6	1946-47	£3,700	£2,500	£700
P3 60	1595/4	1948-49	£5,500	£2,500	£1,000
P3 75	2103/6	1948-49	£4,000	£3,000	£800
P4 75	2103/6	1950-51	£3,200	£1,800	£1,200
P4 75	2103/6	1952-64	£3,500	£1,800	£1,200
P4 60	1997/4	1954-59	£3,200	£1,200	£1,200
P4 90	2638/6	1954-59	£4,000	£1,800	£1,200
P4 75	2230/6	1955-59	£3,800	£1,200	£1,000
P4 105R	2638/6	1957-58	£4,000	£2,000	£1,000
P4 105S	2638/6	1957-59	£4,000	£2,000	£1,000
P4 80	2286/4	1960-62	£3,000	£1,200	£800
P4 95	2625/6	1963-64	£3,000	£1,600	£500
P4 100	2625/6	1960-62	£3,800	£2,000	£1,000
P4 110	2625/6	1963-64	£3,800	£2,000	£1,000
P5 3 litre	2995/6	1959-67	£4,000	£2,500	£1,000
P5 3 litre Coupé	2995/6	1959-67	£5,500	£3,800	£1,000
P5B (V8)	3528/8	1967-74	£6,250	£4,500	£1,500
P5B (V8) Coupé	3528/8	1967-73	£6,250	£4,500	£1,500
P6 2000 SC Series 1	1980/4	1963-65	£2,200	£800	-
P6 2000 SC Series 1	1980/4	1966-70	£2,000	£800	-
P6 2000 SC Auto Series 1	1980/4	1966-70	£1,500	£600	-
P6 2000 TC Series 1	1980/4	1966-70	£2,000	£900	-
P6 2000 SC Series 2	1980/4	1970-73	£2,000	£900	-
P6 2000 SC Auto Series 2	1980/4	1970-73	£1,500	£800	-
P6 2000 TC Series 2	1980/4	1970-73	£2,000	£900	-
P6 3500 Series 1	3500/8	1968-70	£2,500	£1,400	-
P6 2200 SC	2200/4	1974-77	£1,750	£850	-
P6 2200 SC Auto	2200/4	1974-77	£2,500	£1,000	-
P6 2200 TC	2200/4	1974-77	£2,000	£1,000	-
P6 3500 Series 2	3500/8	1971-77	£3,000	£1,700	-
P6 3500 S Series 2	3500/8	1971-77	£2,000	£1,500	-

1971 Rover P5B Saloon, 3528cc,
well maintained, mechanically sound, bodywork
requires some attention, includes manuals and
spare parts, new steering box.
£1,000–1,500 *H&H*

1969 Rover P5B Saloon, black leather trim,
excellent condition.
£3,750–4,250 *AS*

1973 Rover P5B Saloon, 8 cylinders, 3528cc,
43,000 miles recorded, well maintained,
full service history, good condition.
£4,000–5,000 *ADT*

1970 Rover 3500, 8 cylinders, 3528cc, good running
order, always been garaged.
£900–1,200 *ADT*

*Renowned for their reliability, allied to realistic fuel
economy due to the comparatively low weight, these
cars are enjoyable to drive and in V8 form have a
spirited performance.*

1975 Rover P6 SC, 2200cc, 98bhp, good overall
condition, automatic transmission, 71,000 recorded
miles, full history.
£1,200–1,800 *LF*

l. **1975 Rover P6 3500,** unrestored, excellent
condition both bodily and mechanically,
finished in Davos white with tan cloth trim,
98,000 miles recorded.
£2,000–2,500 *ADT*

*The P6 series, as this model was known, made its
debut at the 1963 Motor Show. By 1968 the V8
version was available and the model both in 4 and
8 cylinder guises remained available until 1976.*

SAAB

c1956 Saab 92B Two Door Saloon, fully restored, excellent condition, finished in burgundy.
£4,250–5,000 *BKS*

The Model 92 was introduced in 1950 and was powered by a 764cc twin cylinder 2 stroke engine of DKW type, developing 25bhp. Torsion bar suspension all-round ensured good roadholding.

1977 Saab 96, 4 cylinders, 1498cc, fair all-round condition.
£3,800–4,300 *ADT*

The V4 engined Saab had a long and sporting heritage, effectively being a development from the earlier 2 stroke engined cars which enjoyed so much rally success, most memorably in the hands of Eric Carlsson.

SAAB Model	ENGINE cc/cyl	DATES	CONDITION 1	2	3
92	764/2	1950-53	£3,000	£1,500	£1,000
92B	764/2	1953-55	£3,000	£1,500	£1,000
93-93B	748/3	1956-60	£3,000	£1,500	£1,000
95	841/3	1960-68	£3,000	£1,500	£1,000
96	841/3	1960-68	£3,500	£1,500	£1,000
96 Sport	841/3	1962-66	£3,500	£1,500	£1,000
Sonnett II	1698/4	1967-74	£3,500	£1,500	£1,000
95/96	1498/4	1966-80	£3,000	£1,000	£800
99	1709/4	1968-71	£2,000	£1,200	-
99	1854/4	1970-74	£2,000	£1,000	-
99	1985/4	1972-83	£2,000	£1,000	£500
99 Turbo	1985/4	1978-83	£3,000	£1,000	£500

1980 Saab 99 Turbo, 1985cc, one owner from new, 50,000 recorded miles, finished in red with grey upholstery.
£2,900–3,100 *H&H*

This is one of the later 145bhp models and is believed to be one of the 500 homologation specials built by the factory.

SALMSON

1939 Salmson S4-61 Two Door Coupé, Bendix-Servo operated brakes and independent front suspension, restoration started, needs completing.
£4,150–4,650 *BKS*

Salmson vied with Amilcar in France for the major slice of the light sports car market and in the 1920s had a reputation for developing high output from efficient 4 and 6 cylinder engines.
The 1930s British Salmson Aero Engines Ltd at Raynes Park, London, operated in parallel with the French and by then both French and English versions had become more sophisticated, the twin overhead camshaft model S4 being the mainstay of production.

SIMCA

1953 Simca Vedette V8, 2½ litre side valve, built by Simca for Ford, good original example.
£6,000–7,000 *CRE*

1973 Simca 1000LS, 944cc, warranted 11,700 miles recorded, original spare wheel, good condition.
£900–1,200 *H&H*

SINGER

Via sewing machines and bicycles George Singer produced his first motor car in Coventry in 1905. The Singer Nine of the 1930s had a really fine 972cc engine and in open form was a serious rival to MG offerings. Both designs endured into the 1950s without radical changes. The other great pre-war Singer was the 1.5 litre Le Mans. Post-war, Singer's products were too expensive to compete comprehensively with the likes of BMC and in 1955, the company was acquired by the Rootes empire, and thereby reduced to an upmarket badge that faded away for good in 1970.

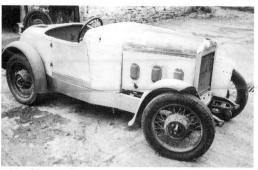

1931 Singer Sports Two Seater, 4 cylinders, overhead camshaft, 972cc, 4 speed gearbox, unrestored.
£2,250–2,750 *DB*

1947 Singer Nine Roadster, 4 cylinders, 1074cc, overhead camshaft, excellent weather equipment, very good condition.
£2,750–3,250 *BRIT*

Singer was another famous Coventry firm whose roots lay in the cycle industry. Their first motor car was produced in 1905 and by the late 1920s they were Britain's third largest private car manufacturer.

1947 Singer Nine Roadster, 4 cylinders, 1074cc, new ash body framework, engine, gearbox, steering and suspension reconditioned, totally rebuilt to original specification.
£10,000–12,000 *BRIT*

In 1939 Singer introduced the 9hp 4 seater Roadster, and was reintroduced immediately after the war with approximately 2,500 being produced, largely for export. Today these cars are quite a rare sight.

1958 Singer Gazelle Series 2, overdrive, rev counter, centre arm rests, wind-up ariel, spot and reversing lights, 2 owners, 82,000 miles recorded, full history, excellent original condition.
£3,000–3,500 *CRE*
Less than 1,600 examples were made.

1964 Singer Chamois Saloon, 875cc, 28,000 miles recorded from new, fully restored.
£950–1,100 *H&H*

SINGER Model	ENGINE cc/cyl	DATES	CONDITION 1	2	3
10	1097/4	1918-24	£5,000	£2,000	£1,000
15	1991/6	1922-25	£6,000	£3,000	£1,500
14/34	1776/6	1926-27	£7,000	£4,000	£2,000
Junior	848/4	1927-32	£6,000	£3,000	£1,500
Senior	1571/4	1928-29	£7,000	£4,000	£2,000
Super 6	1776/6	1928-31	£7,000	£4,000	£2,000
9 Le Mans	972/4	1932-37	£12,000	£8,000	£5,000
Twelve	1476/6	1932-34	£10,000	£7,000	£6,000
1.5 litre	1493/4	1934-36	£3,000	£2,000	£1,000
2 litre	1991/6	1934-37	£4,000	£2,750	£1,000
11	1459/4	1935-36	£3,000	£2,000	£1,000
12	1525/4	1937-39	£3,000	£2,000	£1,000

STANDARD

From modest beginnings Standard was, by 1906, marketing Britain's first inexpensive 6 cylinder car. The company specialised in medium range cars in the 1920s, but it was the Standard 9 that buoyed the company on in the 1930s. In 1945, with Captain John Black at the helm, the company acquired the defunct Triumph marque as an up-market badge. Standard-Triumph was merged into Leyland in 1961 and ironically it was the Standard name that was almost immediately dropped while Triumph soldiered on until 1980.

1932 Standard Nine Swallow Four Seater Saloon, 4 cylinders, 1005cc, blue with red upholstery, restored, very good condition.
£11,000–12,000 *COYS*

It was with cars such as this that William Lyons established the base from which he launched SS Cars, later to become Jaguar. Lyons had gone into partnership with a friend to make motorcycle sidecars and his genius for organisation had seen Swallow Sidecars expand rapidly. Very soon the company began to undertake car bodies.

In the case of the Standard Nine, Lyons transformed a boxy little saloon into a very handsome and distinctive motor car. Instead of the flat windscreen of the original, there was a rakish V screen.

1935 Standard Twelve Saloon, 2 owners, barn stored, suitable for restoration.
£830–1,200 *BKS*

r. **1947 Standard Eight Tourer,** black with beige trim, all-weather equipment, fully restored, excellent condition throughout.
£3,000–3,250 *AS*

STANDARD Model	ENGINE cc/cyl	DATES	CONDITION 1	2	3
SLS	1328/4	1919-20	£5,000	£4,000	£1,000
VI	1307/4	1922	£5,000	£4,000	£1,000
SLO/V4	1944/4	1922-28	£5,000	£4,000	£1,000
6V	2230/6	1928	£10,000	£8,000	£5,000
V3	1307/4	1923-26	£4,000	£3,000	£1,000
Little 9	1006/4	1932-33	£4,000	£2,000	£1,000
9	1155/4	1928-29	£5,500	£3,000	£1,000
Big 9	1287/4	1932-33	£4,500	£3,250	£2,000
15	1930/6	1929-30	£6,000	£4,000	£2,000
12	1337/6	1933-34	£4,000	£3,000	£1,500
10hp	1343/4	1933-37	£4,000	£2,500	£1,000
9	1052/4	1934-36	£4,200	£2,500	£1,000
Flying 9	1131/4	1937-39	£3,200	£1,800	£750
Flying 10	1267/4	1937-39	£3,500	£2,200	£1,000
Flying 14	1176/4	1937-48	£4,500	£2,200	£1,000
Flying 8	1021/4	1939-48	£4,200	£2,400	£1,000

STANDARD Model	ENGINE cc/cyl	DATES	CONDITION		
			1	2	3
12	1609/4	1945-48	£2,000	£950	£250
12 DHC	1509/4	1945-48	£3,200	£2,000	£500
14	1776/4	1945-48	£3,000	£950	£250
Vanguard I/II	2088/4	1948-55	£1,800	£750	£150
Vanguard III	2088/4	1955-61	£1,500	£750	£150
Vanguard III Est	2088/4	1955-61	£2,000	£800	£150
Vanguard III Sportsman	2088/4	1955-58	£2,000	£800	£200
Vanguard Six	1998/6	1961-63	£1,500	£700	-
Eight	803/4	1952-59	£1,250	£500	-
Ten	948/4	1955-59	£1,400	£800	-
Ensign I/II	1670/4	1957-63	£1,000	£800	-
Ensign I/II Est	1670/4	1962-63	£1,000	£850	-
Pennant Companion	948/4	1955-61	£1,800	£850	£300
Pennant	948/4	1955-59	£1,650	£825	£250

l. **1947 Standard Flying Eight Tourer,** 4 seater, 4 cylinders, 1009cc, original leather interior, good condition.
£5,000–5,500 *ADT*

STANLEY

c1924 Stanley Steamer Seven Passenger Sedan, 2 cylinders, double acting, 20bhp, pumps gear driven off rear axle, mechanical internal expanding brakes, front semi-elliptic spring suspension, full elliptic springs rear, left-hand drive, requires restoration.
£11,000–13,000 *C*

The Stanley was America's best known and longest lived steam automobile, and this car represents the last year of full, albeit small, production of the marque. Due to long storage, there is surface rust on the hood. Fenders and running boards are straight and paint on the aluminium body is poor. Upholstery is intact for patterns during restoration. The car will require full restoration in order to bring it to working order and acceptable cosmetic appearance.

> *A rebuilt car is not necessarily more valuable than a car in good original condition, even if the restoration has been costly.*

STEAMOBILE

1901 Steamobile Model A Runabout, twin cylinder, steam-powered, 8hp engine, original black leather wings, new boiler, fuel and air tanks overhauled, original whip holder, brass lamps, fully restored, excellent condition throughout.
£22,000–27,000 *C*

The Steamobile Company of America superseded the Trinity Cycle Manufacturing Company in February 1901, which had been producing a steam powered car since 1900 under the name of Keen Steamobile of New Hampshire. The earliest form of Steamobile was the 2 seater Runabout, and this model was exhibited at the Greenfield Fair, Massachusetts, in September 1901, offered at a price of $850. A Dos-à-Dos with detachable rear seat was offered in the following month at a cost of $900 and in early 1902 a full 4 seater became available. Unfortunately, the Steamobile Company of America went out of business in late 1902, probably the first victim of over-production in the United States.

STELLITE

1914 Stellite 8/10hp Two Seater with Dickey,
2 speed gearbox, non-original upholstery in black
vinyl, side and rear mounted lighting, single
front Powell and Hanmer acetylene,
good condition throughout.
£8,300–9,300 *S*

*Produced by Electric and Ordnance Accessories Co,
a subsidiary of Vickers, the Stellite was a close
relation of the Wolseley and shared many features
with Wolseley cars of the time. The Stellite was a
great success and, despite its 2 speed gearbox,
offered a surprisingly fast turn of speed and would
tackle virtually any gradient in bottom gear.*

STEVENS-DURYEA

**1914/15 Stevens-Duryea Model DD 50hp
Seven Passenger Tourer,** 6 cylinders, L-head,
496cu in, 8129cc, 80bhp at 1800rpm, 3 speed
manual gearbox, left-hand drive, electric lights,
starting system, low mileage recorded, restored,
very good condition throughout.
£27,000–32,000 *C*

*In 1914 the J. Stevens Arms Company withdrew
its support and J. Frank Duryea obtained control
of the company. The company lacked working
capital and the banks were unwilling to provide
financial support at the onset of WWI. Production
halted in January 1915.
   This Model DD is a rare survivor of one of the
last models produced before the factory closed.
According to the Stevens-Duryea Register there are
only 5 models known to exist.*

STUDEBAKER

l. **1947 Studebaker
Champion Starlight
Coupé,** requires
mechanical work,
good condition.
£2,000–2,500 *BC*

STUTZ

1930 Stutz Eight Model M Four Door Sedan,
8 cylinders, in-line, single overhead camshaft,
322cu in, 113bhp, 4 speed manual gearbox,
left-hand drive, rust on bodywork and wheels,
requires restoration.
£10,000–13,000 *C*

1972 Stutz Blackhawk Two Door Coupé,
automatic transmission, air conditioning,
sunroof, 10,000km miles recorded, left-hand
drive, very good condition throughout.
£9,000–12,000 *BKS*

*After a gap of more than 30 years, the once famous
Stutz name reappeared on an automobile in 1969.
The Bearcat replica was followed in 1970 by the
Pontiac Grand Prix based Blackhawk. A modified
Pontiac 6.5 litre V8 provided the power. The already
prodigious power output was raised to 431bhp in
1972, when Pontiac's 7.5 litre unit was adopted. List
price then was more than 3 times that of a Cadillac
Eldorado. Around 55 Blackhawks are thought to
have found customers, among them Elvis Presley
who reputedly had two.*

SUNBEAM

Although its first car was produced in 1901, Sunbeam's real glory years were in the 1920s with a string of successful Grand Prix cars, record breakers and fine sports and touring machines. Rootes bought the company in 1935 and after the war Sunbeam initially continued its sporting tradition. A Sunbeam MkIII won the 1955 Monte Carlo Rally and the Sunbeam Rapiers of the early 1960s proved useful in rallying and touring car racing. Eventually, though, most Sunbeams were nothing more than slightly peppier and posher Hillmans. Chrysler acquired Rootes in 1964 and the Sunbeam marque faded into the sunset in 1976.

1923 Sunbeam Two Seater with Dickey, 14hp, full history and original sales invoice, excellent original condition.
£16,000–18,000   *UMC*

1934 Sunbeam 20hp Four Door Saloon, 6 light sliding-head coachwork, 6 cylinders, overhead valve, 2194cc, 18.2hp, 4 speed gearbox, photographic record of restoration, original purchase receipt and guarantee, servicing receipts, very good condition throughout.
£13,500–15,500   *BKS*

Introduced in 1927 and priced at £750, the first 20hp Sunbeam enjoyed a production life of 6 years, being superseded by a new Twenty in 1933. Unfortunately, the collapse of the Sunbeam-Talbot-Darracq combine in 1935 and its subsequent acquisition by the Rootes brothers meant that the revised Twenty, one of the last true Sunbeams, never got the chance it deserved.

1954 Sunbeam Alpine Drophead, full history, restored, excellent condition.
£12,000–14,000   *UMC*

SUNBEAM Model	ENGINE cc/cyl	DATES	CONDITION		
			1	2	3
12/16	2412/4	1909-12	£25,000	£16,000	£12,000
16/20	4070/4	1912-15	£32,000	£22,000	£15,000
24	4524/6	1919-22	£30,000	£19,000	£11,000
3 litre	2916/6	1925-30	£48,000	£30,000	£20,000
14/40	2200/4	1925-30	£18,000	£10,000	£8,000
16	2040/6	1927-30	£16,000	£12,500	£10,000
20	2916/6	1927-30	£22,000	£15,000	£10,500
Speed 20	2916/6	1932-35	£15,000	£10,000	£8,000
Dawn	1627/4	1934-35	£8,000	£5,000	£3,500
25	3317/6	1934	£10,000	£8,000	£4,000

Prices can vary depending on replica bodies, provenance, coachbuilder, drophead, twin cam etc.

1952 Sunbeam-Talbot 90 MkII Four Door Saloon, 4 cylinder, 2267cc, Humber-derived engine, manual transmission, sunroof, original upholstery, new clutch, exhaust pipes and brake pipes, chromework needs replating, tools, handbook, good condition.
£1,150–1,650 *BKS*

Introduced in 1948 in MkI guise, the Sunbeam-Talbot 90 was offered in sports saloon and drophead coupé form, and was fitted with the larger 1944cc engine. In MkII guise from 1951 onwards, the 90 featured the 2267cc overhead valve 4 cylinder engine, and is recognisable from the twin air intakes flanking the grille. The engine was derived from the latest Humber Hawk type, and was good for 80/85mph.

1954 Sunbeam-Talbot 90, 4 cylinders, 2267cc, chassis, floorpan, panelwork and paint in good condition, electrical system and mechanicals in good order, restored, very good condition throughout.
£1,800–2,200 *ADT*

The Sunbeam-Talbot 90, with its 2.3 litre engine, was a formidable sports saloon in its day.

1956 Sunbeam 90 MkIII Saloon, floor gearchange with overdrive, sunroof, rev counter, fully history, concours winner, excellent condition.
£7,500–8,500 *UMC*

1955 Sunbeam-Talbot MkIII Saloon, 2.2 litres, steering column gearchange, 95mph, grey and burgundy paintwork, carpet and red leather upholstery original, good condition throughout.
£3,000–3,500 *S*

1957 Sunbeam MkIII Saloon, 4 cylinders, 2267cc, overhead valves, 4 speed manual gearbox, 4 wheel drum brakes, independent front suspension, semi-elliptic leaf spring rear, sunroof, 7,900 miles recorded, right-hand drive, excellent condition throughout.
£8,000–10,000 *C*

1957 Sunbeam 90, 4 cylinders, 2267cc, floor gearchange with overdrive, steel sliding sunroof, good condition throughout.
£3,250–3,750 *ADT*

From 1954 the name Talbot was deleted, and subsequent models were badged simply as Sunbeams.

1964 Sunbeam Tiger I Two Door Roadster, 4.7 litre Ford V8 engine, 'mild' cam, tubular exhaust headers, automatic transmission, left-hand drive, restored, excellent condition throughout.
£9,500–11,500 *BKS*

Inspired by Carroll Shelby's success in shoehorning a Ford V8 into the AC Ace to create the Cobra, Rootes asked Shelby to perform the same trick with its Sunbeam Alpine sports car. Ford's 260cu in 4.2 litre unit was chosen, and even though this had 'only' 160bhp on tap, it was approaching double the output of the contemporary Alpine's 1.6 litre four. Tiger performance was vastly superior to that of the Alpine, the former's 9.5 seconds 0–60mph time being 5 seconds quicker than the 4 cylinder car's, the latter peaking at 92mph compared to the Tiger's 117mph.

This car is believed to have been owned briefly by Geoffrey Rootes, and is an experimental automatic transmission car built for evaluation as a possible USA export model.

l. **1969 Sunbeam Rapier,** 4 cylinders, 1725cc, white with black vinyl interior, 27,000 miles recorded, good overall condition.
£1,400–1,800 *ADT*

The original Sunbeam Rapier enjoyed a 12 year production run from 1955 to 1967, and was finally superseded by a completely restyled sleek fast-back coupé.

SUNBEAM-TALBOT/ SUNBEAM Model	ENGINE cc/cyl	DATES	CONDITION 1	2	3
Talbot 80	1185/4	1948-50	£3,500	£2,250	£1,000
Talbot 80 DHC	1185/4	1948-50	£6,000	£4,500	£2,000
Talbot 90 Mk I	1944/4	1949-50	£4,000	£2,100	£750
Talbot 90 Mk I DHC	1944/4	1949-50	£7,000	£4,750	£2,000
Talbot 90 II/IIa/III	2267/4	1950-56	£5,000	£3,000	£1,500
Talbot 90 II/IIa/III DHC	2267/4	1950-56	£7,000	£5,000	£2,250
Talbot Alpine I/III	2267/4	1953-55	£11,000	£7,500	£3,750
Talbot Ten	1197/4	1946-48	£3,500	£2,000	£750
Talbot Ten Tourer	1197/4	1946-48	£7,000	£4,000	£2,000
Talbot Ten DHC	1197/4	1946-48	£6,500	£4,000	£2,000
Talbot 2 litre	1997/4	1946-48	£4,000	£2,500	£1,000
Talbot 2 litre Tourer	1997/4	1946-48	£7,500	£4,000	£2,250
Rapier I	1392/4	1955-57	£1,200	£700	£300
Rapier II	1494/4	1957-59	£1,800	£900	£300
Rapier II Conv	1494/4	1957-59	£3,000	£1,500	£450
Rapier III	1494/4	1959-61	£2,000	£1,200	£400
Rapier III Conv	1494/4	1959-61	£3,500	£1,600	£600
Rapier IIIA	1592/4	1961-63	£2,000	£1,200	£400
Rapier IIIA Conv	1592/4	1961-63	£3,600	£1,700	£650
Rapier IV/V	1592/ 1725/4	1963-67	£2,000	£700	£250
Alpine I-II	1494/4	1959-62	£6,000	£3,500	£1,800
Alpine III	1592/4	1963	£6,500	£4,000	£1,250
Alpine IV	1592/4	1964	£6,500	£4,000	£1,250
Alpine V	1725/4	1965-68	£7,000	£4,000	£1,250
Harrington Alpine	1592/4	1961	£8,000	£4,750	£1,250
Harrington Le Mans	1592/4	1962-63	£10,000	£6,500	£3,000
Tiger Mk 1	4261/8	1964-67	£14,000	£9,000	£5,000
Tiger Mk 2	4700/8	1967	£12,000	£7,500	£5,000
Rapier Fastback	1725/4	1967-76	£1,100	£700	£250
Rapier H120	1725/4	1968-76	£1,500	£800	£300

SUPER

l. **1911 Super Cyclecar Tandem Two Seater,** watercooled 998cc Anzani V twin engine, 42mph, 123½in (314cm) long, 37½in (95cm) wide, good condition throughout.
£6,500–8,000 *BKS*

Believed to be the sole survivor of the 26 Super cyclecars that were built in Asnieres, Seine, during 1911, this remarkably original tandem 2 seater was used as a runabout on a Scottish estate, and had a recorded mileage of just 410 miles when it was acquired by its present owner. The Super was certainly better than many cyclecars in having front seat control and proper Ackermann steering with independently sprung front wheels.

TALBOT

1925 Talbot Model Z 10 10/23hp Four Seater Tourer, overhead valve engine, 1073cc, requires restoration.
£5,750–6,750 *BKS*

Talbot were in dire financial straits in 1925 and pushed hard the maxim, 'quality in a light car is well worth the cost', but with the contemporary 14hp Morris Oxford selling for £260 against £350 for a 10hp Talbot this model looked expensive.

1932 Talbot 14/45 Four Door Saloon, 6 cylinders, overhead valve engine, 1.7 litres, 65mph, stored for 25 years, requires recommissioning, good condition.
£4,750–5,750 *BKS*

r. **1937 Talbot Ten BE Drophead Coupé,** coachwork by Carbodies of Coventry, 1185cc, good condition throughout.
£6,300–7,300 *LF*

l. **1983 Talbot Matra Murena,** 1600cc, left-hand drive, original instruction manual, good condition throughout.
£2,500–3,000 *H&H*

TALBOT Model	ENGINE cc/cyl	DATES	CONDITION 1	2	3
25hp and 25/50	4155/4	1907-16	£35,000	£25,000	£15,000
12hp	2409/4	1909-15	£22,000	£15,000	£9,000
8/18	960/4	1922-25	£8,000	£5,000	£2,000
14/45	1666/6	1926-35	£16,000	£10,000	£5,000
75	2276/6	1930-37	£22,000	£12,000	£7,000
105	2969/6	1935-37	£30,000	£20,000+	£15,000

Higher value for tourers and coachbuilt cars.

TALBOT-LAGO

1953 Talbot-Lago Grand Sport Coupé,
6 cylinders, 4482cc, 170bhp at 4200rpm, top speed
120mph, restored, excellent condition.
£30,000–35,000 *COYS*

Following the collapse of the Sunbeam-Talbot-Darracq combine in 1934, the Rootes Brothers took over the English Sunbeam and Talbot names, while Italian Antonio Lago acquired the French Talbot and Darracq marques. The Talbot-Lago Grand Sport Coupé was launched at the 1952 Paris Salon, with 2 door coachwork designed by Letourneur et Marchand. It was one of the fastest touring cars of its day. This car is one of just 26 examples ever produced.

1938 Talbot-Lago T150C SS Figoni et Falaschi 'Teardrop' Coupé, excellent condition.
£1,400,000+ *BLK*

This car is one of the 6 examples that were taken to Le Mans for the race in 1939. It has been on display at the Brooks Stevens Museum for about 40 years.

TRABANT

l. **c1992 Trabant 601S Two Door Saloon,** twin cylinder 2 stroke engine, 594cc, resin body, front wheel drive, 2 door mirrors, hand rests, rear fog and reversing lights, outside adjustment for headlamp dipping, museum displayed, very good condition.
£250–400 *BKS*

TRIUMPH

In those glory years of the 1950s and 1960s, Triumph's TR roadsters stood out as worthy best-of-breed contenders in the no-nonsense sports car stakes. From the bluff-fronted TR2 to the chisel-chinned TR6 they were as true-Brit as a sports car could be. Yet the company that provided so many memorable motoring sensations for the tweed, cravat and corduroy crew was actually founded by a pair of ex-patriot Germans, Siegfried Bettman and Mauritz Schulte, who formed a partnership to make bicycles. In 1902 they turned to motorcycles, and in 1923 the first Triumph motor car appeared. Triumph's first really successful car was the diminutive Super Seven,

unveiled in September 1927. The car and motorcycle business separated in 1936, and in June 1939 the receivers were called in to close down the car business. That might have been the end of the Triumph story, but in 1944 Sir John Black acquired the remains of Triumph for his Standard Motor Company. What he got was a name, a bit of residual goodwill – and precious little else. Yet somehow, over the next two decades, Triumph built up a sporting reputation to rival MG and Austin-Healey and on the saloon side eclipsed Standard's own offerings. The Triumph name eventually disappeared in 1980.

1934 Triumph Southern Cross, very good condition.
£14,000–18,000 *FHF*

TRIUMPH Model	ENGINE cc/cyl	DATES	CONDITION 1	2	3
TLC	1393/4	1923-25	£6,000	£4,000	£1,500
TPC	2169/4	1926-30	£6,000	£4,000	£2,000
K	832/4	1928-34	£4,000	£2,000	£1,000
S	1203/6	1931-33	£5,000	£3,000	£1,500
G12 Gloria	1232/4	1935-37	£6,000	£4,000	£2,000
G16 Gloria 6	1991/6	1935-39	£11,000	£5,000	£3,000
Vitesse/Dolomite	1767/4	1937-39	£14,000	£10,000	£6,000
Dolomite	1496/4	1938-39	£11,000	£6,000	£3,000

1934 Triumph Gloria Saloon, 1344cc, totally rebuilt, stored, sliding sunroof, very good condition.
£4,750–5,500 *H&H*

1935 Triumph Gloria Six Four Seater Tourer, full engine rebuild, resprayed in dark blue, 1991cc, 4 bearing, 6 cylinder, inlet-over exhaust, F-head Coventry Climax engine, 116in wheelbase, excellent condition.
£31,000–34,000 *BKS*

Only 2,000 Gloria Sixes of all kinds were built between 1934 and 1937. This is believed to be the sole surviving standard Gloria Six tourer.

1939 Triumph Dolomite 14/60 Drophead Coupé, by Salmons, 4 cylinders, 1767cc, repainted, chromework excellent, engine, gearbox, suspension, exhaust system and back axle in good condition, original blue upholstery, new carpets, fully lined black double duck hood, original radio and aerial.
£15,750–18,750 *ADT*

The Dolomite range was noted for its sensational Art Deco style 'waterfall' grille. This example was the 1938 Olympia Show Car.

1947 Triumph 1800 Roadster, 1800cc, grey leather upholstery and trim, added rear lights and indicators, very good condition.
£11,500–13,500 *S*

The post-war Triumph Roadster was the last car in the world to feature a double dickey seat. It also had a three-abreast bench seat.

1948 Triumph Roadster, 1800cc, totally restored, excellent concours condition.
£19,000–20,000 *SW*

1949 Triumph 2000 Roadster Two Door Convertible, modifications include 4 speed gearbox, auxiliary water temperature gauge, very good condition throughout.
£18,500–20,500 *BKS*

The 1800 Roadster was one of the first post-war designs – the other being its sister car, the 1800 Saloon – to bear the Triumph name. They were both launched in March 1946, and the Roadster was not revised until 1948 when it received the 2.1 litre engine, and 3 speed gearbox. Power went up from 65 to 68bhp, and top speed increased from 70 to 77mph. When Roadster production ceased the following year, a total of 4,501 cars had been built.

This example was used by the BBC from 1985 onwards in making the series Bergerac.

1952 Triumph TR2, totally rebuilt, very good condition.
£9,750–10,750 *BLE*

1955 Triumph TR2, 1991cc, new stainless steel exhaust, right-hand drive, restored, museum stored.
£10,500–12,000 *H&H*

1954 Triumph TR2 Supercharged, 2138cc, Shorrocks C142 B supercharger, manual 4 speed gearbox with overdrive on 2nd, 3rd and 4th gears, chrome wire wheel option, Alfin brake drums, oil cooler, engine overhauled, rewired, body-off restoration and repaint, interior retrimmed, modifications include Derrington exhaust, polished con rods, ports and crankshaft, right-hand drive, good condition throughout.
£9,000–11,000 *BKS*

1962 Triumph TR4, 4 cylinders, 2138cc, engine rebuilt, new radiator, black vinyl interior in fair condition, resprayed, panel and paintwork in good order.
£4,500–5,500 *ADT*

1962 Triumph Herald 1200 Estate, 1147cc, restored, full history, serviceable condition, requires some work.
£750–950 *H&H*

r. **1963 Triumph TR4,** 4 cylinders, overhead valve, 2138cc, 100bhp at 4600rpm, 4 speed manual gearbox, front disc brakes, rear drums, £9,000 restoration, including removing body from chassis, shot blasting, priming and painting, engine stripped, bodywork stripped to bare metal, new wiring loom, steel wheels fitted, new tyres and exhaust, 500 miles recorded since restoration, good condition.
£6,750–7,750 *C*

1964 Triumph TR4, coachwork by Michelotti, 4 cylinders, 2138cc, 100bhp at 4600rpm, 127lb.ft at 3350rpm, twin SU carburettors, 0–60mph in 10.9 seconds, top speed of 110mph with optional overdrive, restored in 1988, garaged since, new exhaust system, front shock absorbers, brake calipers and sills, very good condition.
£5,000–6,000 *COYS*

The TR4's 4 speed gearbox was new, as was rack-and-pinion steering which, with the more rigid chassis, provided even better road holding and handling than the TR3.

1965 Triumph 2000, manual gearbox, one owner, 15,000 miles recorded, good original condition throughout.
£2,000–2,500 *PA*

1965 Triumph TR4A, 4 cylinders, 2138cc, optional Surrey top, requires recommissioning, good original condition throughout.
£7,000–8,000 *ADT*

1967 Triumph Spitfire MkIII, 4 cylinders, 1296cc, British Racing Green, restored, optional hard-top, renewed interior trim, steering, suspension and brakes overhauled, tyres and exhaust system replaced, good condition.
£3,250–3,750 *ADT*

Introduced in 1962, the Triumph Spitfire was based on the contemporary Triumph Herald, and achieved phenomenal success. With several updates it remained in production until 1981. The MkIII used the power unit from the 13/60 Herald in mildly tuned form.

1969 Triumph Vitesse 2 Litre MkII Convertible, alloy wheels, locking bonnet, steering column lock, additional instruments, 47,000 miles recorded, good condition.
£5,300–5,800 *BKS*

Revising the Herald's bonnet enabled Standard-Triumph to squeeze an under-bored 1.6 litre version of the Triumph 2000 six into their successful small saloon, the Vitesse, in 1962. A 2 litre version with GT6 engine, gearbox, and running gear was launched in 1966. Although fast and well appointed, the 2 litre Vitesse was dogged by the same handling complaints as its forbear. The arrival of the MkII in the autumn of 1968 at last addressed the problem, the newcomer featuring a superior wishbone type independent rear suspension in place of the original swing-axle set-up.

l. **1969 Triumph Spitfire,** 1293cc, 54,000 miles recorded, very good condition throughout.
£1,700–2,000 *H&H*

1969 Triumph 2000 MkI, 6 cylinders, 1998cc, 56,000 recorded miles, unused for 2 years.
£750–1,000 *JNic*

1969 Triumph TR6, 2498cc, 150bhp, 10,000 miles recorded since restoration, fuel injection system, sports stainless steel exhaust, walnut dash, boot rack, overdrive gearbox, good condition.
£7,000–8,000 *H&H*

TRIUMPH Model	ENGINE cc/cyl	DATES	CONDITION 1	2	3
1800/2000 Roadster	1776/ 2088/4	1946-49	£14,000	£8,000	£5,000
1800	1776/4	1946-49	£4,000	£2,000	£1,000
2000 Renown	2088/4	1949-54	£4,000	£2,000	£1,000
Mayflower	1247/4	1949-53	£2,000	£1,000	£500
TR2 long door	1247/4	1953	£10,000	£8,000	£5,000
TR2	1247/4	1953-55	£9,000	£6,000	£5,000
TR3	1991/4	1955-57	£9,000	£8,500	£3,500
TR3A	1991/4	1958-62	£9,500	£8,500	£3,500
TR4	2138/4	1961-65	£9,000	£6,000	£3,000
TR4A	2138/4	1965-67	£9,000	£6,500	£3,000
TR5	2498/6	1967-68	£9,000	£7,500	£4,000
TR6 (PI)	2498/6	1969-74	£8,000	£7,500	£3,500
Herald	948/4	1959-61	£1,000	£400	£150
Herald FHC	948/4	1959-61	£1,500	£550	£300
Herald DHC	948/4	1960-61	£2,500	£1,000	£350
Herald 'S'	948/4	1961-64	£800	£400	£150
Herald 1200	1147/4	1961-70	£1,100	£500	£200
Herald 1200 FHC	1147/4	1961-64	£1,400	£800	£300
Herald 1200 DHC	1147/4	1961-67	£2,500	£1,000	£350
Herald 1200 Est	1147/4	1961-67	£1,300	£700	£300
Herald 12/50	1147/4	1963-67	£1,200	£600	£250
Herald 13/60	1296/4	1967-71	£1,300	£600	£200
Herald 13/60 DHC	1296/4	1967-71	£2,500	£1,500	£500
Herald 13/60 Est	1296/4	1967-71	£1,500	£650	£300
Vitesse 1600	1596/6	1962-66	£2,000	£1,250	£550
Vitesse 1600 Conv	1596/6	1962-66	£2,800	£1,350	£600
Vitesse 2 litre Mk I	1998/6	1966-68	£1,800	£800	£300
Vitesse 2 litre Mk I Conv	1998/6	1966-68	£4,500	£2,200	£1,000
Vitesse 2 litre Mk II	1998/6	1968-71	£2,000	£1,500	£300
Vitesse 2 litre Mk II Conv	1998/6	1968-71	£5,000	£2,500	£600
Spitfire Mk I	1147/4	1962-64	£2,000	£1,750	£300
Spitfire Mk II	1147/4	1965-67	£2,500	£2,000	£350
Spitfire Mk III	1296/4	1967-70	£3,500	£2,500	£450
Spitfire Mk IV	1296/4	1970-74	£5,000	£2,500	£350
Spitfire 1500	1493/4	1975-78	£3,500	£2,500	£750
Spitfire 1500	1493/4	1979-81	£5,000	£3,500	£1,200
GT6 Mk I	1998/6	1966-68	£5,000	£4,000	£1,200
GT6 Mk II	1998/6	1968-70	£6,000	£4,500	£1,400
GT6 Mk III	1998/6	1970-73	£7,000	£5,000	£1,500
2000 Mk I	1998/6	1963-69	£2,000	£1,200	£400
2000 Mk III	1998/6	1969-77	£2,000	£1,200	£500
2.5 PI	2498/6	1968-75	£2,000	£1,500	£900
2500 TC/S	2498/6	1974-77	£1,750	£700	£150
2500S	2498/6	1975-77	£2,500	£1,000	£150
1300 (FWD)	1296/4	1965-70	£800	£400	£150
1300TC (FWD)	1296/4	1967-70	£900	£450	£150
1500 (FWD)	1493/4	1970-73	£700	£450	£125
1500TC (RWD)	1296/4	1973-76	£850	£500	£100
Toledo	1296/4	1970-76	£850	£450	£100
Dolomite 1500	1493/4	1976-80	£1,350	£750	£125
Dolomite 1850	1854/4	1972-80	£1,450	£850	£150
Dolomite Sprint	1998/4	1976-81	£5,000	£4,000	£1,000
Stag	2997/8	1970-77	£9,000	£5,000	£2,000
TR7	1998/4	1975-82	£4,000	£1,200	£500
TR7 DHC	1998/4	1980-82	£5,000	£3,500	£1,500

l. **1971 Triumph GT6 MkIII,**
6 cylinders, 1998cc, optional
overdrive, resprayed, mechanical
components reconditioned, fully
restored, excellent condition.
Est. £4,500–5,250 *ADT*

*Making its debut in 1966, the GT6 was
a fast-backed fixed head version of the
Spitfire, powered by a 6 cylinder engine
as used in the then contemporary
Vitesse model. When fitted with the
optional overdrive, the car would cruise
comfortably at 90+mph indefinitely.*

1971 Triumph Vitesse MkII Convertible,
6 cylinders, 1998cc, regularly maintained,
optional overdrive, good overall condition.
£3,250–3,750 *ADT*

1971 Triumph TR6, 2500cc, suspension
modified, full uprate to 190bhp, bare shell
restoration, excellent condition.
£10,000–12,000 *SC*

1972 Triumph Stag 4x4, coachwork by
Michelotti, 8 cylinders, 2997cc, anti-lock brakes,
manual gearbox, 6,000 miles recorded since full
restoration, engine rebuilt, bare metal respray,
new hood and factory hard-top, excellent condition.
£7,350–8,350 *COYS*

*Introduced in the early 1970s, the Triumph Stag
was fitted with the new in-house produced 3 litre
V8. The body was designed by Giovanni Michelotti.
In July 1971 two cars, one a manual and one an
automatic, were handed over to FF Developments
Ltd, the industry leader in 4 wheel drive
development, and the 2 cars supplied were
converted to all-wheel control by them. They also
fitted anti-lock brakes, making this model one of
the most sure-footed and safest of Stags.*

Miller's Starter Marque

Starter Triumphs: *Herald and Vitesse
saloons and convertibles, Spitfire, Dolomite,
Toledo and variants.*

- A Triumph Herald's a top-down winner when
  it comes to budget wind-in-the-air motoring –
  an Italian-styled 4 seater convertible with a
  25ft (760cm) turning circle that's tighter than
  a London taxi and an engine that's so
  accessible it's like having your own inspection
  pit. They are very modestly priced too.

- Of course, it's not all good news. The Herald's
  performance is hardly shattering,
  particularly with the early, rather asthmatic
  948cc Standard 10 engine. They're also prone
  to rust and the handling was legendary – for
  being so darned awful (in the earlier models
  at least). In the wet and in sudden throttle-off
  conditions, the car's high-pivot swing-axle
  rear suspension would pitch it suddenly into
  unpredictable oversteer.

- But who would be daft enough to try to race a
  Herald on public roads? What's more relevant
  are the smiles per mile as you and your
  family potter along over hill and dale burning
  fossil fuel at a miserly 35–40mpg.

- Herald's do fray quite ferociously and you will
  want to inspect the separate chassis, which
  provides the structural strength. The front-
  hinged bonnet is both a strength and weakness.
  It gives unrivalled access to front running gear
  and engine, but once the rot sets in it can flap
  around like a soggy cardboard box.

- Finally, because of its separate chassis, the
  Herald saloon is one car that can be safely
  turned into a convertible. The roof literally
  unbolts and there are a number of rag-top
  conversion kits available.

- **Pick of the bunch:** The Herald's certainly
  no winged messenger, so avoid early cars
  with puny 948cc engine, and go for at least
  the 1147cc or preferably the last 1296cc cars.

- The Herald's chassis formed the basis of a
  number of sporting Triumphs, including the
  twin-headlamped Vitesse. Similar in looks to
  the Herald, but with 1600 and 2000cc engines,
  the Vitesse will heave you along with plenty
  more urge – almost to 100mph in 2 litre form.
  The Herald chassis also formed the basis of
  the pretty little 2 seater Triumph Spitfire,
  again with wonderful engine access provided
  by the front-hinged one-piece bonnet. The
  Spitfire ran from 1961 to 1980 and that means
  there are plenty to choose from.

l. **1972 Triumph Stag,** 8 cylinders, 2997cc, optional
manual transmission with overdrive, later type alloy
wheels, fully resprayed, engine reconditioned, gearbox
rebuilt, new power steering rack, suspension rebuilt,
very good condition.
£3,150–3,650 *ADT*

1972 Triumph TR6, very good condition throughout.
£11,000–12,000 *DHAM*

1973 Triumph Stag, resprayed, new power
steering, 52,285 miles recorded, full history,
excellent condition.
£4,300–4,800 *PA*

1974 Triumph TR6, 6 cylinders, 2498cc, outer
wings replaced, complete respray, 9,000 miles
recorded since engine rebuilt, restored,
very good condition throughout.
£5,250–5,750 *ADT*

1972 Triumph Spitfire MkIV Two Door Roadster,
fully restored, excellent condition throughout.
£4,150–4,650 *BKS*

*Launched in 1962, the Triumph Spitfire was such
a success that the basic design remained virtually
unchanged until 1970. A restyled Spitfire, the
MkIV, with revised bonnet and rear end treatments
was announced for 1971. The engine was still the
1296cc overhead valve four as introduced on the
MkIII, but there was new 'swing spring' rear
suspension to tame previous handling quirks, and
an all-synchromesh gearbox. By the time production
ceased in 1980 over 300,000 Spitfires of all types
had been built.*

**1974 Triumph Stag Four Seater Convertible
with Hard-Top,** fully restored and reconditioned
costing £53,067, V8 engine rebuilt, 2 new cylinder
heads, thermostatically controlled oil cooler,
uprated shock absorbers, new alloy wheels, tyres,
handmade stainless steel exhaust system,
chromework and glass, bodyshell painted with
16 coats of paint, all restoration detailed in
20-page invoice, excellent condition.
£16,000–17,500 *S*

*This car was fully restored by S. P. Autos of
Rainham, Essex in June 1989.*

1974 Triumph Stag, right-hand drive, very good condition.
£5,500–6,000 *PAL*

1975 Triumph Spitfire 1500, 4 cylinders, 1493cc, hard-top, overdrive, tonneau cover, 38,700 miles recorded, garage stored, good original condition.
£3,000–3,500 *BCA*

1975 Triumph Stag, 8 cylinders, 2997cc, engine rebuilt, automatic transmission, torque converter, replacement differential, new steering rack and front and rear coil springs, very good condition.
£3,500–4,000 *ADT*

l. **1976 Triumph Stag,** 8 cylinders, 2997cc, full bare metal respray, engine rebuilt, Borg-Warner automatic transmission, stainless steel exhaust system, good overall condition.
£4,000–4,500 *BRIT*

1980 Triumph TR7 Convertible, 4 cylinders, 1998c, 5 speed transmission, new hood, very good condition.
£2,650–3,150 *ADT*

1976 Triumph 2500 TC, 2498cc, one owner from new, 54,500 miles recorded, very well maintained, excellent running order.
£1,850–2,250 *H&H*

1980 Triumph TR7 Convertible, 4 cylinders, 1998cc, new vinyl hood and carpets, 5 speed manual transmission, restored, good condition throughout.
£1,600–2,000 *ADT*

1980 Triumph Dolomite 1850 HL, 4 cylinders, 1854cc, automatic transmission, one owner since new, full history, 37,000 miles recorded, excellent condition throughout.
£2,000–2,400 *ADT*

The Dolomite was a development of the original Triumph 1300, which had first appeared in 1965, and evolved through 1500cc versions – early examples were front wheel drive – and finally into the 1850 and 2000cc Sprint in 1972.

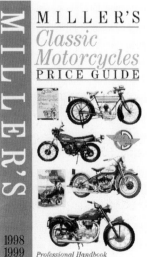

TROJAN

Don't Forget!
If in doubt please refer to the 'How to Use' section at the beginning of this book.

l. **1924 Trojan PB Chummy,** 4 cylinders, 1488cc, good running order, with sound chassis and wooden floorpan, single wheel brake working well, solid and pneumatic tyres, restored, excellent condition.
£3,750–4,500 *ADT*

TVR

Following a period of special building, the Blackpool company of TVR commenced manufacture of its first production car, the Grantura, in 1957. Powered by a Coventry Climax 1100cc engine or a supercharged version of the Ford 100E unit, it was a highly successful machine of particularly distinctive appearance, and its design was to set the format for TVR motor cars for a number of years to come. The company went from strength to strength and offered a fascinating array of models including the Vixen, V6 Tuscan and 2500M.

1969 TVR Vixen S2, 4 cylinders, Ford 1600cc unit, alloy wheels, fully restored from bare chassis, very good condition throughout.
£5,750–6,750 *ADT*

The TVR Vixen replaced the Grantura in 1967 and utilised essentially the same multi-tubular chassis, all independent suspension and glass fibre bodyshell as its predecessor, although now with a kamm-tail. Almost all Vixens were supplied as kits and used either Ford's 1600cc crossflow engine or the MGB 1800cc unit which, although more powerful, did not improve the vehicle's performance as it was somewhat heavier. In the spring of 1968 the Series 2 Vixen was introduced, where the main improvement was that the body was now bolted to the chassis rather than moulded to it on assembly. Series 3 models followed in 1970 and the last Series 4 cars were built in 1973. Only 438 S2 Vixens were built.

1973 TVR 2500M, totally rebuilt including engine, new triple Weber carburettors, repainted, very good condition.
£8,500–9,000 *TVR*

1975 TVR 3000M, 3 litre Ford Essex engine, 2996cc, correct teak dashboard and trim, Wolfrace alloy wheels, factory Webasto sunroof, fibreglass body, very good original condition throughout.
£2,750–3,500 *H&H*

TVR Model	ENGINE cc/cyl	DATES	CONDITION 1	2	3
Grantura I	1172/4	1957-62	£4,000	£3,000	£2,000
Grantura II	1558/4	1957-62	£4,500	£3,000	£2,000
Grantura III/1800S	1798/4	1963-67	£5,000	£3,000	£2,200
Tuscan V8	4727/8	1967-70	£12,000	£7,000	£6,000
Vixen S2/3	1599/4	1968-72	£5,000	£3,000	£1,500
3000M	2994/6	1972-79	£7,000	£4,000	£3,000
Taimar	2994/6	1977-79	£7,500	£5,000	£3,500

1980 TVR 3000S, totally rebuilt, 80,000 miles recorded, right-hand drive, excellent condition throughout. **£12,500–14,000** *TVR*

UNICAR

1959 Unicar Four Wheel Villeres, 328cc twin engine, requires total restoration.
£800–1,100 *DRC*

These cars were produced by S. E. Opperman Ltd at Borehamwood, Hertfordshire, but very few were made.

1966 Vanden Plas 1100 Princess, 1100cc, 2 previous owners, original picnic tables and driver's handbook, very good condition.
£1,000–1,500 *H&H*

VANDEN PLAS

1966 Vanden Plas 1100 Princess, 1100cc, walnut dashboard, door cappings, rear picnic tables and leather all in good order, new rear subframe, excellent restored condition.
£2,500–2,750 *H&H*

The Vanden Plas models were based on the BMC 1100 and 1300 models but offered a much superior level of trim.

1969 Vanden Plas Princess 1300, 4 cylinders, 1275cc, 37,000 miles recorded, full length sliding roof, mechanically good, interior 'as new', very good original condition throughout.
£2,500–3,000 *ADT*

This 1300 version appeared late in 1967 and offered lively performance as well as good road holding.

l. **1974 Vanden Plas 1300 Princess,** 1275cc, one owner, 58,000 miles recorded, requires minor restoration, very good condition.
£1,000–1,300 *H&H*

This 1974 1300 Princess is one of the very last made of this model.

Prices

The price ranges given reflect the average price a purchaser should pay for a similar vehicle. Condition, rarity of model, pedigree, restoration and many other factors must be taken into account when assessing values.

r. **1974 Vanden Plas 1300 Princess,** very good condition.
£3,500–4,000 *DHAM*

1955 Morris Minor Series II Convertible De Luxe, 3 owners from new, 45,000 miles recorded, new speedometer and hood, red leather interior, formerly the property of Tommy Steele, excellent condition.
£4,000–4,500 *BKS*

1968 Ford 'UFO' Aluminium-bodied Car, 1600cc, built by Alan Mann using Ford Zodiac floorpan and components, for the film *Doppelganger*, directed by Gerry Anderson, unrestored.
£3,000–3,500 *DB*

Three similar cars were constructed.

r. **1973 Range Rover Camper,** conversion by Carmichael.
£10,000–12,000 *C*

Designed for a Saudi Arabian prince, this camper is fitted with a shower, basin, double bed, reclining seats, red velour buttoned upholstery, fibre optics in the ceiling for twinkling star effect, stereo, radio, public address system and television.

1946 Chevrolet Fleetmaster Four Door Sedan, 6 cylinders, overhead valve, 3½ litres, 3 speed manual transmission, cosmetically restored, very good condition throughout.
£4,600–5,000 *S*

This vehicle was used in the 1996 film Evita, *starring Madonna.*

1942 GMC CCKW-352 2½ Ton Hard Cab Cargo Truck, 6 cylinders, 94bhp, 5 speed gearbox with 2 speed transfer box, twin wheels on rear axles, 20in tyres, all-steel bodywork covered with canvas canopy, correct markings for the Argentine military, front-mounted winch.
£2,500–3,000 *S*

This vehicle was used in the 1996 film Evita, *starring Madonna.*

l. **c1942 GMC CCKW-353 2½ Ton 6x6 Hard Cab Cargo Truck,** 6 cylinders, 269cu in overhead valve engine, 94bhp at 3000rpm, 5 speed gearbox with 2 speed transfer box with facility to disengage drive to front axle, twin wheels on rear axles, 20in tyres, correct markings for Argentine military, front-mounted winch.
£2,500–3,000 *S*

This vehicle was used in the 1996 film Evita, *starring Madonna.*

1953 Albion Chieftain Flat Platform Lorry, 4 cylinder diesel engine, 75bhp, totally restored to concours standard.
£9,000–11,000 *BKS*

This 1953 Chieftain was in early service with coal merchants Bennetts of Ossett, and later was displayed at the West Yorkshire Transport Museum at Bradford.

c1914 American La France Fire Engine, Type SU engine, 3 speed gearbox, front bench seat, large box-like rear section with standing room for 6 persons, Monogram electric headlights, recently stored.
£5,200–7,000 *S*

1927 Austin Heavy Twelve Van, 4 cylinders, 1861cc, 12.8bhp, 4 speed manual gearbox, original body, restored.
£9,200–10,000 *C*

This vehicle was used to carry inmates to and from Lewes Prison. Commercial vans from this period are particularly sought after due to their rarity and eye-catching presence.

1935 Bedford 2 Ton Dropside Lorry, 6 cylinders, 3530cc, twin rear wheel axle, totally restored, excellent condition.
£6,500–7,500 *ADT*

1954 Bedford Utilicon, low mileage, good condition.
£2,500–2,750 *AS*

1952 Bedford Ambulance, 3530cc, original bell, Notek fog lamp, requires recommissioning.
£1,600–2,000 *BRIT*

This vehicle was supplied new to Dorset County Council, and then went to the St John Ambulance Brigade in Dorchester.

r. 1936 Lanchester Minibus, right-hand drive, very good condition.
£7,000–7,500 *PAL*

This vehicle is a one-off made in 1950s, on a 1936 Lanchester.

1961 BMW Isetta, single cylinder, 300cc, 4 stroke, 4 speed gearbox. **£3,000–4,000** *CRC*

1959 BMW Isetta, excellent condition. **£5,500–6,000** *PC*

1965 Bond, 250cc, good condition. **£700–750** *AS*

1971 Fiat 500 Gamine. **£5,000–6,000** *ScR*

1988 Replicar Cursor, 50cc Honda engine. **£1,500–2,000** *ScR*

1951 Fuldamobil N-1, single cylinder, 247cc, 3 speed gearbox with reverse, 2 wheel cable brakes, transverse leaf front suspension, coil rear suspension, left-hand drive, completely restored, ex-Bruce Weiner Collection. **£10,350–12,000** *C*

1959 Goggomobil TL-400 Transporter, Glas twin cylinder engine, 2 stroke, 392cc, pre-select 4 speed manual gearbox with reverse, left-hand drive, completely restored, ex-Bruce Weiner Collection. **£22,000–24,000** *C*

1957 Heinkel 154 Kabine, single cylinder, 198cc, 4 speed gearbox with reverse, hydraulic front brakes, rear cable, swinging arm and coil spring suspension, left-hand drive, ex-Bruce Weiner Collection. **£4,600–5,000** *C*

This is believed to be one of only 100 examples in existence.

c1977 Invacar Model 70, 500cc Steyr-Puch horizontally opposed twin cylinder, air-cooled engine, Variomatic style transmission, handlebar steering. **£300–500** *ScR*

Built by AC Cars and Invacar Ltd.

1959 Messerschmitt KR200, single cylinder, 191cc, good condition.
£3,200–3,800 *ADT*

1959 Messerschmitt KR200 Cabriolet, 2 recorded owners, very original condition.
£5,500–6,500 *CRE*

1956 Messerschmitt KR200 De Luxe.
£8,000–9,000 *ScR*

1954 Mochet Velocar Grand Luxe, single cylinder, Ydral 2 stroke, 3.5bhp, 125cc, 3 speed gearbox with reverse, 4 wheel brakes, 7,000km recorded from new, left-hand drive, fully restored, excellent condition, ex-Bruce Weiner Collection.
£7,500–9,000 *C*

1957 P. Vallee Chantecler, single cylinder Ydral 2 stroke engine, 125cc, 3 speed manual gearbox with reverse, 4 wheel cable brakes, System Neiman suspension, left-hand drive, requires some restoration, ex-Bruce Weiner Collection.
£7,000–8,000 *C*

c1966 Peel Trident, good condition.
£2,000–2,500 *ScR*

1949 Rolux Baby VB60, single cylinder, 125cc, Ydral 2 stroke, left-hand drive, ex-Bruce Weiner Collection.
£9,200–10,000 *C*

1963 Scootacar MkI, handlebar controls, good condition.
£2,000–2,500 *ScR*

1958 Zundapp Janus 250, single cylinder, 2 stroke, 248cc, 4 speed manual gearbox with reverse, struts and coil springs suspension, 4 wheel hydraulic brakes, left-hand drive, ex-Bruce Weiner Collection.
£9,200–9,800 *C*

1958 Zundapp Janus 250, single cylinder, 2 stroke, 248cc, 4 speed namual gearbox with reverse, struts and coil springs suspension, 4 wheel hydraulic brakes, left-hand drive, ex-Bruce Weiner Collection.
£9,200–9,800 *C*

1965 Abbot SPG, manufactured by Vickers Ltd, Rolls-Royce K60 engine, 105mm self-propelled gun.
£10,000–12,000 *RRM*

1955 Daimler Ferret Scout Car 4x4 Liaison, Rolls-Royce B60 in-line, 6 cylinder engine, 4.25 litres, 116bhp, top speed 45mph, 8–10mpg.
£3,000–4,500 *MVT*

By end of 1971, 4,409 Ferrets were produced .

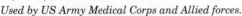

WWII WC 54 Dodge Ambulance, 6 cylinder, 92bhp driving rear or all wheels, 4 speed gearbox.
£3,500–4,000 *RRM*

Used by US Army Medical Corps and Allied forces.

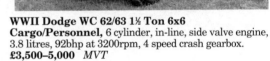

WWII Dodge WC 62/63 1½ Ton 6x6 Cargo/Personnel, 6 cylinder, in-line, side valve engine, 3.8 litres, 92bhp at 3200rpm, 4 speed crash gearbox.
£3,500–5,000 *MVT*

c1956 Ferret Scout Mk 2/3, in United Nations colours, .
£4,500–5,000 *RRM*

1944 Dodge WC 54 ¾ Ton 4x4 Ambulance, 6 cylinders, in-line, side valve engine, 3.8 litres, 92bhp at 3200rpm, 4 speed crash gearbox, 195in long, 5,920lbs unladen weight.
£3,200–4,500 *MVT*

This is the ambulance variant of the weapons carrier. It was able to carry 4 wounded men on litters, or 8 seated.

1942–44 Dodge WC 56/57 ¾ Ton 4x4 Command Reconnaissance Car, 6 cylinders, in-line, side valve engine, 3.8 litres, 92bhp at 3200rpm, 4 speed crash gearbox, no transfer box but selectable front axle, 2½ ton winch.
£8,000–10,000 *MVT*

This is another of the variants on the standard chassis, and is very desirable.

WWII Dodge WC 51/52 ¾ Ton 4x4, 6 cylinders, in-line, side valve engine, 3.8 litres, 92bhp at 3200rpm, 4 speed crash gearbox, no transfer box but selectable front axle, 5,250lbs unladen weight without winch.
£2,800–3,500 *MVT*

1942 Ford Amphibian Jeep GPA ¼ Ton 4x4, 4 cylinders, 15.6bhp, 84in wheelbase, 4,450lbs gross weight, ground-up restoration.
£25,000–30,000 *PETT*

WWII Ford GPA (General Purpose Amphibian), 4 cylinders, in-line, petrol engine, 2.2 litres, 60bhp, 3 speed gearbox with high and low ratio transfer box, with propeller for water use, steering in water by the front wheels, 84in wheelbase.
£16,000–20,000 *MVT*

WWII DUKW GMC 353 Amphibian, 3,000 miles recorded, unrestored, all-original condition.
£16,000–17,500 *RRM*

WWII International Harvester M5 A2 Halftrack, 6 cylinders, in-line, petrol engine, 143bhp, 4 speed gearbox with high and low ratios with optional front axle drive.
£6,000–8,500 *MVT*

WWII GMC DUKW (Duck) Amphibian, 6 cylinders, in-line, petrol engine, 4.4 litres, 104bhp, 5 speed gearbox with 2 speed transfer, with prop shaft and prop shaft and prop for water.
£10,000–15,000 *MVT*

This vehicle could carry 25 men and their equipment, or up to a 5 ton payload.

r. **WWII M16 Halftrack with 4 Guns,** 4.050 calibre machine guns mounted, American.
£13,500–15,000 *RRM*

c1941 Mercedes-Benz G5 Kubelwagen, 4 cylinders, 2006cc, 45hp, side valve engine, 5 speed transmission, completely restored.
£30,000–33,000 *BKS*

Just 320 examples were produced before the model was phased out in 1941.

1943 Sherman M4 Series Grizzly Tank, 5 speed synchromesh transmission, controlled differential, front sprocket drive, vertical volute spring suspension.
£20,000–22,000 *RRM*

1942 Willys MB/Ford GPW Jeep, 3 speed gearbox with high and low ratio transfer box, all-steel 2+2 seater body with folding canvas tilt, ex-British Army.
£4,500–6,000 *MVT*

During WWII over 500,000 Jeeps were built. All the parts of the Willys/Ford Jeeps were interchangeable, with slight variations in construction.

1939/40 Russian T34/85 Medium Tank, 500hp diesel engine, 34mph.
£5,500–7,000 *MVT*

Over 40,000 examples were built, many of which were in active service until the 1980s.

1942 Cadillac Stuart Tank M5 A1, twin V8 cylinder, 110bhp, 4 speed Hydramatic transmission, transfer unit and controlled differential, volute spring suspension, 37mm gun and 4 MGs.
£18,000–20,000 *RRM*

1950–51 Willys MC/M38 Jeep, 4 cylinders, in-line, petrol engine, 2.2 litres, 60bhp, 3 speed gearbox with high and low ratio transfer box, 24 volt electrics, fully waterproofed.
£4,000–4,500 *MVT*

r. **1952 Willys/Ford MD/M38A1 Jeep,** 4 cylinders, in-line, petrol engine, 2.2 litres, 72bhp, 3 speed gearbox with high and low ratio transfer box, 24 volt electrics, fully waterproofed.
£3,000–4,000 *MVT*

l. **1939 Atco Trainer Two Seater,** Villiers 98cc, 2 stroke petrol engine, top speed 10mph, one forward gear, restored, finished in traditional Atco green livery, little used, good condition. **£1,250–1,450** *BKS*

Charles H. Pugh Ltd, better known for their horticultural machinery, designed the Atco Trainer for use in schools for training in car handling and road safety. Very few examples exist today.

1933 Buick Pedal Car, pressed steel body and balloon-type wheels, solid rubber tyres, treadle drive, 42in (107cm) long, 21in (53cm) wide, electric headlights, radiator badge, excellent restored condition. **£900–1,100** *S(S)*

1928 Steelcraft Fire Chief Pedal Car, pressed steel body and balloon-type wheels, solid rubber tyres, treadle drive, 42in (107cm) long, 22in (56cm) wide, chromium radiator, headlights, Fire Chief bell, American, excellent restored condition. **£950–1,100** *S(S)*

1930s Garton Auburn Racer Pedal Car, pressed steel body and balloon-type wheels, solid rubber tyres, treadle drive, 41in (104cm) long, 19in (48cm) wide, opening rear toolbox, chromium headlights and hub-caps, American, excellent restored condition. **£350–400** *S(S)*

1935 Gendron Shark-Nose Skippy Roadster Pedal Car, pressed steel body and artillery-type wheels, solid rubber tyres, treadle ball-bearing drive, chromium steering wheel, lights, bumpers and hub-caps, excellent restored condition. **£675–775** *S(S)*

1955 Austin J40 Pedal Car, pressed steel body, adjustable treadle drive, pneumatic tyres, 60in (152cm) long, 27in (69cm) wide, dummy engine, opening boot and bonnet, good restored condition. **£475–550** *S(S)*

Cooper Bristol Child's Car, built by Star Design, 5.5bhp Honda engine, top speed of 18mph, pneumatic tyres, hydraulic brakes, 4 point safety harness, good condition. **£2,150–2,650** *COYS*

Two model racing cars, a 1929 Bugatti Type 35C and a 1932 Bugatti Type 59.
£3,000–3,300 *CSK*

A Toschi model of a Ferrari, finished in red, features include steering wheel, flyscreen, exhaust vents and transfers.
£970–1,000 *BKS*

Normally supplied as a rubber band driven toy, this model was supplied as a spirit decanter holder, the liquid would have been dispensed from a funnel in the front grille.

A model of an Alfa Romeo P2, manufactured by JEP, painted light red with gold exhaust and black wheels, fuel and oil caps, handbrake, steering and hand-wound clockwork driven rear wheels, with original key, c1928.
£970–1,000 *BKS*

A model of 1957 MG EX181, as driven by Stirling Moss, produced 1980–95.
£230–250 *PC*

A bronze model of a Maserati 250F, depicting Stirling Moss cornering the car at speed, marked 'G. H. Chism '93', 21½in (55cm) long.
£3,650–3,850 *BKS*

A model of a 1979 Budweiser car, as driven by S. Barrett, produced 1980–95.
£200–250 *PC*

Two Tamiya plastic model racing cars, constructed from kits, 14in (35.5cm) long.
£50–65 each *LE*

A model of a McLaren M23, as driven by James Hunt, 1976 World Champion, produced 1980–95.
£175–200 *PC*

A Minic tinplate 1950 Jeep, with clockwork mechanism, 5in (12.5cm) long.
£10–15 *COB*

A model of Jordan's F1 racing car, built by Amalgam of Bristol, one of 3 commissioned by team Jordan representing Barrichello's car number 11, type 196, finished in Benson & Hedges livery with sponsors decals, 20½in (52cm) long.
£2,000–2,300 *BKS*

This model was presented by Eddy Jordan at Estoril.

After Gamy, Bablot le gagnant sur Delage, a print depicting a Delage at speed during the 1913 French Grand Prix, slight fading, framed and glazed, 16 x 32in (40.5 x 81.3cm).
£200–220 *BKS*

After George Meotier, Moto Flirt and Moto Fuite, a pair of comic lithographic prints, c1910, framed and glazed, 21 x 14in (53.5 x 35.5cm).
£950–1,000 *BKS*

Terence Cuneo, Humber Sceptre MkI, Hillman Super Minx and other cars at a pedestrian crossing with children at play, oil on canvas, original artwork for calendar, c1963, 25 x 30in (63.5 x 76cm).
£5,500–5,750 *CSK*

A original oil painting of a Alfa Romeo, 20thC.
£140–160 *BC*

Frank Wootton, Devonshire House, Piccadilly, London W1, oil on canvas, signed 'Wootton', framed, 28¾ x 34⅜in (75.5 x 88cm).
£2,100–2,300 *CSK*

Helen Taylor, an Alfa Romeo Monza at speed, an abstract composition using 'blink of an eye' references, mixed media on board, 20 x 24in (51 x 61cm).
£160–200 *BKS*

r. Michael Turner, a Model T Ford causing havoc in a farmyard, gouache, signed, 8¾ x 14in (22 x 35.5cm).
£575–700 *CSK*

Steven Massey, a study of
Tazio Nuvolari during his last
days as a racing driver, acrylic
on thick paper, framed and
glazed, 17 x 15in (43 x 38cm).
£500–600 *BKS*

Roy Nockolds, W. O. Bentley driving on the Route Nationale
to the South of France in an 8 litre Bentley, hand-coloured silk
screen print, 17 x 27in (43 x 68.5cm).
£200–220 *BKS*

This work was commissioned by W. O. Bentley himself.

After E. Montaut, Michelin –
Le Pneu Michelin a Vaincu le
Rail, full colour lithograph,
printed facsimile signature,
excellent condition, 61 x 43in
(155 x 110cm).
£2,300–2,700 *C*

After E. Montaut, En
Reconnaissance, a linen-backed
lithograph depicting airship,
aeroplane and a Clement-Bayard
in military usage, 62 x 45in
(157.5 x 114.5cm).
£1,400–1,800 *C*

Michael Wright, Glen Kidson in
the 6½ litre Bentley during the
1930 Le Mans 24 hour race,
watercolour, mounted,
framed and signed, 30 x 20in
(76 x 51cm).
£1,500–1,700 *BKS*

A BMC poster, advertising Austin-Healey Sprite MkIV, c1966.
36 x 28in (91.5 x 71cm).
£250–300 *LE*

A poster, advertising the
Louis Vuitton Concours,
framed and glazed, 1993,
27½ x 19⅝in (70 x 50cm).
£55–60 *BKS*

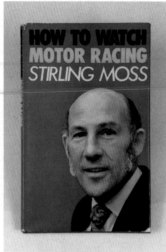

Stirling Moss, *A Turn at the Wheel*, 1961.
£25–30 *GPCC*

Stirling Moss, *How to Watch Motor Racing*, 1975.
£5–6 *GPCC*

C. E. 'Johnny' Johnson, *To Draw a Long Line, My Days with a British Sports & Grand Prix Racing Car Maker*, 1989. **£20–25** *GPCC*

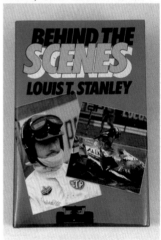

Hans Tanner & Doug Nye, *Ferrari*, Sixth Edition, 1984.
£40–50 *GPCC*

Stirling Moss, *Fangio, A Pirelli Album*, signed by Juan Manuel Fangio and Stirling Moss, 1991.
£75–100 *GPCC*

Louis T. Stanley, *Behind the Scenes*, 1985.
£15–18 *GPCC*

A silver keyless watch, with chronograph and instantaneous 30 minute recorder, used by the Automobile Club to time the Gordon Bennett Cup Race, Ireland, 1903, case engraved, signed, 51mm diam.
£3,250–3,500 *BKS*

A pair of Heuer Rally-Master dashboard instruments, *l.* Master Time, 8-day stop watch, *r.* Monte-Carlo, register with digital jumping hour, 1970s, 58mm diam.
£1,350–1,450 *BKS*

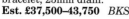

An 18ct gold gentleman's wristwatch, in the shape of a Bugatti radiator grille, with 18ct yellow and white gold bracelet, 23mm diam.
Est. £37,500–43,750 *BKS*

A Jaeger rear-view mirror with an electric watch, signed, 4¾in (12cm) wide.
£960–1,100 *BKS*

A Champion sparking plugs enamel advertising sign, original condition, 1930s, 32 x 54in (81.5 x 137cm).
£30–40 *SW*

A Continental Pneumatic advertising sign, early chromo study published by Niedersedlitz, showing 2 maidens in a garlanded car, unused condition.
£25–30 *SpP*

A Price's Energol illuminated advertising sign, 15 x 12in (38 x 30.5cm).
£200–250 *LE*

Dunlop – lady racing motorist, a colour lithograph depicting a young lady in 1930s period overalls and helmet, wearing Meyrovitz goggles, 54in (137cm) high.
£1,400–1,600 *C*

A Beckmeter Shellmex electric petrol pump, good condition, 1950s, 74in(188cm) high.
£750–1,200 *CRC*

A Wane electric petrol pump, cast iron head and base, 1930s.
£750–1,000 *CRC*

A John Bull Tyres enamel advertising sign, excellent condition, 1930s, 38 x 38in (96.5 x 96.5cm).
£40–50 *SW*

A Tiger plastic petrol pump globe, 1960s, 17 x 16in (43 x 40.5cm).
£100–150 *LE*

A Gamages 5 gallon oil can, 21in (53.5cm) high.
£110–120 *LE*

A two-coloured metal Indian chief car mascot, on a heavy base.
£45–50 *LF*

A Rolls-Royce 'Spirit of Ectasy' showroom display bronze, after Charles Sykes, signed, No. 28, mounted on display base, 19½in (50cm) high.
£1,500–1,700 *S*

A lamp mascot, stamped 'Transviseur C. D. Breveté'.
£40–50
An Indian head mascot, unsigned, French, 1925.
£170–180 *BKS*

A Coq Nain mascot, by René Lalique, brown glass with ruby red centre, maker's mark to base, French, 1928.
£1,600–1,800 *BKS*

A frosted glass Pharoah's head mascot, after a design by Red Ashay, glass, 4⅜in (12cm) high.
£460–500 *S*

A Lalique 'Tete de Bellier' glass mascot, French, 1928–39, 3⅜in (9.5cm) high.
£2,300–2,500 *S*

A 'Centauresse L'Eclair' mascot by Darel, French, 1920s, stamped, 5¾in (14.5cm) high.
£575–625 *S*

A Lalique 'Sanglier' glass mascot, French, 1929–39. 3½in (9cm) long.
£230–260 *S*

A Walt Disney brass Mickey Mouse mascot, by Desmo, base stamped 'Desmo', c1930.
£1,500–1,600 *BKS*

A satin-glass Eagle's head mascot, by René Lalique, marked, number 1138, France, 1928.
£2,400–2,500 *BKS*
These were reputedly fitted to German officers staff cars.

A Lalique 'Coq Nain' clear glass mascot, French, 1928–30, maker's mark 8in (20.5cm) high.
£1,400–1,500 *S*

A Lalique 'Tete D'Aigle' fumee tinted glass mascot, in a metal mounting ring on a chromed radiator cap, French, 1928–39, 6in (15cm) long.
£1,050–1,150 *S*

A bronze elephant mascot, by Charles, signed, superbly detailed and sculpted, with raised trunk, c1920.
£1,200–1,400 *BKS*

A Barrett & Sons wicker fold-fronted four-person picnic set, with original kettle, ornate stand and burner, gilt-rimmed enamel cups, saucers, plates, bottles, sandwich boxes each marked inside lids, c1905.
£3,000–3,500 *BKS*

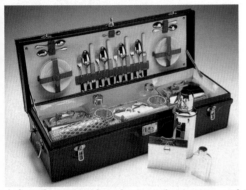

A Coracle running board mounted picnic set, within a wooden case covered in black leather cloth with brass edges, fully fitted for four-persons, with china cups, saucers, wicker-covered glasses, drinks bottle, thermos flask, sandwich boxes, 1907–1910.
£1,800–2,300 *BKS*

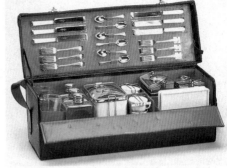

An Edwards & Sons six-person leather fold-fronted picnic set, with original drink flasks, twin kettle burner, kettles, cups and plates, housed in lift-out containers, compartments for preserve jars, c1908.
£2,000–2,500 *BKS*

A Mappin & Webb four-person picnic set, fold-fronted leather case, contents housed in wicker covered wire supports, copper kettle, bottles, containers, cups, saucers and cutlery, 1909.
£5,000–5,200 *BKS*

A Goldsmiths & Silversmiths Company six-person picnic set, in a leather case, with kettle, stand and burner, sandwich box, china cups, saucers, plates and cutlery, c1920.
£3,700–4,300 *BKS*

A four-person green picnic set, with flasks, containers, cups, saucers, plates and cutlery, excellent condition, 1958, 15¾in (40cm) wide.
£60–70 *SW*

r. A four-person picnic set, with plates, cutlery and containers, good condition, 1950s, 21¾in (55cm) wide.
£40–50 *SW*

A Duncan Hamilton motor racing game, 15 x 11in (38 x 28cm).
£50–60 *LE*

A McLaren crankshaft, designed
by Porsche, used condition,
1984–87, 16in (40.5cm).
£350–425 *GPT*

A Le Mans souvenir car badge, 1950s.
£120–150 *LE*

A Panhard-Levassor spirit flask, in the form of
a radiator, hallmarked, very rare.
£280–300 *BC*

An ice bucket, depicting various makes of
racing car, 11in (28cm) high.
£35–40 *LE*

A 54-piece Rolls-Royce boardroom dinner service,
Biarritz pattern by Clarice Cliff, clear glazed with line
decoration and 'RR' symbol in top left corner, factory
marks to base, facsimile signature Clarice Cliff,
registered design 1933.
£1,800–2,300 *S*

VAUXHALL

The Griffin may be a mythical beast, but over the last 95 years the cars that sport this ancient English heraldic emblem have become an enduring fact of motoring life for millions of motorists in Great Britain and across the world. The company's first car was produced in 1903, and in the Edwardian and Vintage years the sporting Prince Henry and 30/98 models stood out as serious road-going rivals to the 3 litre Bentleys, right up there with Invictas and Bugattis. In 1925 the firm's poor finances led to General Motors taking control and successfully moving the marque down market into solid middle-class territory with successful models like the H-type 10 and the J-type 14. In the 1950s the transatlantic influence really became prominent with the gaudy Crestas and F-type Victors so beloved today of ageing teddy-boys. General Motors had also held a majority shareholding in German car-maker Opel since the late 1920s. For many years they remained completely separate operations, but from the mid-1970s the model lines converged with most design input coming from Germany.

1925 Vauxhall 23/60hp OD Kington Tourer,
4 litre D-type engine, body-off restoration, transmission overhauled, electrics rewired, worn chassis components renewed, new radiator core, original instruments, very good condition.
£32,500–37,500 *BKS*

This car was supplied new to Australia, returning to the UK via New Zealand in 1979.

1927 Vauxhall 14/40 Princeton Tourer,
excellent condition throughout.
£20,000–25,000 *DH*

This car has completed many rallies on the Continent in recent years, and is an ideal grand touring car for home or abroad.

VAUXHALL Model	ENGINE cc/cyl	DATES	CONDITION 1	2	3
D/OD	3969/4	1914-26	£35,000	£24,000	£18,000
E/OE	4224/4	1919-28	£100,000	£60,000	£35,000
Eighty	3317/6	1931-33	£10,000	£8,000	£5,000
Cadet	2048/6	1931-33	£7,000	£5,000	£3,000
Lt Six	1531/6	1934-38	£5,000	£4,000	£1,500
14	1781/6	1934-39	£4,000	£3,000	£1,500
25	3215/6	1937-39	£5,000	£4,000	£1,500
10	1203/4	1938-39	£4,000	£3,000	£1,500
Wyvern LIX	1500/4	1948-51	£2,000	£1,000	£500
Velox LIP	2200/6	1948-51	£2,000	£1,000	£500
Wyvern EIX	1500/4	1951-57	£2,000	£1,320	£400
Velox EIPV	2200/6	1951-57	£3,000	£1,650	£400
Cresta EIPC	2200/6	1954-57	£3,000	£1,650	£400
Velox/Cresta PAS/PAD	2262/6	1957-59	£2,850	£1,300	£300
Velox/Cresta PASY/PADY	2262/6	1959-60	£2,700	£1,500	£300
Velox/Cresta PASX/PADX	2651/6	1960-62	£2,700	£1,300	£300
Velox/Cresta PASX/PADX Est	2651/6	1960-62	£2,700	£1,300	£300
Velox/Cresta PB	2651/6	1962-65	£1,600	£800	£100
Velox/Cresta PB Est	2651/6	1962-65	£1,600	£800	£100
Cresta/Deluxe PC	3294/6	1964-72	£1,500	£800	£100
Cresta PC Est	3294/6	1964-72	£1,500	£800	£100
Viscount	3294/6	1964-72	£1,700	£900	£100
Victor I/II	1507/4	1957-61	£2,000	£1,000	£250
Victor I/II Est	1507/4	1957-61	£2,100	£1,100	£300
Victor FB	1507/4	1961-64	£1,500	£900	£200
Victor FB Est	1507/4	1961-64	£1,600	£1,000	£300
VX4/90	1507/4	1961-64	£2,000	£900	£150
Victor FC101	1594/4	1964-67	£1,600	£900	£150
Victor FC101 Est	1594/4	1964-67	£1,800	£1,000	£200
101 VX4/90	1594/4	1964-67	£2,000	£1,500	£250
VX4/90	1975/4	1969-71	£1,000	£600	£100
Ventora I/II	3294/6	1968-71	£1,000	£375	£100
Viva HA	1057/4	1963-66	£1,000	£350	£100
Viva SL90	1159/4	1966-70	£1,000	£350	£100
Viva Brabham	1159/4	1967-70	£2,000	£1,000	£800
Viva	1600/4	1968-70	£500	£350	£100
Viva Est	1159/4	1967-70	£500	£400	£100

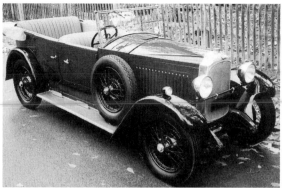

l. **1929 Vauxhall 20/60 R-Type Princeton Tourer,** 2.9 litres, wire wheels, engine rebuilt, new upholstery, side-mounted spare wheel, luggage grid, excellent condition.
£15,600–20,000 *BKS*

This was the first of the new models introduced at Luton following the takeover by General Motors, and superceded the previous 14/40. Customers now had a 6 cylinder car for the same price as they had previously paid for a 'four'. The engine, a 7 bearing pushrod-operated overhead valve 'six', was of British rather than American inspiration, although the 4 speed gearbox was now controlled through a centrally-placed gear lever. Brakes were coupled and worked better than anything tried at Luton in the pre-General Motors days.

Miller's Starter Marque

Starter Vauxhalls: *PA Cresta/Velox, 1957–62; F-type Victor, 1957–61.*

- As our price table shows, all Vauxhalls of the 1950s and 1960s are affordable, but two models that really stand out for their glamorous styling are the Detroit-inspired PA Cresta/Velox and the F-type Victor. A kind of mid-Atlantic meeting between Uncle Stan and Uncle Sam, they are very appealing today to anyone who is nostalgic for the 1950s.

- They look for all the world like classic Yank tanks, yet their flanks clothe ordinary British mechanicals and running gear that are generally readily available and easy to maintain. The earlier E-type Cresta, Velox and Wyvern also offer a touch of star-spangled razzmatazz but their numbers have thinned to a level where they are not quite as practical as the later PA. Later cars, like the PB Cresta and FB Victors, are also practical buys, but compared to the extravagant PA they are almost muted.

- The glorious PA Cresta is a monster by British standards, a genuine 6 seater with enough body rock and roll to please any Elvis fan. Mechanically they offer little to worry about with their strong 2.2 and 2.6 litre engines, and ancillaries like front discs, starter motors and dynamos are straight out of an MGB.

- Pick of the PAs: Some prefer the looks of the pre-1960 models with their three-piece rear window, although later models have slightly more eager 2.6 litre lumps in place of the earlier 2.2.

- But the bodies are a different matter. Legend has it that PA Crestas rusted so rapidly that by the time they reached the end of the Luton production line they would have failed today's MOT test. Actually their resistance to rust was pretty much in line with other cars of the era. The big difference is there's just more metal to rust. When you go and look at one take a metal detector, because a festering rust box will be a labour of love rather than a sound buying proposition.

- The F-type Victor delivers a Detroit dream in a UK-sized package. Compared to contemporary saloon rivals it was a fine car to drive with a tough and flexible engine. The mechanicals are all pretty sturdy, but the early cars really did have a deserved reputation for rusting, as their bodyshells offered more mud traps than a Florida swamp. In fact, by the end of 1959 Vauxhall was already receiving corrosion complaints and in response added underseal and splash panels.

1933 Vauxhall ASX Salmons Tickford Drophead Coupé, 14.7hp, full history, good condition.
£9,000–10,000 *UMC*

1956 Vauxhall Wyvern Four Door Saloon, manual transmission, 24,000 miles recorded, heater fitted from new, right-hand drive.
£2,500–3,000 *BKS*

Introduced in 1951, initially with 1442cc 4 cylinder engine, the Vauxhall Wyvern was styled on the 1949 Chevrolet. It features the traditional Vauxhall flutes, independent front suspension by coil springs and a hypoid rear axle. From April 1952 the short-stroke 1508cc engine was fitted, providing far more urge, and this was followed by recirculating ball steering in 1953 and a redesigned bonnet and grille in 1955. 105,275 examples with the larger engine were sold.

1960 Vauxhall F Series 2 Estate, 1508cc, 51,000 miles recorded, resprayed, very good condition.
£2,200–2,600 *H&H*

This Vauxhall was exhibited at the 1960 Motor Show, and only 5 or 6 examples of this model still exist.

1964 Vauxhall Victor FB, many accessories including headlamp peaks, spotlights, fire extinguisher and wing mirrors, good original condition.
£800–1,000 *CRE*

1975 Vauxhall Viva Deluxe, 4 cylinders, 1256cc, one owner from new, 18,000 miles recorded, very good condition throughout.
£1,000–1,300 *JNic*

VINCENT-HOLLIER

l. **1915 Vincent-Hollier,** V8, 28hp, right-hand drive, wooden artillery wheels, good oil pressure, normal water temperature, excellent condition.
£10,000–11,000 *Bro*
This is one of the very first V8 motor cars built, and was very powerful for Edwardian touring. It is now a very rare car.

VOLKSWAGEN

1957 Volkswagen Beetle, 4 cylinders, 1192cc, headlight cowls, 'cheesegrater' exhaust trims, whitewall tyres, Perspex sun visor, completely restored, excellent condition throughout.
£6,500–7,500 *COYS*

r. **1967 Volkswagen Karmann Ghia Coupé,** 1584cc, engine requires attention, restoration costs of £5,500, right-hand drive, good overall condition.
£2,500–3,000 *H&H*

Miller's Starter Marque

Starter Volkswagens: *Beetle*

- The Volkswagen Beetle is one bug they just can't find a cure for. Produced continuously from 1945, every car that rolls off the remaining South American production line adds to a 21 million+ world production record that's unlikely ever to be beaten.

- As a starter classic the Beetle has the benefit of still being in production, which means readily available cheap spares for most Beetles other than very early cars. That buzzing air-cooled 4 cylinder engine is well nigh unburstable too, and in mechanical terms the cars are easy to work on. One fact says it all: the world record for an engine swap – drive-up to drive-away – is just over 3 minutes.

- If it's first-of-breed purity you're after, there's either the 1131cc 1945–53 split-screen cars or the 1953–57 oval window 1200cc cars. For driveability and less onerous ownership costs, a good mid-way motor is the 1500cc Bug produced from 1966 to 1970. It's old enough to be classic, fast enough to keep up and still pure in design.

- The body's the Beetle's bug though. Although the wings are bolt on and virtually every body panel is available there are a lot of Beetle bodywork bodges around. Check very closely where body attaches to chassis just behind front wheels and immediately ahead of rear ones: severe rust here can make the vehicle unsafe.

1972 Volkswagen Karmann Beetle Convertible, 1600cc, one owner, 67,000 miles recorded, excellent condition throughout. **£4,000–5,000** *H&H*

1972 Volkswagen Beetle 1300, 4 cylinders, 1285cc, good overall condition. **£1,600–2,000** *ADT*

r. **1975 Volkswagen Beetle Two Door Convertible,** coachwork by Karmann, 1584cc, air conditioning, manual transmission, fully restored, left-hand drive, very good conditon. **£7,500–8,000** *BKS*

l. **1975 Volkswagen 1300 Beetle,** 1300cc, one owner, 57,000 miles recorded, stainless steel exhaust, stone guard, headrests, chromework excellent, very good overall condition. **£2,400–2,800** *H&H*

VOLKSWAGEN Model	ENGINE cc/cyl	DATES	CONDITION 1	2	3
Beetle (split rear screen)	1131/4	1945-53	£5,000	£3,500	£2,000
Beetle (oval rear screen)	1192/4	1953-57	£4,000	£2,000	£1,000
Beetle (slope headlamps)	1192/4	1957-68	£2,500	£1,000	£600
Beetle DHC	1192/4	1954-60	£6,000	£4,500	£2,000
Beetle 1500	1493/4	1966-70	£3,000	£2,000	£1,000
Beetle 1302 LS	1600/4	1970-72	£2,500	£1,850	£850
Beetle 1303 S	1600/4	1972-79	£3,000	£2,000	£1,500
1500 Variant/1600	1493/ 1584/4	1961-73	£2,000	£1,500	£650
1500/1600	1493/ 1584/4	1961-73	£3,000	£2,000	£800
Karmann Ghia/I	1192/4	1955-59	£5,000	£3,000	£1,000
Karmann Ghia/I DHC	1192/4	1957-59	£8,000	£5,000	£2,500
Karmann Ghia/I	1192/4	1960-74	£5,500	£3,000	£1,800
Karmann Ghia/I DHC	1192/4	1960-74	£7,000	£4,500	£2,000
Karmann Ghia/3	1493/4	1962-69	£4,000	£2,500	£1,250

1972 Volkswagen Karmann Ghia Fixed Head Coupé, 1600cc, resprayed, very good condition.
£6,000–6,500 *PC*

1977 Volkswagen Beetle 1303 Two Door Karmann Convertible, 1584cc, pull-out stereo, partially stamped service record, original purchase invoice, 50,600 miles recorded, very good condition.
£6,500–7,500 *BKS*

This rare right-hand drive car is finished in silver livery with black interior.

VOLVO

Although founded back in 1927 it wasn't until the post-war era that Volvo reached a wider international audience, initially with the PV444/PV544 which earned admiration both for the accomplished roadholding that made it a rally winner and for the solid build-quality that has become a Volvo hallmark. In the late 1950s the 121 continued in the same mould and endured through various model designations (122/131/132/123GT) up to 1970. Today they are still enjoyed in daily use as a robust and stylish classic workhorse. Perhaps the most unlikely Volvo is the P1800 sports car, a one-time flight of fancy by the sober Swedes. It's certainly stylish, robust too, and terminally typecast as the 'Saint' Volvo after co-starring alongside Roger Moore in the long-running TV series in the 1960s. In estate form it's an uncommonly practical sports car.

1950 Volvo PV444, restored, excellent overall condition.
£4,000–5,000 *Bro*

1963 Volvo PV544, 4 cylinders, 1780cc, good condition throughout.
£2,100–2,600 *ADT*

One of their most widely remembered post-war models was the PV444, a design dating back to 1945 and powered by a 1.4 litre overhead valve engine. The engine size was eventually increased to 1.8 litres and the new model designated PV544. It was to remain in production until 1965.

1966 Volvo Amazon 122S, 1780cc, manual 4 speed gearbox, optional overdrive, restored, good condition.
£3,200–3,800 *H&H*

VOLVO Model	ENGINE cc/cyl	DATES	CONDITION 1	2	3
PV444	1800/4	1958-67	£4,000	£1,750	£800
PV544	1800/4	1962-64	£4,000	£1,750	£800
120 (B16)	1583/4	1956-59	£3,000	£1,000	£300
121	1708/4	1960-67	£3,500	£1,500	£350
122S	1780/4	1960-67	£4,500	£1,500	£250
131	1780/4	1962-69	£4,000	£1,500	£350
221/222	1780/4	1962-69	£2,500	£1,500	£300
123Gt	1986/4	1967-69	£3,000	£2,500	£750
P1800	1986/4	1960-70	£3,500	£2,000	£1,000
P1800E	1986/4	1970-71	£4,000	£2,500	£1,000
P1800ES	1986/4	1971-73	£5,000	£3,000	£1,000

1971 Volvo 1800E Sports Coupé, one owner for 16 years, resprayed, bodywork restored, good condition.
£2,000–2,500 *S*

When Volvo decided to enter the sports car market they combined resources with Pressed Steel in Britain to produce a new bodyshell, instructing Jensen of West Bromwich to assemble the model. Production of the 2 seater sporting car commenced in 1960. The model was progressively updated – the engine was enlarged to 2 litres and Bosch fuel injection incorporated giving 125bhp. There were also design changes to the coachwork. From 1964 assembly reverted to Sweden. The 2 litre version became known as the 1800E and an 1800ES estate was added. Production ended in 1973.

WOLSELEY

Since the dawn of the motor industry Wolseley had been renowned for the production of fine motor cars, many with well engineered overhead camshaft engines. These motor cars were progressively developed until financial difficulties ultimately led to the bankruptcy in 1927 of the Wolseley company. Sir William Morris came to the rescue and purchased Wolseley, bringing it under the wing of the growing Nuffield empire, and the resulting products were not unnaturally to be found sharing many components from Morris and MG vehicles. The inevitable rationalisation process gathered momentum and by 1938 all Wolseleys were effectively upmarket versions of their Morris counterparts.

1938 Wolseley Six 25hp Saloon, 2500cc, original blue leather interior, new flywheel and headlining, rewired, repainted in black and ivory, temperature gauge, very good condition.
£6,300–7,300 *H&H*

This car has been used for wedding hire for the past 6 years.

r. **1939 Wolseley 25hp Saloon,** original brown leather trim, finished in off-white and black, very good condition.
£8,000–9,000 *AS*

1973 Volvo P1800 ES, 1986cc, engine rebuilt, halogen headlamp kit, fully undersealed, full history, good condition.
£1,500–1,800 *H&H*

WALTHAM

1904 Waltham Orient 4hp Runabout, engine rebuilt, new piston, inlet valve, big-end and main bearings, museum stored in US, good condition.
£5,000–7,000 *BKS*

The Runabout was imported from the USA in 1989, and its first UK owner took part in 3 London to Brighton runs with it, but failed to finish on each occasion because of trouble with the engine's atmospheric inlet valve. A simple modification to the inlet valve spring is said to have got it 'running reliably'. The chassis is said to be free from woodworm and dry rot, and the varnished hickory body is in good condition.

1938 Wolseley Saloon, 14hp, original leather trim, history and service records, good condition.
£5,000–6,000 *AS*

WOLSELEY Model	ENGINE cc/cyl	DATES	CONDITION 1	2	3
10	987/2	1909-16	£16,000	£12,500	£9,000
CZ (30hp)	2887/4	1909	£18,000	£13,000	£9,000
15hp and A9	2614/4	1920-27	£12,000	£10,000	£8,000
20 and C8	3921/ 3862/6	1920-27	£11,000	£8,000	£6,000
E4 (10.5hp)	1267/ 1542/4	1925-30	£6,000	£4,000	£3,000
E6 and Viper and 16hp	2025/6	1927-34	£15,000	£12,000	£8,000
E8M	2700/8	1928-31	£18,000	£15,000	£12,000
Hornet	1271/4	1931-35	£10,000	£8,000	£4,500
Hornet Special	1271/ 1604/6	1933-36	£12,000	£8,000	£5,000
Wasp	1069/4	1936	£7,000	£5,000	£3,500
Hornet	1378/6	1936	£8,000	£6,000	£4,000
21/60 and 21hp	2677/ 2916/6	1932-39	£11,000	£6,000	£4,000
25	3485/6	1936-39	£8,500	£5,500	£4,000
12/48	1547/4	1937-39	£5,000	£3,000	£2,000
14/56	1818/6	1937-39	£6,000	£4,000	£2,000
18/80	2322/6	1938-39	£7,500	£5,500	£4,000

Early Wolseley cars are well made and very British and those with coachbuilt bodies command a premium of at least +25%.

l. **1946 Wolseley Fourteen,** 6 cylinders, 1818cc, original leather seats, requires cosmetic restoration, 74,000 miles recorded, not used for 25 years, good original condition.
£2,500–3,000 *ADT*

1960 Wolseley Hornet MkIII, requires cosmetic attention, full history.
£1,400–1,700 *CRE*

l. **1962 Wolseley 1500,** 4 cylinders, 1489cc, well maintained, engine running well, 59,000 miles recorded, good condition.
£1,100–1,500 *BCA*

WOLSELEY Model	ENGINE cc/cyl	DATES	CONDITION 1	2	3
8	918/4	1939-48	£3,000	£2,000	£1,000
10	1140/4	1939-48	£3,500	£2,000	£1,000
12/48	1548/4	1939-48	£4,000	£2,000	£1,250
14/60	1818/6	1946-48	£4,500	£2,500	£1,500
18/85	2321/6	1946-48	£6,000	£3,000	£2,000
25	3485/6	1946-48	£7,000	£4,000	£2,500
4/50	1476/4	1948-53	£2,500	£1,000	£450
6/80	2215/6	1948-54	£3,000	£1,500	£750
4/44	1250/4	1952-56	£2,500	£1,250	£750
15/50	1489/4	1956-58	£1,850	£850	£500
1500	1489/4	1958-65	£2,500	£1,000	£500
15/60	1489/4	1958-61	£2,000	£700	£400
16/60	1622/4	1961-71	£1,800	£800	£400
6/90	2639/6	1954-57	£2,500	£1,000	£500
6/99	2912/6	1959-61	£3,000	£1,500	£750
6/110 MK I/II	2912/6	1961-68	£2,000	£1,000	£500
Hornet (Mini)	848/4	1961-70	£1,500	£750	£400
1300	1275/4	1967-74	£1,250	£750	£400
18/85	1798/4	1967-72	£950	£500	£250

COMMERCIAL VEHICLES

1911 London General Omnibus Company B-Type Double Deck Omnibus, museum displayed, very good condition.
£10,000–15,000 *BKS*

This is another rare survivor of the 1300 B-Type buses that served in France during WWI. After the Armistice it was bought in chassis form by the Essex-based Laindon & District Motor Services. It was then fitted with the body from a National steam bus that was still in place when B-214 was discovered in a garden at Crays Hill, Billericay, in the early 1960s. Fortunately, a genuine LGOC B-Type body was found in use as a house on nearby Canvey Island. It was united with the chassis during a painstaking restoration completed in the early 1970s by a Gloucestershire-based team headed by Captain J. B. Atkinson.

1926 Morris Commercial One Ton Tipper Truck, in working order, restored, good condition.
£6,350–6,850 *S*

According to Morris' literature this vehicle was directed at 'builders and general contractors, who require a vehicle that will carry a ton load and which can be capable of tilting quickly with loose loads'.

1931 Morris One Ton Dropside Truck, restored, good condition.
£5,000–6,000 *H&H*

This vehicle was first registered on 1st January 1931, but is believed to be much older. It is possible that the chassis is an original T type used by the manufacturers' experimental department.

1912 Model T Ford Express Delivery Van, rear lamps rebuilt, white rubber 30 x 3½in tyres, stainless steel valves and seats, aluminium pistons, rebuilt engine, replaced 1912 cylinder block, new body, restoration cost £20,000, very good condition.
£7,000–9,000 *BKS*

Launched on the English market during 1912, the Express delivery van, nicknamed the 'Pie Van', was one of the most expensive variants of the Model T Ford. Rare in Britain, this particular example is the result of a 'no expense spared' restoration in the search for authenticity.

1929 Dennis Platform Truck, fully restored, good running order, roadworthy, engine excellent.
£5,250–6,000 *S*

This truck was at the Dargate Motor Museum until 1989.

Don't Forget!

If in doubt please refer to the 'How to Use' section at the beginning of this book.

1934 Ford Model BF 12cwt Van, very good condition.
£6,250–7,250 *BKS*

The 12cwt van was the most popular body style available of the 14.9hp Ford BF light commercial chassis, representing 5,202 vehicles out of a production total of 8,784 units between 1932–35. It is believed that this nicely presented example of the 2nd series of Briggs-bodied Model BF vans is now one of only 3 survivors.

1935 Guy Wolf 20 Seater Single Decker Bus, coachwork by Guy Motors Ltd, 3308cc, fully restored to original condition, engine overhauled, bodywork restored in 1980, repainted in 1981, interior, transmission, electrics and chassis in good condition.
£7,500–9,500 *BKS*

Guy Motors Ltd of Fallings Park, Wolverhampton, made trucks and buses from 1914 until 1976. The 3 ton Wolf was introduced in 1933, powered by a Meadows 4 cylinder engine, and was also offered as a 20 seater coach. The Meadows engines were also Wolverhampton-produced. Eventually both Guy and Meadows were taken over by Jaguar.

1936 Morris 8 Series I 5cwt Van, 4 cylinders, 918cc, fully restored in 1981, covered less than 5,000 miles since.
£5,000–6,000 *ADT*

The Series I Morris 8 Van was produced from September 1934 until the outbreak of WWII in September 1939.

1936 Citroën Rosaline, 1600cc, 4 speed overhead valve engine, running order, unrestored.
£800–1,000 *DB*

1938 Commer 25cwt Van, 4 cylinders, 2 litre overhead valve engine, 4 speed manual gearbox, rewired electrics, good condition.
£2,300–3,000 *BKS*

Founded in 1905, and established as commercial vehicle manufacturers at its new Luton factory the following year, Commercial Cars Ltd did not acquire the now familiar Commer name until 1926, when the Humber Motor Company took control. This vehicle was originally employed in the service of Lyons' Tea, it has been rallied on the Continent and appeared in the TV series Agatha Christie's Poirot.

l. **1956 Leyland Tipper Truck,** manual transmission, 5005kg unladen taxable weight, good condition overall.
£2,500–3,000 *BKS*

l. **1957 Land Rover Series 1,** 1997cc petrol engine, 88in wheelbase, extensively restored, newly fabricated bulkhead, chassis stripped to bare metal, fully reconditioned, schedule of restoration with costs.
£4,400–5,000 *S*

Maurice Wilkes, technical director of Rover, conceived the idea of a go-anywhere vehicle which became known as the Land Rover. Wilkes acquired 2 war-surplus Jeeps and, clearly impressed by their abilities, proceeded to exploit the potential of all-purpose design. The original Land Rover prototype was essentially a Jeep equipped with a Rover gearbox and powered by the same 4 cylinder engine used for the Rover 60.

1960 Saurer Alpenwagen IIIA, 6 cylinders in-line, diesel, 8720cc, 135bhp, 8 gear pneumatic, preselector, live axle suspension, 4 wheel drum brakes, left-hand drive, restored, interior converted into camper, refrigerator, toilets and wine bar, good condition.
£11,000–13,000 *C*

Adolph Saurer began to manufacture petrol engines in 1888 in Aarbon, Switzerland. He started producing special buses for the Alps (Alpenwagen) in 1921 distinguished by robustness and reliability, a narrow turning radius and passenger compartments offering panoramic views. The motor brake was a crucial innovation enabling Saurer to master the problem of fading brakes when descending passes.

1960 Morris Cowley Van, 1489cc, restored, underside in exceptional condition.
£2,000–2,500 *CRE*

1962 Land Rover Series 2A, 4 cylinders, 2286cc, 4 speed manual gearbox, shaft-driven winch, Safari body and front cab with shooting turret, 88in wheelbase, right-hand drive, recent chassis work, new fuel tank, steering joints, brake overhaul, road springs, oil pump, lights and wipers, and more recently a starter motor and switch, full history, quantity of spares, good condition overall.
£1,100–1,300 *S*

1989 Nissan Escargo Van, 1500cc, very good condition overall.
£7,000–7,500 *RUT*

HORSE-DRAWN VEHICLES

Early 19thC Chichester Carriage, built by Pettle of Barnstaple, enclosed coachwork with remnants of grey silk moiré interior, 2 padded doors each with sliding windows bearing Chichester coat-of-arms, open driver's seat with handbrake, leaf sprung turning wheels, luggage platform.
£1,750–2,000 *S*

c1900 Ralli Car, to suit 13.2hh, rubber tyred wheels, finished in blue with white lining, brass trim, grey upholstery, including a pair of carriage lamps, axle width 140cm, excellent condition.
£1,400–1,800 *P(Sc)*

1962 Trojan 200 Bubble Car, 200cc, left-hand drive, totally restored.
£2,500–3,000 *H&H*

c1897 Horseless Carriage, finished in black with black leather interior, original and excellent condition.
£10,500–11,500 *C*

This beautiful carriage was built by the American coachbuilders Moline Plow Co, of Freeport, Illinois, in 1897 and has remained in the same American family ownership for 91 years. It was motorised in 1910 with a Lauren single cylinder engine and features a single speed chain drive to the rear wheels.

MICROCARS

1953 Reliant Regal MkI, 4 cylinders, 747cc, 4 speed gearbox, aluminium body with ash frame, requires restoration, quantity of spares.
£875–1,025 *C*

Reliant took over production of the Raleigh three-wheeled van in 1934, but it was not until 1953 that the first Reliant three-wheeled car came into being. Glass fibre bodies were not used until 1956. The Regal advanced through 6 designations, adding new features such as synchromesh to the gearbox and curved windscreens.

1962 BMW Isetta 300 Bubble Car, 298cc, 4 speed manual gearbox, chassis-up rebuild, bare metal respray, excellent order throughout.
£2,500–3,000 *H&H*

l. **1960 BMW Isetta Bubble Car,** 295cc, 2 cylinder engine, close-coupled 4 wheel model, fully restored to concours condition.
£3,450–4,000 *H&H*

1957 Victoria 250, single cylinder, 248cc, 14hp,
5 speed gearbox, electric change, 4 wheel hydraulic
brakes, coil spring front suspension, swinging arm
rear, left-hand drive, comprehensive restoration,
excellent condition, ex-Bruce Weiner Collection.
£10,000–11,000 C

*The Victoria was a slightly redesigned Spatz built
by the Victoria Motorcycle firm in Germany,
utilising their 250cc engine and a different
windscreen and hood. Transmission was through
a 5 speed, push-button and switch, electric gearbox
and this particular car is one of only around a
dozen Spatz/Victorias known to the club, and
is the earliest known to exist.*

1960 BMW Isetta, three-wheeler, 3 speed gearbox,
2 owners, original interior, spare working engine,
spare parts, sound condition overall.
£1,400–1,800 S

*Iso SpA, the Milanese firm formerly associated with
the manufacture of scooters and motor cycles,
started the fashion for the aptly named 'bubble' car
with the introduction of the Isetta for the 1953
season. A large swing-up door incorporating the
steering wheel and column was a characteristic of
the oviform body. Production was discontinued in
1955 in Milan but the cars were made under licence
by VELAM of France and BMW of Germany.*

Cross Reference
BMW

1960 FMR TG500 Tiger Bubble Top, twin cylinder, 2 stroke, 490cc, 4 speed gearbox, hydraulic drum
brakes, cable handbrake to front wheels, independent all-round front suspension, with single wishbones
and rubber torsion, single wishbones and coil spring rear, 21,500 miles recorded, completely restored,
good overall condition, ex-Bruce Weiner Collection.
£26,500–28,000 C

*The FMR TG500 was the successor to the well-established and economical Messerschmitt three-wheeler.
It had much improved performance over its predecessor. The narrow body and exceptionally low centre of
gravity, with a 490cc vertical twin 2 stroke Sachs-derived engine at the rear, gave the new model
exceptionally brisk acceleration. Capable of reaching 65mph in 3rd gear and had handling to match.*

c1967 Bond MkG, finished in green and white, good condition.
£1,500–2,000 *ScR*

One of the last Villiers-powered engined Bonds to leave the factory was the Bond MkG Tourer. Engine choice was either as a single or a twin 250cc.

1959 Goggomobil T400 Limousine, Glas twin cylinders, 2 stroke, 392cc, 4 speed gearbox, electric shift, 4 wheel hydraulic brakes, swing axle and coil spring suspension, left-hand drive, meticulous rebuild, ex-Bruce Weiner Collection.
£17,250–19,000 *C*

A microcar limousine may be a contradiction in terms, but Goggomobil built the T400 as a true automobile in miniature. Its rear-mounted 392cc engine and saloon-like coachwork ensured it sold in numbers that surpassed any microcar ever built, with 250,000 produced.

1955 Inter Berline AEMS, rear-mounted single cylinder engine, Ydral 2 stroke, 175cc, 3 speed manual gearbox, System Nieman suspension, 3 wheel cable brakes, resprayed, good overall condition, ex-Bruce Weiner Collection.
£8,000–8,800 *C*

The Inter was launched at the Paris Salon in 1953, manufactured by the SNCAN (Société Nationale de Construction Aeronautique) aircraft factory in Lyon. Powered by an Ydral single cylinder 2 stroke engine via a 3 speed manual transmission, output was 8.5hp, whilst the rear wheel drive propelled the car to 50mph. An optional folding front axle was incorporated to allow the car to pass through narrow gateways.

1959 Scootacar MkI, restored to original condition.
£3,000–3,500 *ScR*

The Bruce Weiner Microcar Collection

Canadian Bruce Weiner already had an interesting but unfocussed collection of motor cars when he unexpectedly became smitten by a BMW Isetta. This fascination with bubble car design and technology led to the rapid acquisition of a Messerschmitt – and thereafter the interest became almost an obsession which motivated a search for more examples resulting in an exceptionally large and varied collection of microcars.

Many of the microcars when found, were subjected to a full restoration. Whilst modern technology was exploited to ensure the highest standards, great care was taken to preserve originality and to avoid flamboyant over-restoration. A better standard of finish than the original has been achieved and the subsequent longevity of each car much enhanced.

The microcars were kept in roadworthy condition and regularly driven by their owner. The fact they all appeared for sale together undoubtedly constitutes a unique event in microcar history. Unfortunately some of the cars sold for very high and unrealistic sums, and therefore the majority of the cars were sold to overseas buyers.

1959 Messerschmitt KR200 Bubble Car, 200cc Sachs engine, designed in 1956, manufactured by FMR (Fahrzeug-und Maschinenbau GmbH Regensburg), white-painted fibreglass canopy, red-painted metal body panels assembled on a steel chassis.
£2,750–3,500 *CSK*

MILITARY VEHICLES

When you first embark on looking for a military vehicle the range is enormous. The most popular vehicles are those that were built and saw service during WWII, those vehicles used by the Allies and those of the axis powers. Those of the American, British and Canadian forces are the most plentiful and perhaps the most reasonable to buy. WWI vehicles are hard to come by. Then there is the classification of post war, which encompasses anything from the end of WWII right up to the present day. This last group is readily available and at sensible prices. Perhaps the favourite vehicle in this classification is the trusty Land Rover, and there are certainly enough around with interesting variants.

Military vehicles come in all shapes and sizes. There are the smaller vehicles like the Jeep and Land Rovers, through various truck sizes including amphibians, right up to the heavy tanks. The bigger the vehicle doesn't necessarily mean the bigger the price tag. The running costs too vary considerably. Spare parts are readily available for all but the rarest of vehicles, petrol costs can be enormous with the bigger vehicles if you use them regularly, but if you are sensible they can be kept within reason.

Take the WWII GMC 2½ ton truck, the backbone of all Allied armies. Over 500,000 of them were built with many different body/chassis/cab combinations. They continued to see active service with many armed forces right through until the 1990s. A running example of a long wheelbase, open cab GMC without winch in need of a little cosmetic work can be had for as little as £1,500. For a truck in pristine condition, with all the accessories, around £3,000–3,500. Then you have the other bodies – tankers, compressors, tippers, radio bodies etc.

Often people buy a military vehicle because they like the rugged no-nonsense design and construction, but then get swept into the other aspects of owning such a vehicle. In many cases they made history, and as a result have shaped our lives. As a consequence there is the fascinating side of why a particular vehicle was built, which army it served with, and with which regiment. It may be marked up as it would have been in the conflict in which it was used. All of them have a story to tell if you are prepared to do a little research. You can liken it to owning a racing car and knowing its track record, which makes it that little bit special.

Over the next few pages there is a sample of some of the most popular vehicles, but these are a fraction of what is available. The membership of the Military Vehicle Trust have over 1,000 different vehicle variants registered. If over the next few pages you don't see what you are looking for then the MVT might be able to help (see Directory of Clubs on page 336).

Simon Johnson

l. **1941 Bantam BRC 40 ¼ Ton 4x4 Jeep,** 4 in-line, petrol, 40bhp, 3 speed gearbox with high and low ratio transfer box, ladder type leaf spring suspension, 80in wheelbase, restored.
£15,000–18,000 *MVT*

Bantam, formerly the Austin Car Company of America, of Butler Pennsylvania, were the originators of the Jeep design and along with the US Army Ordnance Department drew up the specification for a small go-anywhere vehicle. Bantam built the very first jeep in just 49 days, a further 69 vehicles were delivered in 71 days.

When large quantities of Jeeps were wanted, Bantam lost out to Willys Overland who had developed the MA/MB. As a result Bantam only made 2,605 examples of the BRC 40.

Prices

The price ranges given reflect the average price a purchaser should pay for a similar vehicle. Condition, rarity of model, pedigree, restoration and many other factors must be taken into account when assessing values.

r. **1941 Ford GP Slat Grille Jeep,** 4 cylinder side valve engine, good condition.
£7,500–12,000 *PETT*

1941 Willys MA Prototype Jeep,
good condition.
£30,000–33,000 *PETT*

1942–45 Willys MB Jeep, 4 cylinder side valve
engine, good condition.
£3,500–4,000 *PETT*

*Most popular amongst collectors, Ford and Willys
produced approximately 575,000 Jeeps during WWII.*

1942 Willys MB Jeep, total body-off restoration, engine overhauled, re-bored, new pistons, bearings and
cylinder head, gearbox and transmission overhauled, new clutch and universal joints, 12 volt system with
alternator, electric fuel pump and Solex carburettor, modified side and tail lights, rare Hull M4 compass,
correct water jerry on offside, radiator header tank affixed to radiator grill.
£8,650–9,350 *S*

*This vehicle is presented as a Jeep that could have
been adapted by army workshops to form part of the
legend known as the Long-Range Desert Patrol.*

r. **c1960s Ford M151 A1/A2 Military Utility
Tactical ¼ Ton 4x4 Truck (MUTT),** 4 cylinders
in-line, petrol, 2.32 litres, 71bhp.
£3,500–5,500 *MVT*

*The MUTT is a complete break from its predecessors.
Gone is the ladder-type chassis, now an integral
body/chassis. The full floating axles on leaf springs
are replaced by independant suspension all round.*

1955 M38 MP Jeep, good condition.
£7,500–8,500 *PETT*

This vehicle was mainly used in Korea.

c1960 US M42 Mighty Mite, all-aluminium body
and engine, good condition.
£3,800–4,200 *PETT*

*Only 4,000 of these were built to drop behind enemy
lines in Vietnam.*

1953 GAZ M461 Military Truck,
renovated and repaired.
£750–1,000 *S*

*This vehicle was used to ferry children living
in project accommodation following the
Romanian unrest in 1991, this GAZ was then
laid up for 2 years. It was renovated in 1994
in order to drive it to the UK. Since its
arrival in this country it has had shock
absorbers fitted.*

l. **1984 Jeep CJ7,** 4.2 manual
gearbox, right-hand drive,
power-assisted steering.
£4,000–4,500 *CTP*

**l. 1944 GMC CCKW 353
2½ Ton 6x6 Truck,** 6 cylinder
in-line, petrol, 4.4 litres,
104bhp, 5 speed transmission,
cargo-bodied.
£2,200–3,000 *MVT*

*The 'deuce-and-a-half' (2½ ton,
6x6) truck was the work horse
of the US Army during WWII.
In common with many other
standard chassis, there were
many body types and equipment
variations. GMC built over half
a million of these trucks and
after the war they remained
popular all over the world for
many years for both military
and civilian use.*

1950s Austin Champ ¼ Ton FV1800 (WNI),
Rolls-Royce B40 engine, 2.8 litre, 4 cylinders,
petrol, Austin A90, 2.6 litres (civilian), 5 speed
synchromesh gearbox.
£2,000–3,000 each *MVT*

*The Champ was designed for the British Forces to
replace the WWII Jeep. Main production started in
1952 and some 13,000 were built up to 1956 when
production was stopped.*

> **Miller's is a price
> GUIDE not a price LIST**

1941 Diamond T 969 6x6 Wrecker, 6 cylinders
in-line, petrol, 8.6 litres, 119bhp, 5 speed gearbox
with 2 speed transfer.
£8,000–10,000 *MVT*

*The Diamond T was a standardised US Army
4 ton 6x6 truck. The Diamond T Car Company of
Chigago produced the largest number of these
chassis for use by the military.*

WWII Pacific TR 1/M26, 17.8 litre, 6 cylinders
in-line, petrol, 230bhp.
£6,500–8,500 *MVT*

*The Pacific is a 6x6 armoured tractor unit built by
the Pacific Car & Foundary Company of Seattle.
Used primarily in conjunction with a 40 ton
semi-trailer for transporting tanks.*

c1940 AEC Matador, 7.5 litre, 6 cylinders in-line, diesel, 95bhp, 4 speed gearbox with 2 speed transfer.
£4,500–6,000 *MVT*

Over 9,000 Matadors were produced between 1939 and 1945.

1943 M8 Armoured Car, good condition.
£14,000–15,000 *RRM*

WWII M3 A1 White Scout Car, good condition.
£7,000–7,500 *RRM*

c1941 White M5 A1 Half Track Armoured Car, 6 cylinder 128bhp engine driving the rear or both axles, 4 speed gearbox with 2 speed transfer, resprayed in long-range desert patrol livery, Tulsa winch, jerry cans and full canopy, good working order.
£4,600–6,000 *S*

Developed from the 4x4 15cwt personnel truck, a series of experimental limited production armoured half track models were produced for trials during the 1930s. They were produced from 1941 by Autocar, Diamond T, White and latterly International.

WWII GMC CCKW-353 2½ Ton 6x6 Hard Cab Cargo Truck, 6 cylinders, 269cu in overhead valve engine, 94bhp at 3000rpm, 5 speed gearbox, resprayed in combat livery with correct markings for Argentine military, hard cab, cab turret, front-mounted winch.
£1,750–2,250 *S*

This vehicle was one of 4 GMC cabs used in the film Evita.

r. **1943–44 Amphibious DUKW,** good condition.
£15,000–17,000 *RRM*

CHILDREN'S CARS

Jaguar SS100 Miniature Replica,
battery-operated, good condition.
£1,800–2,000 *PAL*

**c1934 Atco Junior Safety First Two Seater
Trainer,** Villiers 2 stroke engine, 0.98hp,
forward and reverse gears, stored for many
years, unrestored condition.
£900–1,100 *HOLL*

Maserati 250F Child's Car, electric model of
Grand Prix car, aluminium body panels, coil spring
and wishbone front suspension, finned brake
drums, knock-off wire wheels, pneumatic tyres,
powered by 12 volt battery, 78in (198cm) long.
£3,700–4,300 *BKS*

Ferrari F40 Child's Electric Car, 6 volt battery-
powered, forward and reverse foot pedal operation,
plastic body shell, rubber solid treaded tyres, Italian.
£200–250 *CARS*

Bugatti Black Bess, child's pedal car modelled on
the legendary chain-driven racing machine, steel
chassis, semi-elliptic spring front suspension, quarter
elliptic springs to rear, pedal drive through chain
transmission, central steering position operating via
drag link and track rod mechanism, outside handbrake
and bulb horn, wire spoke wheels with solid rubber
tyres, distinctive radiator with dummy-cap and badge
to front, finished in semi-matt black paintwork.
£500–600 *C*

1930s Child's Pedal Racing Car, pressed metal
body, steering front wheels, left-hand exhaust
applied to body, black and red number, incomplete.
£210–250 *Hal*

RACING & RALLYING

1947 Cooper FIII HRD Racing Car, 1000cc, Norton HRD engine, full rebuild, stored ever since, ready-to-race order.
£8,250–9,250 *S*

In immediate post-war years, Britain produced a national formula for cheap racing for cars limited to 500cc. It was accepted internationally by the FIA in 1960, classified as Formula 3, and continued for many years, providing a nursery for drivers such as Peter Collins, Stirling Moss, Ivor Bueb, Stuart Lewis-Evans and many more.

1973 Lola-Cosworth T286, 8 cylinders, 2993cc, Cosworth DFV engine, good condition.
£17,750–20,750 *COYS*

The T286 employed a monocoque chassis with a Cosworth DFV V8 mated to a Hewland transaxle. Just 3 T286s were built, all of which were raced with some success. This example was the 4th car built. Originally ordered by Alain de Cadanet in 1977 – when T286 production ended – for use at Le Mans, but the car was never delivered. Subsequently, following an order from the Otford Paper Group, the car was finally assembled in November 1984 with a 3.5 litre Cosworth DFL for use in Thundersports events, competing successfully in the hands of Jim Wallace. It is now fitted with a damaged and incomplete Cosworth DFV.

1934 Lagonda Rapier Single Seater Special, AC 6 cylinder, 1991cc engine, 4 speed manual gearbox, triple SU carburettors, electric starter motor, coil ignition, modern oil filter, rebuilt in 1984, good overall condition.
£16,000–18,000 *C*

1965 Crosslé C7S, 8 cylinders, 4727cc, 4.7 litre Chevrolet engine, maintained in race-prepared condition.
£22,000–23,000 *COYS*

Crosslé ties with Lola and Mallock for the honour of being the world's longest established maker of production racing cars. The C7S was a mid-engined sports racer in the same idiom as the Lotus 23 and Elva Mk 7. This car was originally fitted with a 2 litre BMW engine and it was raced in 1965 by John l'Amie and John Crosslé. Later raced in national and international events by Kinnane and Tony Dean. Recently used for testing.

1967 MGB GT Sebring 2 Litre Competition Coupé, 1950cc, close ratio gearbox, rebuilt, full history.
£21,500–26,500 *BKS*

This ex-Paddy Hopkirk/Andrew Hedges competition MGB GT was built by the factory to compete in the Sebring 12 hours endurance race of 1967. BMC's planners had intended to introduce their aluminium-bodied MGC-based GTS model at that event, but development delays with the aluminium bodies made this impossible, and so this car emerged instead as the only road-racing MGB GT to be produced by the BMC Competition Department.

Paddy Hopkirk and Andrew Hedges co-drove the car in the Floridan endurance classic, finishing handsomely 11th overall. Since the GT had been fitted with the 2004cc special engine intended for the GTS it ran in the Prototype category, and when the overall class results were published it emerged in third place beaten only by the 7 litre Ford Mk IVs.

1960 Lola Formula I, requires restoration.
£15,000–20,000 *FHF*

1953 Staride JAP F3, 500cc, JAP speedway
engine, race-ready condition.
£8,000–9,000 *Car*

1969 Merlyn MkIIA Formula Ford,
1600cc Connaught engine, imported from
USA 1994, restored by Simon Hadfield 1994,
excellent condition.
£15,000–17,000 *Car*

*Second in Historic Formula Ford
Championship 1996.*

1970 March 708 Formula Ford, 1600cc NES
engine, restored by Tony Broster 1993,
superb as-raced condition.
£13,500–14,500 *Car*

1959 Elva Formula Junior, 998cc BMC A Series
engine, condition as found, requires restoration.
£11,000–12,500 *Car*

1951 Cooper MkV, 500cc JAP speedway engine,
ready to race, restored by Ian Scott 1995.
£11,000–12,500 *Car*

1978 Chevron B43 Formula 3, 2000cc Toyota Formula 3 engine, recently restored by Keith Norris, race-ready condition.
£12,000–13,000 *Car*

1960 Cannon Trials Mudplugger, 4 cylinder 1172cc side valve engine, 3 speed gears.
£1,000–1,250 *DB*

This is one of 100 similar cars made by Mike Cannon of Tonbridge, Kent.

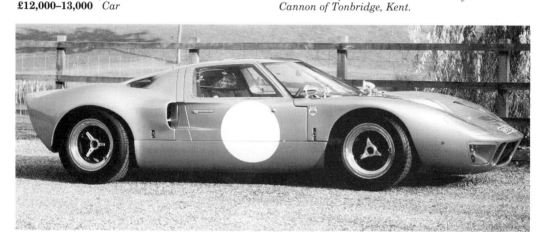

1968 Ford GT40, 5 litre engine, excellent condition.
£250,000+ *DHAM*

1964 Ford Lotus Cortina, 4 cylinders, 1588cc, 184bhp, engine and gearbox fully rebuilt, good condition.
£13,500–17,000 *COYS*

In the early 1960s Ford asked Lotus founder Colin Chapman to produce a sports/racing version of its new Cortina for homologation in Group 2. The Lotus Cortina sported bonnet, bootlid and doors made of alloy, as were clutch and diff housings and the gearbox tailshaft. Front suspension was standard MacPherson strut, lowered and stiffened, but the rear was radical, the leaf springs replaced by an A-bracket, coil springs and trailing arms. Wide wheels and servo-assisted disc front/drum rear brakes, along with 105bhp from the twin-cam 1588cc Ford engine and a close ratio box, completed the package.

The Lotus Cortina's first victory came in the 1964 Motor Six Hours at Brands Hatch. This car is believed to have been an Alan Mann team car early in its life. Its race record is long and impressive, with numerous outright victories until its retirement in the early 1990s.

1990 Minardi M190 F1, 8 cylinders, 3500cc Cosworth engine, excellent condition.
£45,500–48,000 *COYS*

1965 Ginetta G4, Ford 1500cc engine, excellent condition.
£18,000–19,500 *Car*

REPLICA, KIT & REPRODUCTION CARS

c1980 Replica Curved Dash Oldsmobile,
single cylinder, 50cc, 1.6 litres, 2 speed epicyclic transmission, trembler coil ignition, 500rpm.
£2,000–3,000 *S*

The first really successfully mass-produced automobile, the Curved Dash Oldsmobile found 2,100 customers in 1902, and by 1904 was selling at the rate of 5,000 a year. This accurate replica of the renowned Curved Dash is believed to have been constructed by the late Commander Chapman in the early 1980s. The power unit is a motor mower engine of 50cc and he used this vehicle as a support or trailing car on the annual London to Brighton run for a number of years.

1988 Shapecraft Lotus 15 Replica, 2000cc, 2 litre Pinto engine, good condition, unused.
£5,000–6,000 *Car*

1967-type Ferrari P3/4 Sports-Prototype Replica, Ferrari flat 12 Boxer engine, in running order, good condition.
£25,000–30,000 *BKS*

The fabulous Ferrari P3/4 series of sports-prototype racing cars are currently some of the most highly valued and most coveted of all post-war thoroughbreds. This replica combines features of both original Maranello works team models and is ex-USA.

1967/84 Bugatti Replica, by Chiltern Motors, 4 cylinders, 1493cc, twin carburettors, external fly-off handbrake, extremely good condition.
£2,750–3,500 *BRIT*

c1979 Teale Bugatti Type 35 Replica,
Bugatti-style radiator, separate headlamps, aero screens, side-mounted spare wheel, based on Morris Marina running gear, right-hand drive, excellent condition throughout.
£7,000–8,500 *BKS*

l. **1920s Kennedy Squire Replica,** 2 litres, chrome wire wheels, wooden dashboard, leather upholstery, fold-flat windscreen, aluminium panels over wooden frame.
£10,000–12,000 *CARS*

1964/96 Ferrari 250LM Replica.
£41,000–45,000 *COYS*

The 250LM has a special place in Ferrari history. A would-be successor to the great 250GTO, a car which could have dominated GT racing had it been homologated, a car which the factory almost abandoned when it wasn't, but which went on to score Ferrari's last ever Le Mans win, thus earning its name and enduring reputation. Only 32 examples of this beautiful looking and sensational sounding car were built. It was constructed over a lengthy period by a leading Italian restorer, using materials and skills accumulated during the past 30 years. The chassis was scratch built to the exact pattern by factory craftsmen in the Modena area, as were the suspension, pedal box and steering box. The gearbox turret is correct, and the steering column, steering wheel, instruments, knobs, Borrani wire wheels and so forth are totally accurate. The body was faithfully constructed using exact patterns and looks quite superb. Engine, gearbox, brakes and interior are required to complete this exciting project.

1991/75 Dax V12 Cobra Replica, running gear from Jaguar XJ V12, period style wheels, triple spinners, racing type fuel filler, full roll bar, fuel injected, chromed radiator reservoir, cam covers and air filter boxes, side exhaust pipes with heatshields, good condition throughout.
£12,000–13,500 *ADT*

1996 Superformance Cobra SC Replica, V8 engine, 351cu in, 385hp, 5 speed transmission, good condition.
£18,000–22,000 *KI*

> **Don't Forget!**
> *If in doubt please refer to the 'How to Use' section at the beginning of this book.*

1989 GTM Rossa Convertible, 1275cc, 27,000 miles recorded, MOT certificates and workshop build manual, good condition.
£2,100–2,500 *H&H*

This car was built by an engineer in 1989/90 using mainly new parts and it has had only 2 owners since.

1992/3 Beauford Tourer, 2.8 litre Nissan engine, 5 speed manual gearbox, power steering, very good condition.
£8,000–9,000 *AS*

1988 Libra Cobra Replica, Ford Cortina Pinto 2000cc engine, Stage 1 camshaft, twin Weber carburettors, 4 speed Cortina gearbox, front suspension, steering and brakes, Escort steering column and pedal clusters, good condition.
£4,000–5,000 *H&H*

1994 Ford 5 Litre GT40 Replica Two Seater Coupé, State 3 V8 engine, fully balanced with gas-flowed and polished heads, stainless steel valves, Holley 650cfm double pump carburettors, Mallory electronic ignition, 350bhp, 5 speed transaxle gearbox with original gate pattern change, air conditioned, 319 test miles.
£29,000–34,000 *BKS*

Lotus Honda 99T Replica.
£11,500–15,000 *C*

The Lotus 99T was the car with the Honda Type GEV6 turbo engine and active suspension that Senna and Nakajima both drove under the bright yellow and blue Camel livery. R. J. Reynolds, manufacturers of Camel cigarettes, wanted to make a worldwide cinema commercial to highlight the signing of Nelson Piquet, World Formula 1 Champion, to the Camel-sponsored Lotus team. As a turbo-charged Lotus Honda would be completely impractical for the stop/start requirements of filming, a suitable alternative operation had to be formed. As a result a car was built with Team Lotus supplying the bodywork, floor pan, rear wing and turbo scoops from Ayrton Senna's Australian Grand Prix car. Senna had finished second to Gerhard Berger in the race but was later disqualified for an oversized brake duct infringement. The Lotus components were carefully adapted to fit a Ralt RT22 F3000 car which, when completed, bore a striking resemblence to the real thing. The components were then bought from Lotus and stored until recently when, as a project, it was decided to build a show car. It does not have an engine fitted at all and has a moulded gearbox to give the impression of a running car.

RESTORATION PROJECTS

1911 Franklin Body now suitable for 1920s Rolls-Royce Silver Ghost.
£350–500 *BKS*

This Edwardian wide 2 seater body with dickey is believed to be from a 1911 American Franklin. It is fitted to a pre-war Ghost chassis, tailored to fit the later post-war chassis with sloping bonnet. The body is separate from the chassis and in need of some work prior to fitting. The hood, windscreen and floorboards are included, along with running boards, running board/chassis dust trays and gearbox under trays. The interior and bench seats are black leather and in original condition.

c1922 Stutz Touring Car, 4 cylinders, in-line, T-head, 360.8cu in, 80bhp, 3 speed manual gearbox, right-hand drive.
£7,000–8,500 *C*

This car is partially restored with what appears to be an overhauled engine ready to install in the chassis. The body that goes with the car is in fine original condition, including its dark green long grain Spanish leather. Other parts will still require restoration and painting. It presents an opportunity to continue and finish a project which was well on its way to becoming a complete, operating vintage Stutz once again.

1923 Rolls-Royce 20hp Barrel-sided Tourer, coachwork in the style of Barker, original instrumentation, dash and single front seat, wheels and radiator restored.
£10,750–12,250 *S*

This car has been in the same ownership for 20 years and is largely complete mechanically. Restoration is well advanced and should be relatively straightforward.

1912 Daimler TS38 38hp Full Folding Cabriolet, 4 cylinders with sleeve valves, 6282cc, 3 speed manual right-hand gearbox, right-hand drive.
£30,500–35,000 *C*

1922 Ford Model T Rolling Chassis, 4 cylinders, 176.7cu in, 22hp, planetary transmission, 2 speeds forward, one reverse, 3 pedal, one lever, wings, running boards, radiator, bonnet, scuttle, petrol tank, left-hand drive, in working order.
£2,000–3,000 *C*

By 1922 the famous Model T 'Tin Lizzie' had been in continuous development for 14 years and was well on the way to its 16 million+ tota. The rugged design incorporated the sturdy 4 cylinder 20hp side valve engine in the light 100in wheelbase chassis frame. This car has been the subject of some major restoration some 25 years ago, since which time it has been dry stored in a barn. It comprises a complete rolling chassis, with engine and gearbox and all ancillaries installed.

1923 Rolls-Royce 20hp Cockshoot Drophead Three-Quarter Cabriolet, 2 door body, with round edge type radiator.
£6,500–7,500 *RCC*

This rare early example car has been mostly reframed.

1924 Peugeot 190S, 4 cylinders, 1000cc, side valve, gearbox in rear axle.
£2,200–2,600 *DB*

1924 Rolls-Royce Silver Ghost Series T Running Chassis, wheels rebuilt, brakes overhauled, new tyres, front wheel brakes, Barker dipping headlamp system, correct horn, coil and starting carburettor, complete with wings, running boards and spare wheel with side mounting bracket.
£21,250–24,250 *BKS*

c1925 Ford Model T Tractor with Cab, requires total restoration.
£2,500–3,000 *S*

Henry Ford, born on a farm in rural Michigan in 1863, married a farmer's daughter in 1888 and tested his first gasoline engine in the kitchen of the Ford home 3 years later.
The first production Ford, the Model A, appeared in 1903 and the 4 cylinder Model N runabout introduced in 1906 was the forebear of the Model T, constructed by mass-production methods and on sale from 1908. The new model formed the basis for a farm tractor, available from 1916, and within 3 years the American giant accounted for 41 per cent of all motor vehicles registered in Great Britain.

l. **c1926 Ford Model T Tourer,** right-hand drive, probably complete.
£3,800–4,300 *S*

1927 Amilcar CG SS, 4 cylinders, 1100cc, 4 speed gearbox, staggered seat 2 seater, barn discovery.
£8,500–9,500 *DB*

r. **1927 Sunbeam 35hp Estate,** coachwork by Irving & Morris of Salisbury, straight 8 pushrod overhead valve engine, 5447cc, 35hp.
£22,000–26,000 *BKS*

As this car was originally very expensive, it seems unlikely that more than about 65 found customers, and of these only 4 or 5 are known to survive today. This example was used as a mourners' car until the outbreak of WWII. It was then requisitioned, ostensibly for conversion to an ambulance. It was owned at some time by Olympic bobsleigh champion and vintage car racer Keith Schellenberg.

1928 Singer Junior,
950cc, 4 cylinders, overhead camshaft.
£1,150–1,350 *DB*

c1929 Stutz Model M Chassis, 8 cylinders in-line, single overhead camshaft, 322cu in, 113bhp, 4 speed manual gearbox, hydraulic brakes, semi-elliptic suspension, left-hand drive, ideal donor car, with quantity of sheet metal parts such as hood, cowl and wings.
£5,000–6,000 *C*

1930 Rolls-Royce Phantom II Hearse,
long-chassis PII, rebodied by Salmons as a hearse, stored for 25 years.
£7,000–9,000 *S*

1933 Standard Nine, 4 cylinder, 1200cc.
£750–1,000 *DB*

1934 Lagonda 16/80 Special 6 T8 Tourer,
recently discovered, believed complete, engine removed from chassis, overhauled, ENV Preselective gearbox.
£8,000–9,000 *S*

The 16/80 Special 6 announced in August 1932 with a smooth pushrod operated overhead valve unit of 1991cc capacity, effectively adopting the 14/60 Continental chassis with the Silver Crossley engine. This gave 25mpg economy and had a top speed of 75–80mph, acceleration being a notable feature, The Motor recording a 0–60mph time of 19.2 seconds.

r. **1937 Hillman Saloon 20/80,** 6 cylinders, 3 litre engine, unused for 30 years.
£1,000–1,250 *DB*

c1941 Mercedes-Benz G5, chassis only.
£14,750–16,000 *BKS*

This bodyless G5 is a rare example of one of the more sophisticated 4x4 military medium cars to be used by the Wehrmacht in the early stages of WWII. Powered by a 2006cc 4 cylinder 45hp side valve engine, a total of 320 examples were produced before the model was phased out in 1941.

An intriguing restoration project for the dedicated military vehicle enthusiast, who has the choice of fitting it with open-sided Kubelwagen or convertible Kommandeurwagen bodywork.

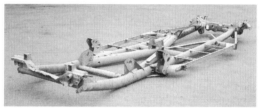

A Ferrari 195 chassis, finished in primer, slightly corroded at rear end, chassis number erased, 4 wheels, less spokes, and rear axle casing.
£4,750–5,750 *BKS*

1951 AC Two Door Saloon.
£1,500–1,800 *H&H*

1952 Rolls Bentley MkVI, 4566cc, manual transmission, dry-stored since 1969, resprayed in 1965, original toolkit.
£5,000–5,800 *DJ*

1959 Volkswagen Two Door Sedan, requires restoration, 4 cylinder horizontally-opposed air-cooled 1300cc engine, 36bhp, 4 speed manual gearbox, hydraulic brakes, torsion bar suspension, left-hand drive.
£475–575 *C*

This is a well used example of the ubiquitous VW Beetle.

1959 Alfa Romeo 2000 Spider Veloce Convertible, left-hand drive, partially restored, believed to be complete, subject of much work, bodywork restored, resprayed, rechromed brightwork, engine overhauled.
£2,500–3,000 *S*

Touring of Milan designed the very pretty 2+2 open bodies for Alfa Romeo's 2000 Spiders, which were introduced in 1958.

AUTOMOBILE ART

Pat Nevin, Tourist Trophy, charcoal sketch, self portrait of the artist seated by the road drawing a Singer with broken axle, signed Frederic Nevin, 1935.
£100–115 *BKS*

A tapestry depicting a motoring and hunting scene on a wooded road, mounted in contemporary frame, some discolouration, c1905, 19 x 19in (48 x 48cm).
£160–180 *C*

Roy Anthony Nockolds, Hurrying South, gouache, signed and dated 1951, 23½ x 19½in (60 x 49.5cm).
£410–450 *MCA*

Michael Wright, 1928 Boillot Cup – Birkin Leads Ivanowski's blown Alfa Romeo at the St Martin Hairpin on the Boulogne Circuit, watercolour and gouache, signed, mounted and glazed, 17½ x 15½in (44.5 x 39.5cm).
£700–750 *C*

Birkin recorded the highest average speed for the race at 73.16mph, but failed to beat his severe handicap and finished fifth.

Roy Anthony Nockolds, 'Scientific' returning from trials in the Alps, a motoring scene, signed and dated 1959, oil on board, 17½ x 23½in (44.5 x 60cm).
£210–230 *MCA*

Bob Murray, watercolour and gouache on board, depicting a Spitfire completing a fly-past over a 1925 3 litre Bentley, framed and glazed.
£440–480 *BKS*

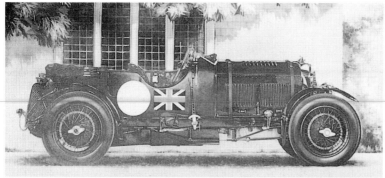

l. Tony Upson, acrylic on board mural of a 4.5 litre Bentley, framed, 48 x 96in (122 x 244cm).
£1,700–1,900 *BKS*

r. Tony Upson, acrylic on board mural of a Ferrari 250 GTO/64, framed, 48 x 96in (122 x 244cm).
£1,000–1,100 *BKS*

Posters

l. Anon, Renault – Billancourt Seine, full colour lithograph poster, linen-backed, depicting various coach styles on the 40CV chassis, 46 x 63in (117 x 160cm).
£750–1,000 *C*

A Dunlop Land Speed Record poster, 12 x 38in (30.5 x 96.5cm).
£400–450 *LE*

l. Geo Ham, Montlhèry – Prix de Paris, April 1956 – poster for the event sponsored by Valvoline, lithograph design, framed and glazed, 30 x 20in (76 x 51cm).
£550–600 *C*

AUTOMOBILIA

A German penknife, depicting a car, c1910.
£85–90 *BC*

r. A Mercedes Ruddspeed decanter, superb original condition, original mascot top.
£230–250 *BKS*

A coffee table constructed from a pair of Rolls-Royce Corniche pattern radiator grilles, stainless steel frame and top surface to table, radiator supports in chromium-plated finish, with 'Spirit of Ectasy' mascots.
£1,500–1,700 *C*

A brooch in the form of a Bentley Blue-Label radiator badge, by Garrard of London, gold and white gold with diamonds set in central 'B' motif, on enamelled blue oval ground, raised beaded pattern border to base, surmounted upon a similar bordered surround, applied stylised wings, with finely chased feather pattern, gold backing to badge, engraved 'Marie', 2in (5cm) wide.
£3,700–4,000 *C*

A silver St Christopher key ring, hallmarked, 1930.
£120–125 *BC*

A Mido Bugatti 18ct gold gentleman's wristwatch, in the form of a Bugatti radiator grille, limited series.
£2,900–3,000 *BKS*

A Morris ashtray, by Les Leston, 7½in (19cm) diam.
£80–90 *LE*

r. A Longines 18ct gold gentleman's wristwatch, in the form of a Rolls-Royce car radiator grille, case and movement signed, 1970s, 44mm wide.
£1,200–1,400 *BKS*

Badges, Mascots & Trophies

A Monte Carlo Rally finisher's award and lapel badge, plaque on wooden base, lapel badge in the form of a miniature rally plate, 1958, plaque 3½ x 6½in (9 x 16.5cm).
£275–300 *LE*

A Royal Automobile Club Rally of Great Britain finisher's award, 1955, 6 x 4in (15 x 10cm).
£50–60 *LE*

An Isle of Man TT Trophy finisher's award, silver plate, 1936, 10½in (27cm) high.
£280–300 *LE*

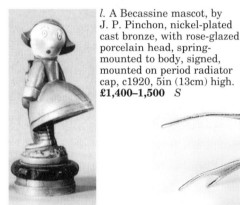

l. A Becassine mascot, by J. P. Pinchon, nickel-plated cast bronze, with rose-glazed porcelain head, spring-mounted to body, signed, mounted on period radiator cap, c1920, 5in (13cm) high.
£1,400–1,500 *S*

An early MG Car Club badge, by J. Fray of Birmingham.
£15–18 *LF*

A swallow on ball mascot, numbered 560298 under tail, with original mounting plinth, 3in (7.5cm) high.
£70–75 *LF*

A Sabino opalescent coloured glass fish mascot, signed on base, slightly damaged, c1930, 2¼in (5.5cm) high.
£350–370 *CSK*

Marius Sabino (1878–1961) was a contemporary of Lalique although very much in his shadow. Sabino's glass is instantly recognisable from the crystal blue and honey hues in his glass which was obtained by using a 6 per cent solution of arsenic compared to Lalique's use of 1 per cent.

A chrome-plated winged goddess on wheel mascot, signed C. H. Soudant, inscribed, c1920, 6in (15cm) high.
£160–180 *HOLL*

A silver-plated bronze car mascot, 'La Renommée', by Ballot, good condition, 1922–28.
£1,375–1,450 *BKS*

Designed by Emile Peynot, this was awarded the silver medal of Journal l'Auto *in 1922. This example is complete with the original integral radiator cap mounting and trumpet. Many of these mascots were reproduced in later years – however, this example has a correct threaded end section.*

r. A flying bird mascot, with nickel-plated body, action movement for each aluminium wing, beak slightly shortened, good condition, unmounted.
£140–150 *BKS*

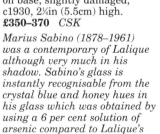

A brass Robert policeman mascot, signed 'Hassall', registered No. 611941 on base, head replaced, 4½in (11.5cm) high.
£65–70 *CSK*

A chrome-plated eagle mascot seated upon a ball, and a Ford Bantam mascot, unmounted.
£95–100 *BKS*

A Rolls-Royce Spirit of Ectasy bronze showroom model, on a double step marble base, inscribed on base 'Charles Sykes', 1924.
£520–540 *BKS*

A crafted bronze sculptured Bugatti mascot, by motoring artist Keith Oney, No. 003/250, mounted on a turned base.
£275–295 *BKS*

A Rolls-Royce 20/25hp chrome on brass mascot, stamped 'R-R Ltd 6.2.11.' and indistinctly signed 'C. Sykes', possibly re-chromed or reproduction.
£110–125 *LF*

A Lalique Longchamps glass mascot, double-maned version, introduced by René Lalique on 12th June, 1929, withdrawn when single maned version introduced on 10th September, 1929.
£2,300–2,700 *S*

l. A Mickey Mouse mascot, probably British, nickel-plated bronze, with 4 fingers on each hand and a tail, on a 1920s bronze radiator cap, 3¾in (9.5cm) high.
£1,150–1,350 *S*

A Rolls-Royce 'Spirit of Ectasy' kneeling lady mascot, by Charles Sykes, nickel-plated brass or chromed bronze, mounted upon radiator pressure cap.
£250–350 *CARS*

This mascot was designed for the higher bonnet line of the 1920–30s cars, so as not to obscure the driver's vision.

A René Lalique 'Perche' mascot, amber tinted glass, etched 'R. Lalique' to base, c1930, 6in (15cm) long.
£1,800–2,200 *C*

A W. O. Bentley 8 litre style winged 'B' mascot, nickel-silver on brass, later plating, some repairs, 8in (20.5cm) wide.
£230–250 *BKS*

Components

A pair of Marchal Agrolux chrome-plated headlamps, manufacturer's emblems to rim and centre of vertical bar, 10in (25cm) diam.
£105–115 *HOLL*

A cast boa constrictor snake's head bulb horn, with painted tongue, glass eyes, label and rubber bulb, 42in (107cm) long.
£260–300 *BKS*

A single turn, polished brass flared trumpet, with gauze, bulb horn, with 28in (71cm) flexible extension and rubber bulb.
£140–180 *BKS*

A pair of Powell and Hanmer polished brass acetylene gas lamps, self-contained, largely complete condition, with internal carbide containers and burners, slight damage, c1914.
£620–700 *BKS*

A Bakelite dashboard watch, with chronograph and registers, by Hamilton Watch Co, USA, graduated in 24 hours and 60 minutes, auxiliary dials for elapsed time, civil date, with radiumed Arabic numerals, good condition, 1940s.
£600–650 *BKS*

A Jaeger rear-view mirror with watch, excellent condition, c1930, 4¾in (12cm) wide.
£820–850 *BKS*

A bus ticket machine and a footbell, c1930.
£40–50 *LF*

l. A BRC Alpha acetylene gas projector set, comprising: a pair of sided projectors, with solid nickel full span reflectors, atmospheric burner, central condenser lens and polished plain front glass, good condition.
£2,500–2,750 *BKS*

A Birglow auto signal, with illuminating hand and cable operation, full working condition, original paint, plating, lighting switch and brackets, c1920–30.
£440–480 *CSK*

A pair of Lucas Windtone short trumpet horns, restored to high standard, suitable for fast touring cars of late 1920s–30s.
£325–350 *BKS*

An Edwardian brass double bend horn, c1905.
£30–35 *GAZE*

An ignition and switch panel for a Bugatti, oval box with multi-terminal unions at rear, starter button, light switch, ignition light and 4 fuse apertures on the fascia.
£230–270 *BKS*

A Boa-constrictor type horn, with flared trumpet and fly gauze, 52in (132) long.
£350–380 *BKS*

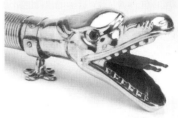

A Boa-constrictor snake's head bulb horn, open-mouthed head, vibrating tongue, glass eyes, crows foot mounting bracket, 54in (137cm) flexible tube, rubber bulb, one eye missing, otherwise good order.
£600–640 *BKS*

A pair of J & R Oldfield veteran brass oil rear lamps, complete, in working order, suitable for c1908 car.
£460-520 *BKS*

A French interior division vanity unit, wooden case, leather lined, fitted with silver topped bottles, cigarette case, manicure set, card wallet, mirror, case fitted with white enamel faced watch with Arabic numerals and subsidiary seconds dial, c1910, 9½in (24.5cm) wide.
£750–900 *S*

A pair of early vintage Rotax electric side lamps, numbered 203, nickel plated over brass, original reflectors, front glasses and mounting brackets.
£230–270 *BKS*

Picnic Sets

A Coracle four-person wicker picnic basket, with partitioned interior housing accessories including ceramic food box with metal lid, glasses, ceramic cups and saucers, butter jar, the lid fitted with cutlery and enamel plates, c1910 basket 19¾in (50cm) wide, with locking rod.
£750–900 *S*

r. A Drew & Sons 'En Route' six-person wicker picnic basket, with kettle, saucepan, ornate burner, large and small food boxes, ceramic cups and saucers, Autotherm jug, 2 wicker covered bottles, stacking metal beakers, condiment jars, cutlery, the lid with ceramic plates, c1910, 28¼in (72cm) wide.
£2,500-3,000 *S*

A Finnigans six-person fold-fronted picnic set, with centrally mounted copper kettle burner, twin wicker covered drinks flasks, nest of 6 glasses in wicker containers, 6 china cups and saucers, cutlery housed in lid, twin sandwich ceramic boxes with ceramic bases and nickel lids, food boxes, central wicker covered flasks, vesta case, c1920.
£2,000-2,750 *BKS*

l. A Drew & Sons gentleman's vanity/overnight case, with ivory-backed brushes, ivory shoe horn, letter opener, glove stretcher, mirror, manicure set, writing case, inkwell and vesta case, case and silver tops initialled 'G.E.C.', 1913, 17½in (44.5cm) wide.
£400-450 *S*

A four-person picnic set, by John Bagshaw & Sons of Liverpool, with silver fittings, London 1928, crocodile skin lid, with 'MB' monogram, 2 locks with central handle, suede lining and protection board, several items missing, good overall condition, c1928.
£5,600-6,400 *BKS*

Petrol Pump Globes

A National Benzole Mixture glass petrol pump globe, good colour and condition.
£140–150 *BKS*

A Pratts Ethyl Petrol pump globe, good condition, c1934 20in (51cm) high.
£450–500 *LE*

An Avery Hardoll petrol pump, requires total restoration.
£280–300 *DRC*

A Super Fina shield-shaped opaque glass petrol pump globe, c1950.
£220–260 *HOLL*

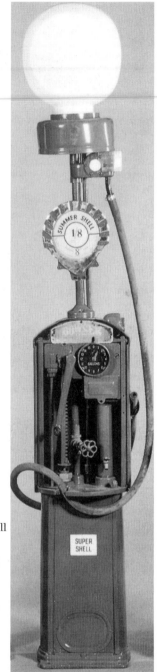

r. A Bowser hand-cranked petrol pump, finished in Shell livery, numbered N35727, plain glass globe, 16 gallon gauge, replica price flag and hose, lacking nozzle, pump 80⅜in (205cm) high.
£500–600 *S*

Models

A bronze model depicting Tazio Nuvolari driving an Alfa Romeo P3, by Gordon Chism, marked 'G. H. Chism 93' to chassis.
£1,400–1,600 *BKS*
Nuvolari won the 1932 Monaco Grand Prix.

A bronze model of a Bugatti T57 Atalante, after Franco Guibara, on polished black marble base and wood plinth.
£6,400–7,400 *C*

l. A collection of ERA model racing cars, and a Riley, good condition.
£3,000–3,500 *CSK*

A Bugatti Type 59 GP model, by Henri Baigent, metal with wooden hand-carved bodywork, 'glow plug' type integral drive motor, piano-wire spoked wheels, rubber tyres, engine-turned dashboard, louvred bonnet, drilled chassis and plated radiator.
£4,600–5,300 *C*

An Ahrens Fox Fire 1:24 scale model engine, wooden panel driver's compartment, chrome-plated pump and engine, 1922.
£50–60 *BKS*

A Benz Motorwagen 1:8 scale model, painted green, working engine and steering, 1886.
£140–170 *BKS*

Specially commissioned by Rob Walker, this model featured among the famous 'indoor races' at the Walker household.

r. A WMF deskpiece, depicting a chain-driven racer at speed, the bonnet opening to reveal storage space, signed, correct marks to base, 7½ x 16¼in (19 x 41cm).
£1,100–1,300 *BKS*

A silver model of a Ford Model T, by Comyns, London 1989, hallmarked, opening bonnet and doors, detailed engine, working steering, various accessories including lamps, horn, moulded upholstery, toolkit, finished in matt and polished silver, mounted on mirror topped wooden base, 1913.
£1,600–1,900 *S*

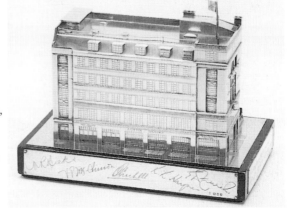

r. A silver presentation piece in the form of Stanhope House and the Little Georgian House, signed on silver strips by board of directors of The Car Mart Ltd, 1962.
£800–1,000 *BKS*

This model depicts the headquarters of The Car Mart Ltd (later Kennings) the Rolls-Royce distributors with the Royal Warrant. This was presented to the then chairman upon his retirement.

A Pocher model of an Alfa Romeo 8C 2300 Monza, in display case with mirrored base and perspex cover, 1931.
£520–560 *S*

l. A Ford Model A 1:16 scale model, with *faux* brass detailing, rear opening door, wooden floor and mahogany steering wheel.
£115–130 *BKS*

A 2in scale model of an articulated Clayton undertype wagon, built by F. Lynn, with brazed superheated copper boiler, centre fuelling chute and fittings, water and pressure gauges, safety blower, injector, whistle, main stop, clack and blowdown valves, twin cylinders with enclosed valve gear and cranks, ratchet-operated lubricator, eccentric driven feed pump and by-pass, single speed chain drive to rear axle, 18 x 64in (46 x 162.5cm), and a trailer.
£1,400–1,600 *CSK*

A collection of 4 Bentley Specials for Brooklands Outer Circuit, 1930s Birkin Bentley and Barnato Hassan Bentley, 1936 Pacey Hassan and Bentley Jackson.
£3,450–3,750 *CSK*

A collection of 4 models, 1937 Mercedes W125, 1938 Mercedes W154, 1939 Mercedes W163, 1938 Auto Union D-Type.
£3,450–3,750 *CSK*

Photographs

A black and white photograph of Scuderia Ferrari Dinos at the British Grand Prix 1958, by Edward Eves, mounted and framed, 24 x 28in (71 x 61cm).
£160–170 *JAR*

A black and white photograph of Karl Kling in a Mercedes Benz W196 at the French Grand Prix in Reims 1954, by Alan Smith, mounted, 8 x 11⅜in (20.5 x 29cm).
£50–60 *JAR*

Make the most of Miller's

Price ranges in this book reflect what you should expect to pay for a similar example. When selling, however, you should expect to receive a lower figure. This will fluctuate according to a dealer's stock and salability at a particular time. It is always advisable, when selling a collectable, to approach a reputable dealer or an auction house which has specialist sales.

r. A black and white photograph of Graham Hill at the Monaco Grand Prix 1964, by Colin Waldeck, unframed, 20 x 16in (51 x 40.5cm).
£125–140 *JAR*

Enamel Signs

An enamel Avions Voisin three-colour sign, outstretched wings supporting central Voisin motor vehicle front view, with Issy-Seine beneath, some deterioration and chipping to edges, 12 x 63in (30.5 x 160cm).
£1,200–1,400 *BKS*

A double-sided enamel Price's Motor Oils 3-colour wall sign, good condition but some scratching, 24in (61cm) wide.
£230–250 *BKS*

A double-sided enamel Shell Motor Spirit sign, 1940s.
£70–80 *GAZE*

A double-sided enamel Talbot advertising sign, with blue, yellow and black badge motif, Talbot logo in black on white ground, French, c1930, 17 x 48in (43 x 122cm).
£700–750 *C*

An enamel Esso sign, c1920, 47½ x 72½in (121 x 184cm).
£150–250 *CRC*

An enamel Rootes Service sign, excellent condition, 1950s, 28 x 48in (70 x 122cm).
£220–250 *SW*

r. An enamel Dragonfly sign, c1920, 36 x 60in (92 x 153cm).
£200–300 *CRC*

RACING AUTOMOBILIA
Prints

Nicholas Watts, Ferrari – The First Grand Prix Victory, limited edition print, signed by José Gonzalez and Gigi Villoresi, 24½ x 33in (63 x 84cm).
£120–130 *MPG*

It was at the British Grand Prix at Silverstone in 1951 that Ferrari achieved its first Grand Prix victory.

The image depicts the tremendous battle between the eventual winner José Gonzalez, driving the Ferrari 375/F1 and Juan Fangio in the Alfa Romeo. Gigi Villoresi also in a Ferrari finished third.

Nicholas Watts, Tribute to Jochen Rindt – World Champion 1970, limited edition print, signed by Jackie Ickx, 24¾ x 33in (63 x 84cm).
£90–100 *MPG*

A controversial and charismatic character, Jochen Rindt's career ended tragically when he was killed during final practice for the 1970 Italian Grand Prix at Monza. The image depicts his last Grand Prix victory at Hockenheim in which he out-manoeuvred the Ferrari of Jackie Ickx on the final lap.

Books

r. Enzo Ferrari, *The Enzo Ferrari Memoirs*, first edition, with dust cover, 1963.
£20–25 *LF*

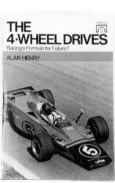

Denis Jenkinson & Cyril Posthumus, *Vanwall – The story of Tony Vandervell and his racing cars*, foreword by Stirling Moss, 1975.
£45–50 *GPCC*

Jean-Claude Hallé, *Francois Cevert – A Contract with Death*, 1974.
£50–65 *GPCC*

Adriane Galisteu, *Adriane – My Life with Ayrton*, 1994.
£10–20 *GPCC*

Alan Henry, *The 4-Wheel Drives – Racing's Formula for Failure?*, 1975.
£8–10 *GPCC*

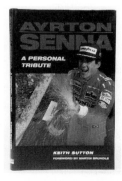

r. Keith Sutton, *Ayrton Senna – A Personal Tribute*, foreword by Martin Brundle, 1994.
£25–28 *GPCC*

Clothing

A Jordan team shirt, 1995.
£35–40 *GPT*

A Cerruti Ferrari cap, signed by Schumacher and Irvine, 1997.
£300–360 *GPT*

A Ralf Schumacher personal Jordan shirt, signed, 1997.
£95–115 *GPT*

A Ralf Schumacher Jordan race suit, 1997.
£800–1,000 *GPT*

Components

A Jordan front wing flap, 1994, 14 x 12in (35.5 x 30.5cm).
£45–55 *GPT*

A Prost Ferrari piston and con rod, 1990.
£350–400 *GPT*

A Lotus Formula 1 rear wing end plate, 1994, 23 x 13in (58.5 x 33cm).
£150–185 *GPT*

l. A Benetton exhaust, 1994, 24in (61cm) long.
£75–125 *GPT*

A Benetton carbon fibre front wing end plate, 1995, 21 x 13in (53.5 x 33cm).
£85–125 *GPT*

Miscellaneous

l. An Onyx model of a Williams Renault FW16, signed by Damon Hill, 1994, 4¼ x 4in (10.5 x 10cm).
£75–100 *GPT*

A Williams fuel churn, 1994, 21in (53.5cm) high.
£95–135 *GPT*

A Williams pressurised fuel churn, 1995, 34in (86.5cm) high.
£125–150 *GPT*

GLOSSARY

We have attempted to define some of the terms that you will come across in this book. If there are any terms or technicalities you would like explained or you feel should be included in future please let us know.

All-weather: A term used to describe a vehicle with a more sophisticated folding hood than the normal Cape hood fitted to a touring vehicle. The sides were fitted with metal frames and transparent material, in some cases glass.

Barchetta: Italian for 'little boat', an all-enveloping open sports bodywork.

Berline: Originally a 4 wheeler with hooded seat behind, more recently French usage for English term saloon (Berlina in Italian).

Boost: The amount of pressure applied by a supercharger or turbocharger.

Boxer: Engine configuration with horizontally opposed cylinders.

Brake Horsepower – bhp: This is the horse power of the combustion engine measured at the engine flywheel (See Horsepower).

Brake: A term dating from the days of horse drawn vehicles. Originally the seating was fore and aft, with the passengers facing inwards.

Cabriolet: The term Cabriolet applies to a vehicle with a hood which can be closed, folded half way, or folded right back. The Cabriolet can be distinguished from the Landaulette as the front of the hood reaches the top of the windscreen whereas the Landaulette only covers the rear quarter of the car.

Chain drive: A transmission system in which the wheels are attached to a sprocket, driven by a chain from an engine powered sprocket usually on the output side of a gearbox.

Chassis: A framework to which the car body, engine, gearbox, and axles are attached.

Chummy: An open top 2 door body style usually with 2 front seats and one at the rear.

Cloverleaf: A 3 seater open body style usually with a single door, 2 seats in the front and one at the rear.

Concours: *Concours d'Elegance* is a competition of cars of aesthetic qualities. *Concours d'Etat* is a competition of condition. Concours has become a byword for a vehicle in excellent condition.

Cone Clutch: One in which both driving and driven faces form a cone.

Connollising: Leather treatment produced by British firm Connolly to rejuvenate and restore suppleness to old and dry leather.

Convertible: A general term (post-war) for any car with a soft top.

Continental: This is a car specifically designed for high speed touring, usually on the Continent. Rolls-Royce and Bentley almost exclusively used this term during the 1930s and post-WWII.

Coupé: In the early Vintage and Edwardian period, it was only applied to what is now termed a Half Limousine or Doctor's Coupé which was a 2 door, 2 seater. The term is now usually prefixed by Drophead or Fixed Head.

Cubic Capacity: The volume of an engine obtained by multiplying the bore and the stroke.

De Ville: Almost all early coachwork had an exposed area for the driver to be in direct control of his horses, and so the motor car chauffeur was believed to be able to control the vehicle more easily if he was open to the elements. As the term only refers to part of the style of the car, i.e. the front, it is invariably used in connection with the words Coupé and Sedanca.

Dickey Seat: A passenger seat, usually for 2 people contained in the boot of the car without a folding hood (the boot lid forms the backrest). Known in America as a rumble seat.

Doctor's Coupé: A fixed or folding head coupé without a dickey seat and the passenger seat slightly staggered back from the driver's to accommodate the famous black bag.

Dog Cart: A horsedrawn dog cart was originally used to transport beaters and their dogs to a shoot (the dogs were contained in louvred boxes under the seats, the louvres were kept for decoration long after the dogs had gone).

Dos-à-dos: Literally back-to-back, i.e. the passenger seating arrangement.

Double duck: double layered fabric used in construction of soft tops.

Drophead Coupé: Originally a 2 door 2 seater with a folding roof, see Roadster.

Dry Sump: A method of lubricating engines, usually with 2 oil pumps, one of which removes oil from the sump to a reservoir away from the engine block.

Engine: Engine sizes are given in cubic centimetres (cc) in Europe and cubic inches (cu in) in the USA. 1 cubic inch equals 16.38cc (1 litre = 61.02cu in).

Fender: American usage for the English word wing.

Fixed Head Coupé: FHC, a coupé with a solid fixed roof.

Golfer's Coupé: Usually an open 2 seater with a square-doored locker behind the driver's seat to accommodate golf clubs.

Hansom: As with the famous horse drawn cab, an enclosed 2 seater with the driver out in the elements either behind or in front.

Homologation: To qualify for entry into some race series rules can require that a minimum number of road-going production versions of the race car are built. These are generally known as 'homologation specials'.

Hood: American usage for English term bonnet. English usage for a retracting soft top.

Horsepower: The unit of measurement of engine power. One horsepower represents the energy expended in raising 33,000lb by one foot in 60 seconds.

Landau: An open carriage with a folding hood at each end which would meet in the middle when erected.

Laudaulette: Also Landaulet, a horsedrawn Landaulette carried 2 people and was built much like a coupé. A Landau was a town carriage for 4 people. The full Landau was rarely built on a motor car chassis because the front folding hood took up so much room between the driver's seat and the rear compartment. The roof line of a Landaulette has always been angular, in contrast to the Cabriolet and the folding hood, and very often made of patent leather. A true Landaulette only opens over the rear compartment and not over the front seat at all.

Limousine: French in origin, always used to describe a closed car equipped with occasional seats and always having a division between the rear and driver's compartments. Suffixes and prefixes are often inappropriately used with the term Limousine and should be avoided.

Monobloc engine: An engine with all cylinders cast in a single block.

Monocoque: A type of construction of car bodies without a chassis as such, the strength being in the stressed panels. Most modern mass-produced cars are built this way.

Monoposto: Single seater (Italian).

Nitrided: Hardening of engine components, particularly crankshafts, to stand up to the stresses of racing.

OHC: Overhead camshaft, either single (SOHC) or double (DOHC).

OHV: Overhead valve engine.

Phæton: A term dating back to the the days of horsedrawn vehicles for an open body, sometimes with a Dickey or Rumble Seat for the groom at the rear. It was an owner/driver carriage and designed to be pulled by 4 horses. A term often misused during the Veteran period but remains in common use, particularly in the United States.

Post Vintage Thoroughbred (PVT): A British term drawn up by the Vintage Sports Car Club (VSCC) for selected models made in the vintage tradition between 1931 and 1942.

Roadster: A 2 seater sports car. The hood should be able to be removed totally rather than folded down as a drophead coupé.

Roi des Belges: A luxurious open touring car with elaborately contoured seat backs, named after King Leopold II of Belgium. The term is sometimes wrongly used for general touring cars.

Rotary engine: An engine in which the cylinder banks revolve around the crank, for example the Wankel engine with its rotating piston.

Rpm: Engine revolutions per minute.

Rumble Seat: A folding seat for 2 passengers, used to increase the carrying capacity of a standard 2 passenger car.

Runabout: A low powered light open 2 seater from the 1900s.

Saloon: A 2 or 4 door car with 4 or more seats and a fixed roof.

Sedan: See Saloon.

Sedanca de Ville: A limousine body with the driving compartment covered with a folding or sliding roof section, known in America as a Town Car.

Sociable: A cycle car term meaning that the passenger and driver sat side-by-side.

Spider/Spyder: An open 2 seater sports car, sometimes a 2+2 (2 small seats behind the 2 front seats).
Spider is generally the Italian usage, and Spyder the German spelling.

Stanhope: A term from the days of horsedrawn vehicles for a single seat 2 wheel carriage with a hood. Later, a 4 wheeled 2 seater, sometimes with an underfloor engine.

Station Wagon: See Brake.

Stroke: The distance a piston moves up-and-down within the cylinder. This distance is always measured in millimetres.

Supercharger: A device for forcing fuel/air into the cylinder for extra power.

Superleggera: Italian for 'super lightweight' method of construction devised by Touring of Milan, whereby a lightweight aluminium skin was attached to a framework of tubes to produce a light yet strong structure. One of the best known proponents of this method was Aston Martin who employed Superleggera construction in some of their DB series cars.

Surrey: An early 20thC open 4 seater with a fringed canopy. A term from the days of horse drawn vehicles.

Tandem: A cycle car term, the passengers sat in tandem, with the driver at the front or at the rear.

Targa: A coupé with a removable centre roof section.

Tonneau: A rear entrance tonneau is a 4 seater with access through a centrally placed door at the rear. A detachable tonneau meant that the rear seats could be removed to make a 2 seater. Tonneau nowadays usually means a waterproof cover over an open car used when the roof is detached.

Torpedo: An open tourer with an unbroken line from the bonnet to the rear of the body.

Tourer: An open 4 or 5 seater with 3 or 4 doors, folding hood, with or without sidescreens, generally replaced the term torpedo, with seats flush with the body sides. This body design began in about 1910, but by 1920 the word tourer was used instead – except in France, where 'torpédo' continued until the 1930s.

Unitary Construction: Vehicle with integral body and chassis – the chassis is no longer a separate item. See monocoque.

Veteran: All vehicles manufactured before 31st December 1918, only cars built before 31st March 1904 are eligible for the London to Brighton Commemorative Run.

Victoria: Generally an American term for a 2 or 4 seater with a very large folding hood. If a 4 seater, the hood would only cover the rear seats.

Vintage: Any vehicles manufactured between the end of the veteran period and 31st December 1930. See Post Vintage Thoroughbred.

Vis-à-Vis: Face-to-face, an open car where one or 2 passengers sit opposite each other.

Voiturette: A French term meaning a very light car, originally used by Léon Bollée.

Wagonette: A large car for 6 or more passengers, in which the rear seats faced each other. Entrance was at the rear, and the vehicles were usually open.

Waxoyled: Treatment of underside of car with Waxoyl, a proprietary oil and wax spray that protects against moisture and rust.

Weyman: A system of construction employing Rexine fabric panels over a Kapok filling to prevent noise and provide insulation.

Wheelbase: The distance between the centres of the front and rear wheels.

MOTOR BOOKS

Leading specialists in automotive books for enthusiasts throughout the world.
Many thousands of general, technical, tuning and rating books in our catalogue for £1.00

MOTOR BOOKS, 33 St Martin's Court, St Martin's Lane, London WC2N 4AL Tel: 0171-836 5376/6728/3800 Fax: 0171-497 2539

MOTOR BOOKS, 8 The Roundway, Headington, Oxford OX3 8DH Tel: (01865) 766215 Fax: (01865) 763555

MOTOR BOOKS, 10 Theatre Square, Swindon SN1 1QN Tel: (01793) 523170 Fax: (01793) 432070

INTERNET: http://www.solnet.co.uk/motor-books

FREEPHONE: ORDERLINE 0800 0267890 E-MAIL: motor_books@compuserve.com

Postage & Packing:	Standard Rate	Minimum Charge	1st Class/Air/Express
UK Delivery	10% of order value	£1.50 over £50 post free (Manuals £5.00)	On Request
Overseas Delivery	15% of order value	£5.00	Please ask for quote

CREDIT CARDS: Visa, Access, Mastercard, Eurocard, Diners Club, TSB, AMEX Please quote full card number and expiry date.

Official technical books. These are all originals or unedited re-issues of official factory publications, including workshop manuals and parts catalogues. Far more detailed than the condensed literature widely available, they are essential possessions for owners and restorers and are highly recommended.

Audi Fox Official Service Manual: 1973–79. 562 pages, 1,020 illus/diagrams, 27 pages of electrical wiring diagrams. SB. (XO92) (ISBN 083760 0979) £24.95

Austin Healey 100/6 & 3000 Official Workshop Manual. Covers 100/6, 3000 Mks I & II. Plus Mk II and Mk III sports convertible (series BJ7 and BJ8). Detailed upkeep and repair, tools, general info. 400 pages, fully illustrated. SB. (AKD1179H) (ISBN 094820 7477) £21.95

Daimler 2.5 V-8 & 250 Saloon Official Service Manual. Detailed upkeep and repair, tools, general information. 548 pages, photos, drawings, SB. (E1002) (ISBN 185520 0082) £29.95

Daimler 2.5 V-8 & 250 Saloon Official Parts Catalogue. Fully illustrated and indexed guide to all parts. 328pp, drawings. SB. (D4) (ISBN 185520 0090) £24.95

Ford Capri Official Workshop Manual 1974 on. Covers: 1300cc, 1600cc, 2000cc, 2300cc, 3000cc. 600 pages. Well illus. SB.(ISBN 185520 2018). . . £29.95

Ford Capri 2.8 Injection Official Workshop Manual. Supplement to the above. 84 pages, illustrated. SB. (ISBN 185520 2026) £7.95

Jaguar XK120, XK140, XK150, XK150S & Mk VII, VIII & IX Official Service Manual. Massive publication compiled from 9 different previous official manuals. 784 pages, photos, drawings, wiring diagrams. SB. (ISBN 187064 2279). £46.95

Jaguar Mk 2 Official Service Manual. 4th edition covering all 2.4, 3.4, 3.8, 240 and 340 models. 545 pages, drawings. SB. (E121/7)(ISBN 187064 2953) . £29.95

Jaguar E-Type V-12 Series 3 Official Service Manual. Well illustrated with drawings, charts and diagrams. Ringbinder (E165/3)(ISBN 185520 0015). £27.95

Jaguar S-Type Parts Catalogue. Covers 3.4 & 3.8 models. 248 pages, drawings, diagrams. SB. (J35) (ISBN 185520 1569). £24.95

Jaguar E-Type V-12 Series 3 Open 2 Seater Official Parts Catalogue. All parts illustrated and numbered. 240 pages, drawings. SB. (RTC9014) (ISBN 186982 6841) £15.95

Land Rover Series 1 Official Workshop Manual. Covers all petrol and diesel

models up to 1958. 384 pages, drawings, charts. SB. (4291) (ISBN 090707 3980) £21.95

Land Rover Discovery Official Workshop Manual. A detailed guide to maintenance, etc. Covers petrol models V-8, 3.5 & 3.9 and diesel models Mpi and 200 Tdi. 844 pages. Over 1,000 illustrations. SB. (ISBN 185520 312X) £39.95

Land Rover Series 1 1948–53 Official Parts Catalogue. Section 1 – 1948–51 models, Section 2 – 1952–53 models, Section 3 – extra equipment. Covers home and export models: part numbers and illustrations. 446 pages (4051) SB. (ISBN 185520 1194) £19.95

Land Rover Series 1 1954–58 Official Parts Catalogue. 86, 88, 107 & 109 petrol and diesel models. Covers home and export. Contains part numbers and illustrations. 442 pages. (4107) SB. (ISBN 185520 1070) £19.95

High Performance Lotus Cortina Official Workshop Manual 1969. Information on all repair and adjustment procedures on the Mk 2. 316 pages, illustrated with photos and diagrams. SB. (ISBN 185520 1461) £27.95

MG Midget Series TD & TF Official Workshop Manual. Covers all components and tasks in great detail, for both minor and major repairs. 240 pages, photos, drawings, diagrams. SB. (AKD580A) (ISBN 185520 2115) £17.95

MGB Official Workshop Manual. Maintenance, lubrication chart, general data, engine tuning, all components, service tools, plus emission control supplement. Pub. 76. 425 pages, diagrams. SB. (AKD3259) (ISBN 185520 1747) £21.95

MGC Workshop Manual. Covers the six-cylinder MGC 1967–69. Full maintenance, repair, troubleshooting, tune-up instructions. 336 pages, drawings. SB. (ISBN 185520 1852) £19.95

MGB Tourer, GT & V-8 Official Parts Catalogue, up to Sept 1976. All parts numbered, illustrated. 440 pages. SB. (AKM0039) (ISBN 094820 706X) £19.95

Mini Official Workshop Manual (1959–76). 9th edition. The complete

professional or amateur mechanic's guide to all repair and servicing procedures. Covers Saloon, Countryman, Traveller, Clubman, Estate, 1275GT, Van Pick-up, Moke, Cooper 'S'. 362 pages. SB. (AKD4935) (ISBN 185520 1488) £19.95

Morris Minor Series MM, Series II & 1000 Official Workshop Manual. Highly detailed maintenance and repair instructions for service supervisors, qualified & less experienced mechanics. Pub. 70. 440 pages, drawings. SB. (AKD530) (ISBN 185520 1577) . £16.95

Range Rover (Two Door) Official Repair Operation Manual. Covers years 1970–85. Detailed instructions for all components, also incorporating 5 speed and automatic gearbox supplement. 508 pages, drawings. SB. (AKM3630) (ISBN 185520 1224) £28.95

Triumph TR4 Official Workshop Manual (Incorporating supplement for TR4A). The complete professional or amateur mechanic's guide to all repair and servicing procedures. 360 pages, photos and drawings. SB. (510322) (ISBN 094820 7957) £23.95

Triumph Stag Official Repair Operation Manual. Complete guide to all components and their repair and upkeep. Pub. 1977. 640 pages, drawings. SB. (AKM3966) (ISBN 185520 0139) £24.95

Triumph TR2 & TR3 Official Spare Parts Catalogue. All parts illustrated, identified and numbered. 4th edition. 369 pages, drawings. SB. (501653) (ISBN 090707 3999) £18.95

Austin A40 Devon/Dorset WSM . . £17.95
Austin A40 Somerset WSM £24.95
Austin A55 MkII & A60/Oxford V & VI/ Wolseley 15/60 & 16/60 WSM. . . £31.95
AustinMorris & Vanden Plas etc. 1100/1300 WSM £25.95
Austin Healey 100 BN1 & BN2 WSM £19.95
Austin Healey 100/4 Parts £30.00
Austin Healey 3000 MkII 61–67 Parts £28.95
Austin Healey 3000 MkII 62–68 Parts £34.95
Austin Healey 100/6 & 3000 WSM £21.95

Austin Healey 100/6 Parts £28.95
Austin Healey Sprite MkI 'Frogeye'
  WSM. £17.95
Austin Healey Sprite I/II & Midget I
  Body Parts £15.95
Austin Healey Sprite I/II & Midget I
  Mechanical Parts £34.95
Austin Healey Sprite Mk 2, 3 & 4 &
  Midget WSM. £18.95
Austin Healey Sprite Mk 3 & 4 Parts . . . .
  . . . . £18.95
BMW 1502/2002 WSM £87.95
BMW 2500/3.3 Litre WSM £92.95
BMW 320/323i 6 cyl (2 vols) WSM £87.95
BMW 520 6 cylinder WSM £67.95
BMW 518-520 4 cylinder WSM . . £60.95
BMW 628/630/633Csi WSM £97.00
BMW 728/730/733i (2 vols) WSM £109.95
Citroën 12 & 15 WSM £19.95
Citroën 2CV (2 vols) £49.90
Citroën 2CV Parts £31.00
Daimler 2.5L V8 & 250 Saloon WSM . . .
  . . . . £29.95
Daimler 2.5L V8 & 250 Saloon Parts . . .
  . . . . £24.95
Daimler Dart Parts £19.95
Fiat Uno All Models £68.95
Fiat X1/9 Technical Data WSM . . £26.95
Fiat 500 1957–72 WSM £31.95
Ford Anglia/Prefect/Popular 1939–59 . . .
  . . . . £28.95
Ford Anglia 100E WSM £27.95
Ford Capri 1.3/1.6/2.0/2.3 & 3.0 from
  1974 WSM £29.95
Ford Capri 2.8i Supplement WSM . £7.95
Jaguar 1.5, 2.5, 3.5 1946–48 WSM £14.95
Jaguar Mk V Parts. £33.00
Jaguar XK 120/140/150 & Mk 7/8/9
  WSM. £46.95
Jaguar XK 120 Parts £38.95
Jaguar XK 140 Parts £36.95
Jaguar XK 150 Parts (2 vols) £70.00
Jaguar Mk 2/240/340 WSM £29.95
Jaguar Mk 2 3.4, 3.8, 340 Parts . . £33.95
Jaguar Mk 2 2.4 Parts £46.00
Jaguar E-Type 3.8/4.2 Ser. 1/2 WSM . . .
  . . . . £35.95
Jaguar E-Type V12 Ser. 3 WSM . £25.95
Jaguar 420 WSM £27.95
Jaguar XJ6 Ser. 1 WSM. £29.95
Jaguar XJ6 Ser. 2 WSM. £29.95
Jaguar XJ12 Ser. 2 WSM. £29.95
Jaguar XJ6 & XJ12 Ser. 3 WSM . £52.00
Jaguar XJS V12 (+HE Supp)WSM£36.95

Jaguar Mk 2 3.4/3.8/340 Parts . . . £33.95
Jaguar E-Type Ser. 1 Parts £19.95
Jaguar E-Type 4.2 Ser. 1 Parts . . £19.95
Jaguar E-Type Ser. 2 GT Parts . . £24.95
Jaguar XJ6 Ser. 1 Parts. £16.95
Jaguar XJ6 Ser. 2 Parts. £29.95
Jaguar XJ6 Ser. 3 Parts. £29.95
Lamborghini Espada WSM £27.95
Lamborghini Countach 5000 WSM . . . .
  . . . . £27.95
Lamborghini Countach 5000 Parts£28.95
Lamborghini Countach 5000 4V Parts . .
  . . . . £27.95
Lancia Delta & HF WSM £49.00
Lancia Delta HF/Prisma/Integrale 4WD
  WSM. £91.95
Lancia Fulvia all models WSM . . £49.95
Lancia Beta WSM £33.00
Lancia Montecarlo WSM £35.95
Lancia Flaminia WSM £33.95
Lancia Flavia WSM £33.95
Lancia Stratos WSM £36.95
Lancia Stratos Parts £36.95
Lancia Thema WSM. £64.95
Lancia Dedra WSM £69.00
Lancia Prisma WSM £64.95
Maserati Ghibli WSM £27.95
Maserati Bora WSM. £27.95
Maserati 3500GT WSM £23.00
Maserati 3500GT Parts £27.95
Maserati Biturbo WSM £75.95
Mazda RX2 WSM £22.95
Mazda RX3 WSM £29.95
Mazda RX7 to 1985 WSM £49.95
Mercedes Benz 170 (M136) 1950–53
  WSM. £63.00
Mercedes Benz 190 1956–61 WSM£43.00
Mercedes Benz 190SL supplement£26.95
Mercedes Benz 300SL WSM. £63.00
MG Midget TD & TF WSM £17.95
MG Midget Mk 1, 2 & 3 WSM . . . £18.95
MG Midget 1500 WSM. £17.95
MGA WSM £18.95
MGA 1500 Parts. £18.95
MGA 1600 Parts. £20.95
MGB & GT to Sept '76 WSM £21.95
MGB & GT 1978 on WSM £17.95
MG Midget Mk 2 & 3 Parts £17.95
MGB Tourer GT & V8 to Sept '76 Parts.
  . . . . £19.95
MGB Tourer & GT Sept '76 on Parts . . .
  . . . . £13.95
Mini 1959–76 WSM £19.95
Morris Oxford Series 'MO' WSM . £25.95

Reliant Scimitar GTE SE5 . . . . . . £41.95
Reliant Scimitar GTE SE6 . . . . . . £41.95
Reliant SST & SS1 WSM £33.95
Reliant SST & SS1 Parts £29.95
Renault 8 WSM £37.95
Renault Dauphine WSM £35.00
Riley 1 1/2 – 2 1/2 WSM £26.95
Riley 1 1/2 Parts £32.95
Land Rover Series 1 WSM £21.95
Land Rover Series 1 1948–53 Parts . . . .
. . . . £19.95
Land Rover Series 1 1954–58 Parts . . . .
. . . . £19.95
Land Rover Series 2 & 2A WSM . £46.90
Land Rover Series 3 WSM £23.95
Land Rover Series 3 Parts £12.95
Land Rover 90/110 Defender to 1993
  WSM £39.95
Range Rover 1970–85 WSM Parts £24.95
Range Rover 1986–93 WSM £49.95
Rover P4 WSM £43.95
Rover 3 & 3.5L Saloon & Coupé WSM . .
. . . . £28.95
Rover 3 & 3.5L Saloon & Coupé Parts . .
. . . . £28.95
Rover 2000 & 2200 (P6) WSM . . . £25.95
Rover 2000 Series 2 Parts £15.95
Rover 2200 Parts £17.95
Rover 3500 & 3500S (P6) WSM . . £26.95
Rover 3500 & 3500S (P6) Parts . . £23.95
Standard Eight & Ten £25.95
Sunbeam Alpine Series I to V WSM . . . .
. . . . £33.00
Sunbeam Alpine Series I to V Parts . . .
. . . . £34.00
Triumph Dolomite Range from 1976
  Parts £29.95
Triumph TR2 & 3 WSM £23.95
Triumph TR4 & TR4A WSM £23.95
Triumph TR6 WSM £24.95
Triumph Spitfire 1, 2, 3, Vitesse 6 &
  Herald WSM £20.95
Triumph Spitfire Mks I & II Parts £28.95
Triumph Spitfire 4 WSM £17.95
Triumph Spitfire 1500 WSM £17.95
Triumph Stag WSM £24.95
Triumph TR2 & 3 Parts £18.95
Triumph TR4 Parts £18.95
Triumph TR6 Parts £18.95
Triumph TR7 1975–78 Parts £19.95
Triumph TR7 1979 on Parts £19.95
Triumph Spitfire Mk 3 Parts £15.95
Triumph Spitfire 1500 (75+) Parts £15.95
Triumph Stag Parts £22.95

Volvo P1800 WSM £34.95
Volvo P1800ES WSM £39.95
Volvo Amazon 120 WSM £41.95
Volvo 121/122S WSM £28.95
Volvo PV544 (P210) WSM £40.95
Wolseley 1500 & Riley 1.5 WSM . £25.95

We can also supply many handbook
  reprints for the above range of vehicles
  as well as the original factory manuals
  for many other vehicles old and new.

ORIGINAL RESTORER'S GUIDE
SERIES FROM BAY VIEW BOOKS
Original AC Ace & Cobra £19.95
Original Aston Martin DB4/5/6 . . £19.95
Original Austin Healey 100, 100/6 &
  3000 . . . . £19.95
Original Austin Seven £19.95
Original Citroen DS £19.95
Original Ferrari V8 . . . . £19.95
Original Jaguar E-Type £19.95
Original Jaguar Mk 1 & 2 . . . . . . £19.95
Original Jaguar XK £19.95
Original Land Rover Series 1 . . . . £19.95
Original Mercedes SL to 1971 . . . £19.95
Original MGA £19.95
Original MGB, C & V8 . . . . £19.95
Original MG T Series £19.95
Original Mini Cooper & Cooper 'S' £19.95
Original Morgan 4/4, Plus 4 & Plus 8 . . .
. . . . £19.95
Original Morris Minor £19.95
Original Porsche 911 . . . . £19.95
Original Porsche 356 1950-65 . . . £19.95
Original Sprite & Midget 1958-79 £19.95
Original Triumph TR £19.95
Original VW Beetle £19.95
Original VW Bus 1950-79 . . . . . . £19.95

9000+ MOTORING BOOKS, ROAD
  TESTS, VIDEO'S, WORKSHOP
  MANUALS & PARTS CATALOGUES!
Any title not in stock can usually be
  obtained in a few days.

THE FOLLOWING LIST ARE NOW
  AVAILABLE FREE ON REQUEST
Alfa Romeo, BMW, Ferrari, Jaguar,
  Mercedes Benz, MG, Porsche, RR &
  Bentley, Triumph, Motorsport.

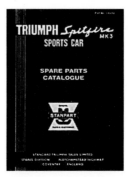

DIRECTORY OF CAR CLUBS

If you would like your Club to be included in next year's directory, or have a change of address or telephone number, please inform us by 30th June 1998. Entries will be repeated unless we are requested otherwise.

105E Anglia Owners Club Middlesex Group, 9 Evelyn Avenue, Ruislip, Middlesex HA4 8AR Tel: 01895 672251

1100 Club, Paul Vincent, 32 Medgbury Road, Swindon, Wiltshire SN1 2AS

2CVGB Deux Chevaux Club of GB, PO Box 602 Crick, Northampton, Northamptonshire NN6 7UW

750 Motor Club Ltd, Courthouse, St Winifreds Road, Biggin Hill, Kent TN16 3H Tel: 01959 575812

A C Owners Club, R A Morpeth, The Clovers, Mursley, Buckinghamshire MK17 0RT

A40 Farina Club, Membership Secretary, 2 Ivy Cottages, Fullers Vale, Headley Down, Bordon, Hampshire GU35 8NR

ABC Owners Club, D A Hales, The Hedgerows, Sutton St Nicholas, Hereford HR1 3BU Tel: 01432 880726

Alexis Racing and Trials Car Register, Duncan Rabagliati, 4 Wool Road, Wimbledon, London SW20 0HW

Alfa Romeo 1900 Register, Peter Marshall, Mariners, Courtlands Avenue, Esher, Surrey KT10 9HZ

Alfa Romeo Owners Club, Michael Lindsay, 97 High Street, Linton, Cambridgeshire CB1 6JT

Alfa Romeo Section (VSCC Ltd), Allan & Angela Cherrett, Old Forge, Quarr, Nr Gillingham, Dorset SP8 5PA

Allard Owners Club, Miss P. Hulse, 1 Dalmeny Avenue, Tufnell Park, London N7

Alvis Owners Club, 1 Forge Cottages, Bayham Road, Little Bayham, Lamberhurst, Kent TN3 8BB

Alvis Register, Mr J. Willis, The Vinery Wanborough Manor, Nr Guildford, Surrey GU3 2JR Tel: 01483 810308

American Auto Club UK, 11 Wych Elm, Colchester, Essex CO2 8PR Tel: 01206 564404

Amilcar Salmson Register, RAF King, Apple House, Wildmoor Lane, Sherfield on Lodden, Hampshire RG27 0HA

Armstrong Siddeley Owners Club Ltd, Peter Sheppard, 57 Berberry Close, Bourneville, Birmingham, West Midlands B30 1TB

Assoc of British Volkswagen Clubs, 66 Pinewood Green, Iver Heath, Buckinghamshire SL0 0QH

Association of Healey Owners, Don Griffiths, The White House, Hill Pound, Swanmore, Hampshire SO32 2PS Tel: 01489 895813

Association of Old Vehicle Clubs in Northern Ireland Ltd, Secretary Trevor Mitchell, 38 Ballymaconnell Road, Bangor, Co Down, Ireland BT20 5PS Tel: 01247 467886

Association of Singer Car Owners, Anne Page, 39 Oakfield, Rickmansworth, Hertfordshire WO3 2LR Tel: 01923 778575

Aston Martin Owners Club Ltd, Jim Whyman, AMOC Ltd, 1A High Street, Sutton, Nr Ely, Cambridgeshire CB6 2RB Tel: 01353 777353

Atlas Register, 38 Ridgeway, Southwell, Nottinghamshire NG25 0DJ

Austin A30-35 Owners Club, Barbara Scott (membership secretary), 16 Dene View, Ashington, Northumberland NE63 8JT Tel: 01670 853347

Austin Atlantic Owners Club, 124 Holbrook Road, Stratford, London E15 3DZ Tel: 0181 534 2682 (home) 0171 833 7907 (work)

Austin Big 7 Register, R. E. Taylor, 101 Derby Road, Chellaston, Derbyshire DE73 1SB

Austin Cambridge/Westminster Car Club, Mr J Curtis, 4 Russell Close, East Budleigh, Budleigh Salterton, Devon EX9 7EH Tel: 01395 446210

Austin Eight Register, Ian Pinniger, 3 La Grange Martin, St Martin, Jersey, Channel Islands JE3 6JB

Austin Gipsy Register 1958-1968, Mike Gilbert, 24 Green Close, Rixon, Sturminster Newton, Dorset DT10 1BJ

Austin Healey Club, 47 George Crescent, Muswell Hill, London N10 1AL Tel: 0181 444 0156

Austin Healey Club, Mike Ward, Midland Centre, 9 Stag Walk, Sutton Coldfield, West Midlands B76 1JZ Tel: 0121 382 3223

Austin J40 Car Club, BG Swann, 19 Lavender Avenue, Coudon, Coventry CV6 1DA

Austin Maxi Club, Mrs C J Jackson, 27 Queen Street, Bardney, Lincolnshire LN3 5XF

Austin Seven Mulliner Register, Mike Tebbett, Little Wyche, Walwyn Road, Upper Colwall, Nr Malvern, Hereford & Worcester WR13 6PL

Austin Seven Owners Club (London), Mr and Mrs Simpkins, 5 Brook Cottages, Riding Lane, Hildenborough, Kent TN11 9QL

Austin Seven Sports Register, CJ Taylor, 222 Prescot Road, Aughton, Ormskirk, Lancashire L39 5AQ

Austin Seven Van Register 1923-29, NB Baldry, 32 Wentworth Crescent, Maidenhead, Berkshire SL6 4RW

Austin Sheerline & Princess Club, Ian Coombes 44 Vermeer Crescent, Shoeburyness, Essex S53 9TJ

Austin Swallow Register, G. L. Walker, School House, Back Way, Great Haseley, Oxfordshire OX44 7JP

Austin Ten Drivers Club Ltd, Mrs Patricia East, Brambledene, 53 Oxted Green, Milford, Godalming, Surrey GU8 5DD

Battery Vehicle Society, Keith Roberts, 29 Ambergate Drive, North Pentwyn, Cardiff, Wales CF2 7AX

Bean Car Club, G. Harris, Villa Rosa, Templewood Lane, Farnham Common, Buckinghamshire SL2 3H

Bentley Drivers Club, 16 Chearsley Road, Long Crendon, Aylesbury, Buckinghamshire HP18 9AW

Berkeley Enthusiasts Club, Paul Fitness, 9 Hellards Road, Stevenage, Hertfordshire SG1 3PN Tel: 01438 724164

Biggin Hill Car Club with XJ Register of JDC, Peter Adams, Jasmine House, Jasmine Grove, London SE20 8JY Tel: 0181 778 7531

BMW Car Club, PO Box 328, Andover, Hampshire SP10 1YN Tel: 01264 337883

BMW Drivers Club, Sue Hicks, Bavaria House PO Box 8, Dereham, Norfolk NR19 1TF Tel: 01362 694459

Bond Owners Club, Stan Cornock, 42 Beaufort Avenue, Hodge Hill, Birmingham, West Midlands B34 6AE

Borgward Drivers Club, Mr D. C. Farr, 19 Highfield Road, Kettering, Northamptonshire NN15 6HR Tel: 01536 510771

Brabham Register, Ed Walker, The Old Bull 5 Woodmancote, Dursley, Gloucestershire GL11 4AF Tel: 01453 543243

Bristol Austin Seven Club, 1 Silsbury Hill Cottages, West Kennett, Marlborough, Wiltshire SN8 1QH

Bristol Microcar Club, 123 Queens Road, Bishopsworth, Bristol, Avon BS13 8QB Tel: 0117 964 2901

Bristol Owners Club, John Emery, Uesutor Marringdean Road, Billingshurst, Sussex RH14 9HD

British Ambulance Preservation Society, Roger Leonard, 21 Victoria Road, Horley, Surrey RH6 9BN

British Automobile Racing Club, Thruxton Circuit, Andover, Hampshire SP11 8PN Tel: 01264 772607 & 772696/7

British Racing and Sports Car Club, Brands Hatch, Fawkham, Dartford, Kent DA3 8NG

British Saab Enthusiasts, Mr M Hodges, 75 Upper Road, Poole, Dorset BH12 3EN

British Salmson Owners Club, John Maddison 86 Broadway North, Walsall, West Midlands WS1 2QF Tel: 01922 29677

Brooklands Society Ltd, Reigate Lodge, Chartway, Reigate, Surrey RG2 0NZ

Brough Superior Club, P Staughton, Secretary, 4 Summerfields, Northampton, Northamptonshire NN4 9YN

BSA Front Wheel Drive Club, Barry Baker, 164 Cottimore Lane, Walton-on-Thames, Surrey KT12 2BL

Buckler Car Register, Stan Hibberd, 52 Greenacres, Woolton Hill, Newbury, Berkshire RG15 9TA Tel: 01635 254162

Bugatti Owners Club Ltd, Sue Ward, Prescott Hill, Gotherington, Cheltenham, Gloucestershire GL52 4RD

Bullnose Morris Club, Richard Harris, P O Box 383, Hove, Sussex BN3 4FX

C A Bedford Owners Club, G. W. Seller, 7 Grasmere Road, Benfleet, Essex SS7 3HF

Cambridge-Oxford Owners Club, 32 Reservoir Road, Southgate, London N14 4BG

Capri Club International, Field House, Ipsley Church Lane, Redditch, Hereford & Worcester B98 0AJ Tel: 01527 502066

Capri Club International North London Branch, 12 Chalton Road, Edmonton, London N9 8EG Tel: 0181 364 7845/0181 804 6326

Capri Drivers Association, Mrs Moira Farrelly (Secretary), 9 Lyndhurst Road, Coulsdon, Surrey CR5 3HT

Chiltern Vehicle Preservation Group, Chiltern House, Aylesbury, Buckinghamshire HP17 8BY Tel: 01296 651283

Citroen Car Club, P O Box 348, Bromley, Kent BR2 2QT

Citroen Traction Owners Club, Steve Reed, 1 Terwick Cottage, Rogate, Nr Petersfield, Hampshire GU31 5EG

Clan Owners Club, Chris Clay, 48 Valley Road, Littleover, Derbyshire DE23 6HS Tel: 01332 767410

Classic and Historic Motor Club Ltd, Tricia Burridge, The Smithy, High Street, Ston Easton, Bath, Avon BA3 4DE

Classic Corvette Club (UK), Ashley Pickering, The Gables, Christchurch Road, Tring, Hertfordshire HP23 4EF

Classic Crossbred Club, Alan Easto, 7 Wills Hill, Stanford Le Hope, Essex SS17 7AY Tel: 01375 679943

Classic Saloon Car Club, 7 Dunstable Road, Luton, Bedfordshire LU1 1BB Tel: 01582 31642

Classic Z Register, Lynne Godber, Thistledown, Old Stockbridge Road, Kentsboro, Wallop, Stockbridge, Hampshire SO20 8LB Tel: 01264 781979

Club Alfa Romeo 2600/2000 International, Roger Monk, Knighton, Church Close, West Runton, Cromer, Norfolk NR27 9QY

Club Alpine Renault UK Ltd, 71 Bedford Avenue, Barnet, Hertfordshire EN5 2ES

Club Lotus, Lotus Lodge, PO Box 8, Dereham, Norfolk NR19 1TF Tel: 01362 694459

Club Marcos International, Mrs I Chivers, Membership Secretary, 8 Ludmead Road, Corsham, Wiltshire SN13 9AS Tel: 01249 713769

Club Peugeot UK, Club Regs 504 Cab/Coupe, Beacon View, Forester Road, Soberton Heath, Southampton, Hampshire SO32 3QG Tel: 01329 833029

Club Peugeot UK, (General Secretary), 2 Sunnyside, Priors Hill, Tinsbury, Bath, Avon BA3 1HE

Club Triumph, Derek Pollock, 86 Waggon Road, Hadley Wood, Hertfordshire EN14 0PP Tel: 0181 440 9000

Club Triumph Eastern, Mr D. A. Davies, 72 Springwater Road, Eastwood, Leigh-on-Sea, Essex SS9 5BJ

Clyno Club, Swallow Cottage, Langton Farm, Elmesthorpe, Leicestershire LE9 7SE

Commercial Vehicle and Road Transport Club, Steven Wimbush, 8 Tachbrook Road, Uxbridge, Middlesex UB8 2QS

Connaught Register, Duncan Rabagliati, 4 Wool Road, Wimbledon, London SW20 0HW

Cortina MkII Register, Mark Blows, 78 Church Avenue, Broomfield, Chelmsford, Essex CM1 7HA

Cougar Club of America, Barrie S Dixon, 11 Dean Close, Partington, Greater Manchester M31 4BQ

Crayford Convertible Car Club, 58 Geriant Road, Downham, Nr Bromley, Kent BR1 5DX Tel: 0181 461 1805

Crossley Climax Register, Mr G Harvey, 7 Meadow Road, Basingstoke, Hampshire RG21 3LL

Crossley Register, Malcolm Jenner, Willow Cottage, Lexham Road, Great Dunham, Kings Lynn, Norfolk PE32 2LS

DAF Owners Club, S. K. Bidwell (Club Sec), 56 Ridgedale Road, Bolsover, Chesterfield, Derbyshire S44 6TX

Daimler and Lanchester Owners Club, John Ridley, Trewyn Manor, Pandy, Abergavenny, Gwent, Wales NP7 7PG Tel: 01873 890737

De Tomaso Drivers Club, Chris Statham, 2-4 Bank Road, Bredbury, Stockport, Cheshire SK6 1DR Tel: 0161 430 5052

Delage Section of the VSCC Ltd, Peter Jacobs (Secretary) Clouds' Reach, 17 The Scop, Almondsbury, Bristol, Avon BS12 4DU

Delahaye Club, A. F. Harrison, 34 Marine Parade, Hythe, Kent CT21 6AN Tel: 01303 261016

Dellow Register, Douglas Temple Design Group, 4 Roumelia Lane, Bournemouth, Dorset BH5 1EU Tel: 01202 304641

Delorean Owners Club, Linehill House, Sapey Common, Clifton-upon-Teme, Worcestershire WR6 6EP Tel: 01886 853294

Diva Register, Steve Pethybridge, 8 Wait End Road, Waterlooville, Hampshire PO7 7DD Tel: 01705 251485

DKW Owners Club, C. P. Nixon, Rose Cottage, Rodford, Westerleigh, Bristol, Avon BS17

Droop Snoot Group, 41 Horsham Avenue Finchley, London N12 9BG.Tel: 0181 368 1884

Dunsfold Land Rover Trust, Dunsfold, Surrey GU8 4NP Tel: 01483 200058

Dutton Owners Club, Rob Powell, 20 Burford Road, Baswich, Stafford, Staffordshire ST17 0BT Tel: 01785 56835

Early Ford V8 Club, 12 Fairholme Gardens, Cranham, Upminster, Essex RM14 1HJ Tel: 01708 222729

Elva Owners Club, R. A. Dunbar, Maple Tree Lodge, The Hawthorns, Smock Alley, West Alley, West Chiltington, Sussex RH20 2QX

Enfield & District Veteran Vehicle Trust, Whitewebbs Museum, Whitewebbs Road, Enfield, Middlesex EN2 9HW Tel: 0181 367 1898

ERA Club, Guy Spollon, Arden Grange, Tamworth-in-Arden, Warwickshire B94 5AE

F and FB Victor Owners Club, Wayne Parkhouse, 5 Farnell Road, Staines, Middlesex TW18 4HT

F-Victor Owners Club, Alan Victor Pope, 34 Hawkesbury Drive, Mill Lane, Calcot, Reading, Berkshire RG3 5ZR Tel: 01635 43532

Facel Vega Owners Club, Roy Scandrett, Windrush, 16 Paddock Gardens, East Grinstead, Sussex RH19 4AE

Fairthorpe Sports Car Club, Tony Hill, 9 Lynhurst Crescent, Uxbridge, Middlesex UB10 9EF

Ferrari Club of GB, Betty Mathias, 7 Swan Close, Blake Down, Kidderminster, Hereford & Worcester DY10 3JT Tel: 01562 700009

Fiat 130 Owners Club, Michael Reid, 28 Warwick Mansions, Cromwell Crescent, London SW5 9QR Tel: 0171 373 9740

Fiat Dino Register, Mr Morris, 59 Sandown Park, Tunbridge Wells, Kent TN2 4RT

Fiat Motor Club (GB), H. A. Collyer, Barnside, Chilkwell Street, Glastonbury, Somerset BA6 8D Tel: 01458 31443

Fiat Osca Register, Mr M. Elliott, 36 Maypole Drive, Chigwell, Essex IG7 6DE Tel: 0181 500 7127

Fiat Twin-Cam Register, 3 Anderson Place, Bagshot, Surrey GU19 5LX

Fire Service Preservation Group, Andrew Scott, 50 Old Slade Lane, Iver, Buckinghamshire SL0 9DR

Five Hundred Owners Club Association, David Docherty, Oakley, 68 Upton Park, Chester, Cheshire CH2 1DQ Tel: 01244 382789

Ford 105E Owners Club, Sally Harris, 30 Gower Road, Sedgley, Dudley, West Midlands DY3 3PN Tel: 01902 671071

Ford Avo Owners Club, D. Hensley, 11 Sycamore Drive, Patchway, Bristol, Avon BS12 5DH

Ford Capri Enthusiasts Register, Liz Barnes, 46 Manningtree Road, South Ruislip, Middlesex HA4 7LB Tel: 0181 842 0102

Ford Classic and Capri Owners Club, 30 Jersey Road, Mowmacre Hill, Leicester, Leicestershire LE4 2LR Tel: 0116 236 5498/0116 252 8394

Ford Corsair Owners Club, Mrs E Checkley, 7 Barnfield, New Malden, Surrey KT3 5RH

Ford Cortina 1600E Enthusiasts Club, D. Wright, 32 St Leonards Avenue, Hove, Sussex BN3 4QL

Ford Cortina 1600E Owners Club, Dave Marston, 23 Cumberland Road, Bilston, West Midlands WV14 6LT Tel: 01902 405055

Ford Escort 1300E Owners Club, Robert Watt, 65 Lindley Road, Walton-on-Thames, Surrey KT12 3EZ

Ford Executive Owners Register, Jenny Whitehouse, 3 Shanklin Road, Stonehouse, Coventry, Warwickshire CV3 4EE

Ford Granada MkI Owners Club, Paul Bussey, Bay Tree House, 15 Thornbera Road, Bishops Stortford, Hertfordshire CM23 3NJ

Ford GT Owners, c/o Riverside School, Ferry Road, Hullbridge, Hockley, Essex SS5 6ND

Ford MkII Independent O/C, 173 Sparrow Farm Drive, Feltham, Middlesex TW14 0DG Tel: 0181 384 3559

Ford MkIII Zephyr and Zodiac Owners Club, John Wilding, 10 Waltondale, Telford, Shropshire TF7 5NQ Tel: 01952 580746

Ford MkIV Zephyr & Zodiac Owners Club, 29 Ruskin Drive, Worcester Park, Surrey KT4 8LG Tel: 0181 649 0685

Ford Model T Ford Register of GB, Mrs Julia Armer, 3 Strong Close, Keighley, Yorkshire BD21 4JT Tel: 01535 607978

Ford RS Owners Club, PO Box 135, Newport, Gwent, Wales NP6 2YU Tel: 01633 412626

Ford Sidevalve Owners Club, Membership Secretary, 30 Earls Close, Bishopstoke, Eastleigh, Hampshire SO50 8HY

Ford Y&C Model Register, Bob Wilkinson, Castle Farm, Main Street, Pollington, Goole, Humberside DN14 0DJ Tel: 01405 860836

Frazer-Nash Section of the VSCC, Mrs J Blake, Daisy Head Farm, South Street, Caulcott, Bicester, Oxfordshire OX6 3NE

Friends of The British Commercial Vehicle, c/o BCVM, King Street, Leyland, Preston, Lancashire PR5 1LE

Gentry Register, Frank Tuck, 1 Kinross Avenue, South Ascot, Berkshire SL5 9EP Tel: 01990 24637

Gilbern Owners Club, P. C. Fawkes, 24 Mayfield Buckden, Huntingdon, Cambridgeshire PE18 9SZ Tel: 01480 812066

Ginetta Owners Club, Dave Baker, 24 Wallace Mill Gardens, Mid Calder, Livingstone, West Lothian, Scotland EH53 0BD Tel: 01506 8883129

Gordon Keeble Owners Club, Ann Knott, Westminster Road, Helmdon, Brackley, Northamptonshire NN13 5QB Tel: 01280 702311

Granada MkII and MkIII Enthusiasts' Club, 10 Alder Grove, Halesowen, West Midlands B62 9TL Tel: 0121 426 2346

Grand Prix Contact Club, David Hayhoe, 28 Pine Avenue, West Wickham, Kent BR4 0LW Tel: 0181 777 6479

Gwynne Register, H. K. Good, 9 Lancaster Avenue, Hadley Wood, Barnet, Hertfordshire EN4 0EP

Heinkel Trojan Owners and Enthusiasts Club, Y Luty, Carisbrooke, Wood End Lane, Fillongley, Coventry, Warwickshire CV7 8DF

Hillman Commer Karrier Club, A. Freakes, Kingfisher Court, Bridge Road, East Molesey, Surrey KT8 9HL Tel: 0181 941 0604

Historic Commercial Vehicle Society (HCVS), Iden Grange, Cranbrook Road, Staplehurst, Kent TN12 0ET

Historic Lotus Register, Nyes Place, Newdigate, Surrey RH5 5BX Tel: 01737 767371/01293 871541

Historic Rally Car Register RAC, Martin Jubb, 38 Longfield Road, Bristol, Avon BS7 9AG

Historic Sports Car Club, Cold Harbour, Kington Langley, Wiltshire SN15 5LY

Historic Volkswagen Club, 11a Thornbury Lane Church Hill, Redditch, Hereford & Worcester B98 7RP Tel: 01527 591883

Holden UK Register, G. R. C. Hardy, Clun Felin, Woll's Castle, Haverfordwest, Pembrokeshire, Dyfed, Wales SA62 5LR

Honda S800 Sports Car Club, Chris Wallwork, 23a High Street, Steeton, Yorkshire BD20 6NT Tel: 01535 653845

Hotchkiss Association GB, Michael Edwards, Wootton Tops, Sandy Lane, Boars Hill, Oxford, Oxfordshire OX1 5HN Tel: 01865 735180

HRG Association, I J. Dussek, Little Allens, Allens Lane, Plaxtol, Sevenoaks, Kent TN15 0QZ

Humber Register, R. N. Arman, Northbrook Cottage, 175 York Road, Broadstone, Dorset BH18 8ES

Imp Club, Michelle Ross, 71 Evesham Road, Stratford-upon-Avon, Warwickshire CV37 9BA Tel: 01789 204778

Isetta Owners Club, 19 Towcester Road, Old Stratford, Milton Keynes, Buckinghamshire MK19 6AH Tel: 01908 569103

Jaguar Car Club, R. Pugh, 19 Eldorado Crescent, Cheltenham, Gloucestershire GL50 2PY

Jaguar Drivers Club, Jaguar House, Stuart Street, Luton, Bedfordshire LU1 2SL Tel: 01582 419332

Jaguar Enthusiasts Club, 176 Whittington Way, Pinner, Middlesex HA5 5JY Tel: 0181 866 2073

Jaguar/Daimler Owners Club, 130/132 Bordesley Green, Birmingham, West Midlands B9 4SU

Jensen Owners Club, Caroline Clarke, 45 Station Road, Stoke Mandeville, Buckinghamshire HP22 5UE Tel: 01296 614072

Jensen Owners Club, Brian Morrey, Selwood, Howley, Nr Chard, Somerset Tel: 01460 64165

Jowett Car Club, Ian Preistly, Membership Secretary, 626 Huddersfield Road, Wyke, Bradford, Yorkshire BD12 8JR

Junior Zagato Register, Kenfield Hall, Petham, Nr Canterbury, Kent CT4 5RN Tel: 01227 700555

Jupiter Owners Auto Club, Steve Keil, 16 Empress Avenue, Woodford Green, Essex IG8 9EA Tel: 0181 505 2215

Karmann Ghia Owners Club, Astrid Kelly (Membership Secretary), 7 Keble Road, Maidenhead, Berkshire SL6 6BB Tel: 01628 39185

Kieft Racing and Sports Car Club, Duncan Rabagliati, 4 Wool Road, Wimbledon, London SW20 0HW

Lagonda Club, Colin Bugler (Hon Secretary), Wintney House, London Road, Hartley Wintney, Hampshire RG27 8RN Tel: & Fax 01252 845451

Lancia Motor Club, Dave Baker (Membership Secretary), Mount Pleasant, Penrhos, Brymbo, Wrexham, Clwyd, Wales LL11 5LY

Land Rover Register (1947–1951), Membership Secretary, High House, Ladbrooke, Leamington Spa, Warwickshire CV33 0BT

Land Rover Series One Club, David Bowyer, East Foldhay, Zeal Monachorum, Crediton, Devon

Land Rover Series Two Club, P O Box 1609, Yatton, Bristol, Avon

Landcrab Owners Club International, Bill Frazer, PO Box 218, Cardiff, Wales

Landrover Series 3 Owners Club Ltd, 23 Deidre Avenue, Wickford, Essex SS12 0AX Tel: 01268 560818

Lea Francis Owners Club, R. Sawers, French's, High Street, Long Wittenham, Abingdon, Oxfordshire OX14 4QQ

Les Amis de Panhard et Levassor GB, Denise Polley, 11 Arterial Avenue, Rainham, Essex RM13 9PD

Lincoln-Zephyr Owners Club, Colin Spong, 22 New North Road, Hainault, Ilford, Essex IG6 2XG

London Bus Preservation Trust, Cobham Bus Museum, Redhill Road, Cobham, Surrey KT11 1EF

London Vintage Taxi Association, Steve Dimmock, 51 Ferndale Crescent, Cowley, Uxbridge, Berkshire UB8 2AY

Lotus Cortina Register, Fernleigh, Hornash Lane, Shadoxhurst, Ashford, Kent TN26 1HX

Lotus Drivers Club, Lee Barton, 15 Pleasant Way, Leamington Spa, Warwickshire CV32 5XA Tel: 01926 313514

Lotus Seven Owners Club, David Miryless, 18 St James, Beaminster, Dorset DT8 3PW

Malaysia & Singapore Vintage Car Register, 2 Asimont Lane, Singapore 1130

Manta A Series Register, Mark Kinnon, 112 Northwood Avenue, Purley, Surrey, CR8 2EQ

Marcos Owners Club, 62 Culverley Road, Catford, London SE6 2LA Tel: 0181 697 2988

Marendaz Special Car Register, John Shaw, 107 Old Bath Road, Cheltenham, Gloucestershire GL53 7DA Tel: 01242 526310

Marina/Ital Drivers Club, Mr J G Lawson, 12 Nithsdale Road, Liverpool, Merseyside L15 5AX

Marlin Owners Club, Mrs J. Cordrey, 14 Farthings Went, Capel St Mary, Ipswich, Suffolk IP9 2UJ

Maserati Club, Michael Miles, The Paddock, Old Salisbury Road, Abbotts Ann, Andover, Hampshire SP11 7N Tel: 01264 710312

Masters Club, Barry Knight, 2 Ranmore Avenue, East Croydon, Surrey CR0 5QA

Matra Enthusiasts Club, MEC, 19 Abbotsbury, Orton Goldhay, Peterborough, Cambridgeshire PE2 5PS Tel: 01733 234555

Mercedes-Benz Club Ltd, P. Bellamy, 75 Theydon Grove, Epping, Essex CM16 4PE Tel: 01992 573304

Messerschmitt Enthusiasts Club, Mrs Brenda Anstey, 10 Litchaton Way, Plymouth, Devon PL7 4RD Tel: 01752 339022

Messerschmitt Owners Club, Mrs Eileen Hallam, Birches, Ashmores Lane, Rusper, Sussex RH12 4PS Tel: 01293 871417

Metropolitan Owners' Club, Nick Savage, The Old Pump House, Nutbourne Common, Pulborough, Sussex RH20 2HB Tel: 01798 813713

MG Car Club, 7 Chequer Lane, Ash, Canterbury, Kent CT3 2ET Tel: 01304 240380/01304 813863

MG Octagon Car Club, Unit 19, Hollins Business Centre, Rowley Street, Stafford, Staffordshire ST16 2RH Tel: 01785 251014

MG Owners Club, Octagon House, Swavesey, Cambridgeshire CB4 5QZ Tel: 01954 231125

MG 'Y' Type Register, Mr J. G. Lawson, 12 Nithsdale Road, Liverpool, Merseyside L15 5AX

Midget & Sprite Club, Nigel Williams, 15 Foxcote, Kingswood, Bristol, Avon BS15 2TX

Mini Cooper Club, Joyce Holman, 1 Weavers Cottages, Church Hill, West Hoathly, Sussex RH19 4PW

Mini Cooper Register, 141 Church Lane, Cheshunt, Hertfordshire EN8 0DX Tel: 01992 627863

Mini Marcos Owners Club, Roger Garland, 28 Meadow Road, Worcester, Hereford & Worcester WR3 7PP Tel: 01905 58533

Mini Moke Club, Paul Beard, 13 Ashdene Close, Hartlebury, Hereford & Worcester DY11 7TN

Mini Owners Club, 15 Birchwood Road, Lichfield, Staffordshire WS14 9UN

MKI Consul, Zephyr and Zodiac Club, 180 Gypsy Road, Welling, Kent DA16 1JQ Tel: 0181 301 3709

MkI Cortina Owners Club, R. J. Raisey, 51 Studley Rise, Trowbridge, Wiltshire BA14 0PD

MkII Consul, Zephyr and Zodiac Club, 170 Conisborough Crescent, Catford, London SE6 2SH

MkII Granada Owners Club, 58 Jevington Way, Lee, London SE12 9NQ Tel: 0181 857 4356

Model A Ford Club of Great Britain, Mr S. J. Shepherd, 32 Portland Street, Clifton, Bristol, Avon BS8 4JB Tel: 0117 973 9355

Morgan Sports Car Club Ltd, Mrs Christine Healey (Registrar), 41 Cordwell Close, Castle Donington, Derby, Derbyshire DE74 2JL

Morgan Three-Wheeler Club Ltd, K. Robinson, Correction Farm, Middlewood Road, Poynton, Stockport, Cheshire SK12 1TX

Morris 12 Club, D Hedge, Crossways, Potton Road, Hilton, Huntingdon, Cambridgeshire PE18 9NG

Morris Cowley and Oxford Club, Derek Andrews, 202 Chantry Gardens, Southwick, Trowbridge, Wiltshire BA14 9QX.

Morris Marina Owners Club, Nigel Butler, Llys-Aled, 63 Junction Road, Stourbridge, West Midlands DY8 4YJ

Morris Minor Owners Club, Jane White, 127-129 Green Lane, Derby, Derbyshire DE1 1RZ

Morris Register, Greenstones, 205 Main Road, Great Leighs, Chelmsford, Essex CM3 1NS Tel: 01245 361517

Moss Owners Club, David Pegler, Pinewood, Weston Lane, Bath, Avon BA1 4AG Tel: 01225 331509

Naylor Car Club, John W. Taylor (Secretary), c/o Naylor Brothers Restoration, Airedale Garage, Hollins Hill, Shipley, Yorkshire BD17 7QN

North East Club for Pre War Austins, Tom Gatenby, 9 Townsend Crescent, Morpeth, Northumberland NE61 2XW

North London MG Club, 2 Duckett Road, Harringey, London N4 1BN Tel: 0181 366 6655/0181 341 7436

Nova Owners Club, Ray Nicholls, 19 Bute Avenue, Hathershaw, Oldham, Lancashire OL8 2AQ

NSU Owners Club, Rosemarie Crowley, 58 Tadorne Road, Tadworth, Surrey KT20 5TF Tel: 01737 812412

Ogle Register, Chris Gow, 108 Potters Lane, Burgess Hill, Sussex RH15 9JN Tel: 01444 248439

Old Bean Society, PP Cole, 165 Denbigh Drive, Hately Heath, West Bromwich, West Midlands B71 2SP

Opel GT UK Owners Club, Dean Hayes, 11 Thrale Way, Parkwood, Rainham, Kent ME8 9LX Tel: 01634 379065

Opel Manta Owners Club, 14 Rockstowes Way, Bristol, Avon BS10 6JE

Opel Vauxhall Drivers Club, The Old Mill, Dereham, Norfolk NR20 5RT

Panther Car Club, George Newell (Secretary), 91 Fleet Road, Farnborough, Hants GU14 9RE Tel: 01252 540217

Pedal Car Collectors Club, c/o A. P. Gayler, 4-4a Chapel Terrace Mews, Kemp Town, Brighton, Sussex, BN2 1HU Tel: 01273 601960

Piper (Sports and Racing Car) Club, Clive Davies, Pipers Oak, Lopham Rd, East Harling, Norfolk, NR16 2PE Tel: 01953 717813

Porsche Club Great Britain, Robin Walker, c/o Cornbury House, Cotswold Business Village, London Road, Moreton-in-Marsh, Glos GL56 0JQ Tel: 01608 652911/01296 688760

Post 45 Group, Mr R Cox, 6 Nile Street, Norwich, Norfolk NR2 4JU

Post Office Vehicle Club, 7 Bignal Rand Close, Wells, Somerset BA5 2EE

Post War Thoroughbred Car Club, 87 London Street, Chertsey, Surrey KT16 8AN

Post-Vintage Humber Car Club, 32 Walsh Crescent, New Addington, Croydon, Surrey CR0 0BX Tel: 01689 849851

Potteries Vintage and Classic Car Club, B. Theobald, 78 Reeves Avenue, Cross Heath, Newcastle, Staffs ST5 9LA

Pre-1940 Triumph Owners Club, Jon Quiney, 2 Duncroft Close, Reigate, Surrey RH2 9DE

Pre-67 Ford Owners Club, Mrs A. Miller, 100 Main Street, Cairneyhill, Dumfermline, Scotland KY12 8QU

Pre-War Austin Seven Club Ltd, Mr J. Tatum, 90 Dovedale Avenue, Long Eaton, Nottingham G10 3HU Tel: 0115 972 7626

Pre-50 American Auto Club, Alan Murphy, 41 Eastham Rake, Wirral, Merseyside L62 9AN Tel: 0151 327 1392

Radford Register, Chris Gow, 108 Potters Lane, Burgess Hill, Sussex RH15 9JN Tel: 01444 248439

Range Rover Register, Chris Tomley, Cwm/Cochen, Bettws, Newtown, Powys, Wales SY16 3LQ

Rapier Register, D. C. H. Williams, Smithy, Tregynon, Newtown, Powys, Wales SY16 3EH Tel: 01686 650396

Rear Engine Renault Club, R. Woodall, 346 Crewe Road, Cresty, Crewe, Cheshire CW2 5AD

Register of Unusual Micro-Cars, Jean Hammond, School House Farm, Hawkenbury, Staplehurst, Kent TN12 0EB

Reliant Owners Club, Graham Close, 19 Smithey Close, High Green, Sheffield, Yorkshire S30 4FQ

Reliant Sabre and Scimitar Owners Club, PO Box 67, Teddington, Middx TW11 8QR Tel: 0181 977 6625

Renault Frères, J. G. Kemsley, Yew Tree House, Jubliee Road, Chelsfield, Kent BR6 7QZ

Renault Owners Club, C. Marsden, Chevin House, Main Street, Burley-in-Wharfedale, Ilkley, Yorkshire LS29 7DT Tel: 01943 862700

Riley Motor Club, 37 Gibbon Road, Acton, London W3 7AF Tel: 0181 743 9585

Riley Register, J. A. Clarke, 56 Cheltenham Road, Bishops Cleeve, Cheltenham, Glos GL52 4LY

Riley RM Club, Mrs Jacque Manders, Y Fachell, Ruthin Road, Gwernymynydd, Mold, Clwyd, Wales CH7 5LQ

Ro80 Club GB, Simon Kremer, Mill Stone Cottage, Woodside Road, Winkfield, Windsor, Berkshire SL4 2DP Tel: 01344 890411

Rochdale Owners Club, Brian Tomlinson, 57 West Avenue, Birmingham, West Midlands B20 2LU

Rolls-Royce Enthusiasts' Club, Peter Baines, The Hunt House, Paulerspury, Northamptonshire NN12 7NA

Ronart Car Club, Simon Sutton (Membership Secretary), Orchard Cottage, Allan Lane, Fritchley, Derbyshire DE56 2FX Tel: 01773 856901

Ronart Drivers Club, Chalk Dell House, Batchworth Hill, London Road, Rickmansworth, Herts WD3 1JP Tel: 0171 722 1212/01923 779966

Rootes Easidrive Register, M. Molley, 35 Glenesk Road, London SE9 1AG

Rover P4 Drivers Guild, 54 Ingaway, Lee Chapel South, Basildon, Essex SS16 5QR Tel: 01268 413395

Rover P5 Owners Club, G. Moorshead, 13 Glen Avenue, Ashford, Middx TW15 2JE Tel: 01784 258166

Rover P6 Owners Club, PO Box 11, Heanor, Derbyshire DE75 7YG

Rover SD1 Club, PO Box 12, Owlsmoor, Sandhurst, Berkshire GU47 4WZ Tel: 01344 761791

Rover Sports Register, Cliff Evans, 8 Hilary Close, Great Boughton, Chester, Cheshire CH3 5QP

Saab Enthusiasts Club, PO Box 96, Harrow, Middx HA3 7DW Tel: 01249 815792

Saab Owners Club of GB Ltd, Mrs K. E. Piper, 16 Denewood Close, Watford, Herts WD1 3SZ Tel: 01923 229945

Salmons Tickford Enthusiasts Club, Keith Griggs, 40 Duffins Orchard, Ottershaw, Surrey KT16 0LP

Savage Register, Trevor Smith, Hillcrest, Top Road, Little Cawthorpe, Louth, Lincolnshire LN11 8NB

Scimitar Drivers Club, c/o Mick Frost, Pegasus Main Road, Woodham Ferrers, Essex CM3 8RN Tel: 01245 320734

Scootacar Register, Stephen Boyd, Pamanste, 18 Holman Close, Aylsham, Norwich, Norfolk NR11 6DD Tel: 01263 733861

Simca Owners Register, David Chapman, 18 Cavendish Gardens, Redhill, Surrey RH1 4AQ

Singer Owners Club, 3 Riverhill, Watton-at-Stone, Herts SG14 3SD Tel: 01920 830517

Skoda Owners Club of Great Britain, Ray White, 78 Montague Road, Leytonstone, London E11 3EN

Small Ford Club, 115 Woodland Gardens, Isleworth, Middx TW7 6LU Tel: 0181 568 3227

Solent Austin Seven Club Ltd, F. Claxton, 185 Warsash Road, Warsash Hants SO31 9JE

South Devon Commercial Vehicle Club, Bob Gale, Avonwick Station, Diptford, Totnes, Devon TQ9 7LU Tel: 01364 73130

South Hants Model Auto Club, C Derbyshire, 21 Aintree Road, Calmore, Southampton, Hants SO40 2TL

South Wales Austin Seven Club, Mr and Mrs J. Neill, 302 Peniel Green Road, Peniel Green, Swansea, Wales SA7 9BW

Spartan Owners Club, Steve Andrews, 28 Ashford Drive, Ravenhead, Notts NG15 9DE Tel: 01623 793742

Sporting Escort Owners Club, 26 Huntingdon Crescent, Off Madresfield Drive, Halesowen, West Mids B63 3DJ

Stag Owners Club, 4 Channel Close, Folkestone, Kent CT19 6QN Tel: 01303 241090/01303 252941

Standard Motor Club, 12 Majors Close, Chedburgh, Bury St Edmunds, Suffolk IP29 4U Tel: 01284 850896

Star, Starling, Stuart and Briton Register, D. E. A. Evans, New Wood Lodge, 2A Hyperion Rd, Stourton, Stourbridge, West Midlands DY7 6SB

Sunbeam Alpine Owners Club, Pauline Leese, 53 Wood Street, Mow Cop, Stoke-on-Trent, Staffs ST7 3PF Tel: 01782 519865

Sunbeam Rapier Owners Club, Peter Meech, 12 Greenacres, Downton, Salisbury, Wiltshire SP5 3NG Tel: 01725 21140

Sunbeam Talbot Alpine Register, Derek Cook, Membership Secretary, 47 Crescent Wood Road, Sydenham, London SE26 6SA

Sunbeam Talbot Darracq Register, R. Lawson, West Emlett Cottage, Black Dog, Crediton, Devon EX17 4QB

Sunbeam Tiger Owners Club, Brian Postle, Beechwood, 8 Villa Real Estate, Consett, Co Durham DH8 6BJ Tel: 01207 508296

Surrey Classic Vehicle Club, 55a Ditton Road, Surbiton, Surrey KT6 6RF Tel: 0181 390 3570

Swift Club and Swift Register, John Harrison, 70 Eastwick Drive, Bookham, Leatherhead, Surrey KT23 3NX Tel: 01372 452120

Tame Valley Vintage and Classic Car Club, Mrs S. Ogden, 13 Valley New Road, Royton, Oldham, Lancashire OL2 6BP

Tornado Register, Dave Malins, 48 St Monica's Avenue, Luton, Bedfordshire LU3 1PN Tel: 01582 37641

Toyota Enthusiasts Club, c/o Billy Wells (Secretary & Treasurer), 28 Park Road, Feltham, Middlesex TW13 6PW Tel: 0181 898 0740

TR Drivers Club, Bryan Harber, 19 Irene Road, Orpington, Kent BR6 0HA

TR Register, 1B Hawksworth, Southmead Industrial Park, Didcot, Oxfordshire OX10 7HR Tel: 01235 818866

Traction Enthusiasts Club, Preston House Studio, Preston, Canterbury, Kent CT3 1HH

Traction Owners Club, Peter Riggs, 2 Appleby Gardens, Dunstable, Bedfordshire LU6 3DB

Trident Car Club, Ken Morgan, Rose Cottage, 45 Newtown Rd, Verwood, Dorset BH31 6EG Tel: 01202 822697

Triumph 2000/2500/2.5 Register, M. Aldous, 42 Hall Orchards, Middleton, King's Lynn, Norfolk PE32 1RY Tel: 01553 841700

Triumph Dolomite Club, 39 Mill Lane, Upper Arncott, Bicester, Oxfordshire OX6 0PB Tel: 01869 242847

Triumph Mayflower Club, T. Gordon, 12 Manor Close, Hoghton, Preston, Lancashire PR5 0EN

Triumph Razoredge Owners Club, Stewart Langton, 62 Seaward Avenue, Barton-on-Sea, Hampshire BH25 7HP Tel: 01425 618074

Triumph Roadster Club, Paul Hawkins, 186 Mawnay Road, Romford, Essex RM7 8BU Tel: 01708 760745

Triumph Spitfire Club, Mr Cor Gent, Anemoon 41, 7483 AC Haaksbergen, Netherlands.

Triumph Sporting Owners Club, G. R. King, 16 Windsor Road, Hazel Grove, Stockport, Cheshire SK7 4SW

Triumph Sports Six Club Ltd, 121B St Mary's Road, Market Harborough, Leicestershire LE16 7DT

Trojan Owners Club, Derrick Graham, Troylands, St Johns, Earlswood Common, Redhill, Surrey RH1 6QF Tel: 01737 763643

Turner Register, Dave Scott, 21 Ellsworth Road, High Wycombe, Buckinghamshire HP11 2TU

TVR Car Club, c/o David Gerald, TVR Sports Cars, Hereford & Worcester Tel: 01386 793239

UK Buick Club, Alf Gascoine, 47 Higham Road, Woodford Green, Essex IG8 9JN Tel: 0181 505 7347

United States Army Vehicle Club, Dave Boocock, 31 Valley View Close, Bogthorn, Oakworth Rd, Keighley, Yorkshire BD22 7LZ

Vanden Plas Owners Club, Old School House, Sutterton Drove, Amber Hill, Boston, Lincolnshire PE20 3RQ Tel: 01205 290436

Vanguard 1&2 Owners Club, R. Jones, The Villa, The Down, Alviston, Avon BS12 2TQ Tel: 01454 419232

Vauxhall Cavalier Convertible Club, Ron Goddard, 47 Brooklands Close, Luton, Bedfordshire LU4 9EH

Vauxhall Owners Club, Roy Childers (Membership Secretary), 31 Greenbanks, Melbourn, Nr Royston, Cambridgeshire SG8 6AS

Vauxhall PA/PB/PC/E Owners Club, G. Lonsdale, 77 Pilling Lane, Preesall, Lancashire FY6 0HB Tel: 01253 810866

Vauxhall VX4/90 Drivers Club, c/o 43 Stroudwater Park, Weybridge, Surrey KT13 0DT

Vectis Historic Vehicle Club, 10 Paddock Drive, Bembridge, Isle of Wight PO35 5TL

Veteran Car Club Of Great Britain, Jessamine Court, High Street, Ashwell, Baldock, Hertfordshire SG7 5NL Tel: 01462 742818

Victor 101 FC (1964–1967), 12 Cliff Crescent, Ellerdine, Telford, Shropshire TF6 6QS

Vintage Austin Register, Frank Smith, The Briars, Four Lane Ends, Oakerthorpe, Alfreton, Derbyshire DE5 7LN Tel: 0773 831646

Vintage Sports Car Club Ltd, The Secretary, 121 Russell Road, Newbury, Berkshire RG14 5JX Tel: 01635 44411

Viva Owners Club, Adrian Miller, The Thatches, Snetterton North End, Snetterton, Norwich, Norfolk NR16 2LD

Volkswagen '50-67' Transporter Club, Peter Nicholson, 11 Lowton Road, Lytham St Annes, Lancashire FY8 3JD Tel: 01253 720023

Volkswagen Cabriolet Owners Club (GB), Emma Palfreyman (Sec), Dishley Mill, Derby Road, Loughborough, Leicestershire LE11 0SF

Volkswagen Owners Caravan Club (GB), Mrs Shirley Oxley, 18 Willow Walk, Hockley, Essex SS5 5DQ

Volkswagen Owners Club (GB), PO Box 7, Burntwood, Walsall, West Midlands WS7 8SB

Volkswagen Split Screen Van Club, Brian Hobson, 12 Kirkfield Crescent, Thorner, Leeds, Yorkshire LS14 3EN

Volvo Enthusiasts Club, Kevin Price, 4 Goonbell, St Agnes, Cornwall TR5 0PH

Volvo Owners Club, North View, Broadmoor Road, Carbrooke, Thetford, Norfolk IP25 6SZ Tel: 01953 885591

Vulcan Register, D. Hales, The Hedgerows, Sutton St Nicholas, Hereford & Worcester HR1 3BU Tel: 01432 880726

VW Type 3 and 4 Club, Jane Terry, Pear Tree Bungalow, Exted, Elham, Canterbury, Kent CT4 6YG

Wanderers (Pre-War Austin Sevens), D. Tedham, Newhouse Frm, Baveney Wood, Cleobury, Mortimer, Kidderminster, Hereford & Worcester DY14 8JB

Wartburg Owners Club, Bernard Trevena, 55 Spiceall Estate, Compton, Guildford, Surrey GU3 Tel: 01483 810493

Wolseley 6/80 and Morris Oxford Club, John Billinger, 67 Fleetgate, Barton-on-Humber, Lincolnshire DN18 5QD Tel: 01652 635138

Wolseley Hornet Special Club, S. Ellin, The Poppies, 9 Cole Mead, Bruton, Somerset BA10 0DL

Wolseley Register, M. Stanley (Chairman), 1 Flashgate, Higher Ramsgreave Road, Ramsgreave, Nr Blackburn, Lancashire BB1 9DH

X/19 Owners Club, Sally Shearman, 86 Mill Lane, Dorridge, Solihull, West Midlands B93 8NU

XR Owners Club, Paul Townend, 50 Wood Street, Castleford, Yorkshire WF10 1LJ

XR Owners CLub, 20a Swithland Lane, Rothley, Leicestershire LE7 7SE

Yankee Jeep Club, 8 Chew Brook Drive, Greenfield, Saddleworth, Lancashire OL3 7PD

Yorkshire Thoroughbred Car Club, Bob Whalley, 31 Greenside, Walton, Wakefield, Yorkshire WF2 6NN

Zephyr and Zodiac Mk IV Owners Club, Richard Cordle, 29 Ruskin Drive, Worcester Park, Surrey KT4 8LG Tel: 0181 330 2159

DIRECTORY OF AUCTIONEERS

Academy Auctioneers & Valuers, Northcote House, Northcote Avenue, Ealing, London W5 3UR Tel: 0181 579 7466

Aylesbury Motor Auctions, Pembroke Road, Stocklake, Aylesbury, Buckinghamshire HP20 1DB Tel: 01296 339150

British Car Auctions Ltd, Classic & Historic Automobile Division, Auction Centre, Blackbushe Airport, Blackwater, Camberley, Surrey GU17 9LG Tel: 01252 878555

Brooks, 81 Clapham Common Westside, London SW4 9AY Tel: 0171 228 8000

C. Boisgirard, 2 Rue de Provence, Paris, France 75009 Tel: 010 33 147708136

Central Motor Auctions plc, Central House, Pontefract Road, Rothwell, Leeds, Yorkshire LS26 0JE Tel: 01532 820707

Chapman, Moore & Mugford, 9 High Street, Shaftesbury, Dorset SP7 8JB Tel: 01747 852400

H. C. Chapman & Son, The Auction Mart, North Street, Scarborough, Yorkshire YO11 1DL Tel: 01723 372424

Christie Manson & Woods International Inc, 502 Park Avenue, (including Christie's East), New York, NY 10022, USA Tel: (212) 546 1000

Christie, Manson & Woods Ltd, 8 King Street, St James's, London SW1Y 6QT Tel: 0171 839 9060

Christie's (Monaco), SAM, Park Palace, Monte Carlo 98000 Tel: 00 337 9325 1933

Christie's Pty Ltd, 1 Darling Street, South Yarra, Melbourne, Victoria, Australia 3141 Tel: 010 613 820 4311

Christie's South Kensington Ltd, 85 Old Brompton Road, London SW7 3LD Tel: 0171 581 7611

Classic Automobile Auctions BV, Goethestrasse 10, 6000 Frankfurt 1, Germany Tel: 010 49 69 28666/8

Coys of Kensington, 2/4 Queens Gate Mews, London SW7 5QJ Tel: 0171 584 7444

Dickinson Davy and Markham, Wrawby Street, Brigg, Humberside DN20 8JJ Tel: 01652 653666

David Dockree, Cheadle Hulme Business Centre, Clemence House, Mellor Road, Cheadle Hulme, Cheshire SK7 1BD Tel: 0161 485 1258

Dreweatt Neate Holloways, 49 Parsons Street, Banbury, Oxon OX16 8PF Tel: 01295 253197

Eccles Auctions, Unit 4, 25 Gwydir Street, Cambridge CB1 2LG Tel: 01223 561518

Evans & Partridge, Agriculture House, High Street, Stockbridge, Hampshire SO20 6HF Tel: 01264 810702

Greens (UK) Ltd, Hereford & Worcester WR14 2AY Tel: 01684 575902

H & H Classic Auctions Ltd, 134 Roseneath Road, Urmston, Greater Manchester M41 5AZ Tel: 0161 747 0561

Hamptons Antique & Fine Art Auctioneers, 93 High Street, Godalming, Surrey GU7 1AL Tel: 01483 423567

Andrew Hartley, Victoria Hall Salerooms, Little Lane, Ilkley, Yorkshire LS29 8EA Tel: 01943 816363

Kidson Trigg, Estate Office, Friars Farm, Sevenhampton, Highworth, Swindon, Wiltshire SN6 7PZ Tel: 01793 861000

Kruse International, PO Box 190, 5400 County Road 11A, Auburn, Indiana, 46706 USA Tel: 219 925 5600

Lambert & Foster, 77 Commercial Road, Paddock Wood, Kent TN12 6DR Tel: 01892 832325

Lawrences Auctioneers, Norfolk House, 80 High Street, Bletchingley, Surrey RH1 4PA Tel: 01883 743323

Thomas Mawer & Son, The Lincoln Saleroom, 63 Monks Road, Lincoln, Lincolnshire LN2 5HP Tel: 01522 524984

Morphets of Harrogate, 6 Albert Street, Harrogate, Yorkshire HG1 1JL Tel: 01423 530030

Neales, 192-194 Mansfield Road, Nottingham, Nottinghamshire NG1 3HU Tel: 0115 962 4141

Onslow's, The Old Depot, The Gas Works, off Michael Road, London SW6 2AD Tel: 0171 371 0505

Orion Auction House, Victoria Bdg 13, Bd. Princess Charlotte, Monte Carlo, Monaco Tel: 010 3393 301669

Palmer Snell, 65 Cheap Street, Sherborne, Dorset DT9 3BA Tel: 01935 812218

Parkes Auctions Ltd, 2/4 Station Road, Swavesey, Cambridgeshire CB4 5QJ Tel: 01954 232332

J. R. Parkinson Son & Hamer Auctions, The Auction Rooms, Rochdale Road (Kershaw Street), Bury, Lancashire BL9 7HH Tel: 0161 761 1612/761 7372

Paul McInnis Inc, Auction Gallery, Route 88, 356 Exeter Road, Hampton Falls, New Hampshire, 03844, USA Tel: 010 603 778 8989

Phillips, Blenstock House, 101 New Bond Street, London W1Y 0AS Tel: 0171 629 6602

Rogers Jones & Co, The Saleroom, 33 Abergele Road, Colwyn Bay, Wales LL29 7RU Tel: 01492 532176

Martyn Rowe, The Truro Auction Centre, Calenick Street, Truro, Cornwall TR1 2SG Tel: 01892 260020

RTS Auctions Ltd, 35 Primula Drive, Eaton, Norwich, Norfolk NR4 7LZ Tel: 01603 505718

Silver Collector Car Auctions, E204, Spokane, Washington, USA 99207 Tel: 0101 509 326 4485

Sotheby's, 34-35 New Bond Street, London W1A 2AA Tel: 0171 493 8080

Sotheby's, 1334 York Avenue, New York, NY 10021, USA Tel: 212 606 7000

Sotheby's, B.P. 45, Le Sporting d'Hiver, Place du Casino, Monaco/Cedex MC 98001 Tel: 0101 3393 30 88 80

Sotheby's Sussex, Summers Place, Billingshurst, Sussex RH14 9AD Tel: 01403 783933

Sotheby's Zurich, Bleicherweg 20, Zurich, Switzerland CH-8022 Tel: 41 (1) 202 0011

Specialised Postcard Auctions, 25 Gloucester Street, Cirencester, Gloucestershire GL7 2DJ Tel: 01285 659057

Henry Spencer & Sons (Phillips), 20 The Square, Retford, Nottinghamshire DN22 6BX Tel: 01777 708633

G. E. Sworder & Sons, 14 Cambridge Road, Stansted Mountfitchet, Essex CM24 8BZ Tel: 01279 817778

The Auction, 3535 Las Vegas Boulevard, South Las Vegas, Nevada, USA 89101 Tel: 0101 702 794 3174

Thimbleby & Shorland, 31 Great Knollys Street, Reading, Berkshire RG1 7HU Tel: 01734 508611

Walker, Barnett & Hill, 3/5 Waterloo Road Salerooms, Clarence Street, Wolverhampton, West Midlands WV1 4JE Tel: 01902 773531

Welsh Bridge Salerooms, Welsh Bridge, Shrewsbury, Shropshire SY3 8LH Tel: 01743 231212

Wintertons Ltd, Lichfield Auction Centre, Wood End Lane, Fradley, Lichfield, Staffordshire WS13 8NF Tel: 01543 263256

World Classic Auction & Exposition Co, 3600 Blackhawk Plaza Circle, Danville, California 94506, USA

DIRECTORY OF MUSEUMS

AVON

Bristol Industrial Museum,
Princes Wharf, City Docks, Bristol BS1 4RN
Tel: 0117 925 1470

BEDFORDSHIRE

Shuttleworth Collection, Old Warden
Aerodrome, Nr Biggleswade SG18 9EP
Tel: 01767 627288

BUCKINGHAMSHIRE

West Wycombe Motor Museum,
Cockshoot Farm, Chorley Road,
High Wycombe, West Wycombe HP14 3AR

CHESHIRE

Mouldsworth Motor Museum, Smithy
Lane, Mouldsworth, Chester CH3 8AR
Tel: 01928 731781

COUNTY DURHAM

North of England Open Air Museum,
Beamish, Stanley DH9 0RG

CORNWALL

Automobilia Motor Museum,
The Old Mill, Terras Road, St Stephen,
St Austell PL26 7RX

CUMBRIA

Cars of the Stars Motor Museum,
Standish Street, Keswick CA12 5LS
Tel: 01768 73757

Lakeland Motor Museum, Holker Hall,
Cark-in-Cartmel, Nr Grange-over-Sands
LA11 7SS Tel: 01448 53314

DERBYSHIRE

The Donnington Collection, Donnington
Park, Castle Donnington DE74 2RP
Tel: 01332 810048

DEVON

Totnes Motor Museum, Steamer Quay,
Totnes TT9 5AL Tel: 01803 862777

ESSEX

Ford Historic Car Collection,
Ford Motor Co, Eagle Way, Brentwood
CM13 3BW

GLOUCESTERSHIRE

The Bugatti Trust, Prescott Hill,
Gotherington, Cheltenham GL52 4RD
Tel: 01242 677201

Cotswold Motor Museum,
Sherbourne Street, Bourton-on-the-Water,
Nr Cheltenham GL54 2BY
Tel: 01451 821255

GREATER MANCHESTER

Manchester Museum of Transport,
Boyle Street M8 8UW

HAMPSHIRE

Gangbridge Collection, Gangbridge
House, St Mary Bourne, Andover SP11 6EP

National Motor Museum,
Brockenhurst, Beaulieu SO42 7ZN
Tel: 01590 612123/612345

HUMBERSIDE

Bradford Industrial Museum, Moorside
Mills, Moorside Road, Bradford BD2 3HP
Tel: 01274 631756

Hull Transport Museum,
36 High Street, Hull HU1 1NQ

Museum of Army Transport,
Flemingate, Beverley HU17 0NG
Tel: 01482 860445

Peter Black Collection,
Lawkholme Lane, Keighley BD21 3BB

Sandtoft Transport Centre,
Sandtoft, Nr Doncaster DN8 5SX

KENT

Dover Transport Museum,
Old Park, Whitfield, Dover CT16 2HL

**Historic Vehicles Collection of
C. M. Booth**, Falstaff Antiques,
63-67 High Street, Rolvenden TN17 4LP
Tel: 01580 241234

The Motor Museum, Dargate,
Nr Faversham ME13 9EP

Ramsgate Motor Museum,
West Cliff Hall, Ramsgate CT11 9JX
Tel: 01843 581948

LANCASHIRE

British Commercial Vehicles Museum,
King Street, Leyland, Preston PR5 1LE
Tel: 01772 451011

Bury Transport Museum,
Castlecroft Road, off Bolton Street, Bury

Tameside Transport Collection,
Warlow Brook, Friezland Lane,
Greenfield, Oldham OL3 7EU

LONDON

British Motor Industry Heritage Trust,
Syon Park, Brentford

Science Museum, Exhibition Road,
South Kensington SW7 2DD
Tel: 0171 589 3456

NORFOLK

Caister Castle Car Collection,
Caister-on-Sea, Nr Great Yarmouth

NOTTINGHAMSHIRE

Nottingham Industrial Museum,
Courtyard Buildings, Wallaton Park

SHROPSHIRE

Midland Motor Museum, Stanmore Hall, Stourbridge Road, Bridgnorth WV15 6DT Tel: 01746 762992

SOMERSET

Haynes Sparkford Motor Museum, Sparkford, Yeovil BA22 7LH Tel: 01963 440804

SURREY

Brooklands Museum, The Clubhouse, Brooklands Road, Weybridge KT13 0QN Tel: 01932 857381

Dunsfold Land Rover Museum, Dunsfold GU8 4NP Tel: 01483 200567

SUSSEX

Bentley Motor Museum, Bentley Wild Fowl Trust, Harvey's Lane, Ringmer, Lewes BN8 5AF

Foulkes-Halbard of Filching, Filching Manor, Filching, Wannock, Polegate BN26 5QA Tel: 01323 487838

TYNE & WEAR

Newburn Hall Motor Museum, 35 Townfield Garden, Newburn NE15 8PY

WARWICKSHIRE

Heritage Motor Centre, Banbury Road, Gaydon CV35 0YT Tel: 01926 645040

Museum of British Road Transport, St Agnes Lane, Hales Street, Coventry CV1 1PN Tel: 01203 832425

WEST MIDLANDS

Birmingham Museum of Science & Industry, 136 Newhall Street, Birmingham B3 1RZ Tel: 0121 235 1651

Black Country Museum, Tipton Road, Dudley DY1 4SQ

WILTSHIRE

Science Museum, Red Barn Gate, Wroughton, Nr Swindon SN4 9NS Tel: 01793 814466

YORKSHIRE

Automobilia Transport Museum, Huddersfield. Tel: 01484 559086

IRELAND

Kilgarven Motor Museum, Kilgarven, County Kerry Tel: 00 353 64 85346

National Museum of Irish Transport, Scotts Garden, Killarney, County Kerry

ISLE OF MAN

Manx Motor Museum, Crosby Tel: 01624 851236

Port Erin Motor Museum, High Street, Port Erin Tel: 01624 832964

JERSEY

Jersey Motor Museum, St Peter's Village

NORTHERN IRELAND

Ulster Folk and Transport Museum, Cultra Manor, Holywood, County Down Tel: 01232 428428

SCOTLAND

Doune Motor Museum, Carse of Cambus, Doune, Perthshire FK16 6HG.

Grampian Transport Museum, Main Street, Alford, Aberdeenshire AB33 8AD Tel: 019755 62292

Highland Motor Heritage, Bankford, Perthshire

Melrose Motor Museum, Annay Road, Melrose TD6 9LW Tel: 01896 822 2624

Moray Motor Museum, Bridge Street, Elgin IV30 2DE Tel: 01343 544933

Museum of Transport, Kelvin Hall, 1 Bunhouse Road, Glasgow G3 8DP Tel: 0141 357 3929

Myreton Motor Museum, Aberlady, Longniddry, East Lothian EH32 0PZ Tel: 018757 288

Royal Musuem of Scotland, Chambers Street, Edinburgh EH1 1JF Tel: 0131 225 7534

INDEX TO ADVERTISERS

BIBLIOGRAPHY

Baldwin, Nick; Georgano, G. N.; Sedgwick, Michael; and Laban, Brian; The World Guide to Automobiles, Guild Publishing, London, 1987.

Colin Chapman Lotus Engineering, Osprey, 1993.

Flammang, James M; Standard Catalog of Imported Cars, Krause Publications Inc, 1992.

Georgano, G. N.; ed: Encyclopedia of Sports Cars, Bison Books, 1985.

Georgano, Nick; Military Vehicles of World War II, Osprey 1994.

Harding, Anthony; Allport, Warren; Hodges, David; Davenport, John; The Guinness Book of the Car, Guinness Superlatives Ltd, 1987.

Hay, Michael; Bentley Factory Cars, Osprey, 1993.

Hough, Richard; A History of the World's Sports Cars, Allen & Unwin, 1961.

Isaac, Rowan; Morgan, Osprey, 1994.

McComb, F. Wilson; MG by McComb, Osprey, 1978.

Nye, Doug; Autocourse History of the Grand Prix Car 1966–1991, Hazleton Publishing, 1992.

Posthumus, Cyril, and Hodges, David; Classic Sportscars, Ivy Leaf, 1991.

Robson, Graham; Classic and Sportscar A–Z of Cars of the 1970s, Bay View Books, 1990.

Sedgwick, Michael; Gillies, Mark; Classic and Sportscar A–Z of Cars of the 1930s, Bay View Books, 1989.

Sedgwick, Michael, Gillies, Mark; Classic and Sportscar A–Z of Cars 1945–70, Bay View Books, 1990.

Sieff, Theo; Mercedes Benz, Gallery Books, 1989.

Vanderveen, Bart; Historic Military Vehicles Directory, After the Battle Publications, 1989.

Willson, Quentin; Selby, David; The Ultimate Classic Car Book, Dorling Kindersley, 1995.

INDEX

Italic page numbers denote colour pages, **bold** numbers refer to information and pointer boxes

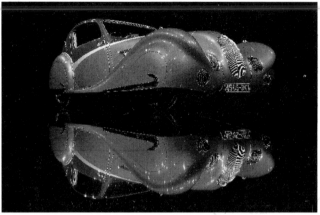